I0817264

NEW STUDIES IN BIBLICAL THEOLOGY 65

‘YOU SHALL BE CLEAN’

'When the psalmist declares that only those who have "clean hands and a pure heart" can ascend into God's presence (Psalm 24:4), he highlights the significance of the concepts of defilement and cleansing. Addressing this much-neglected topic, Dr Harper skilfully engages with its ubiquitous presence throughout the Bible. By offering new perspectives on the biblical text, this careful study enriches our understanding of the Bible. Importantly, it sheds fresh light on the scope and impact of Christ's atoning ministry, reminding readers of the necessity of engaging with the whole canon of Scripture.'
T. Desmond Alexander, Senior Lecturer in Biblical Studies and Director of Postgraduate Studies, Union Theological College, Belfast

'The biblical laws and language about purity and impurity are so utterly foreign to us and we struggle to know what to do with them. But Geoff Harper's study of the relevant materials provides insight and clarity on the subject and helps us to understand what it means to have hearts cleansed by faith and to be white as snow before God. A book that will open up vistas of study for understanding a confusing topic.'
Michael F. Bird, Deputy Principal, Ridley College, Melbourne, Australia

'With clarity, insight and humility, Geoff Harper demonstrates that the theme of defilement and cleansing is woven into the whole of Scripture. Far from being an obscure part of the Old Testament, it has vital connections to Christian theology, discipleship and witness. This is a study that deserves to be widely read for both the challenges and encouragement it provides.'
David G. Firth, Tutor in Old Testament, Trinity College Bristol

'Geoffrey Harper has written a robust and readable study on Israel's purity system, filling the scholarly gap on a vital and yet heretofore neglected topic. Without equal in its breadth, *'You Shall Be Clean'* will surely become a frequently consulted standard on purity. More than this, Harper's fine treatment will open up significant, canon-wide avenues of meaning in Scripture, as well as a greater view of the wondrous incarnation of God's Son and the marvel of his cleansing work.'
L. Michael Morales, Professor of Biblical Studies, Greenville Presbyterian Theological Seminary

‘Geoffrey Harper skilfully draws the reader into an often neglected, yet vital aspect of the Bible’s redemptive narrative. In insightful exposition, he demonstrates how the dynamic categories of defilement and cleansing shape the biblical world and frame the theological vision of its eschatological hope. As a result, the person and work of Christ emerge in clearer relief, as does the Lord’s unwavering commitment to make his people fit for his holy presence. This significant contribution to biblical theology will inspire faithful preaching and discipleship in the church and open productive pathways to present the gospel to a world longing to be made clean.’
Christine Palmer, Faculty in Old Testament, Gordon-Conwell Theological Seminary

‘Issues of defilement, cleansing and purity were central to the daily lives of the ancient Israelites. Yet today, these themes are often overlooked and misunderstood by readers of the Bible. In this insightful and timely study, Geoff Harper builds on his important work on Leviticus to skilfully trace the themes of defilement and cleansing across both the Old and New Testaments. The result is a deeper understanding of these themes across the Bible, a richer appreciation for the person and work of Jesus, and fresh insights for Christian life and mission.’
Anthony R. Petterson, Morling College, Australian University of Theology

‘As one of the leading scholars on Leviticus today, Geoff Harper is well positioned to write a biblical theology of purity and impurity. With tremendous clarity, he shows us what the concepts of purity and impurity mean and how they play out, not just in the Old Testament, but in the entire biblical story. In doing so, he helps us to understand that story better – and does so in a way that is academically strong, theologically rich and pastorally warm. Even in places where I came to different conclusions, Harper still challenged me to see just how pervasive the themes of purity and impurity are – and how important it is to understand them if we are to understand the text. Harper’s book will help you to gain that understanding.’
Jay Sklar, Professor of Old Testament, Covenant Theological Seminary

NEW STUDIES IN BIBLICAL THEOLOGY 65

Series editors: D. A. Carson and Benjamin L. Gladd

'YOU SHALL BE CLEAN'

A biblical theology of defilement and cleansing

G. Geoffrey Harper

First published in Great Britain in 2025

Apollos
Studio 101, The Record Hall, 16–16A Baldwin's Gardens, London EC1N 7RJ
https://ivpbooks.com

Published in the USA by B&H Academic®, Brentwood, Tennessee

Scripture acknowledgments can be found on p. 246.

British Library Cataloguing-in-Publication Data
A catalogue record for this book is available from the British Library

ISBN 978–1–78974–272–5
eBook ISBN 978–1–78974–273–2

Library of Congress Cataloging-in-Publication Data is on file at the Library of Congress, Washington, DC

B&H Academic ISBN 979–8–3845–3132–6
eBook ISBN 979–8–3845–3133–3

30 29 28 27 26 25 VP 1 2 3 4 5 6 7 8 9 10

1 3 5 7 9 10 8 6 4 2

Typeset by Fakenham Prepress Solutions, Fakenham, Norfolk NR21 8NL
First printed in the USA

eBook by Fakenham Prepress Solutions, Fakenham, Norfolk NR21 8NL
Produced on paper from sustainable sources

Inter-Varsity Press publishes Christian books that are true to the Bible and that communicate the gospel, develop discipleship and strengthen the church for its mission in the world.

IVP originated within the Inter-Varsity Fellowship, now the Universities and Colleges Christian Fellowship, a student movement connecting Christian Unions in universities and colleges throughout Great Britain, and a member movement of the International Fellowship of Evangelical Students. Website: www.uccf.org.uk. That historic association is maintained, and all senior IVP staff and committee members subscribe to the UCCF Basis of Faith.

In memory of Richard Hibbert (1963–2020)
Encourager, friend and collaborator

Contents

Illustrations

Tables

Figures

Series preface

New Studies in Biblical Theology is a series of monographs that address key issues in the discipline of biblical theology. Contributions to the series focus on one or more of three areas: (1) the nature and status of biblical theology, including its relations with other disciplines (e.g. historical theology, exegesis, systematic theology, historical criticism, narrative theology); (2) the articulation and exposition of the structure of thought of a particular biblical writer or corpus; and (3) the delineation of a biblical theme across all or part of the biblical corpora.

Above all, these monographs are creative attempts to help thinking Christians understand their Bibles better. The series aims simultaneously to instruct and to edify, to interact with the current literature and to point the way ahead. In God's universe, mind and heart should not be divorced: in this series we will try not to separate what God has joined together. While the notes interact with the best of scholarly literature, the text is uncluttered with untransliterated Greek and Hebrew, and tries to avoid too much technical jargon. The volumes are written within the framework of confessional evangelicalism, but there is always an attempt at thoughtful engagement with the sweep of the relevant literature.

As of late, scholars have increasingly become interested in ritual purity, and the time is ripe for a biblical-theological presentation. Dr Harper wisely guides the reader through the maze of biblical passages that speak to this issue. The result is a greater appreciation of Christ, his work and our identity.

D. A. Carson
Trinity Evangelical Divinity School

Benjamin L. Gladd
The Carson Center for Theological Renewal

Author's preface

While writing this book many people asked what I was researching. Replying 'Impurity' sent the conversation in one of two directions. For some, glazed eyes signalled the need to shift to a more germane topic. Yet, for those who deigned to hear me ramble about Egypt and defilement, or about Jesus and a haemorrhaging woman, something interesting happened: a dawning sense of wonder and curiosity. Those interactions became needed encouragements to persist, especially when daydreams increasingly fixated on setting the project aside. I hope that those conversations might prefigure the experience of readers who decide to give this book a try: initial scepticism, perhaps, giving way to a sense of discovery as one of the Bible's core themes becomes a little clearer. I am grateful to Don Carson and Philip Duce for initially accepting my proposal and for their early input. Benjamin Gladd and Tom Creedy have admirably continued that trend, and the book has benefited much from the editorial skills of Rima Devereaux and Amanda Kay.

As the years go by, I become increasingly thankful to have colleagues and friends who are willing to engage in robust conversation. Several – Kit Barker, Janson Condren, Katy Davis, Karl Deenick, Ed Grudier, Jay Sklar, Mark Stephens and Alan Thompson – sacrificed time and energy to discuss ideas and read early drafts. Their probing has prevented many an error. I am also grateful to the board of Sydney Missionary & Bible College (an affiliated college of the Australian University of Theology) for study leave granted in the first half of 2024, which allowed me to finish the project.

This book cannot be and is not intended to be a definitive statement on defilement and cleansing, neatly summing up all that can and has been said. Instead, I offer it in the spirit of the great Medieval exegete Maimonides as a guide for the perplexed. Like all guidebooks, it points out the main features and attractions – things a traveller ought not to miss. Beyond that remit, however, exploration is left to the curiosity and energy of those who opt to journey further through this fascinating terrain. In the end, I hope readers better understand the intricacies of these themes and, through them, gain a clearer vision of the God who makes his people clean. The ready applicability of that truth to global mission is a topic I miss ruminating upon with my former colleague, Richard Hibbert. This book is dedicated to his memory.

G. Geoffrey Harper

Abbreviations

[ ]	Denotes English versification where different to MT
1 En.	1 Enoch
AB	Anchor Bible
ABRL	Anchor Bible Reference Library
ABS	Archaeology and Biblical Studies
AcBib	Academia Biblica
ACTMS	Australian College of Theology Monograph Series
AD	Anno Domini
Ag. Ap.	Josephus, *Against Apion*
AGJU	Arbeiten zur Geschichte des antiken Judentums und des Urchristentums
AIL	Ancient Israel and Its Literature
AJSR	*Association for Jewish Studies Review*
ANE	Ancient Near East(ern)
Ant.	Josephus, *Jewish Antiquities*
AOTC	Apollos Old Testament Commentary
ATSDS	Adventist Theological Society Dissertation Series
BASOR	*Bulletin of the American Schools of Oriental Research*
BBR	*Bulletin of Biblical Research*
BBRSup	Bulletin of Biblical Research Supplement
BC	Before Christ
BCOTWP	Baker Commentary on the Old Testament Wisdom and Psalms
BDAG	Danker, Frederick W., Walter Bauer, William F. Arndt and F. Wilbur Gingrich. *Greek-English Lexicon of the New Testament and Other Early Christian Literature*. 3rd ed. Chicago: University of Chicago Press, 2000.
BECNT	Baker Exegetical Commentary on the New Testament
BETL	Bibliotheca ephemeridum theologicarum lovaniensium
BI	*Biblical Interpretation*
BibSem	The Biblical Seminar
BIS	Biblical Interpretation Series

BR	*Biblical Research*
BTS	Biblical Tools and Studies
BZABR	Beihefte zur Zeitschrift für altorientalische und biblische Rechtsgeschichte
BZAW	Beihefte zur Zeitschrift für die alttestamentliche Wissenschaft
CAT	Commentaire de l'Ancien Testament
CBQ	*Catholic Biblical Quarterly*
ConBNT	Coniectanea Biblica: New Testament Series
CR:BS	*Currents in Research: Biblical Studies*
CSB	Christian Standard Bible
DHR	Dynamics in the History of Religions
DRCS	Daniel and Revelation Committee Series
Dreams	Philo, *On Dreams*
DSS	Dead Sea Scrolls
EBT	Explorations in Biblical Theology
ECC	Eerdmans Critical Commentary
EDIS	Edition Israelogie
EJL	Early Judaism and Its Literature
EMQ	*Evangelical Missions Quarterly*
Ep. Bar.	Epistle of Barnabas
Ep. Jer.	Epistle of Jeremiah
EQ	*Evangelical Quarterly*
ESV	English Standard Version
EV(V)	English version(s)
FAT	Forschungen zum Alten Testament
Flight	Philo, *On Flight and Finding*
GFS	GlossaHouse Festschrift Series
Gk.	Greek
HALOT	*The Hebrew and Aramaic Lexicon of the Old Testament.* L. Koehler, J. J. Stamm, B. Hartmann, M. E. J. Richardson and W. Baumgartner. 3rd ed. 5 vols. Leiden: Brill, 1994.
HBM	Hebrew Bible Monographs
HBS	Herders Biblische Studien
HCOT	Historical Commentary on the Old Testament
HCSB	Holman Christian Standard Bible
Hebr.	Hebrew
HipNov	*Hiphil Novum*

HTKAT	Herders Theologischer Kommentar zum Alten Testament
HTR	*Harvard Theological Review*
ICC	International Critical Commentary
IDB	*The Interpreter's Dictionary of the Bible: An Illustrated Encyclopedia.* Edited by George Arthur Buttrick. 5 vols. Nashville: Abingdon, 1962.
IVP	Inter-Varsity Press
JAJ	*Journal of Ancient Judaism*
JBL	*Journal of Biblical Literature*
Jdt.	Judith
JESOT	*Journal for the Evangelical Study of the Old Testament*
JETS	*Journal of the Evangelical Theological Society*
JHS	*Journal of the Hebrew Scriptures*
JJMJS	*Journal of the Jesus Movement in Its Jewish Setting*
JLRS	*Journal of Law, Religion and State*
JPS	Jewish Publication Society
JPSTC	JPS Torah Commentary
JRDH	*Journal of Religion, Disability and Health*
JSHJ	*Journal for the Study of the Historical Jesus*
JSNTSup	Journal for the Study of the New Testament Supplement Series
JSOT	*Journal for the Study of the Old Testament*
JSOTSup	Journal for the Study of the Old Testament Supplement Series
JTISup	Journal of Theological Interpretation Supplement Series
Jub.	Jubilees
J.W.	Josephus, *Jewish Wars*
KJV	King James Version
LAE	The Life of Adam and Eve
Let. Aris.	Letter of Aristeas
LHBOTS	Library of Hebrew Bible/Old Testament Studies
lit.	literally
LNTS	The Library of New Testament Studies
LSJ	Liddell, Henry G., Robert Scott, Henry S. Jones. *A Greek-English Lexicon.* 9th ed. With revised supplement. Oxford: Clarendon, 1968.
LXX	The Septuagint
Macc.	Maccabees

Mos.	Philo, *De vita Mosis*
MS(S)	Manuscript(s)
MT	Masoretic Text
NA^{28}	*Novum Testamentum Graece*, Nestle-Aland, 28th ed.
NASB	New American Standard Bible
NETS	New English Translation of the Septuagint
NIBC	New International Biblical Commentary
NICNT	The New International Commentary on the New Testament
NICOT	The New International Commentary on the Old Testament
NIDNTT	*New International Dictionary of New Testament Theology.* Edited by Colin Brown. 4 vols. Grand Rapids: Zondervan, 1975–1978.
NIDOTTE	*New International Dictionary of Old Testament Theology and Exegesis.* Edited by W. VanGemeren. 5 Vols. Grand Rapids: Zondervan, 1997.
NIGTC	New International Greek Testament Commentary
NIV	New International Version
NIV84	New International Version (1984 edition)
NIVAC	New International Version Application Commentary
NLT	New Living Translation
NovTSup	Supplements to Novum Testamentum
NPNF^{2}	*Nicene and Post-Nicene Fathers, Series 2.* Edited by Philip Schaff and Henry Wace. Peabody: Hendrickson: 1979.
NSBT	New Studies in Biblical Theology
NTC	New Testament Commentary
NTS	*New Testament Studies*
OBT	Overtures to Biblical Theology
OSAR	Oxford Studies in the Abrahamic Religions
OTL	Old Testament Library
par(s).	parallel(s)
PEQ	*Palestine Exploration Quarterly*
PNTC	Pillar New Testament Commentary
RBL	*Review of Biblical Literature*
RBS	Resources for Biblical Study
REJ	*Revue des études juives*
RQ	*Revue de Qumran*
RSV	Revised Standard Version
SANT	Studien zum Alten und Neuen Testaments

SBL	Society of Biblical Literature
SBLDS	Society of Biblical Literature Dissertation Series
SBLMS	Society of Biblical Literature Monograph Series
SBLSS	Society of Biblical Literature Symposium Series
SFSHJ	South Florida Studies in the History of Judaism
SGBC	Story of God Bible Commentary
SHJ	Studying the Historical Jesus
SIDA	*Scripta Instituti Donneriani Aboensis*
Siph.	Siphrut: Literature and Theology of the Hebrew Scriptures
Sir.	Sirach
SJOT	*Scandanavian Journal of the Old Testament*
Spec.	Philo, *On the Special Laws*
SNTSMS	Society for New Testament Studies Monograph Series
StBibLit	Studies in Biblical Literature (Lang)
STDJ	Studies on the Texts of the Desert of Judah
STR	*Southeastern Theological Review*
Syr.	Syriac
TDOT	*Theological Dictionary of the Old Testament*. Edited by Gerhard Kittel and Gerhard Friedrich. Translated by Geoffrey W. Bromiley. 10 vols. Grand Rapids: Eerdmans, 1964–1976.
T. Iss.	Testament of Issachar
T. Levi	Testament of Levi
TLZ	*Theologische Literaturzeitung*
Tob.	Tobit
TOTC	Tyndale Old Testament Commentary
TrinJ	*Trinity Journal*
TynBul	*Tyndale Bulletin*
UBS[5]	*The Greek New Testament*, United Bible Societies, 5th ed.
Unchange.	Philo, *That God is Unchangeable*
Vg.	Latin Vulgate
VT	*Vetus Testamentum*
VTSup	Supplements to Vetus Testamentum
WBC	Word Biblical Commentary
Wis.	Wisdom of Solomon
WUNT	Wissenschaftliche Untersuchungen zum Neuen Testament
WWS	*When Women Speak*
ZAW	*Zeitschrift für die alttestamentliche Wissenschaft*
ZECNT	Zondervan Exegetical Commentary on the New Testament

Introduction

Was Jesus ever impure? Did he ever require cleansing? How one responds is telling. Reticence to reply 'yes' raises concerns about what exactly it meant for the second person of the Trinity to be incarnated as a *Jewish* man living in the first century. Indeed, one might recall the early church's rejection of Docetism with its declaration that Jesus only *seemed* human. Yet, the alternative also raises questions. If Jesus was, at times, impure, what implications did that have for accessing the temple he termed 'my Father's house' (John 2:16)? And what about Jesus' moral perfection and sinlessness, or his portrayal as high priest who enters heaven to make atonement (Heb. 9 – 10)? Would these virtues and roles, essential to Christology, thereby be compromised? After thirteen years teaching Old Testament studies at undergraduate and graduate levels, it strikes me that Western Christians are often ill-equipped to engage with such Christological queries.

The larger issues raised by pondering Jesus' susceptibility to defilement are determining what impurity is and whether the concept still applies. It is immediately apparent that purity language pervades the canon; frequency alone signals the importance of the theme. Less immediately clear, however, is what the category entails. The point is accentuated by considering countermeasures. In biblical texts, impurity – or uncleanness (the terms are synonymous) – is not remedied by better sanitation. Nor is it resolved (straightforwardly, at any rate) by repentance and forgiveness. Instead, a complex suite of alternate remedial measures indicates that this category remains conceptually distinct from hygiene and sin. What, then, is impurity and how can it be resolved? These are the central questions this book explores.

Recovering a crucial theme

Why write (or read, for that matter) a book on impurity? In short, because defilement and cleansing are essential aspects of the biblical authors' worldviews. Moreover, correctly understanding these concepts directly impacts overlapping areas of theology: sacrifice, atonement and the ritual use of blood; relationship with God, oneself, the community and the earth; the task of world evangelism and testifying to all that God has accomplished; and, as above, one's conception of Jesus. Impurity and its amelioration directly impinge upon vital areas of Christian thought and practice.

However, importance does not always match depth of reflection. Impurity – especially when one removes any hygienic or moral connotations – remains, at best, of marginal Christian interest.[1] Indeed, deliberate neglect has an established pedigree.[2] For example, because Leviticus 11 (par. Deut. 14:1–21) designates certain animals like pigs 'impure', eating kosher became (and remains) culturally formative for Jewish communities (see 1 Macc. 1:62–63; cf. Tob. 1:10–11; 2 Macc. 6:18–31; 4 Macc. 5:16–27; m. Ḥul. 3–10). However, and perhaps even because of their importance to Judaism, Christian rejection of dietary limitations has been equally determined.[3] The early Christian Epistle of Barnabas (c. AD 100) even asserts Israel erred in understanding Leviticus 11 as prohibiting literal meats. Instead, Christians should rightly comprehend that God intended only a *symbolic* proscription of *moral* vices (v. 10). Jiří Moskala charts a wider trend among the early Church Fathers to de-judaize Old Testament passages such as Leviticus 11 to free Christians from observing their demands.[4] Likewise, he finds that none of the major Protestant confessions contain any discussion of pure and impure animals.[5]

Notwithstanding the Jewish-Christian polemics that increasingly marked the early decades of the church (or nineteenth- and early twentieth-century biblical studies, for that matter[6]), it is at least worth pondering what potential gap might be left by failing to adequately grapple

[1] That some dissident Christian communities in the Middle Ages observed Jewish rituals is noted by Watts 2017: 206.

[2] See Harper 2020.

[3] For a contrary position, see McDonald 2013. Some understand Lev. 11 as banning *harmful* foods, with implications for ancient and contemporary diet (e.g. Kellogg 1891: 290–94; Craigie 1976: 230–31; Harrison 1980: 124–29). The problems facing a hygiene/health reading of Lev. 11 are outlined by Moskala 2001: 31–37.

[4] Moskala 2000: 51.

[5] Moskala 2000: 68–69.

[6] A sense of this period and its enduring legacy can be gained from Brueggemann and Hankins 2013; Strawn 2017: 103-29; Edwards 2019; Bergen 1996; Robinson 1944.

with the concepts of defilement and cleansing. To begin answering that question, I focus the results of this study onto three representative areas of Christian thinking in which there are demonstrable gains and losses (see chapter 9).

The first concerns the incarnation. What was Jesus' relationship to impurity? While Christians rightly maintain Jesus' sinlessness, that is not a sufficient response. Impurity is conceptually distinct from sin; one could be impure and innocent at the same time. With that in mind, should Jesus be understood within the Jewish purity system or separate from it? What is at stake either way? These are important questions to ponder. Matthew Thiessen's comment serves as both caution and invitation:

> I am persuaded that we often misunderstand the Gospel writers' depictions of Jesus because we naturally and unthinkingly transfer him and the people of the literary world of the Gospels into our own conceptual world. … But modern readers of the Gospels will not rightly understand Jesus apart from a more thorough comprehension of ancient Jewish (and non-Jewish) ritual purity concerns, precisely because these purity concerns map out the reality of the world as the Gospel writers conceived it.[7]

The second area is atonement. The intensity which attends discussions of atonement is proportional to the doctrine's importance. Much hangs on decisions made here. Yet, as Scot McKnight rightly recognizes, 'We cannot discuss atonement until we define the problem that atonement remedies.'[8] However, the category of defilement is frequently missing, despite the vital connection between impurity and atonement in the biblical texts. While Graham Cole, for instance, identifies the detrimental impact of sin, wrath, judgment, broken relationships, evil powers and cosmic decay upon the experience of *shalom*, impurity does not feature.[9] Moreover, while Cole recognizes a connection between atonement and cleansing, cleansing is understood only as the removal of sin.[10] More needs to be said.

A robust understanding of defilement and cleansing also proves beneficial for global mission, especially evangelism to non-Western peoples

[7] Thiessen 2020: 3.

[8] McKnight 2007: 23.

[9] Cole 2009: 67–84.

[10] Cole 2009: 164-66; likewise, Craig 2020: 2–3.

whose felt needs may not be addressed by typical gospel explanations. Indeed, a former colleague, Richard Hibbert, suggests a better approach for engaging Muslim people is to frame the gospel in terms of pollution and purity.[11] If Hibbert is on to something (and I think he is), then Western Christians may have some catching up to do to enable more faithful witness to Christ in our multicultural global village.

For all these reasons and more, grappling with defilement and cleansing is crucial. Thankfully, since the publication of Wilfried Paschen's seminal *Rein und Unrein* in 1970, the volume of literature devoted to exploring biblical (and extra-biblical) conceptions of purity has markedly increased.[12] That is good news. Nevertheless, very few studies consider how the themes of defilement and cleansing play out across the canon. This is the gap the current volume addresses.

The task of biblical theology

To undertake a canonical-level survey is to embark on a biblical-theological reading of Scripture. However, biblical theology is an elastic label that has been appropriated by several distinct, even mutually exclusive, approaches. For this reason, it is better to speak of possible biblical theolo*gies*. Outlining and evaluating these differing conceptions has been done elsewhere.[13] As expected, understanding what biblical theology is and how to do it are shaped by prior commitments regarding the provenance of texts, the supervening effects of canonical order, one's systematic framework, and so on. It is naïve to imagine stepping outside such influences, let alone coming to the biblical texts objectively. In lieu of that potential, what remains is to clarify one's own approach and assumptions while being cognisant of inherent weaknesses and limitations. At least then neither author nor reader is left wondering.

First, while this study recognizes historical development it is not diachronic in a strict sense. There is simply too much uncertainty when it comes to the absolute or even relative dating of biblical texts, especially

[11] Hibbert 2008: 352.

[12] Paschen 1970. Introductory surveys are provided by Wright 1992: 6:729–41; Averbeck 1997: 4:477–86; Klawans 2010: 377–402; Kazen 2018b: 220–44; deSilva 2013. Competing methodological approaches are evaluated by Kazen 2018a; Watts 2023.

[13] See Frei 1974: 165–82; Reid 2011; Klink and Lockett 2012; cf. Bruno, Compton, and McFadden 2020.

those of the Old Testament. The reasons for lack of clarity are threefold: (1) ancient writing conventions did not require the clear demarcation of author and date that modern copyright demands;[14] (2) the relationship between oral and written traditions is complex and non-linear; both media may co-exist, mutually influencing one another; and (3) there is an unavoidable paucity of data: the earliest extant, and often fragmentary, Old Testament manuscripts date to the third century BC.[15] Hence, while representing impressive archaeological discoveries, there is still up to a millennium (depending on one's final dating decisions) between textual composition and the earliest surviving copies. In light of these realities, Benjamin Sommer wisely cautions against what he terms 'pseudo-historicism', that is, the tendency to emphasize certain aspects of a text to corroborate presuppositions regarding dating.[16] Instead, Sommer advises interpreters to be content with less precise provenances, perhaps utilizing 'pre-exilic' rather than 'seventh-century', for example.[17] Thus, I remain content to follow a broad movement from pre-exilic, exilic and post-exilic texts, to Second Temple and New Testament documents.

Second, for reasons that become clear below, I begin with Leviticus and Numbers. From there, I loosely follow the trifold division of the Hebrew canon (Torah, Prophets and Writings) before moving on to consider Second Temple texts, the Gospels and Acts, and the New Testament epistles. Privileging literary placement over date of composition in this manner acknowledges the foundational importance of the Pentateuch for the Old Testament and of the Gospels for the New.[18] It also recognizes that for those reading Scripture sequentially, material following the Torah (the Prophets and Writings) and Gospels (the New Testament letters) is encountered as elaboration on these foundational corpora.[19]

Third, as an evangelical Christian interpreter, I affirm the dual authorship of the Bible. Thus, I assume there are always two levels of intent in play. Hence, while human authors and redactors influence meaning at

---

[14] See Carr 2005; Walton and Sandy 2013.

[15] Inscriptions push the date back further, but the evidence is disputed. Regarding whether the Ketef Hinnom amulets (c. 600 BC), for instance, reflect Num. 6:24–26, see Smoak 2015.

[16] Sommer 2011: 85–108; also, Sommer 2001: 57.

[17] Sommer 2011: 106.

[18] See Watts 2017: 95–99; cf. Kruger 2012: 202–32.

[19] Contra Kazen 2015b: 443 who argues that Leviticus and Numbers (which he dates to the Persian period) cannot inform pre-exilic notions of impurity.

the level of book or collection of books (e.g. the Book of the Twelve), and even deliberately develop or add to prior revelation, God alone controls meaning at the level of canon. Accordingly, 'coherence' became a vital criterion for determining canonicity.[20] This has a direct bearing on any analysis of defilement and cleansing across texts that display significant diversity of language, culture, style, idiom and theology. There are twin dangers to navigate: the Scylla of collapsing differing usages into one homogenous and undifferentiated whole, and the Charybdis of viewing Scripture as a discordant collection of competing truth claims. While Scripture may be multi-hued and polyphonic, it is not (in my estimation, at least) a cacophony. Symphony is my preferred metaphor. This does not presume the biblical presentation of purity is monochrome or resistant to development. It does, however, require one to assume and look for coherence even if not always neat, complete or fitting easily with pre-existing expectations.

Considering these commitments, my approach in this study takes seriously the third form of biblical theology outlined in the Series Preface; that is, 'the delineation of a biblical theme across all or part of the biblical corpora'.

The language of defilement and cleansing

The dangers inherent to word study analyses of biblical themes have been well rehearsed.[21] Any comprehensive grasp of defilement and cleansing in the biblical canon cannot simply be derived by surveying the key lexemes. Contextual use is crucial. Additionally, the wider semantic fields reveal associated terminology, which evinces change over time. Moreover, as defilement and cleansing may feature even in the absence of specific vocabulary, other textual features must also be considered: images, metaphors, allusions, and so forth. Nevertheless, defilement and cleansing are often signalled by technical terms. Hence, an initial survey of the lexical landscape of both Old and New Testaments provides a working vocabulary that subsequent chapters will elaborate. At the same time, some readers may prefer to skip this section and the next, referring back as needed.

---

[20] Kruger 2012: 133–58.

[21] See, seminally, Barr 1961.

Defilement

Table 0.1 Terms for defilement, listed by verbal root, adjective and noun

Terms for defilement			
	Verbal root	Adjective	Noun
Hebrew	*ṭmʾ* ('to be impure, to defile, to defile oneself')	*ṭāmēʾ* ('impure')	*ṭumʾâ* ('impurity')
	ḥnp ('to pollute')	*ḥānēp* ('godless')	*ḥōnep* ('perversity') *ḥănuppâ* ('perversity')
	ḥll ('to profane, desecrate')		*ḥōl* ('common, profane')
	gʿl ('to consider as filth')		*gōʿal* ('loathing')
			niddâ ('impurity')
			piggûl ('tainted [food]')
Greek	*miainō* ('to stain, defile')		*miasmos* ('pollution') *miasma* ('defilement')
	bebēloō ('to profane')		
	koinoō ('to make common, defile')	*koinos* ('impure')	
	molynō ('to stain, defile')		*molysmos* ('defilement')
		akathartos ('impure')	*akatharsia* ('impurity')

In the Old Testament, impurity is most commonly indicated by the verb *ṭmʾ*. Together with its related noun (*ṭumʾâ*) and adjective (*ṭāmēʾ*), *ṭmʾ* occurs almost 300 times, with Leviticus and Numbers accounting for two-thirds of the total. The qal verb indicates a status or state: to be, or to become, impure. Both animate and inanimate entities could be(come) impure, including men (Lev. 15:16), women (Lev. 12:2), priests (Ezek. 44:25), Gentiles (Lev. 17:15), furniture (Lev. 15:4), garments (Lev. 15:17), objects (Num. 19:22), food (Hag. 2:12), cities (Ezek. 22:3), land (Lev. 18:25) and time periods (Num. 6:12). Piel forms of *ṭmʾ* often indicate the act of defiling persons,[22] places,[23] or objects,[24] or pronounce someone or something

[22] E.g. Gen. 34:5; Lev. 11:44; Ezek. 18:6, 11; 20:26; 22:11. The defiling of Yahweh's 'holy name' in Ezek. 43:7–8 may function as a synecdoche for Yahweh's person.

[23] E.g. Lev. 15:31; 18:28; 20:3; Num. 5:3; 19:13; 35:34; Deut. 21:23; Jer. 2:7; Ezek. 5:11; 9:7; 23:38; 36:17; Ps. 79:1; 2 Chr. 36:14.

[24] E.g. 2 Kgs 23:8, 13, 16; Isa. 30:22.

impure.[25] One could also 'be defiled'[26] or could, reflexively, 'defile oneself'.[27] The adjective *ṭāmēʾ* ('impure') has a similar range to the verb, describing both animate[28] and inanimate referents.[29] The noun *ṭumʾâ* ('impurity' or 'uncleanness') occurs thirty-six times. The Greek Old Testament (LXX) often translates *ṭmʾ* and its derivatives (especially qal and niphal forms, the noun, and adjective) with nouns from the *akathar-* word-group used in conjunction with the verb 'to be' (approx. 150x). Alternatively, on more than sixty occasions, the verb *miainō* ('to stain, defile') is used (primarily for niphal, piel, pual and hithpael).[30] Notable exceptions include the use of *hamartia* ('sin') to translate *ṭumʾâ* in Leviticus 14:19.

Several other terms are also important. The verb *ḥnp* (11x), as well as its related adjective (*ḥānēp*, 13x) and nouns (*ḥōnep* [only Jer. 32:16] and *ḥănuppâ* [only Jer. 23:15]), can denote 'godlessness' (Dan. 11:32) or 'defilement'. The verb often depicts land pollution (Num. 35:33; Isa. 24:5; Jer. 3:1, 2, 9), but also defilement of 'prophet and priest' (Jer. 23:11) and 'Zion' (Mic. 4:11). The adjective appears in parallel with the unrighteous (Isa. 10:6; Job 20:5; 34:30), or in contrast to the righteous (Ps. 35:16; Job 17:8; Prov. 11:9), and thus often demarcates persons in danger with respect to God (Isa. 9:16; 33:14; Job 8:13; 13:16; 15:34; 27:8; 36:13). The LXX translates *ḥnp* and its derivatives with a variety of terms, most frequently 'ungodly' (*asebēs*) or 'lawless' (*anomos* and *paranomos*).[31]

The verb *ḥll*, which can mean 'to begin' (e.g. Gen. 4:26; 6:1), more often indicates 'to profane' or 'desecrate' (75x), predominantly in Leviticus and Ezekiel. Yahweh (Ezek. 13:19) and his holy name can be 'profaned' (Lev. 20:3; Ezek. 20:39), as can temple (Ezek. 7:22), sanctuary (Lev. 21:12), Sabbath (Ezek. 20:13), priests (Lev. 21:4) and offerings (Lev. 19:8). With this sense, *ḥll* and its related noun (*ḥōl*) serve as antonyms to holiness.

---

[25] E.g. Lev. 13:3, 8, 11, 15, 20, 22, 25, 27, 30, 44, 59.

[26] Passive defilement is conveyed by the pual (Ezek. 4:14) and hothpaal (Deut. 24:4).

[27] Reflexive action is conveyed by the niphal (Lev. 11:43; 18:24; Num. 5:13, 14, 20, 27–29; Jer. 2:23; Ezek. 20:30, 31, 43; 23:7, 13, 30; Hos. 5:3; 6:10) and hithpael (Lev. 11:24, 43; 18:24, 30; 21:1, 3, 4, 11; Num. 6:7; Ezek. 14:11; 20:7, 18; 37:23; 44:25; Hos. 9:4).

[28] For example, men (Num. 9:6), women (Lev. 15:25), animals (Lev. 7:21), birds (20:25), fish (Deut. 14:10), and insects (Deut. 14:19).

[29] Objects include garments (Lev. 13:51), ovens (Lev. 11:35), furniture (Lev. 15:26), containers (Num. 19:15), seed (Lev. 11:38), foodstuffs (Judg. 13:4), offerings (Hag. 2:14), houses (Lev. 14:44), places (Lev. 14:40), and land (Josh. 22:19). Impure lips (Isa. 6:5) and names (Ezek. 22:5) function synecdochally for persons.

[30] *NIDOTTE* 2:374.

[31] *NIDOTTE* 2:209.

Profanation indicates a loss of holy status.[32] Leviticus 10:10 (cf. Ezek. 22:26; 44:23) articulates the resulting double binary between 'holy' (*qōdeš*) and 'profane' (*ḥōl*) and between 'impure' (*ṭāmēʾ*) and 'pure' (*ṭāhôr*). Nevertheless, the holy-profane and pure-impure binaries are not always neatly distinguishable. In many instances, there is a close correspondence between defilement (*ṭmʾ*) and profanation (*ḥll*). Molech worship, for example, means a person has simultaneously 'defiled' (*ṭammēʾ*) the sanctuary 'and profaned' (*ûlĕḥallēl*) Yahweh's name (Lev. 20:3). Jeremiah 16:18 employs *ḥll* to describe the desecration of land through idolatry, paralleling the use of *ḥnp* ('to defile') in 3:1, 2, 9. The LXX generally employs *bebēloō* ('to violate sanctity, desecrate, profane') to render *ḥll*.[33]

Other, less common, terms also appear. The verb *gʿl* (10x)[34] denotes disgust: to consider something as 'dung and filth'[35] or as 'covered with impurity'.[36] The related noun, *gōʿal*, is attested only in Ezekiel 16:5 where it means 'loathing'. The noun *piggûl* is reserved for food deemed 'foul' or 'tainted' (Lev. 7:18; 19:7; Isa. 65:4; Ezek. 4:14). Although *niddâ* concretely denotes 'menstruation' (e.g. Lev. 12:2; 15:19; 18:19; Ezek. 18:6),[37] its extended meaning 'impurity' is applied to gold (Ezek. 7:19), idols (Ezek. 7:20; cf. 2 Chr. 29:5), Jerusalem (Lam. 1:17; cf. the use of *dāweh* ['menstruating'] in 1:13; 5:17) and land (Ezra 9:11). Although *niddâ* remains distinct from sin in Zechariah 13:1, it can designate moral corruption: 'like the impurity of menstruation (*kĕṭumʾat hannīdâ*) was their way before me' (Ezek. 36:17; my tr.; cf. Isa. 64:6[5]).

The New Testament, in large part, adopts the terms used in the LXX and deuterocanonical works. The adjective *akathartos* corresponds to the Hebrew *ṭāmēʾ* ('impure'). In the Gospels, *akathartos* is used only for 'impure' spirits (e.g. Matt. 10:1; Luke 11:24; cf. LXX Zech. 13:2). Elsewhere, the adjective modifies food (Acts 10:14), Gentiles (Acts 10:28) and children (1 Cor. 7:14), in addition to immoral actions (Eph. 5:5; Rev. 17:4). *Akatharsia* ('impurity'; cf. Hebr. *ṭumʾâ*), however, only designates proscribed behaviours (e.g. Matt. 23:27; Rom. 1:24; 2 Cor. 12:21). The verb *miainō* ('to stain, defile') is used for

[32] Reeve 2018: 245–52 argues that *ḥll* signals a public loss of reputation.

[33] BDAG 173.

[34] Lev. 26:11, 15, 30, 43, 44; 2 Sam. 1:21; Jer. 14:19; Ezek. 16:45(2x). In Job 21:10, *gʿl* is parallel to 'miscarry'.

[35] *TDOT* 3:47.

[36] *NIDOTTE* 1:883.

[37] The variant form *ʿiddâ* appears in Isa. 64:6[5] and Ezek. 16:7.

both ritual (e.g. John 18:28) and moral (e.g. Tit. 1:15) impurity. The cognate forms *miasmos* ('pollution') and *miasma* ('defilement') occur only in 2 Peter 2:10, 20 respectively, in relation to moral failings (cf. Jdt. 9:2, 4; 13:16; Wis. 14:26; 1 Macc. 4:43; 13:50). *Koinoō* ('to make common or impure, defile'[38]) is applied to people (Matt. 15:11; Acts 11:9; Heb. 9:13) and places (Acts 21:28). The related adjective *koinos* ('impure') describes unwashed hands (Mark 7:2, 5), non-kosher food (Acts 10:14; 11:8), foodstuffs considered off-limits (Rom. 14:14), Gentiles (Acts 10:28) and mishandling the blood of the covenant (Heb. 10:29).[39] The verb *molynō* ('to stain, defile') and noun *molysmos* ('defilement') appear four times (1 Cor. 8:7; Rev. 3:4; 14:4; and 2 Cor. 7:1 respectively).[40]

Cleansing

Table 0.2 Terms for cleansing, listed by verbal root, adjective and noun

Terms for cleansing			
	Verbal root	Adjective	Noun
Hebrew	*ṭhr* ('to be pure, to purify, to purify oneself')	*ṭāhôr* ('pure') *ṭāhōr* ('pure')	*ṭōhar* ('purity') *ṭāhŏrâ* ('purification') *ṭĕhar* ('cleanness')
Hebrew	*ḥṭʾ* ('to purify')		
Hebrew	*qdš* ('to consecate')		
Hebrew	*brr* ('to purify, purge')	*bōr* ('pure') *bar* ('pure')	*bārûr* ('purity')
Hebrew	*zkh/zkk* ('to be clean')	*zak* ('pure, clear')	
Hebrew		*ḥap* ('clean')	
Greek	*katharizō* ('to cleanse, purify')	*katharos* ('pure')	*katharismos* ('cleansing')
Greek	*hagnizō* ('to cleanse, purify')	*hagnos* ('pure')	*hagnismos* ('purification') *hagnotēs* ('purity') *hagneia* ('purity')
Greek	*aphagnizō* ('to purify oneself by offerings')		
Greek	*exilaskomai* ('to propitiate')		
Greek		*amiantos* ('undefiled')	

[38] *NIDNTT* 1:448.

[39] Paschen 1970: 165 suggests collocation with *akathartos* in Acts 10:14, 28; 11:8 explains the less familiar *koinos*.

[40] BDAG 657.

The Old Testament employs numerous terms for cleansing. Foremost, is *ṭhr* (qal), which signifies be(com)ing 'pure' or 'clean' and functions as the antonym of *ṭmʾ* ('to be impure'; esp. Lev. 10:10; Deut. 12:15; Ezek. 22:26; 44:23). To purify or declare pure is typically conveyed by *ṭhr* (piel) with the hithpael conveying reflexive action ('purifying oneself'). As with *ṭmʾ*, a wide range of animate and inanimate objects can be, or be made, 'pure': men (Lev. 15:13), women (Lev. 15:28), priests (Lev. 22:7), Gentiles (2 Kgs 5:10), animals (Gen. 7:2), clothing (Lev. 11:32), precious metals (Num. 31:21–22), wooden articles (Lev. 11:32), rooms (Neh. 13:9), houses (Lev. 14:48), city gates (Neh. 12:30), temple (2 Chr. 29:18), altar (Ezek. 43:26), Jerusalem (2 Chr. 34:5) and even the land itself (Ezek. 39:12). The associated adjective *ṭāhôr*/*ṭāhōr* ('pure, clean'), together with nouns *ṭōhar* ('purity'), *ṭāhŏrâ* ('purity, purification') and *ṭĕhar* ('cleanness'), occur over one hundred times. The terms concretely describe the 'pure' gold of the tabernacle (26x in Exod.) and the clarity of the sky (Exod. 24:10; cf. Job 37:21), as well as ritual (e.g. Lev. 12:4; Num. 6:9) and, occasionally, moral (Hab. 1:13; Prov. 15:26) purity.[41] The LXX utilizes two main roots to translate *ṭhr*: (1) the *kathar-* word-group (esp. *katharizō* ['to cleanse, purify'], *katharos* ['pure'] and *katharismos* ['cleansing']); and, less frequently, (2) the *hagn-* word-group (esp. *hagnizō* ['to cleanse, purify'] and *hagnos* ['pure, holy']).

Also important is the widely attested Semitic root *ḥṭʾ*, which has primarily religious overtones. Although the qal verb means 'to commit a sin', piel and hithpael forms can mean 'to purify' or 'to purify oneself' respectively.[42] The altar (Exod. 29:36; Lev. 8:15; Ezek. 43:20, 22–23) and sanctuary (Ezek. 45:18) could be 'purified' (*ḥṭʾ* piel), as could infected houses (Lev. 14:49, 52) and corpse-defiled persons (Num. 19:19). Levites (Num. 8:21) and corpse-contaminated people (Num. 19:12, 13, 20; 31:19) also purify themselves (*ḥṭʾ* hithpael) or other objects (Num. 31:20, 23). Psalm 51:7[9] envisions purification from sin as the psalmist petitions 'Cleanse me' (*tĕḥaṭṭĕʾēnî*).[43] The LXX utilizes a range of terms to render piel and hithpael forms of *ḥṭʾ*: *katharizō* ('to cleanse'), *hagnizō* ('to purify'),

[41] Regarding ritual and moral uses of the *ṭhr* word group, as well as 'transitional' forms, see *NIDOTTE* 2:345–46. I justify 'ritual' and 'moral' as heuristic categories in chapter 2.

[42] There is significant debate regarding how best to understand the piel and hithpael of *ḥṭʾ*. In Job 41:17, the hithpael means 'to withdraw'. See chapter 1 for further discussion.

[43] The parallel language of washing away sin (Ps. 51:7b[9b]) is rare in the Old Testament. See chapter 5.

aphagnizō ('to purify oneself by offerings') and *exilaskomai* ('to appease'[44] or 'propitiate'[45]).

Several other terms are noteworthy. *Qdš* (piel) means 'to consecrate' (i.e. to make holy) and functions as antonym to *ḥll*, 'to profane' (e.g. Lev. 10:10; 21:15; 22:32; Ezek. 36:23). In several occurrences, *qdš* (piel) works in parallel with verbs of purification. In Leviticus 8:15, blood 'purifies' (*ḥṭ'* piel) and 'consecrates' (*qdš* piel) the altar. Similarly, on the Day of Atonement, sprinkled blood 'cleanses' (*ṭhr* piel) and 'consecrates' (*qdš* piel) the altar from 'the impurities of the Israelites' (Lev. 16:19 my tr.). In 2 Chronicles 29:5, Yahweh's house is 'consecrated' (*qdš* piel) by bringing out 'impurity' (*niddâ*) from the sanctuary. The verb *brr* (18x[46]) means to purify, cleanse, purge. With associated adjectives (*bōr* [5x], *bar* [6x]) and noun (*bārûr*), the root has both concrete and figurative senses, describing 'pure' arrows (Isa. 49:2; NIV 'polished') as well as those 'pure' in hands (2 Sam. 22:21) or heart (Pss. 24:4; 73:1).[47] The verb *zkh* (8x; also attested 4x as *zkk*), 'to be clean' (qal) or 'to cleanse' (piel, hithpael), generally denotes moral purity, appearing in parallel with righteous conduct (Ps. 51:4[6]; 73:13; 119:9; Job 15:14; 25:4) or contrasted with wickedness (Isa. 1:16; Mic. 6:11;[48] Prov. 20:9). The related adjective, *zak* (11x), 'pure, clear', can describe oil (Exod. 27:20; Lev. 24:2), but also actions (Prov. 20:11) or a general demeanour (Job 8:6; 33:9).[49] The adjective *ḥap* ('clean') occurs only in Job 33:9 in parallel with *zak*, 'pure'.

The New Testament also adopts Old Testament cleansing terminology. The most widespread term is *katharos* ('pure') and derivatives, used to render eighteen different Hebrew lexemes in the LXX, most commonly *ṭāhôr*.[50] Cognates appear in almost all the New Testament documents and relate to the full spectrum of physical (e.g. Matt. 27:59; Rev. 15:6; 21:18), ritual (e.g. Matt. 8:2–4; Rom. 14:20) and moral (e.g. John 13:11; Acts 20:26) purity. Hence, there is considerable variety in how Old Testament language is used. The *hagn-* word-group is also important. *Hagnizō* ('to

---

[44] BDAG 350.

[45] LSJ 594. Ezek. 43:23 uses the cognate noun *exilasmos* ('propitiation').

[46] The exact number of occurrences is difficult to ascertain (cf. *NIDOTTE* 1:772–73).

[47] *NIDOTTE* 1:772–73.

[48] Reading as qal with MT.

[49] The cognate Aramaic adjective *zākû* ('pure') appears only in Dan. 6:22[23] to describe Daniel's innocence before God and king.

[50] *NIDNTT* 3:103.

purify'; e.g. John 11:55; Acts 21:24) and *hagnismos* ('purification'; only Acts 21:26) are used in connection with ritual cleansing. Additionally, *hagnizō* can also refer to moral purification (e.g. Jas. 4:8; 1 Pet. 1:22). The same ethical dimension is also apparent in cognate forms: *hagnos* ('pure'; e.g. 1 Pet. 3:2), *hagnōs* ('purely'; only Phil. 1:17), *hagnotēs* ('purity'; e.g. 2 Cor. 11:3) and *hagneia* ('purity'; e.g. 1 Tim. 4:12). *Amiantos* functions as antonym to *miasmos* and means 'undefiled, pure' (Heb. 7:26; 13:4; Jas. 1:27; 1 Pet. 1:4).

Holiness is closely related to the concept of purity. In Greek, three main word-groups convey the idea.[51] *Hieros*, and derivatives, is reserved for what is intrinsically holy (i.e. God/the gods) or for what has been consecrated to, or sanctified by, God/the gods. Although commonplace in Classical Greek literature, most of this word-group occurs rarely in the New Testament.[52] Also uncommon (although frequent in the LXX) is the *hosios* group, used to define that which accords with the transcendent.[53] The *hagios* word-group appears much more frequently in the New Testament. In the LXX, *hagios* occurs extensively in cultic and ritual contexts where it functions spatially (defining what belongs to Yahweh's realm), rather than ethically. New Testament usage includes this sense as God's people are indwelt and made holy by the Holy Spirit (*to pneuma to hagion*).

What to expect from this book

Although the foregoing survey of terminology is provisional and remains to be tested against the biblical texts, it sets helpful parameters and expectations. First, the concepts of defilement and cleansing employ a diversity of language, which appears throughout the canon from Genesis to Revelation. Second, the biblical (and Second Temple) material evinces many close affinities with, as well as significant divergence from, both ANE and Greco-Roman concepts.[54] Due care is required to hear the biblical authors clearly. Third, there are intersecting concepts, which

[51] For discussion, see *NIDNTT* 2:224–38.

[52] The exceptions are *to hieron* ('the temple') and *hiereus*/*archiereus* ('priest'/'high priest').

[53] *Hosios* ('holy, devout') appears in Acts 2:27; 13:34–35; 1 Tim. 2:8; Tit. 1:8; Heb. 7:26; Rev. 15:4; 16:5; *hosiotēs* ('holiness, devoutness') in Luke 1:75; Eph. 4:24; and *hosiōs* ('devoutly') in 1 Thess. 2:10.

[54] Appropriation of purity in post-biblical rabbinic and Christian traditions is beyond the scope of this investigation. Readers can consult Klawans 2000; Hayes 2002; Latz and Ermakov 2014: 177–271; Furstenberg 2023.

interpreters must be careful not to conflate. Impurity is not synonymous with sin, or vice versa, and holiness is not identical to purity. There is overlap, but also distinction. Fourth, in relation to the language of purity and impurity (or holiness for that matter), a moral connotation is possible, but cannot simply be assumed. The range of possible options, from concrete to figurative, necessitates careful exegesis.

The remainder of this volume considers how the themes of defilement and cleansing operate and develop across the Scriptures. Although each biblical book is unique, a discernible canonical logic emerges. While a full articulation must await the retrospection possible in the final chapter, it is useful at this point to outline how the following chapters contribute to that end.

Chapter 1 begins with Leviticus and Numbers. And for good reason. Although often neglected, these books contain the most concentrated explanation of the causes, objects, scope and implications of defilement, as well as the various means God allocates for cleansing. Chapter 2 synthesizes these initial soundings to construct a provisional conceptualization of purity. Doing so is essential. Readers unfamiliar with the dynamics of defilement and cleansing will not fully appreciate how the concepts are utilized by the biblical authors. In the Pentateuch and Former Prophets (chapter 3), purity, or lack of, becomes a key characterization technique. In often subtle ways, narrative portrayal shapes perceptions of God, Israel and the nations. Moral and ritual faithfulness mark one as belonging to Yahweh. Accordingly, the Latter Prophets (chapter 4) foreground the moral defilement produced by bloodshed, idolatry and sexual immorality to warn about, and explain, the necessity of exile. But they also provide important indicators that Yahweh will one day conclusively purify his people. Unsurprisingly, therefore, the mainly post-exilic collection of books known as the Writings (chapter 5) continues to wrestle with issues of defilement and cleansing. There is greater definition and reframing of concepts as various communities work out the purity implications of being God's holy people. This diversity is also a hallmark of the Second Temple literature (chapter 6). While some forms and causes of impurity are simply assumed, there is also significant expansion. The immediate context of the New Testament, therefore, is one of increasing interest in defilement and cleansing. Thus, the Gospels and Acts (chapter 7) repeatedly employ purity dynamics as they present their respective portraits of Jesus and the nascent church. Jesus is the supreme purifier who readies people for the arrival of God's kingdom. In him, and through the pouring out of the Holy Spirit, prophetic hope is realized. Accordingly, the New Testament epistles (chapter 8) appropriate defilement and cleansing for Christological and eschatological ends. Purity informs social and ethical boundaries and drives exhortation for transformation. The purity of God must be reflected in the purity of his people. Finally, with the benefit of canonical hindsight, chapter 9 articulates a biblical theology of defilement and cleansing and grounds this in three representative areas of Christian thought and practice. Far from being superseded or laid aside, purity of body and spirit remains essential in the Christian age. Why that is the case, and what it might entail, become clearer as we work through the biblical material.

1

Defilement and cleansing in Leviticus and Numbers

For many readers of the Old Testament, Leviticus and Numbers remain obscure. After all, these books have a long history of, sometimes wilful, neglect.[1] Yet, when constructing a biblical theology of defilement and cleansing, Leviticus and Numbers prove crucial. Although purity lexemes are distributed across the canon, there are notable concentrations – pre-eminently Leviticus and Numbers, which account for up to two-thirds of key terms. Moreover, large blocks of material are devoted to purity (Lev. 11 – 16; 18; 20 – 22; Num. 5 – 6; 19). For this reason, any canonical investigation must grapple with the priestly texts.[2] At the same time, unfamiliarity with both texts and concepts can make this a daunting task. The reward, however, is a better foundational grasp of a crucial biblical theme.

In Leviticus and Numbers purity, pollution and purification are fundamental aspects of life in biblical Israel.[3] Various sources of defilement could negatively affect individuals, the sanctuary, the entire community, and even the land itself. While some forms of pollution could be eradicated by ritual measures, others could not. Purity, therefore, had significant social entailments. Accordingly, priests were tasked with establishing and

[1] Strawn 2017 provides a sobering analysis of the contemporary North American church in this regard.

[2] In this volume I use 'priestly' in a non-technical sense as an umbrella term for Leviticus and Numbers (rather than to differentiate P and/or H from non-P).

[3] Frymer-Kensky 1983: 399. The extent to which textual presentation matches ancient social reality is contested. The phrase 'biblical Israel' is my attempt to distinguish between 'history' (a sequence of space-time events) and 'historiography' (the written accounts of those events). Determining the rhetorical purposes of the biblical presentation is crucial. This has come sharply to the fore in recent years in relation to ritual texts. Watts's statement has become axiomatic: 'Texts are not rituals and rituals are not texts' (Watts 2007: 29; italics removed). The implications are explored in Nihan and Rhyder 2021.

maintaining strict boundaries and performing purification where possible. The impetus for this concern is the immanent presence of Yahweh that had come to reside in the tabernacle at the heart of the Israelite camp. Purity and presence are inseparably intertwined.

Defilement and cleansing in Leviticus

Presence, priests and purity

Themes of presence and purity dominate the opening sections of Leviticus. Chapters 1 – 9 portray the inception of a cultic system replete with offerings and priests. A repeated speech formula (e.g. 1:1; 4:1; 5:14) works rhetorically to emphasize the divine origin of the institutions.[4] A sevenfold occurrence of 'as Yahweh commanded' throughout the priests' ordination rite works similarly (8:4, 9, 13, 17, 21, 29, 34 my tr.; cf. Exod. 29). Yahweh desires both sacrifice and priesthood.[5] These exist so 'Yahweh's glory might appear' (9:6 my tr.), a potential realized as the gathered community beholds the divine radiance (9:23). Moreover, cultic purification rituals performed by the newly inaugurated priests (9:8–21) enable Moses and Aaron to *enter* the tabernacle and survive the encounter with Yahweh's presence within (9:23). This begins to resolve the narrative dilemma posed by Exodus 40:34–35, which records the exclusion of everyone from Yahweh's glory when it fills the newly erected tabernacle.[6] In this way, Yahweh's 'dwelling' (*miškān*) starts to function as a 'tent of meeting' (*ʾōhel môʿēd*).[7] Increasing proximity to the divine presence characterizes the new reality that Leviticus describes.[8]

Proximity, however, quickly proves catastrophic. In a stunning reversal, Aaron's sons, Nadab and Abihu, did 'what [Yahweh] had *not* commanded

[4] Whether Leviticus has thirty-six (Luciani 2005: 12–13) or thirty-seven (Warning 1999: 39) instances depends on how 16:1–2 is categorized.

[5] The legitimation of an Aaronic priesthood in Lev. 8 – 10 is widely recognized, even if opinions regarding historical setting and textual function differ. Such legitimation is made necessary in view of vying claims regarding priestly authority, lineage, and capability (e.g. Num. 16 – 17; 1 Kgs 12; Mal. 1:6 – 2:9; Ezra 2:61–63). For representative reconstructions, see Ulrich et al. 1992; Watts 2001; Tiemeyer 2006; Malone 2017.

[6] Contra Bolt 2004: 127 who supposes Old Testament rituals *created* distance between God and humanity.

[7] Regarding terminological use in Exodus–Leviticus, see Morales 2015: 195–97.

[8] The trajectory is traced by Nihan 2007: 46–47, 99–105 and Morales 2024: 15–18.

them' (10:1 my tr. and emphasis).[9] The fire that 'issued forth' (*yṣ'*) from Yahweh to 'consume' (*'kl*) the sacrifices upon the altar (9:24) 'issues forth' (*yṣ'*) once more to 'consume' (*'kl*) Nadab and Abihu (10:2). Yahweh's subsequent statement, 'Among those who draw near to me, I will be holy' (10:3 my tr.), reveals a necessary correlate of divine closeness: danger to those who breach holiness and purity boundaries. As Sommer wryly comments, 'In this fire the *fascinans* that attracts humans is brutally tempered with *mysterium* and *tremendum*'.[10] This sobering incident occasions Yahweh's commission, spoken to Aaron alone (10:8), 'to separate between holy and common and between impure and pure' (10:10 my tr.). Moreover, Aaron and sons must 'teach the Israelites all the statutes that Yahweh spoke to them' (10:11 my tr.). Maintaining strict boundaries and instructing others to do likewise become core priestly responsibilities.[11]

Canonical connections further nuance this priestly duty. Leviticus frequently utilizes verbal and conceptual allusion to Genesis 1 – 3 as a rhetorical device.[12] Of interest in 10:10 is the rare verbal form *lĕhabdîl* ('to separate'; NIV 'distinguish'), which occurs elsewhere only in Genesis 1:14, 18 and in texts that address pure-impure (Lev. 11:47) or holy-common boundaries (Ezek. 42:20). The allusion implies a conceptual correspondence between creation, portrayed as successive acts of separation (Gen. 1:4, 6, 7, 14, 18), and the boundaries that Israel must maintain. Separating pure from impure and holy from common are thus set within a broader conceptual framework, making them acts of alignment – or perhaps *re*alignment – along creation lines. Constraining impurity becomes an expression of *imitatio Dei.*

Leviticus 12

Establishing purity boundaries is quickly delimited along specific lines. The short passage in Leviticus 12:1–8 provides an entry point. Verse 2 identifies childbirth as a source of impurity: 'A woman who conceives and bears a male will be impure for seven days. Like the days of her menstruation, she will be impure' (my tr.). Following the boy's circumcision

[9] What the brothers did or did not do has long puzzled interpreters. Options are assessed by Kiuchi 1987: 68–85; Hartley 1992: 132–33; Rendtorff 2003b: 359–63.

[10] Sommer 2001: 61.

[11] It is precisely this point that Ezek. 22:26 highlights: Israel's priests failed to separate between holy and common and did not make known the difference between pure and impure.

[12] See Harper 2018.

on day eight (12:3), the woman must complete an additional thirty-three days 'until the days of her purification are over' (12:4). Giving birth to a girl, however, inaugurates an alternate timeframe: an initial fourteen days of impurity followed by sixty-six days to finish purification (12:5).[13] When the forty- or eighty-day term is over, the mother must present an ascension offering (NIV 'burnt offering') and a purification offering (NIV 'sin offering') at the tabernacle's entrance (12:6, 8).[14] The priest offers these to Yahweh to make atonement. Consequently, 'she will be pure from the flow of her bloods' (12:7 my tr.). Yahweh concludes: 'This is the *tôrâ* for her who bears a male or a female' (12:7 my tr.).

Although brief, this passage elucidates several fundamental aspects of the Levitical purity system. The cause of impurity in this case is a natural event: birth. The resulting defilement is inevitable; hence, there are no avoidance commands. The logic is simple: *every* new mother becomes impure, regardless of age or social status. At the same time, no rationale is provided. *Why* birth generates impurity is simply not explained. Importantly, becoming impure does not *eo ipso* make the woman a sinner.[15] On the contrary, childbirth is evidence of divine blessing (e.g. Gen. 1:28; 4:25; 21:1–6; Ps. 127:3–5); it is childlessness that consistently instigates shame and lament (e.g. Gen. 30:1; 1 Sam. 1; Prov. 30:15–16). Instead, 12:7 identifies 'the flow of her bloods' (my tr.), not sin, as the source of defilement. Yet the problem is not blood loss per se. Nothing is said here or elsewhere about blood from cuts or grazes. Likewise, connecting childbirth impurity to a close encounter with death remains an insufficient explanation. While mother mortality was high and giving birth dangerous (cf. Gen. 35:16–18; 1 Sam. 4:19–20), other, explicitly life-threatening blood loss (e.g. serious arterial bleeding) is never associated with impurity. The underlying reasoning remains obscure.[16]

Nevertheless, childbirth instigates a temporary change in the mother's status or state of being.[17] That she *becomes* impure for either forty or eighty

---

[13] These gendered timeframes have generated considerable, albeit inconclusive, debate. Valuable new avenues are explored by Erbele-Küster 2017; Thiessen 2018.

[14] See Harper 2022b and forthcoming-b for my choice of sacrificial terminology. See also Watts 2013: 4–7.

[15] Although recognizing the absence of wrongdoing, Shepherd 2021: 166 nevertheless reads Lev. 12 against the 'sin of the first parents'.

[16] Thus, simply to equate impurity with death is overly simplistic.

[17] Averbeck 1997: 4:482 prefers 'condition' to conceptualize impurity, reserving 'status' for the holy-common binary.

days means the woman's normal status is pure. Moreover, a formerly pure woman who becomes impure through childbirth can be purified by the prescribed rites. Impurity is a dynamic and reversible category; it is a state one can enter, and exit.

Yet, impurity in Leviticus 12 also has negative entailments. Women made impure by childbirth are forbidden from touching holy objects or entering the sanctuary (12:4).[18] Thus, while impurity in this case is not connected to sin, and cannot be avoided, it is dangerous nonetheless (cf. Lev. 15:31). The problem is not defilement per se, but impurity in proximity to the holy. Divine closeness problematizes the impurity of those who dwell in the camp. Mandated separation indicates a degree of threat to God–human relations (see further below). Moreover, impurity could also be transmitted to others, as implied by the phrase, 'like the days of her menstruation' (12:2 my tr.). While this could indicate an analogous timeframe (i.e. 'seven days', 12:2; cf. 15:19), the fourteen-day impurity following the birth of a girl is also said to be 'like her menstruation' (12:5 my tr.). This suggests something else is intended. Leviticus 15 clarifies: a woman impure from menstruation transmits impurity through contact, either directly (15:19–20, 24) or indirectly (15:21–23). Childbirth impurity has the same potential.[19] This observation highlights the social dimension of impurity: transmission threatens *corporate* access to the sacred.

Yahweh, accordingly, specifies remedial measures. The woman's blood loss functions as a passive means of cleansing. For thirty-three/sixty-six days, 'she will sit in the bloods of purification' (*tēšēb bidmê ṭāhŏrâ*, 12:4 my tr.; also 12:5).[20] Postpartum blood loss is a purgative process.[21] Hence, when 'the days of her purification … are over' (12:6) – that is, after forty or eighty days – the woman may approach the tabernacle previously off-limits (12:4). In fact, she must do so to make the requisite offerings (12:6, 8).

---

[18] The prohibition reveals women could normally touch sacred objects and enter the tabernacle (cf. Exod. 38:8).

[19] Likewise, Levine 1989: 72. The text is silent regarding the purity status of the child. Transmission, however, makes this a moot point: whether through birth or contact, both mother and child become impure.

[20] The LXX obscures the force of the MT with its rendering *haimati akathartō autēs* ('her impure blood'). The NIV similarly implies the mother's blood is impure ('to be purified from her bleeding'). The debate is an ancient one with Pharisees and Sadducees taking opposing sides (Hartley 1992: 165).

[21] Erbele-Küster 2017: 70.

These active purification measures complete the process. Although not specified in 12:7, the normal sacrificial order is purification offering first, ascension offering second (e.g. Lev. 8:14–21; 9:8–17; 14:19–20). The purification offering atones for the woman's impurity, restoring relational connection with Yahweh (12:7; cf. Lev. 4:1 – 5:13).[22] The ascension offering functions primarily as an act of obeisance, demonstrating her ongoing loyalty to God (cf. Lev. 1).[23] With these offerings, the woman's purification is completed, fully reintegrating her into the worshipping community.

The function of Leviticus 12, therefore, is not to prevent impurity or explain its existence. Rather, the legislation itemizes the severity, longevity and transmissibility of childbirth-related defilement to safeguard boundaries between impure and holy (cf. Lev. 10:10). To borrow a medical analogy, Leviticus 12 manages impurity's symptoms rather than treating its underlying cause(s). The legislation specifies the means for rectifying the effects of impurity so that the normal, pure status of an Israelite woman might be regained. Thus, Leviticus 12 does not simply codify patriarchal uneasiness regarding women's health. Rather, the legislation grants a new mother significant moral agency with respect to her own body, her society, and her God.[24] This individual-focused scenario can be extrapolated outwards to clarify a community-wide rationale for impurity rules: preserving ongoing, safe habitation with a holy God. Crucially, this necessitates *bodily* fidelity as much as spiritual, outward observance as much as inward. Leviticus declares all dimensions of human existence to be equally 'God's business'.

Leviticus 13 – 15

Leviticus 13 – 14 continues the focus on diagnosing and remedying impurity, this time with respect to *ṣāraʿat* (ESV: 'leprous disease'). I reason elsewhere,

> Paying heed to the Hebrew is helpful, as English versions make it appear that different topics are being considered. For instance,

[22] I discuss the dynamics of atonement below at Lev. 16.

[23] On the purpose(s) of the ascension offering, see Morales 2019; Harper 2022b: 60–66.

[24] Note the preponderance of feminine verb forms (*she* remains, touches, enters, brings). The mother may also perform her son's circumcision (the verb is passive and without a marked subject).

> the NIV variously translates *tsara'at* as 'defiling skin disease' (13:2), 'spreading mold' (14:34), and 'defiling molds' (14:55). Even the consistent rendering in the ESV ('leprous disease') or NASB ('leprosy') is problematic: In what sense can a woollen jumper or house contract 'leprosy' (13:47; 14:34)? Moreover, historical data suggest that leprosy (i.e., Hanson's Disease) did not exist in ancient Israel.[25]

Determining a suitable English gloss for *ṣāraʿat* is difficult. The term likely serves as an umbrella category that incorporates several related phenomena. Nevertheless, commonalities are evident: *ṣāraʿat* in Leviticus 13 – 14 affects surfaces, penetrates below the surface, is a spreading infection, and renders the afflicted person or object impure.[26] *Ṣāraʿat* also occurs naturally and is, therefore, beyond the control of individuals (although 14:34 reserves a place for divine causation).

The priests perform a crucial role in examining suspected cases (cf. 10:10). Assessment of people (13:2–44), clothing (13:47–59) and houses (14:33–48) elicits a pronouncement regarding status: 'pure' (e.g. 13:6, 23) or 'impure' (e.g. 13:3, 11). As in Leviticus 12, 'pure' is the default; it is *ṣāraʿat* that conveys impurity. The scope is remarkably narrow. Not all skin infections, let alone illnesses generally, render a person impure.[27] Hence, persons with non-*ṣāraʿat* diseases are declared 'pure' (e.g. 13:6, 23, 28, 38). In fact, a person's body may be entirely covered with skin disease and yet be deemed pure (13:13). There is no blanket correlation between sickness and impurity. Some diseases defile; most do not. The defiling potential of *ṣāraʿat* seems to reside in its ability to penetrate surfaces and to spread unchecked (13:3, 7–8, 35–36, 51; 14:37–40). On people, surface penetration exposes 'living flesh' (NIV 'raw flesh'), which 13:15 declares defiling: 'The living flesh is impure' (my tr.; cf. 13:10–11, 14, 16–17).[28]

Ṣāraʿat-defilement lasts indefinitely. In marked contrast to other ancient texts that discuss defiling skin diseases, no healing rites are provided.[29] Instead, the infected are banished (13:45–46); compromised

---

[25] Harper 2022b: 194. Regarding the occurrence of Hanson's Disease (leprosy) in the ancient world, see Hulse 1975; Thiessen 2020: 43–46.

[26] Harper 2022b: 195.

[27] Contra Levine 1989: 92; Blomberg 2023: 255–56.

[28] A cognitive linguistic reading leads Trevaskis 2011: 108–71 to conclude that impurity in Lev. 13 – 14 is connected to the concept of 'flesh', which is used with negative symbolic connotations. In this way, *ṣāraʿat* legislation teaches that sinful humanity ('flesh') is under divine judgment.

[29] See Feder 2015.

fabrics are destroyed (13:52, 56–57); and contaminated building materials are removed outside the town (14:40, 45).[30] Although transmission is not specified for people and objects, requiring the *ṣāra ʿat*-infected to live alone and cry out, 'Impure! Impure!' (13:45–46 my tr.), suggests contact mitigation. Transmission is made explicit in the case of dwellings: 'Anyone who goes into the house while it is closed up will be unclean till evening. Anyone who sleeps or eats in the house must wash their clothes' (14:46-47).

Although indefinite, cleansing *ṣāra ʿat*-impurity is possible. Leviticus 14:2–32 (cf. 14:49–53) outlines purification rites, but only for when the infection had dissipated (14:3, 48). Israel's priests were not doctors; they could not cure *ṣāra ʿat*, only remedy its defiling effects. The complexity of the ritual corresponds to the severity of the impurity. As in Leviticus 12, passive and active measures are employed: waiting (14:8), a blood sprinkling rite (14:6–7), release of a live bird (14:7), washing (14:8–9), shaving (14:8–9), a reparation offering (14:12), a blood smearing rite (14:14), an oil sprinkling/smearing rite (14:15–17), a purification offering (14:19), an ascension offering (14:19–20) and a tribute offering (14:20). By these measures the impure person is purged of their defilement and reintegrated into society (14:20). The protracted, public nature of the ritual, climaxing with an appearance 'before Yahweh' (14:11 my tr.), functions to affirm the cleansed person's status before both God and people. They have successfully transitioned from impure to pure.

Leviticus 15 establishes a frame with chapter 12 by returning to a related topic. The primary concern is identified in 15:2–3: 'flux' (*zôb*), 'flowing from his flesh' (*zāb mibĕśārô*), makes a man impure (my tr.). The legislation is again specific: 'flesh' (*bāśār*) is best understood euphemistically as 'penis' rather than the entire 'body' (contra NIV, ESV). *Genital* discharge is the problem; nothing is said about snot or sweat. The passage differentiates normal (15:16–24) from abnormal 'flux' (15:2b–15, 25–30), for men and women. Normal discharges produce quantifiable impurity. Emission of semen defiles by contact: the man himself (15:16), affected objects (15:17), or a woman he is with (15:18). The resulting impurity is mitigated by a combination of waiting ('till evening') and washing (15:16–18). A woman, when 'her flux is blood' (i.e. during her regular monthly

[30] Thus, the legislation explicitly expands beyond the narrative setting of life in the camp (cf. 13:46–59) to settled life in Canaan (cf. 14:34).

period), becomes impure for seven days (15:19 my tr.). Indirect contact with menstrual blood, by touching the woman or furniture she has used, transmits a lower grade impurity that lasts 'till evening' and is cleansed by washing and/or waiting (15:19–23). Direct contact with 'her menses' (*niddātāh*), however, transmits a seven-day impurity that has sufficient potency to create secondary defilement (15:24 my tr.). No active measures are prescribed for a menstruating woman to regain her pure status.[31]

Abnormal discharges, however, defile indefinitely – for as long as the underlying condition persists. Moreover, men (15:4–12) and women (15:26–27) in this situation also transmit secondary impurity.[32] Secondary defilement is less potent, requiring ablution and waiting 'till evening' (15:5–12, 27). Notably, as with *ṣāraʿat*, cleansing from abnormal discharges is possible only *after* the underlying condition resolves. The man or woman must wait seven days post-healing before washing and making sacrifice (15:13–15, 28–30). Atonement restores relational harmony with Yahweh following the breach caused by the abnormal 'flow' (15:15, 30).

Leviticus 15:31 serves as a summary rationale for 11 – 15 (cf. 10:10). Yahweh declares: 'Thus you will hold the Israelites back from their impurity (*miṭṭumʾātām*) so they will not die in their impurity (*bĕṭumʾātām*) by making impure (*ṭmʾ* piel) my tabernacle which is in their midst' (my tr.). This is the dilemma that necessitates the Day of Atonement: impurity, albeit naturally occurring and unavoidable, endangers individuals and the community. 'Defilement is lethally contagious'.[33] Thus, 15:31 establishes the underlying tenor of Leviticus 11 – 15 as gracious and needed guidance for those invited to approach a holy God.

Leviticus 11

Having examined Leviticus 12 – 15, we are better placed to appreciate the contours of Leviticus 11. The chapter is connected to 12 – 15 through the *Leitmotif* of impurity.[34] Indeed, *ṭmʾ* ('to be impure') occurs more times in Leviticus 11 than anywhere in the Old Testament. Moreover, while the

---

[31] Later tradition required various purification procedures for menstruants. Milgrom 1991: 935 suggests ablutions are omitted here because they are assumed.

[32] Accordingly, Hieke 2014: 526–47 argues that the literary symmetry of Lev. 15 establishes gender neutrality *vis-à-vis* impurity.

[33] Douglas 1993b: 24.

[34] A majority of commentors consider Lev. 11–15 as a major sub-division within the book (Harper 2018: 73).

summary statement in 11:47 explicitly evokes the priests' commission to separate impure from pure (cf. 10:10), the command is democratized. Correctly separating animals is required of *every* Israelite (cf. 11:2), perhaps signalling one aspect of what it means to be a priestly nation (Exod. 19:4–6; cf. Lev. 20:25–26).[35] Yahweh's purview incorporates the mundane as well as sacred. From pantry (Lev. 11) to bedroom (Lev. 15), all of life impacts divine–human relations.

And yet, similarities aside, Leviticus 11 stands apart from chapters 12 – 15. Most notable are avoidance commands. Unlike the naturally occurring and unavoidable impurities itemized in 12 – 15, preventing animal-related impurity is possible. Thus, those creatures declared impure by Yahweh are explicitly prohibited: 'You must not eat their meat or touch their carcasses' (Lev. 11:8; cf. 11:4, 11, 13). This need not signal intrinsic impurity; banned creatures are classified as 'impure *for you*' (*ṭāmēʾ hûʾ lākem*, 11:4, emphasis mine).[36] Either way, disobedience results in defilement: 'by these you will defile yourselves (*ṭmʾ* hithpael)' (11:24 my tr.). Impurity, conveyed to persons (11:24–28, 31, 39–40) or clothing (11:25, 28, 40), is minor, lasting 'till evening' (11:24, 25, 27–28, 31–32, 39–40). Active purification procedures are provided only for objects (e.g. 11:28, 32, 40), not people.

The rationale for why some animals convey impurity is unstated.[37] Nevertheless, Leviticus 11 suggests some connection between impurity and death.[38] When an animal ordinarily allowed to be touched or eaten dies (of natural causes), its carcass conveys impurity by contact (11:39–40; cf. 17:15). Impurity in this case is explicitly *postmortem*. Death generates defilement.

Creation themes are also prominent in Leviticus 11. The passage is saturated with allusions to Genesis 1 – 3.[39] Among these, the conjunction

[35] Péter-Contesse 1993: 181 surmises this is why the legislation is easy to understand and comprehend. The implications of Israel's communal priesthood are explored by Malone 2017: 125–46.

[36] Intrinsic impurity is also challenged by metaphors and similes, which equate Yahweh with animals prohibited by Lev. 11, e.g., a lion (Hos. 13:7–8) or eagle (Deut. 32:11).

[37] For analysis of fourteen distinct rationales (none without problem), see Moskala 2001; cf. Harper 2013; Firmage 1990.

[38] The clustering of key words in 11:24–40 emphasizes the correlation: 25/34 occurrences of the *ṭmʾ* root ('to be impure'), 11/13 uses of *nĕbēlâ* ('corpse'), and 3/3 appearances of *mwt* ('to die') occur here. While many also note that the flying creatures banned in 11:13–19 are predominantly predators, translation difficulties (compare EVV) render any conclusions made on this basis tentative.

[39] For analysis, see Harper 2018: 118–48; Moskala 2000: 199–233.

of second-person verbs used to forbid 'eating' and 'touching' in 11:8 (par. Deut. 14:8) occurs elsewhere only in Genesis 3:3.[40] In each instance, a larger set of potential foods is limited: fruit from any tree bar one in the Garden (Gen. 2:16–17); lists of excluded creatures for Israel (cf. Gen. 9:3). Furthermore, the consequences are conceptually analogous: banishment from the divine presence.[41] As the primordial couple were expelled from the garden where Yahweh 'walked' (Gen. 3:8, 23–24), so impure Israelites are (temporarily) exiled from the tabernacle where Yahweh also 'walks' (Lev. 26:12; 2 Sam. 7:6). Allusion to Genesis heightens the affective power of Levitical legislation as parallels between Adam and Israel provoke remembrance of primordial banishment and reinforce the text's demand for compliance. Israel must learn to avoid that which requires separation from Yahweh.[42] By connecting purity to obedience and presence, and impurity to disobedience and distance, Leviticus 11 anticipates 18 – 20.

Leviticus 16

Yom Kippur is crucially important in Judaism.[43] The significance of the pericope in Leviticus is flagged by unique ritual elements, distinctive terminology,[44] and the appearance of key words in multiples of seven.[45] Furthermore, many commentators regard Leviticus 16 as a standalone unit,[46] and often position it at the book's centre.[47] Rolf Rendtorff even

[40] The syntax is identical in each instance: *ʾkl* negated by *lōʾ* used in conjunction with *min*; followed by *ngʿ* negated by *lōʾ* used with the preposition *bĕ* (Harper 2018: 124).

[41] Harper 2013: 191–93; Trevaskis 2011: 99–101.

[42] Nonetheless, becoming impure through touching and eating is permitted (Lev. 11:39; 17:15), perhaps as a concession, although it is forbidden for priests (Lev. 22:8). Purification, however, is essential (Lev. 17:16).

[43] Yom Kippur, reflecting MT's 'the day of the atonements', is the rite's modern Hebrew name. The *piyyutim* has 'day of forgiveness'. See, further, Stökl Ben Ezra 2003: 15.

[44] See Harper 2018: 155–56.

[45] These include 'holy place' (7x), 'clothing' (7x), 'mercy seat' (7x), 'sin [offering]' (14x), and 'goat' (14x). Moreover, Milgrom 1991: 1038–39 deduces, 'The total number of [blood] manipulations adds up to forty-nine, or seven times seven. Seven, the number that stands for completion and perfection, is multiplied by itself.'

[46] Harper 2018: 73. Recent German scholarship tends to combine Lev. 16 with 17 (e.g. Gerstenberger 1996: 19; Zenger 2008: 65; Zenger and Frevel 2008: 40; Hieke 2014: 61).

[47] E.g. Shea 1986; Smith 1996; Warning 1999: 178; Luciani 2005: 288–334; Ferch 2013. Douglas 1995: 251, followed by Milgrom 2000b: 1364, instead argues that Lev. 19 is the book's centre. Douglas's proposal has not been widely accepted. Alter, for instance, concludes that Douglas's analysis is 'more the product of interpretative ingenuity than of persuasive reading' (2004: 541). Determining Leviticus's structure is made difficult by the presence of overlapping structural features (Harper 2018: 71–77).

argues the Day of Atonement constitutes the theological and structural centre of the Torah.[48]

The deaths of Nadab and Abihu on the first day of priestly service provide the exigency for the ritual (16:1; cf. 9:23 – 10:2).[49] Their demise functions as a sobering reminder of the danger posed by divine holiness (cf. 10:3). It also creates significant problems. Yahweh's termination of recently installed priests, essential to the proper functioning of the cult, allows no opportunity for repentance or purification. Moreover, the brothers' corpses defile the newly consecrated tabernacle, threatening its viability as a tent of meeting for Yahweh and his people. The interposing material of 11 – 15 only heightens tension by itemizing other, usually uncontrollable, sources of impurity, which similarly threaten Israel's corporate life (cf. 15:31). Nadab and Abihu's fate could prefigure that of the nation.

The Day of Atonement comprehensively addresses the Israelites' accumulated 'impurities and rebellions' (16:16 my tr.). This is good news considering the ubiquity of bodily impurities and the defiling effects of rebellion (see below at Lev. 18 – 20). Moreover, Leviticus 16 deals with the effect of these things *on the tabernacle* (16:16, 19; cf. 15:31). The language of 'forgiveness' (*slḥ*) is absent, however, even though the rite's purification offerings (16:11–19) mirror those of 4:1 – 5:13, which explicitly enable forgiveness (e.g. 4:20, 26, 31, 35). Instead, Leviticus 16 emphasizes *cleansing*. The command for annual re-enactment explicitly identifies this goal: 'on this day, he will atone for you to purify you. You shall be pure from all your sins before Yahweh' (16:30 my tr.). Yom Kippur cleanses the community ('you' in 16:30 is plural); this is a purity reset point for the nation.[50]

But in what way are sins dealt with on Yom Kippur? Throughout the year, unintentional sins (4:1–35; 5:14–19) and minor transgressions (5:1–13, 20–26 [6:1–7]) could be atoned. Ignorance or reticence to confess are overcome through the mechanism of 'suffering guilt's consequences' (e.g. 5:17).[51] Requisite offerings enable divine forgiveness (4:20, 26, 31, 35; 5:10, 13, 16, 18, 26 [6:7]; cf. 19:22). However, 'high-handed' sins (cf. Num.

[48] Rendtorff 2003a: 258. See also Morales 2015: 27–32.

[49] The LXX makes the connection explicit by adding the phrase *pyr allotrion* ('strange fire') to 16:1 (cf. 10:1).

[50] This becomes an apt moment to initiate Jubilee with its redistribution of people (25:9–10).

[51] For this rendering of *ʾšm* see Sklar 2005: 24–41; Greenberg 2019: 25–26; cf. Harper forthcoming-a.

15:30) were beyond the remit of the cult to remedy. The penalty for individuals or groups is typically either death (e.g. Lev. 24:23; Num. 16:31–35) or being 'cut off' (*krt*; e.g. Lev. 18:29; 20:3), itself a termination of life, childbearing, or residence in the land.[52] The immediacy and unavoidability of punishment is frequently emphasized. However, while rebels may be summarily expunged, their wrongdoing defiles the tabernacle (cf. Lev. 20:3) and land (Lev. 18:25; Num. 35:33). Thus, while forgiveness may be superfluous for already-dead perpetrators, the residual impurity arising from their actions is problematic. Left unchecked, it would threaten Israel's ability to continue with Yahweh.[53]

This clarifies what Leviticus means by 'atonement'. The etymology of the Hebrew verb (*kpr*) and its precise mechanism are contested.[54] However, what *kpr* accomplishes is easier to ascertain. The verb occurs forty-nine times in Leviticus and is always enacted by a priest on behalf of either the community (4:13–16; 16:30) or an individual (including the high priest for himself [4:3; 16:11]). Thus, 'the priest … becomes *de facto* the indispensable mediator between God and human beings.'[55] In Leviticus, the priests enact *kpr* by means of blood manipulation. Leviticus 17:11 provides the essential rationale: 'the life of the flesh (*nepeš*) is in the blood, and I myself have given it to you upon the altar to atone for your lives (*napšōtêkem*)' (my tr.). Blood sacrifice is Yahweh's gift to Israel. The atonement (*kpr*) it achieves enables two key outcomes. First, atonement removes, or expiates, sin; forgiveness is the result (e.g. 4:20, 26). But second, atonement also removes, or purges, major impurity; purification is the result (e.g. 12:7; 14:19). The same means (blood sacrifice) performs the same act (atonement) with two possible results (expiation or purgation). While related, these functions remain distinct. Depending on context, *kpr* overcomes sin and/or impurity to restore relationship with Yahweh.[56]

---

[52] Sklar 2005: 15–17. Boda 2009: 56–57 argues, based on Lev. 20:18 and Num. 19:11–13, that 'cutting off' is not synonymous with death, but rather indicates estrangement from either assembly or Yahweh.

[53] In Leviticus, impurity consistently threatens Israel's removal not the departure of Yahweh's presence as is frequently assumed (Harper 2022a).

[54] Greenberg 2019 provides a recent summary and evaluation.

[55] Gerstenberger 1996: 61.

[56] Greenberg 2019: 192. Sklar 2005: 187 attempts to connect the functions: 'Since both inadvertent sin and major pollution endanger (requiring ransom) and pollute (requiring purgation), sacrificial atonement must both ransom and cleanse.'

The results of *kpr* are graphically realized in Leviticus 16 with the so-called 'scapegoat'.[57] This goat is not a sacrifice;[58] three times it is identified as the 'living' goat (16:10, 20, 21; cf. m. Yoma 6:6). Nevertheless, this animal performs a crucial ritual role. As Eric Gilchrest notes, 'The goat … suffers an evil meant for the Israelites'.[59] Crucially, the 'scapegoat' not only bears the iniquities confessed over it (16:21), but also the *consequence* of egregious sins and their resulting impurity – namely, exile from Yahweh's presence.[60] The goat is effectively 'cut off', dispatched 'to a cut-off land' (*ʾel-ʾereṣ gĕzērâ*, 16:22 my tr.).[61] Instead of expected death, the 'living' goat endures banishment in Israel's stead.[62] This act of substitution functions as a means of disposal as sin and its defilement are removed, repairing relationship with Yahweh. Leviticus 16 thus becomes the pre-eminent rite of restoration.

Creation themes heighten the significance of Yom Kippur:

> the Sabbath rest enjoined on the Day of Atonement evokes the seventh-day rest of creation's climax *at the very same time* that the high priest enters the divinely-indwelled adytum. In this way Lev 16 ritually recapitulates the time and space of the original creation and, in so doing, brings aspects of that primordial past into the present.[63]

For Christophe Nihan, therefore, Leviticus 1 – 16 functions as 'the grand climax' to the priestly writings as they chart the 'gradual redefinition in Israel of a cosmic order more in conformity with the original order'.[64] This inaugurates a new creation, albeit microcosmically. Even as Yom Kippur mitigates the after-effects of Nadab and Abihu's error (16:1), and the effects of Israel's sins and impurities thereafter (16:29–34), it also

---

[57] There are three main options for understanding *ʿăzāʾzēl*: (1) *ʿăzāʾzēl* is the name of a demon (cf. 1 En. 8:1; 9:6); (2) *ʿăzāʾzēl* is related to the Arabic *azazu* ('rough ground'), perhaps with the sense of 'precipice' (cf. m. Yoma 6:6); and (3) *ʿăzāʾzēl* derives from *ʿēz* ('goat') and *ʾzl* ('to go away'), hence 'go-away goat' or '(e)scape-goat'.

[58] Although the 'scapegoat' constitutes a singular *ḥaṭṭāʾt* ('purification offering') with the goat that is sacrificed (16:5).

[59] Gilchrest 2013: 41.

[60] Gilchrest 2013: 41–42; cf. Harper 2018: 168–74.

[61] Regarding translation of the hapax *gĕzērâ*, see Wenham 1979: 233.

[62] Harper 2018: 169.

[63] Harper 2018: 168.

[64] Nihan 2007: 609.

anticipates cosmic renewal and a conclusive end to sin and impurity.[65] Until that day, Yom Kippur ensures Israel would be cleansed annually from all its sins (16:30).

Yet, 16:30 raises questions about the connection between cleansing and sin. Is cleansing a metaphor for forgiveness? Or does sin generate impurity? These questions segue to Leviticus 18 – 20.

Leviticus 18 – 20

Leviticus 18 – 20 complicates the concept of impurity. In Leviticus 11 – 15, impurity is naturally occurring, generally unavoidable, often short term, and removable through various means. However, while similar terminology occurs in 18 – 20, the concept of impurity is entirely different.[66]

Leviticus 18:6–17 forbids 'uncovering the nakedness' of a close relative, that is, engaging in incestuous sexual activity. Doing so brings 'dishonour' (18:7, 8, 10, 14, 16) and is termed *zimmâ* ('shameful behaviour', 18:17), a word that conveys connotations of deliberate wrongdoing.[67] A second panel (18:18–23) expands beyond close relatives and explicitly employs impurity terms. Sex with a woman is forbidden 'during the uncleanness of her monthly period' (18:19).[68] Intercourse with a neighbour's wife (18:20) or an animal (18:23) would cause a man to 'become defiled by her/it' (*lĕṭām'â-bāh*, my tr.). Homosexual sex is labelled 'an abomination' (*tô'ēbâ*, 18:22; also 20:13) and bestiality a 'perversion' (*tebel*, 18:23; cf. 20:12). The chapter's final verses (18:24–30) demand pure conduct. Repetition of *kōl* ('any/all'; 18:24 [2x], 26, 27, 29) evokes all the chapter's prohibitions. The strong term 'abomination', previously used in 18:22, is applied to every listed transgression (18:26, 27, 29, 30). Avoidance is commanded by framing admonitions: 'Do not defile yourselves (*ṭm'* hithpael)

[65] Daniel 9 exploits this forward-leaning dimension of Yom Kippur (Harper 2015: 53–55). To the degree that the tabernacle (and later temple) should be viewed as representative of the cosmos, the cleansing of the earthly sanctuary on the Day of Atonement anticipates purification of the world. (I am grateful to Benjamin Gladd for this observation.)

[66] While the *ṭm'* root is used in relation to defilement throughout Leviticus, other terms, especially *tô'ēbâ* ('abomination'), are reserved for the impurities detailed in Lev. 18 and 20 (Klawans 2006: 55–56).

[67] The repetition of 'close relative' (*šĕ'ar/ša'ărâ*) in 18:6, 17 (cf. 18:12, 13) frames the intervening material and allows the final phrase, *zimmâ hiw'* ('that is shameful behaviour'; NIV 'wickedness'), to conclude the entire panel.

[68] The variance in consequence between 15:24 and 20:18 is best viewed as the result of accidental and deliberate action respectively.

by any of these' (18:24); 'Do not defile yourselves (*ṭm*ʾ hithpael) by them' (18:30; my tr.).

The consequences of these abominable behaviours are severe. The Canaanites are emblematic. Not only did these prior inhabitants defile themselves by their behaviour (18:24), they defiled the land (18:25, 27).[69] Consequently, the land vomited them out (18:25, 28). Graphic imagery aids the rhetorical point: those who act similarly will, likewise, be regurgitated (18:28). Thus, both native-born and resident foreigners must heed Yahweh's decrees (18:26) lest they be 'cut off' to safeguard national existence (18:29). Leviticus 20 clarifies what 'cutting off' entails, in decreasing severity: execution of perpetrators by divine or human means, whether male or female, Israelite or Gentile, human or animal (20:1–16, 27); banishment from the community (20:17–19);[70] and childlessness – that is, extirpation of a family line (20:20–21). Verse 3 further justifies these severe measures. To offer one's child to Molech, Yahweh says, would 'defile my sanctuary' (my tr.).[71]

Although impurity in Leviticus 18 and 20 bears similarities to impurity in 11 – 15, especially in relation to death for those who defile Yahweh's abode (15:31; 20:3–5), the concept is markedly different. The sources of impurity are no longer naturally occurring, bodily phenomena, but are instead volitional acts. Avoidance is therefore possible and is, in fact, commanded. The resulting defilement is long term, perhaps permanent; no purification rites are prescribed. Yet, nothing is said about transmission to other people. Intriguingly, the impure are not explicitly barred from contact with sacred places (contrast 12:4).[72] I return to the question of how to reconcile these divergent conceptions of impurity in chapter 2.

The remainder of Leviticus

The remaining data from Leviticus and Numbers nuance the above analysis. Leviticus 17:15 and 22:8 reflect 11:39–40. Eating a permitted

[69] See my excursus on land defilement in chapter 4. Although Walton and Walton 2017: 128 claim Canaanite defilement of the land indicates only failure to ritually cleanse it, they do not sufficiently grapple with this wider biblical motif.

[70] Such 'cutting off' is synonymous with death: 'In the wilderness period this would have entailed separation from the manna-fed community, thus increasing risk of death; similarly, within the land, banishment would mean exclusion from agricultural produce and its means of production' (Harper 2018: 170 n. 47).

[71] There is debate regarding whether sanctuary defilement happens remotely (Milgrom 2000b: 1734), only by entering (t. Šebu 1:8), or not at all (Greenberg 2019: 55–63).

[72] In Num. 5 those suspected of immorality are brought *to the sanctuary* for investigation (see below). Similarly, in 1 Kings 2:28–31, Joab, guilty of bloodshed, flees *to the altar* (cf. Exod. 21:14).

animal that died without being correctly slaughtered ('found dead or torn by wild animals') makes one impure. The issue is that the animal's blood is not drained (17:13–14). Because of its defiling potential, priests must avoid this source of food altogether (22:8) or risk death for violating holiness boundaries (22:9; cf. 12:4).[73] The resulting short-term ('till evening'), non-transmissible impurity affects Israelites and non-Israelites equally and must be addressed by washing and waiting (17:15). To refuse cleansing increases the seriousness of the matter: 'he shall bear his iniquity' (17:16 ESV). Thus, 17:16 further reveals the permeable boundary between impurity and sin. While becoming impure is not by itself sinful, foregoing purification is.

The potential of dismissing cleansing rites is also addressed in 5:2–3. Listed infractions are not inadvertent (contra NIV 'unwitting'); rather, a person contacts impurity, but then forgets about it – 'it is hidden from him' (*wĕne ʿlam mimmenû*, 5:2; also 5:3, 4).[74] Leviticus 5:2–3 problematizes flippant attitudes towards cleansing. Hence, whenever such a person 'suffers guilt's consequences', he or she must respond by confessing sin and presenting a purification offering to secure atonement (5:5–13) and experience forgiveness (*slḥ*, 5:10, 13).[75] Yahweh's people must not willingly remain defiled when provided a means of purification.

Purity is also prerequisite for sacrifice. Animals must be from the pure creatures identified in 11:1–23: from herd, flock or permitted birds.[76] Officiating priests must be careful to avoid defilement while carrying out their tasks. Any of the impurities listed in 22:4–8 must be ameliorated before a priest approaches the holy things offered by the people (22:3), including sacrificial meat (22:6–7). Failure would 'profane' (*ḥll* piel) Yahweh's name (22:2), that is, diminish his status in the eyes of onlookers, resulting in death (22:9). Offerers, likewise, must also be pure to share in sacrificial meals (7:19–21). Again, the consequences are stark: 'if anyone

---

[73] Exod. 22:31 operates with the same logic, although it applies the ban more universally.

[74] For this idiomatic reading, see Wenham 1979: 92–93; Milgrom 1991: 298–99.

[75] See Peres 2021 regarding bloodless atonement and forgiveness.

[76] Lev. 1:1 – 5:26 [1:1 – 6:7]; 12:6–8; 14:4–7, 10–11, 21–22; 15:14–15, 29–30; 16:3–15; cf. 27:11, 27. Even though there is a resulting affinity between Yahweh's 'diet' and Israel's, it is not exact and cannot serve as a rationale for food prohibitions (contra Firmage 1990: 196–97). Fish and deer, for example, were eaten by the Israelites, but were not suitable for sacrifice. Klawans 2006: 85–87 argues with appeal to 2 Sam. 24:24 that ownership is fundamental to sacrifice: one cannot offer what one does not own by rearing or cultivating. The same logic lies behind Lev. 27:26–29: listed items *already* belong to Yahweh and cannot therefore be (re)gifted.

who is unclean eats any meat of the fellowship offering belonging to the LORD, they must be cut off from their people' (7:20). Persons are not cut off for becoming impure, but for eating holy food while defiled. These stipulations reveal an overarching logic to Leviticus 1 – 16: Israel's sacrifices (Lev. 1 – 7), the priests who present them (Lev. 8 – 10), and the precincts in which they are offered (Lev. 16), must remain separate from sources of impurity (Lev. 11 – 15). In fact, a core function of Leviticus 11 – 15 is to safeguard the efficacy of Israel's cult. Purity and sacrifice work together.[77] This remains the case even though some cultic processes render people impure; for example, the person who leads the 'scapegoat' away from the camp (16:26) or the one who disposes of the animal carcasses on the same day (16:27–28).

Although articulated more clearly in Numbers, Leviticus also regards human death as defiling. Corpses convey direct and indirect impurity by touch (22:4). Therefore, priests must limit exposure to close relatives only (21:1–3). For anybody else, 'he must not defile himself (*ṭmʾ* hithpael)' (21:4). The rationale is twofold: priests have been set apart as holy (21:6, 8; 22:9; cf. 8:1–36) and they offer up the food of God (21:6, 8, 21).[78] The high priest, however, is understood as permanently connected to the tabernacle (21:12; cf. 10:7). Hence, he must never make himself impure by corpse-contact, even for father or mother (21:11; cf. Num 19:14). He is not even to mourn for the dead (21:10; cf. 10:6; 19:27–28; 21:5). Moreover, a high priest may only marry a virgin lest he 'profane his offspring among his people' (21:14–15 ESV; cf. 21:7).[79] Because the high priestly line is hereditary (16:32), its purity must be maintained.

Defilement and cleansing in Numbers

Numbers operates with the same twofold conception of impurity as Leviticus. Thus, I move through the material more quickly while noting important clarifications and expansions.

In Numbers 5:1–4, Yahweh commands the removal of anyone, male or female, who is *ṣāraʿat*-infected (cf. Lev. 13 – 14), who has a genital discharge (cf. Lev. 15), or who is corpse-contaminated (cf. Lev. 22:4; Num.

[77] The point is carefully explored by Klawans 2006.

[78] There is, again, a strong connection between purity and sacrifice.

[79] I explore the connection between Lev. 21:15 and 1 Cor. 7:14 in chapter 8.

19; 31:19).[80] The community must send such people outside the camp, Yahweh says, 'so they will not defile (*ṭmʾ* piel) their camp where I dwell among them' (5:3 my tr.). Miriam is likewise banished for seven days following her punitive affliction with *ṣāraʿat* (Num. 12:9–15). Thus, as in Leviticus, it is Yahweh's proximate presence that problematizes impurity. His dwelling must be kept separate from defilement. Nonetheless, those with minor impurities are allowed to remain (cf. Num. 19:7). Exclusion is limited to sources of major impurity, most likely to curtail secondary transmission.[81]

Corpse-pollution receives its most sustained treatment in Numbers 19 (cf. Num. 31:19–24). Dead bodies, whether Israelite or Gentile, produce major impurity.[82] Direct contact conveys a seven-day impurity to Israelites and Gentiles alike (19:10–11, 16), and any person entering a 'tent' containing a corpse, or who touches a human bone or grave, also becomes defiled (19:14, 16). The cause of death is immaterial (19:16); whether at home or on the battlefield, corpses defile. Secondary defilement, albeit of lower grades, also features: 'Anything that an unclean person touches becomes unclean, and anyone who touches it becomes unclean till evening' (19:22).[83] However, because Israelite culture valued burial (e.g. Gen. 23:4–20; Num. 20:1; Josh. 24:29–31), becoming impure by handling human remains was not only necessary but praiseworthy (e.g. 2 Sam. 2:5).[84] Therefore, contracting major impurity and being righteous are not mutually exclusive. In fact, Yahweh, at times, commands burial (e.g. Deut. 21:23) and, intriguingly, even buries bodies himself (Deut. 34:6).

[80] Here, I read *nepeš* as short for *nepeš mēt* ('dead body'; cf. 6:6; Milgrom 1990: 33). Notably, neither menstruants nor new mothers are banished. Although specifying the wilderness camp, 5:1–4 shaped Second Temple purity boundaries (see chapter 6; Furstenberg 2023: 27–34). Furthermore, Morales 2024: 20 argues that Num. 5 anticipates the removal of all impurity from the eschatological city in Rev. 21 – 22.

[81] The context is important: imminent departure from Sinai and the movement of the ark among the people (10:33–36; cf. Deut. 23:9–14). Similarly, because divine fire consumed some of the inner edges of the camp (i.e. the areas proximate to the tabernacle, 11:1), the Levites are appointed to guard the tabernacle perimeter (18:2–5).

[82] The pollution mitigated in Num. 31:19 relates to *non-Israelite* corpses; cf. 31:49 (Hayes 2002: 38).

[83] Maccoby 1999: 6 provides an itemized list of polluting effects and timeframes. In rabbinic discourse, corpse-pollution was termed the 'Father of fathers of impurity' due to its potential to cause subsidiary defilement.

[84] For analysis of Israelite funerary rites and the societal importance of touching the dead, see Sonia 2020.

Nevertheless, corpse-impurity is problematic and Numbers 19 proceeds to stipulate mandated cleansing. The ritual is complex. A 'red cow' (*pārâ ʾădummâ*), donated by the people, is slaughtered by a priest outside the camp (19:2–3). Some of the blood is sprinkled towards the tent of meeting before the entire animal is burned with other red items: cedar wood, hyssop and scarlet wool (19:4–6). Although not turned to smoke on the altar, 'it is a purification offering' (*ḥaṭṭāʾt hiwʾ*, 19:9 my tr.; cf. 19:17). The resulting ashes are stored 'in a pure place' (*bĕmāqôm ṭāhôr*) outside the camp, where they are kept 'for waters of impurity' (*lĕmê niddâ*, 19:9 my tr.; contra NIV 'water of cleansing')[85] – that is, a combination of ash and 'fresh [lit. 'living'] water' (19:17). The ash-water mixture is made effective by sprinkling upon corpse-defiled objects or persons on the third and seventh days (19:12, 18–19; cf. 31:19–24). Sprinkling does not require a priest; any 'pure man' (*ʾîš ṭāhôr*) may perform the rite (19:18). Then, on the seventh day, after washing body and clothes and waiting until evening, defiled persons become 'pure' (19:20; cf. 19:12). Although sprinkling is enacted by a third party, the onus remains on individuals to purify themselves (*ḥṭʾ* hithpael; 19:13, 20). One must seek cleansing when required. Refusing to undergo purification is considered defiant, for the person deliberately 'defiles Yahweh's tabernacle/sanctuary' (*miškan/miqdaš yhwh ṭimmēʾ*, 19:13, 20 my tr.). Accordingly, 'that person will be cut off from Israel', 'from the midst of the assembly' (19:13, 20 my tr.). Becoming impure for the sake of the dead may be laudable; deliberately remaining so is not.

Numbers 9 addresses the potential of corpse-defilement inhibiting participation in an obligatory festival. Such clashes were inevitable, especially considering the possible range of mid- to long-term impurities. Numbers 9 thus speaks to the broader matter of weighing mutually exclusive requirements. In this case, the piety of those appealing to Moses and Aaron is unquestionable: they do not conceal impurity, but declare their desire to present Yahweh's Passover offering at the appointed time (9:6–7). Henceforth, Yahweh permits the temporarily impure to celebrate Passover one month later (9:10–11). Purity is, again, a non-negotiable for cultic activity, whether at the tabernacle or in the homes where Passover

---

[85] Touching the 'waters of impurity' conveys minor impurity ('till evening', 19:21). Thus, as observed in Lev. 16, ritual participants in Num. 19 are rendered impure by engaging in a mandatory process (19:21; cf. 19:7–8, 10).

was celebrated (cf. Exod. 12:46). The appointed time for Passover could be set aside; ritual purity could not.[86]

Numbers also assumes that impurity stems from (some) moral transgressions. Numbers 5:11–31 outlines the process for wives suspected of unfaithfulness.[87] As in Leviticus 18, sexual immorality, whether disclosed or not, defiles (5:13). Hence, if the woman had engaged in extramarital sex, she is understood to have 'defiled herself' (*ṭmʾ* niphal, 5:14, 20, 27, 29) and to have 'turned aside to impurity' (*śāṭît ṭumʾâ*, 5:19 my tr.). The problem is not contact with semen; no washing or waiting is prescribed (cf. Lev. 15:18). Moreover, presumed impurity does not bar the woman from the sanctuary (cf. Lev. 12:4; 15:31).[88] Instead, proximity to holiness increases risk as she is presented to the priest (5:15) and stands 'before Yahweh' (5:16, 18, 30 my tr.) to ingest dust from the tabernacle floor mixed with 'holy water' (5:17, 24). The juxtaposition is highlighted by the sevenfold uses of both 'Yahweh' and 'impurity'.[89] If the woman had defiled herself through infidelity, then 'her womb shall swell, and her thigh shall fall away' (5:27 ESV), an idiom for barrenness as 5:28 makes clear (cf. Lev. 20:20–21). As per Leviticus 18 and 20, no means of purification are provided. The passage simply concludes that, if guilty, 'the woman shall bear her iniquity' (5:31 ESV).[90]

Numbers 35 differentiates between deliberate and accidental killing and the resultant need for cities of refuge. In addition to sexual immorality and idolatry (Lev. 18), wrongful shedding of blood (murder) also defiles the land: 'Bloodshed pollutes the land' (35:33; cf. 35:30–32). The resulting plea to preserve land purity is stated twice – 'Do not pollute (*ḥnp*) the land' (35:33); 'Do not defile (*ṭmʾ* piel)' it (35:34) – with appeal to Yahweh's residence as rationale (35:34).

Many of the impurity themes observed in Numbers and Leviticus coalesce in Numbers 6. The passage outlines the 'law of the Nazarite' (6:21). Becoming a Nazarite entailed a special vow of separation to Yahweh (6:2). Dedication, for a specified time (6:13), was available to

86 The importance of Passover is indicated in 9:13, which stipulates that any able celebrant who avoids participation must be cut off.

87 This text's seeming bias against women and assumed protection of patriarchal power has been rebutted elsewhere. See Milgrom 1990: 346–50; Ashley 2022: 96–99; Morales 2024: 149–58.

88 Contra Romney Wegner 2003: 459–60.

89 Morales 2024: 155.

90 Because the adultery remains humanly unknown, the death penalty is not enacted (Milgrom 1990: 349–50).

both men and women (6:2) and elevated a person's holiness: 'All the days of his separation he is holy to the LORD' (6:8 ESV). This enabled non-priests to approximate priestly holiness.[91] Accordingly, purity became more pressing (cf. Lev. 21 – 22). Nazarites were to avoid 'wine and strong drink' (*yayin wĕšēkar*, 6:3), the same beverages forbidden to Aaron and sons during tabernacle service (*yayin wĕšēkar*, Lev. 10:9). They could not cut their hair (6:5; cf. Lev. 21:5) or touch a dead body, even of father or mother (6:6–7; cf. Lev. 21:11). Indeed, corpse-contact, inadvertent or otherwise,[92] defiled the hair the Nazarite had dedicated and necessitated restarting the entire process (6:12), following a seven-day cleansing from corpse-contamination (6:9; cf. Num. 19). This sustained extolling of ritual purity works in tandem with the concern for moral purity in Numbers 5 to underscore that the Israelite camp has become a heavenly dwelling centred on Yahweh's presence and holiness.[93]

Summary

Leviticus and Numbers contain the most systematic discussion of defilement and cleansing within Scripture and deserve the considered attention we have given them. Nevertheless, the purity dynamics revealed are alien to many Western Christians for whom this is a foreign and complicated set of ideas. Some may perceive only an impenetrable morass. However, as the next chapter demonstrates, there is a discernible logic at work, despite the (perhaps) overwhelming level of detail. Moreover, there are indications that purity, in its various forms, is a common *human* concern, not just an Old Testament or Jewish proclivity. Therefore, chapter 2 provides an initial synthesis of the data surveyed in this chapter before progressing further.

[91] This was not functional equality. Nazarites still required priests to perform cultic procedures on their behalf (see 6:10–11, 16–17).

[92] Inadvertent exposure is nevertheless regarded as sinful and required purification, ascension, and reparation offerings (6:10–12).

[93] See Morales 2024: 145, 173. Morales argues that the strayed woman of Num. 5 and the Nazarite of Num. 6 map two divergent alternatives that lie before Israel (149).

2

Conceptualizing defilement and cleansing

The exploration of Leviticus and Numbers in chapter 1 reveals the diversity and complexity of purity in biblical Israel. Nevertheless, there is an inherent logic at work.[1] These texts project a worldview in which people, places and objects exist along a pure–impure spectrum.[2] That spectrum is dynamic. While purity is the default state, a range of naturally occurring, uncontrollable phenomena defile persons and objects, rendering them impure for specified, but occasionally indefinite, periods. Various cleansing rites are outlined to restore a person's or object's purity. Additionally, specific moral transgressions defile. Yet this impurity is long lasting, even permanent, and, in addition to persons, defiles land and sanctuary. In these cases, human means of purification are noticeably scant. Thus, while Leviticus and Numbers provide an initial sketch of purity, indeed a crucial foundation for assessing other biblical and extra-biblical materials, the data nevertheless raise important questions that must be addressed before moving forward.

This chapter therefore presents an important distillation of the analysis thus far. Some readers will find it a helpful orientation before proceeding further. Others, however, may find it too abstract at this point. For these readers, it may be better to return to this discussion having read through the subsequent chapters. The difference may simply reflect whether one prefers to learn inductively, from details to ideas, or deductively, by establishing a conceptual map before engaging the particulars.

[1] This point has not always been granted. The current consensus that biblical purity represents a coherent system is, in many respects, directly creditable to Mary Douglas's pioneering work. See Douglas 1966; 1993a; 1993b; 1999.

[2] Whether the ritual texts of the Pentateuch are best understood as prescriptive, descriptive, or idealistic, is debated. Irrespective, a distinction between ritual practice and ritual text must be preserved (cf. Nihan and Rhyder 2021).

Clarifying concepts and terminology

Defining im/purity as well as selecting the most germane English gloss(es) is not straightforward. Leviticus and Numbers reveal alternate forms of impurity that operate simultaneously, even though this distinction is not always recognized or maintained by scholars.[3] Table 2.1 summarizes the key differences.

Table 2.1 The alternate forms of impurity in Leviticus and Numbers

Impurity A	Impurity B
Natural	Unnatural
Unavoidable	Avoidable
Not a result of sin	Only stems from (some) sins
Often short term	Long term
Secondary transmission possible	No secondary transmission
Does not pollute the land	Pollutes the land
The impure are explicitly barred from sacred places	The impure are not explicitly barred from sacred places
Cleansing always possible	Cleansing usually not possible

In Leviticus and Numbers, Impurity A is predominantly located in Leviticus 12 – 16, 21 – 22 and Numbers 6, 9 and 19. Impurity B occurs in Leviticus 18, 20 and Numbers 5, 35.[4] There are either *two* purity systems that work in tandem,[5] or, as is sometimes argued, one overarching system with two major subdivisions.[6] Irrespective of how one articulates the relationship, it is imperative not to conflate types A and B. Despite lexical overlap (esp. the *ṭm*ʾ root), the two conceptions of

[3] The oversight is discussed by Klawans 2000: 6. For one example of muddled conceptions, see Welch 2012: 65–75.

[4] Leviticus 11 sits somewhere between A and B: animal impurity is naturally occurring, but also avoidable. Thus, many ancient Jews did not think that eating non-kosher animals transmitted *ritual* impurity; rather, ingesting non-kosher meat was an act of disobedience that generated *moral* impurity (Furstenberg 2008; Williams 2024: 374).

[5] So Hoffmann 1905–1906: 303–4; Frymer-Kensky 1983: 404; Klawans 2000.

[6] So Douglas 1973: 140 who identifies different sets of rules that nevertheless display 'systematic interrelatedness'. See also Wright 1991: 170–73. Klawans 2000: 36–38 lists problems inherent to maintaining one overarching system.

purity are markedly different. However, because vocabulary is shared, one must choose English terms that distinguish Impurity A from Impurity B to avoid confusion.[7] However, there is no consensus on the most appropriate phrasing. Significant alternatives are summarized in Table 2.2.

Table 2.2 Proposed glosses for Impurity A and Impurity B

Advocate	Impurity A	Impurity B
Büchler[8]	levitical	religious, spiritual, moral
Paschen[9]	cultic (*kultischer*)	moral (*moralischer*)
Neusner[10]	cultic	ethical
Frymer-Kensky[11]	pollution beliefs, contagious pollutions, ritual pollutions	danger beliefs, danger pollutions
Wright[12]	tolerated	prohibited
Milgrom[13]	physical	spiritual
Averbeck[14]	physical	moral
Maccoby[15]	ritual	metaphorical
Klawans[16]	ritual	moral
Kazen[17]	outer	inner
Philip[18]	real	metaphorical, abstract
Erbele-Küster[19]	cultic, bodily, cult disabled, ritual	?
Furstenberg[20]	bodily	Sin-impurity

[7] Klawans 2000: 22.

[8] Büchler 1928: ix, 214, 29.

[9] Paschen 1970: 13.

[10] Neusner 1973: 25.

[11] Frymer-Kensky 1983: 404.

[12] Wright 1991: 158; 1992: 729–30.

[13] Milgrom 1991: 254 ('spiritual impurity' is linked to the inadvertent sins of Lev. 4).

[14] Averbeck 1997: 4:478–79.

[15] Maccoby 1999.

[16] Klawans 2000: 22–31; 2006: 53–56.

[17] Kazen 2002: 219.

[18] Philip 2006: 64.

[19] Erbele-Küster 2017; 2021.

[20] Furstenberg 2023: 21.

For reasons clarified below, I favour 'ritual' and 'moral' as the least problematic labels. Nonetheless, it is crucial not to assume an anachronistic separation between ritual and moral (let alone smuggle in a relative value judgment). Ritual and moral remain closely intertwined in Old Testament ethics.[21] Conformity in *both* spheres is essential for life 'before Yahweh'.

Scholars frequently resort to evolutionary models to account for alternative forms of impurity. The relationship has been construed both ways. Many consider ritual purity to be original, only later developing moral connotations.[22] Others, however, insist purity first had a moral sense, which (d)evolved into a ritual category – a position classically advocated by Julius Wellhausen.[23] These differing chronological reconstructions rest, in large measure, on prior assumptions regarding textual provenance. However, as Jonathan Klawans observes, the Old Testament gives little or no insight into this supposed progression (either way).[24] Even what little can be gained is frustrated by a lack of consensus regarding the relative (and absolute) dating of biblical texts. Nonetheless, differences between Old and New Testaments or between Second Temple and tannaitic literature are easier to discern and are, in contrast to the vexed dating of Hebrew canonical books, based on actual chronological progression.[25] Given the methodological problems that beset evolutionist schemes, Klawans instead advocates for an original complexity in the biblical texts that can be described and investigated without resolving how it emerged.[26] This aligns with the text immanent and thematic approach I adopt in this volume. Prehistory aside, the received texts of Leviticus and Numbers attest a twofold conception of purity. Responsible exegetes must resist simplifying the inherent complexities.

A related question concerns ontology. Should impurity be understood through an essentialist or non-essentialist lens? How this question is answered usually correlates with the assumed relationship between ritual and moral impurity. Many suggest ritual impurity is literal whereas moral

[21] Barton 2014: 185–210; Kazen 2015c.

[22] E.g. Hayes 2002: 42–43. Kazen 2014 proposes a base notion of 'dirt/disgust', which accumulated metaphorical applications to ritual and moral concerns.

[23] Wellhausen 1885: 420–25; cf. Neusner 1973: 25.

[24] Klawans 2006: 3–10; likewise, Barton 2014: 190.

[25] Accordingly, chapters 6 – 8 map shifting conceptions of purity in later literature.

[26] Klawans 2006: 35–36, following Hubert and Mauss 1964.

impurity is figurative. Hyam Maccoby, for instance, claims texts such as Leviticus 18 'use the term "uncleanness" in a metaphorical non-ritual sense'.[27] Likewise, 'pollution of the Land is a metaphorical, not a real pollution.'[28] David Hoffmann, however, asserts the converse: defilement caused by transgression is concrete; ritual impurity is the symbolic extension.[29] Common to both positions is an assumed progression from (earlier) concrete reference to (later) metaphorical meaning, albeit with differing starting points. Accordingly, Klawans' reservations regarding evolutionist schemes are again applicable. He warns, 'It is no longer sound to assume that metaphor is historically secondary. Quite often the reverse can be demonstrated, even within the Hebrew Bible.'[30] For this reason, and considering terminological overlap, Klawans prefers to consider both types of impurity as real even while allowing for figural expression.[31]

> [W]e ought to understand that with both kinds of impurity, we are dealing with the perceived effects that result from actual physical processes. In the case of ritual impurity, a real, physical process or event (e.g., death or menstruation) has a perceived effect: impermanent contagion that affects people and certain objects within their reach. In the case of moral impurity, a real, physical process or event (e.g., child sacrifice or adultery) has a different perceived effect: a noncontagious defilement that affects persons, the land, and the sanctuary. In both cases, the impurity is conveyed by contact: ritual impurity is conveyed by direct and indirect human contact, and moral impurity is conveyed to the land by sins that take place upon it.[32]

What, however, is conveyed to persons or land in the act of defilement? What *is* impurity? The question is difficult to resolve. A common mistake is to suppose that ancient cultures were unable to develop sophisticated symbolic conceptualizations. They were. At the same time, language can

[27] Maccoby 1999: 12; similarly, Neusner 1973: 108.

[28] Maccoby 1999: 200; also Milgrom 1991: 37; 2000b: 1327.

[29] Hoffmann 1905–1906: 2:22, 59. For Hoffmann, moral impurity defiles both body and soul ('Körper und Seele').

[30] Klawans 2006: 66. See also Lakoff and Johnson 1980.

[31] For metaphorical appropriation of purification language, see DiFransico 2016.

[32] Klawans 2000: 34.

also be used concretely. In fact, both concrete and symbolic dimensions may work simultaneously (as, for instance, with the concept of 'sacrifice').[33] There is, therefore, divergence of opinion regarding the ontology of impurity. Kazen, following Paschen, proposes 'dirt' as the base concept from which other extended meanings developed.[34] Jacob Milgrom employs the term 'miasma' (or 'noxious ray'[35]) to conceptualize impurity as a physical contagion that could be transferred aerially as well as by physical touch.[36] Erbele-Küster follows Milgrom, but argues that impurity 'goes beyond pure physical contact' to become a quasi-real phenomenon, which exists as social-theological construct.[37] Klawans opts for 'potent force' to describe moral impurity, thereby deeming it more than mere metaphor, but still intangible (like the *force* of gravity).[38] And, as noted above, many understand impurity, especially moral impurity, as metaphor only.[39]

Physical substance — Quasi-physical — Force — Metaphor →

Thankfully, resolving the issue is not crucial. Whatever the biblical authors imagined as they wrote 'pure' or 'impure', the terms still fulfil important literary, rhetorical and theological functions, which can be assessed.

Impurity and sin

The relationship between impurity and sin needs to be carefully defined for there is a widespread tendency to conflate or otherwise misconstrue category boundaries. There are two forms of impurity, each of which displays a different correlation to sin. The correspondence between *moral* impurity and sin is clear. Certain heinous sins – sexual immorality, idolatry and

[33] See Lam 2016: 189–90.

[34] Kazen 2014; Paschen 1970: 27.

[35] Milgrom 2000a: 729.

[36] '[I]mpurity was a physical substance, an aerial miasma' (Milgrom 1991: 257). Likewise, Schellenberg 2014: 168–69.

[37] Erbele-Küster 2021: 248; similarly, Eberhart 2011: 90. Accordingly, Erbele-Küster concludes, 'The purity regulations in Lev. 12 and 15 are primarily not descriptions of physiological processes. Rather, with the aid of the body, they construct ritual purity/impurity' (252).

[38] Klawans 2000: 29.

[39] Maccoby 1999: 127 understands Lev. 14:36 to necessarily demand a non-essentialist conception of impurity.

bloodshed – automatically pollute persons, sanctuary and land.[40] Thus, perpetrators simultaneously become guilty, morally impure and a source of moral defilement. Nevertheless, Klawans laments, 'Scholars of ancient Judaism have not paid enough attention to the question of the defiling force of sin.'[41] There is a tendency to dismiss the issue, often by assuming a metaphorical meaning, or to avoid it entirely.[42] David Wright, for instance, concludes that sin does not defile people in any real sense.[43] While a figurative conception of moral impurity may align more neatly with the abstract concept of sin favoured in Western thinking, Leviticus and Numbers treat this type of defilement as being as real as ritual impurity.[44]

Clarifying the relationship between *ritual* impurity and sin is more difficult. Angel Rodriguez, for example, blurs the distinction by claiming that if a Nazarite contacts death, 'ritual impurity could be considered a sin.'[45] However, as Milgrom rightly counters, the sin in view is desecration of the holy, not becoming ritually impure.[46] While there are pathways between ritual impurity and sin (see below), the categories are mutually distinct. Boundaries between sin and ritual impurity can also be collapsed in more subtle ways. Commenting on Leviticus 12, Jerry Shepherd concludes, 'even when an individual presents a sin offering and there is no real question of some personal sin … [s]in is always in the background. … [T]he purification offering is indeed a sin offering because [the mother's] contact with death is the result of the sin of the first parents.'[47] Shepherd assumes a connection between childbirth and death (based on maternal mortality). However, even if granted, reminding readers of a 'theological-symbolic world' threatened by sin and death still falls short of making ritual impurity itself sinful.[48] Ritual impurity may lead to sin, but is not itself sinful.

[40] Maccoby 1999: 199 argues that these acts were not deemed reprehensible only because they defiled the land. Rather, they defiled because they were objectively abhorrent.

[41] Klawans 2000: 13.

[42] Klawans 2000: 12. Correcting this lacuna is the major focus of Klawans' work.

[43] Wright 1987b; 1991: 162–63.

[44] Schellenberg 2014: 170–72; Klawans 2000: vii.

[45] Rodriguez 1979: 104.

[46] Milgrom 1991: 256.

[47] Shepherd 2021: 166.

[48] The quoted phrase is from Boda 2009: 74. Klawans 2000: 37 itemizes instances where ritual symbolism is explained (e.g. Num. 15:37–41) and notes its absence in ritual purity legislation. However, as I argue elsewhere (Harper 2018), allusion and intertextuality can also function as indirect explanations of ritual.

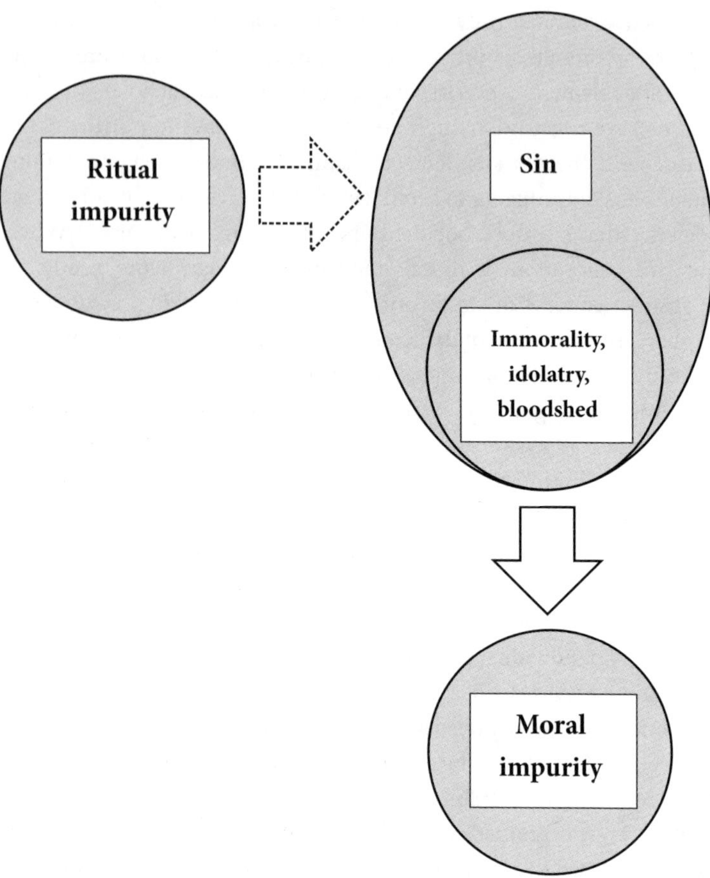

Figure 2.1 A pictorial representation of how sin and impurity relate in Leviticus and Numbers

The relationship between sin and impurity in Leviticus and Numbers is pictorially represented in Figure 2.1.

Impurity and sin remain distinct categories. Nevertheless, the dotted arrow represents instances where ritual impurity may lead to sin. This is most obviously the case when a person deliberately becomes impure (e.g. Lev. 20:18), eschews purification rites (e.g. Lev. 5:2–3; 17:16; Num. 19:13, 20), or violates holiness boundaries while in an impure state (e.g. Lev. 7:20–21; 22:3). In Leviticus and Numbers, 'Defiant disregard for ritual purity laws is considered a moral violation.'[49] The arrow is one-way,

[49] Boda 2009: 53. This observation has significant implications for reading the Gospels.

however. Sinning, by itself, does not render a person ritually impure.[50] However, within the larger field of 'Sin' there is a subset consisting of sexual immorality, idolatry and bloodshed. In Old Testament perspective, these are the most egregious transgressions. The solid downward arrow indicates that those who commit such acts automatically become morally impure. The resulting entailments are worth clarifying. In Leviticus and Numbers, one can sin without becoming ritually or morally impure. On the other hand, one can become ritually impure, but not be guilty of sin. But if one is morally impure, then, by definition, one is also a sinner. Of course, someone could qualify on all three counts. A murderer who failed to purify the resulting corpse-contamination would not only be guilty, but also ritually *and* morally defiled.

Impurity and holiness

Holiness is often defined negatively as *separation from*. However, the concept is more essentially a positive statement of 'god-ness' (cf. Isa. 6:3).[51] Yahweh alone is intrinsically holy. For all other entities, holiness is derivative. This is the logic behind invitations for Israel to become holy as Yahweh is holy (Lev. 11:44–45; 19:2; 20:7, 26) and assertions that it is God who makes holy (e.g. Lev. 20:8; 21:23). Furthermore, holiness is not primarily a moral category. While ethical conduct is sometimes explicit (e.g. Lev. 19), non-moral use of holiness terminology is more common and is used to describe objects (Lev. 12:4; Num. 16:38), places (Lev. 6:16; 7:30), times (Gen. 2:3; Lev. 23) and the ritual status of persons (Num. 6:8). Holiness demarcates that which belongs to Yahweh's realm (cf. Num. 16:5). It is also graded: there is a spectrum of diminishing holiness from Yahweh *in se* (*qādôš qādôš qādôš* ['holy, holy, holy'], Isa. 6:3), to 'most holy' (*qōdeš qădāšîm*), to 'holy' (*qādôš*).[52] This spectrum is mapped out spatially in the tabernacle and temple with their accommodation of Yahweh's presence in the 'most holy place'.

Leviticus and Numbers insist that holiness be kept separate from impurity.[53] Moreover, only limited and tightly controlled interaction

[50] For later variations on this, see chapter 6.

[51] Cf. Jenson 1992: 48 n. 4 who notes that linking the etymology of holiness to notions of separation has been abandoned.

[52] Jenson 1992.

[53] Following Douglas's seminal *Purity and Danger* (1966), it is commonplace to find holiness equated with wholeness. Thus, whatever is not 'whole' corresponds to the non-holy and impure

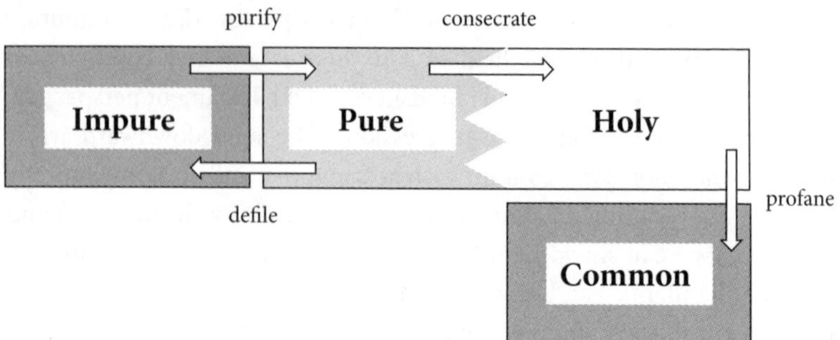

Figure 2.2 The interactions between impure, pure, holy and common

between pure and holy is allowed; for example, presenting animals at the tabernacle's entrance (Lev. 1:3; 3:2) or laypersons eating holy portions of the fellowship offerings (Lev. 7:16–21).[54] The driving concern is protection, not of the holy as is commonly assumed,[55] but of the pure and impure for whom unauthorized contact with holiness results in death (Num. 4:19–20; cf. 1 Sam. 6:19; 2 Sam. 6:6-7).[56] 'The describable presence of God is revealed as holy precisely insofar as it relentlessly threatens the survival of unholy participants.'[57] The relationship between these categories is mapped (in simplified form) in Figure 2.2.[58] In this figure, I assume the category 'common' is not simply an umbrella term that includes both 'impure' and 'pure'.[59] Rather, holy-common works as a distinct binary in

– including physical disability. For instance, deSilva 2022: 278–79 states, 'Defilement and unholiness separated people from contact with the pure and whole God. Thus blemished and deformed persons are barred from the sanctuary, since it would affront holiness to be presented with unwholeness'. However, regarding Lev. 21:17–23, Douglas's (and deSilva's) formulation simply does not work. As Reeve 2018: 181 convincingly demonstrates, a holiness-wholeness paradigm 'fails to notice that blemished (i.e., "un-whole") priests are implicitly declared *holy* by the text'. There is no straightforward connection between physical impairment and impurity. Otherwise, as Cox 2011: 247-48 reasons, disabled priests would be prohibited from eating 'most holy' and 'holy' offerings (Lev. 21:22; cf. 22:1–9).

[54] Frymer-Kensky 1983: 404. Klawans 2006: 58 reasons that ritual purity separated people from what made them least Godlike: being subject to death with the corresponding need for preservation through sexual intercourse and childbirth. Moreover, impurity excluded the whole cycle of life and death from cultic operations (Maccoby 1999: 49–50).

[55] E.g. Frymer-Kensky 1983: 403; Milgrom 1991: 50; Wright 1992: 729; Hundley 2011; Cranz 2017: 122, 41–42.

[56] See, further, Harper 2022a: 488–91.

[57] Radner 2016: 172.

[58] Reproduced from Harper 2022b: 174.

[59] Contra Wenham 1979: 19; Boda 2009: 51.

which 'common' is a negative descriptor that indicates the diminishment or public devaluing of something 'holy'.[60]

Impurity and social control

While much of the purity legislation in Leviticus and Numbers stipulates individual requirements, there are important social dimensions. This is obvious with ritual purity.[61] Entering sacred precincts or contacting holy items while ritually impure endangers an individual's life (Lev. 12:4; 15:31; 16:2; 22:3). However, the contagious nature of many impurities threatens others' wellbeing. While avoiding ritual impurity may, in many cases, be impossible, awareness of one's status and corresponding likelihood of defiling others is crucial.[62] Moral impurity, likewise, endangers the body politic. Frymer-Kensky clarifies the threat:

> One does not share the danger of an adulterer or of someone who has eaten blood by touching him. There is no immediate danger to others in allowing these people to walk around, and therefore there are no prescribed patterns of avoidance. There is, however, an ultimate danger to the people, for if too many individuals commit these deeds, then the whole society might be considered polluted and might thus be in danger of a collective catastrophe.[63]

In these ways, purity laws exercise a controlling influence on the society they govern and directly impact human behaviours. Regulations limit communal interactions, make forbidden deeds taboo, and restrict the places persons may frequent.[64] Mary Douglas highlights the resulting potential:

---

[60] Cf. Jenson 1992: 47–48. For analysis of *ḥōl* ('common') and *ḥll* ('to profane') in Leviticus, see Reeve 2018: 245–52.

[61] The implications of discrete diet for sociocultural boundaries are recognized in the texts (Lev. 11:43–45; 20:25–26; Deut. 14:21).

[62] At the risk of confusing medical and impurity categories, the experience of COVID in 2019–2022 helps conceptualize the social entailments that purity systems instigate. This encompasses the more careful and less careful attitudes displayed by individuals and groups, with corresponding repercussions for others.

[63] Frymer-Kensky 1983: 404. See chapter 4 for realisation of 'collective catastrophe'.

[64] There is, therefore, overlap between purity and the communal function of shame, which also serves to guard and delimit social boundaries. Nevertheless, Lau goes too far to assert, 'That which is pure is honored and desired; that which is defiled is shamed and avoided' (Lau 2020: 68). Even though the language of humiliation (*klm*) appears in connection to Miriam's *ṣāraʿat*-infection (Num. 12:14), this single incident is insufficient to carry the weight Lau apportions. Indeed, as

> As to all the manifold rules which attribute impurity to women, in menses or childbirth, if in doubt ask the Women's Liberation Movement about the intention to sustain male dominance. And to declare adultery and all improper sex impure, is not that a blow struck in defence of marriage and family?[65]

The spectre of protecting those in positions of control and privilege looms large, especially to postmodern minds conditioned to operate with a hermeneutic of suspicion. However, while purity beliefs, and the texts that regulate them, *can* be used as a coercive tool, this is not inherently necessary. Indeed, an evangelical doctrine of Scripture is premised on dual authorship. While this allows for persuasive aims on the part of human authors and redactors it also establishes limits. The purity legislation in Leviticus and Numbers must also be heard as *divine discourse*.[66]

Taking the potential for female subjugation as a test case, do purity regulations in Leviticus and Numbers instigate social inequality along gendered lines? Many conclude that they do.[67] However, without needing to imagine biblical Israel as an egalitarian society (which it was not), significant caveats are nevertheless required.[68] Leviticus 15 addresses genital discharges that affect both women (15:19–30) *and* men (15:2–17), or both together (15:18, 24). The longer timeframe associated with menstruation (7 days) over ejaculation (1 day) is directly correlated to the longevity of the discharge. In fact, Ross Kraemer argues that menstrual taboos may even empower women by allowing them to avoid sexual relations by claiming ritual impurity.[69] Likewise, regulations concerning Nazarite vows (Num. 6), *ṣāraʿat* (Lev. 13–14) and corpse-contamination (Num. 19) are identical for men and women. As Eilberg-Schwartz concludes, impurity is 'a state which both genders generate and occupy.'[70] Even those regulations that uniquely impact women (e.g. childbirth) nevertheless ascribe women moral agency to monitor and ameliorate defilement.

---

noted in chapter 1, some cultic procedures rendered persons impure. Yet, defilement does not result in the 'diminished status within society' (shame) that Lau supposes (69).

[65] Douglas 1973: 141; cf. Kazen 2014: 80 'a worldview is constructed and formulated through particular applications of impurity language.'

[66] For a defence of this approach to reading biblical texts, see Wolterstorff 1995; Barker 2016.

[67] See the literature cited by Philip 2006: 9 n. 43.

[68] I am indebted to Klawans 2000: 7–12, 38–41, for this paragraph.

[69] Kraemer 1992: 103; cf. Lapsley 2005: 21–34.

[70] Eilberg-Schwartz 1990: 182.

Self-control is assumed. Accordingly, even though impurity legislation *could* be used to subjugate women, this would constitute a misappropriation of biblical texts that demonstrate an overt concern to facilitate purity for *all*.[71] Presented as direct divine speech, Levitical purity laws contribute to Yahweh's invitation to men and women to dwell with him.

Impurity and non-Israelites

Another key question relates to ethnic scope: does impurity affect Israelites alone or Gentiles too? This issue becomes especially important when considering Second Temple and New Testament texts (as well as thinking about contemporary implications). Maccoby states his conclusion directly: 'The Hebrew Bible knows nothing of unclean Gentiles or unclean Gentile lands.'[72] The data from Leviticus and Numbers, however, suggest Maccoby is incorrect in both respects.

In Leviticus non-Israelites are depicted as morally impure, irrespective of awareness on their part. This is the underlying logic of 18:24–30. Yahweh states, with reference to sexual immorality and idolatry, 'by all these the nations (*haggôyim*) defiled themselves (*ṭm*ʾ niphal)' (18:24 my tr.). The listed 'abominations' (*tôʿēbōt*) pollute Gentiles as much as Israelites and are the reason why 'the land vomited out its [Canaanite] inhabitants' (18:25; cf. Ezra 9:11). Ritual impurity, likewise, affects non-Israelites. Leviticus 17:15 is explicit: 'Every person' (*kōl-nepeš*) who eats torn animals, 'whether native or foreign resident' (*bāʾezrāḥ ûbaggēr*), will become impure (*ṭm*ʾ qal) until evening (my tr.).[73] Similarly, Numbers 19:10 applies instructions about ritual corpse-impurity 'to the sons of Israel' (*libnê yiśrāʾēl*) and 'to the foreign resident' (*laggēr*) among them (my tr.). Irrespective of whether one limits ritual defilement to matters of food and corpse-pollution only, the wider point remains: non-Israelites could become ritually and morally impure and require purification.[74]

Although a muted theme, there are also hints that Gentile lands were regarded as liable to defilement. The crisis addressed in Joshua 22:16–20 is

[71] In a later work, Douglas concludes: 'We have observed how very remarkable it is that the purity laws of Numbers and Leviticus do not make distinctions between persons. The inference from this would be that the community for which the purity laws were written was not a hierarchy, because purity is not being used to shore up social distinctions' (Douglas 1993b: 48).

[72] Maccoby 1999: 12.

[73] On the meaning of *gēr* ('foreign resident') in Leviticus, see Joosten 1996: 54–73.

[74] Joosten 1996: 68, 72 notes that fear of defiling land or sanctuary is the driving concern. Regarding Ezra 6:21 ('the impurity of the nations of the land'), see chapter 5.

perceived unfaithfulness to Yahweh on the part of the Transjordan tribes, epitomized by recalling the examples of idolatry at Baal Peor (22:17) and Achan's acquisition of items devoted to God (22:20). In this context, the tribes are invited to relocate west of the Jordan, to 'the land of Yahweh's possession', if 'the land of your possession is impure (*ṭāmēʾ*)' (22:19, my tr.). The underlying reasoning is that Gilead's former inhabitants may have defiled their land through moral transgression (the only source of land defilement).[75]

Joshua 22:19 also challenges those who insist impurity exists as a meaningful category only within the geographical bounds of Canaan.[76] Klawans, for example, avers that the land of Israel is holy (citing Zech. 2:16; Ps. 78:54–55), which bequeaths to it a unique status as Yahweh's residence (Num. 35:34). For this reason, inhabitants (foreign immigrants included) must heed purity laws.[77] Yet, Joshua 22:19 hints that divine residence per se is not the issue. Rather, proximity to sacred place – whether tabernacle, temple or land – problematizes impurity that is seemingly ubiquitous. In contrast, Gentile lands are not, or at least not yet, at risk from the holy. However, the eschatological trajectory of the Old Testament renders that situation temporary. Expanding Yahweh's kingdom will have significant repercussions.[78] Therefore, rather than lessening the importance of purity, eschatological realities raise the stakes considerably. Matters of ritual and moral impurity are not simply cultural aspects of being Israelite/Jewish (as diet may be) and cannot simply be dismissed by Gentiles on those grounds. Rather, the texts discussed above make impurity a *human* concern.[79]

Summary

This chapter provides an initial synthesis of defilement and cleansing as the themes appear in Leviticus and Numbers. The results render Henton

[75] See my discussion in chapter 3.

[76] Frankel 2011: 52–56 adduces a tendency to increasingly restrict law observance to life in the land, both in biblical and extra-biblical texts.

[77] Klawans 2000: 33.

[78] This is foreshadowed in divine judgment of Egypt and the overthrow of the kingdoms of Sihon and Og (Josh. 9:9–10), as well as in the extensive domain promised to Moses in Josh. 1:4 (from Mediterranean to Euphrates). Daniel makes what was proleptic a universal expectation (e.g. 2:44; 7:13–14).

[79] See also chapter 6.

Davies' summary of Leviticus 11 – 15 anaemic: 'These chapters are, of course, very unattractive and in part decidedly repulsive. They are mainly of interest to the anthropologist and sociologist. … [They are] meaningless and irrelevant.'[80] On the contrary, grappling with what Leviticus and Numbers communicate about Israel's ritual and moral purity, with all its inherent complexity, grants a deeper understanding of the Scriptures and of the relational God who acts to purify his people. Moreover, even though these books are Israelite texts, originally addressing Israelite audiences, they provide tantalizing hints that defilement and cleansing may have universal applications. The following chapters explore the implications, beginning with the Pentateuch and Former Prophets.

[80] Davies 1962: 120–21.

3

Defilement and cleansing in the Pentateuch and Former Prophets

Leviticus and Numbers do not contain the first references to defilement and cleansing in the Bible. However, commencing with the priestly texts proves beneficial for at least three reasons. First, we have options for how to understand purity lexemes encountered elsewhere. Second, we can be more sensitive to instances where purity themes operate *implicitly*, apart from the use of technical terms. Third, we can assess the degree of affinity with, or divergence from, the conception of purity emerging from Leviticus and Numbers.

This chapter expands the scope of investigation to the remainder of the Pentateuch and the Former Prophets. Engaging with these foundational texts is essential: every major biblical theme has its origins here. Moreover, the largely narrative portrayals of defilement and cleansing in these books provide a different perspective. At the same time, I make no attempt to exhaustively analyse every occurrence of each purity lexeme (which would be tedious). Instead, I sample a range of passages and usages to investigate the literary, theological and rhetorical ends achieved by employing purity concepts. Within the unfolding storyline of these books, plummeting to the nadir of 2 Kings, purity is an important characterization device. The developing portraits of God, Israel and the nations are enhanced by indicating affinity with ritual and moral purity, or their opposites. Accordingly, I explore these sometimes-subtle narrative portrayals to expose the composite picture. It is worth noting, however, that the arrangement of books does not neatly align with compositional history. Thus, readers must carefully distinguish the assumed knowledge of characters within the narrative from that of the audience addressed by the narrative. An Israelite hearing the book of Genesis was familiar with the concept of purity irrespective of whether the Patriarchs were.[1] The authors wrote accordingly.[2] Historical development cannot simply be deduced from the unfolding story even if the narratives can speak to that development.

The Pentateuch

Genesis

Purity language first appears to distinguish creatures. Yahweh commands Noah to take seven pairs from 'the pure animals' (*habbĕhēmâ haṭṭĕhôrâ*) into the ark, along with two of every creature deemed 'not pure' (*lōʾ ṭĕhōrâ*, Gen. 7:2; cf. 7:8).[3] The reason for numerical discrepancy – seven (pairs) versus two (pairs) – becomes clear following the flood when Noah sacrifices 'some of all the pure animals and some of all the pure birds' (8:20 my tr.). The resulting 'pleasing aroma' provokes a divine commitment to never again curse the ground or destroy all living things (8:21). Purity in Genesis 6 – 8 thus relates to sacrifice, not diet.[4] As in Leviticus and Numbers, purity is prerequisite for cultic activities. The text therefore presents Noah as an ideal worshipper. Not only does he prefigure ritual fidelity (offering *pure* animals and birds), but he also, in a context of sexual deviance (6:1–5) and endemic violence (6:11–13), embodies moral purity ('a righteous, perfect man'; 6:9 my tr.; cf. 7:1). This need not mean Noah was understood as a prototypical Israelite. Non-Israelites could also present offerings to Yahweh so long as they followed correct procedure.[5] In fact, Noah, as representative human, embodies the potential for anyone to approach Yahweh sacrificially.

Other supposedly 'Jewish' distinctives are also universalized. Noah is prohibited from eating blood (9:4) and enters a covenant with God

[1] Wellhausen would disagree with this conclusion based on his post-exilic dating of priestly material and contention that ritual purity concerns were correspondingly late. Barton 2014: 189–90, however, exposes the weakness of this position by highlighting texts that Wellhausen dated early, but which nevertheless operate with an understanding of ritual purity.

[2] A similar issue arises with use of the tetragrammaton, YHWH, in texts (e.g. Gen. 4:1) narratively prior to the name's disclosure in Exod. 6:2–3.

[3] The adjective *ṭāmēʾ* ('impure') appears first in Lev. 5:2.

[4] Within the narrative world of Genesis, eating meat, or at least doing so with permission, begins after the deluge (9:3).

[5] Likewise, Joosten 1996: 68. For the similar presentation of Job's 'Yahwistic' cultic devotion (as opposed to Israelite/Judahite), see Awabdy and Häner 2022: 155.

(9:9–11). Animals are classified according to purity in both antediluvian (7:2) and postdiluvian (8:20) worlds, even outside Canaan. More subtly, the entire flood narrative is shaped according to the Israelite liturgical calendar.[6] Furthermore, the explicit exigencies for the deluge, sexual immorality (6:1–4) and violent bloodshed (6:11–13), are acts that later threaten Canaan's purity (Lev. 18:24–25; Num. 35:33). There is, in light of this, an ancient tradition of interpreting the flood as divine *cleansing*.[7] Intriguingly, therefore, post-judgment restoration of the world is framed in purity language replete with cultic overtones: atop a high place (Ararat), a morally pure man offers ritually pure animals on a purified earth.[8] As I discuss in chapter 8, this forms a striking correspondence with John's final vision of the new creation in Revelation 21 – 22.

The theme of ritual purity embedded in the flood narrative appears infrequently elsewhere in Genesis. Occurrences centre around the Patriarchs who, like Noah, functioned in a quasi-priestlike manner. The common pattern of altar building (e.g. 12:7, 8; 13:18; 22:9; 33:20) occasionally evokes purity concerns. The well beside Isaac's altar at Beersheba perhaps facilitates ritual washing (26:25).[9] More explicitly, Jacob, when commanded to settle at Bethel ('House of God') and build an altar, urges his family to put away foreign gods, to purify themselves (*ṭhr* hithpael) and to change their clothes (35:1–2). Although a muted motif, the Patriarchs nevertheless 'fit' within the bounds of ritual purity.

Much more prevalent throughout Genesis is the defiling nature of egregious sin. Cain's act of fratricide evokes Yahweh's indictment, 'the voice of your brother's blood cries out to me from the ground' (4:10 my tr.). In the Pentateuch, the implied rationale for Cain's subsequent banishment from both land and God's presence is that bloodshed permanently defiles murderer and place alike (4:12, 14, 16; cf. Num. 35:33–34). If

[6] LeFebvre 2020: 117–19, 23–24 notes the ark resting on Mt Ararat during the Feast of Booths (8:4); the mountaintops becoming visible at New Moon (8:5); and the ark's cover being removed on New Year's Day (8:13). He concludes, 'these dates are provided to relate the flood events to the liturgical observances of Israel … there is, in fact, remarkable congruity among the Pentateuch's dates – but it is liturgical, not historical, congruity' (124, 128).

[7] See the excursus in chapter 4.

[8] In this way, Noah's 'ascension offerings' (*ʿōlōt*) are perhaps best understood as the procedural climax to purifying the earth, just as the *ʿōlâ* functions in cases of major impurity elsewhere (Lev. 12:6–8; 14:19–20, 30–31; 15:15, 30). Forgiveness is not required: the violent and immoral have been expunged; Noah is righteous and blameless. Deluge and postdiluvian sacrifice resolve the defilement caused by egregious sin, analogous to Yom Kippur (see chapter 1).

[9] Threefold repetition of *šām* ('there') suggests altar and well were proximate.

correct, then Cain's dread of being killed (4:14) is, perhaps, less about wanton violence than it is about defiled land being atoned by shedding the murderer's blood (Num. 35:33). A pattern of violent bloodshed ensues, often interwoven with sexual deviance: Lamech boasts to his *two* wives about killing a 'youth' (*yeled*) (4:23); the flood is required to cleanse the earth of the immoral (6:1–4) and violent (6:11–13); Ham's brutal act of incest (9:20–23) becomes aetiological of Canaan's future judgment for sexual perversion (9:25; cf. Lev. 18:24–25);[10] Shechem defiles (*ṭm'*, piel) Dinah by raping her (34:2, 5), instigating the massacre of the town where she had been treated like a prostitute (34:26–27, 31) and the subsequent excoriation of that violence (49:5–7); Judah demands Tamar be burned for prostitution (38:24), evoking the fate of a priest's daughter for similar defilement (Lev. 21:9); and Reuben's move to secure family dominance by sexual means (35:22) is met with a curse for defiling (*ḥll*, piel) his father's bed (49:4). In these depictions, the Genesis stories enact a formative role as they shape readers' imaginations with respect to purity. Acts leading to ritual and moral purity are extolled and thereby invited; causes of impurity are disavowed. Correspondence with Leviticus and Numbers supports this aim by allowing a consistent portrait of ideal worshippers to emerge.

Depiction of the ideal is ultimately tied to the opening chapters of Genesis.[11] As chapter 1 demonstrated, links are formed between purity boundaries and creation patterns. Lexical and thematic affinities, for instance, connect Genesis 1 – 3 to both the flood narrative and passages that outline dietary laws.[12] The phrase 'according to kind' (*lĕ* + *mîn*) is a case in point.[13] That Israel, following Noah's example, was to separate animals according to Genesis 1 'kinds' suggests maintaining, guarding and restoring purity distinctions was a (re)creative endeavour.[14] This creation-purity symbolism functions *textually*. That is, irrespective of ancient Israelite belief or practice, this is the effect of intertextuality in the

[10] For this understanding of 9:20–23, see Gagnon 2001: 63–71.

[11] The paradigmatic function of Gen. 1 – 3 is widely noted. Noah and Abraham, for example, are presented as Adam redivivus, appointed for fruitful multiplication (Gen. 1:28; 9:7; 17:2, 6). For elaboration, see Postell 2011; Beale 2004: 81–121.

[12] For details, see Harper 2013; 2018: 118–25.

[13] Gen. 1:11, 12(2x), 21(2x), 24(2x), 25(3x); Lev. 11:14–16, 19, 22(4x), 29; Deut. 14:13–15, 18. The only non-Pentateuch use of the phrase is Ezek. 47:10.

[14] Watkin 2017: 104 notes the Torah extends a divine invitation to humans to 'paracreate, participating in the ordering work of creation under God's direction and mandate.'

received texts. Extra-textual practices need not have reflected these layers of symbolism, but the written Torah does.[15] To adapt James Watts's well-known qualifier: we do not have purity taboos, we have purity texts.[16] The distinction is important to maintain. One rhetorical function of purity texts is to establish a connection to creation.

However, this observation raises an important consideration: in the biblical worldview, does impurity stem from humanity's primordial rebellion? Arguably, this *is* the case for moral impurity that results only from wilful sin. Ritual impurity, however, as Leviticus and Numbers clarify, typically arises involuntarily and is not deemed sinful. No repentance or forgiveness is required. Nevertheless, the selectivity of purity legislation is striking. Not all blood or bodily discharges defile, only those connected to reproduction: childbirth (Lev. 12) and genital secretions (Lev. 15). Not all diseases pollute, only *ṣāraʿat* (ESV: 'leprous disease'; Lev. 13 – 14). Additionally, it is the human corpse that generates the most potent impurity (Num. 19).[17] That these matters correspond with the aspects of life judged by Yahweh God in the Garden – reproduction (Gen. 3:16) and longevity (Gen. 3:19) – is notable.[18] Moreover, Jesus' deliberate activity to overcome these sources of ritual impurity further implies an alien rather than intrinsic status in the created order (see chapter 7). Ritual impurity signals the need for re-creation and physical transformation.[19]

Exodus

A connection between impurity and distorted creation is used to powerful effect in Exodus 7 – 12. Ten 'signs and wonders' wrought by Yahweh progressively unravel the fabric of creation as Egypt descends into chaos, darkness and death (7:3; 10:21–22; 11:4–6).[20] The Egyptian hordes being 'covered' (*ksh*) by the Sea is the *coup de grâce* (14:28; cf. Gen. 7:19–20).[21] In these ways, 'YHWH the cosmic creator dislocates his creation in the sense

[15] It is difficult to decide whether purity legislation is inceptive, beginning something new, or reiterative in relation to existing practices.

[16] Cf. Watts 2007: 29 'texts are not rituals and rituals are not texts' (emphasis removed).

[17] The defiling nature of animal death is acknowledged in Lev. 11:39–40.

[18] Much more tentatively, Gen. 3:18 might provide a conceptual link to *ṣāraʿat* if 'mould' is intended (as many EVV and commentators aver).

[19] See my discussion of resurrection in chapter 8.

[20] The encroachment of primordial chaos is pre-empted in 7:9–10 when Aaron's staff becomes a 'sea monster' (*tannîn*), recalling Gen. 1:21 (cf. Isa. 27:1; Ps. 74:13).

[21] Morales 2020: 44–45.

of reversing creation, undoing its order and boundaries by unleashing chaos'.[22] Egypt is thereby 'ruined' (*šḥt*) by Yahweh (Exod. 8:20[24]), a verb that recalls both the flood and Sodom's demise.[23]

Yahweh's de-creation of Egypt takes on additional weight by evoking impurity motifs: the Nile becomes blood and all its fish die (7:20–21);[24] blood is 'everywhere in Egypt' (7:19, 21; cf. Num. 35:33),[25] even 'in … wood and stone' (7:19);[26] the land swarms with impure frogs (8:2[6]; cf. Lev. 11:10–11) and is littered by their carcasses (8:9–10[13–14]); Egypt is inundated with impure gnats and flies (8:13[17], 20[24]; cf. Lev. 11:20); the Egyptians' livestock dies from plague (9:6), rendering animals defiling to consume (cf. Lev. 11:39–40); boils afflict people and animals (9:9–10), resembling *ṣāraʿat*-infection (cf. Lev. 13:18–23);[27] hail fills Egypt's fields with corpses (9:19, 23–25; cf. Num. 19:16); and firstborn children and animals die in every house (12:29–30), polluting the remaining occupants (cf. Num. 19:14).[28] Egypt is not only 'destroyed' (10:7 NASB); from the perspective of Israelite readers, it is systematically defiled. The *whole* land becomes ritually polluted, as do its human and animal inhabitants.[29] Yet, defilement is asymmetrical; Yahweh 'separates' (*plh*) Israelite from Egyptian (8:18[22]; 9:4; 11:7),[30] pre-empting the separation Israel must continue vis-à-vis Egypt and its impure ways (Lev. 18:3; cf. Lev. 24:10–23[31]). The theological point is clear: Yahweh, as cosmic creator, can

[22] Boorer 2016: 258–59. For her analysis of the plague narrative, see 252–67.

[23] Prior to Exod. 8:20[24], all but one use of *šḥt* appears in relation to either deluge (Gen. 6:11–13, 17; 9:11, 15) or Sodom (Gen. 13:10; 18:28, 32; 19:13–14, 29).

[24] The seven-day flow of blood (7:25) perhaps invokes menstruation (cf. Lev. 15:19).

[25] Even every *miqweh* is blood-filled (7:19; here: 'reservoir', but later 'purification pool').

[26] 'In wood and stone' could designate drinking vessels (so NIV). However, Boorer 2016: 256 n. 119 suggests the phrase could refer to everything on the face of the earth or, more specifically, to idols of wood and stone now polluted through Yahweh's agency. Elsewhere, 'wood and stone' often depicts idolatry (Deut. 4:28; 28:36, 64; 29:17; 2 Kgs 19:18; Isa. 37:19; Jer. 2:27; 3:9; Ezek. 20:32; Hab. 2:19; cf. Eccl. 10:9). If idols are intended in 7:19, this furthers the text's polemic against the gods of Egypt (cf. 12:12).

[27] *Šĕḥîn* ('boil') with *prḥ* ('to break out') occurs only in Exod. 9:9–10 and Lev. 13:20, connecting the pericopes.

[28] On the extension of Num. 19:14 to dwellings other than 'tent', see Maccoby 1999: 13–29.

[29] Note the frequent repetition of 'all the land of Egypt' (7:19, 21; 8:12[16], 13[17], 20[24]; 9:9, 22, 24, 25; 10:14, 15, 22; 11:6).

[30] Separation is also achieved by the Egyptians regarding Israelites as detestable in relation to occupation (Gen. 46:34), diet (Gen. 43:32), and cultic practices (Exod. 8:22[26]).

[31] The strong anti-Egyptian polemic of this pericope is explored by Rooke 2015.

choose to unleash chaos, reverse creation and deliberately defile.[32] But he can also deliver from impurity.

Deliverance from impurity is accentuated by the conception of Egypt as the land of the dead. Culturally, 'Egyptians were the leading experts on death, religiously as well as scientifically.'[33] Mummification was prevalent, as were cults of the dead (cf. Gen. 50:26).[34] Moreover, in the Old Testament, one consistently *descends* (*yrd*) into Egypt and *ascends* (*ʿlh*) from there (e.g. Gen. 46:4), just as one goes down into, or is raised up from, Sheol (e.g. 1 Sam. 2:6). Nicholas Wyatt concludes in relation to this spatial movement, 'Going down to Egypt is like going down into the underworld; being in Egypt is like being in the tomb.'[35] Exodus exploits this association by framing Israel's sojourn in Egypt with reference to waters conceptually linked to death – the Nile (Exod. 2) and the Sea (Exod. 14). Israel descended into Egypt/Sheol and must be brought up from there. Thus, Exodus portrays rescue from Egypt, in part, as a deliverance from death and impurity. Consequently, passing through the Sea becomes more than spatial description. As many note, Exodus constructs a rich symbolic tapestry that exhibits Yahweh's defeat of the Egyptian army as a crushing victory over sea monsters and chaos – a motif to which the Old Testament returns frequently (e.g. Isa. 51:9–10; Ezek. 29:3; Ps. 74:12–17; 89:9–11[8–10]; Job 26:12–13).[36] The ANE conceptual backdrop is judgment by river ordeal: the wicked are overcome by the waters while the righteous pass through.[37] However, crossing the Sea also functions as a *rite de passage*. On analogy with ritual cleansing, the Israelites move from a place characterized by death and defilement, through the waters, towards life and purity. Thus, the Sea functions figuratively as a *miqweh*, a source of lustral waters.

'Purification' of Israel by means of the Sea is essential ahead of appearing before Yahweh at Sinai. The idea is heightened in Exodus by reserving purity terminology for use only in relation to the Sinai

[32] See also Boorer 2016: 523.

[33] Morales 2020: 50. This paragraph is indebted to Morales' analysis (48–54).

[34] See, further, Assmann 2003.

[35] Wyatt 2014: 38.

[36] Morales 2020: 58–60 notes in this respect: (1) Pharaoh's characterization as an anti-creation figure; (2) Aaron's *tannîn* ('sea dragon') swallowing the magicians' *tannîn* (7:8–13); (3) Moses confronting Pharaoh as he wades in the river (7:14–25); and (4) the serpent emblem worn by Pharaoh. Miller 2018 explores the wider cosmic allusions.

[37] McCarter 1973; Morales 2012: 27–32.

theophany and tabernacle construction.[38] Because he will appear to all (19:11), Yahweh commands Moses to consecrate (*qdš* piel) the people by having them wash their clothes (19:10) and abstain from sex (19:15). Limits are set around the mountain to ensure even purified people do not encroach upon holy space until summoned (19:12–13, 23). Encountering Yahweh is inherently dangerous (19:21–24).[39]

Yet even though the Sinai encounter dominates the Pentateuchal narrative, forming the setting for Exodus 19 – Numbers 10, it remains penultimate. Instead, 'The goal of the exodus is ultimately a deliverance of a people … to the Promised Land.'[40] Hence, the tabernacle becomes crucial. The 'cloud' and 'glory' atop the mountain (Exod. 24:15–16) transition to the newly constructed tent in Exodus 40:34. Just as Yahweh formerly called to Moses from bush (3:4), mountain (19:3) and cloud (24:16), he continues to call to him from the tent of meeting (Lev. 1:1; cf. Exod. 29:42). The tabernacle becomes a portable Mount Sinai, enabling Yahweh's glory to journey with the people to Canaan. It must therefore be a fitting abode. Twenty-four of the twenty-eight occurrences of *ṭāhôr* in Exodus refer to the 'pure' gold used for the tabernacle furnishings. Remaining instances describe the 'pure' lampstand (31:8; 39:37) and the 'pure' incense used in the holy place (30:35; 37:29). Thus, Exodus utilizes *ṭāhôr* only in relation to items connected to the tabernacle's interior. While the best ('pure') gold is eminently suitable for a royal palace,[41] *ṭāhôr* also invokes a place free from impurity. Accordingly, Yahweh's presence has implications for Israel's future environs, whether that be tabernacle, camp or Canaan. Indeed, 15:17 employs cosmic mountain symbolism to portray Canaan as sacred space: 'You will bring [the people] in and plant them on the mountain of your inheritance: the place for your dwelling you have made, O Yahweh; the sanctuary, O Lord, your hands established' (my tr.). Guarding and maintaining the purity of these sacred

---

[38] The sole exception is the twofold use of *tô ʿēbâ* ('abomination') in 8:22[26], which nevertheless imagines *future* offerings made to Yahweh (at Sinai). Additionally, the verb *ḥṭʾ* means 'to purify' only in 29:36. The other nine instances mean 'to sin' (5:16; 9:27, 34; 10:16; 20:20; 23:33; 32:30, 31, 33). This pattern of language use aligns with Dozeman's observation that divine presence is the governing rubric of the second half of Exodus (Dozeman 2009: 45–46). In chapter 7, I explore the implications of this purity-theophany theme for understanding baptism in John's Gospel.

[39] See, further, Smith 2017: 46–51; DeLapp 2018; Harper 2022a.

[40] Estelle 2018: 94.

[41] So Sklar 2013: 37.

locales becomes paramount (Lev. 12:4; 15:31; 18:24–28; 20:3; Num. 5:1–4; 19:20; 35:33–34).[42]

In Exodus, the purity requirements for safely approaching Yahweh at 'holy' Sinai (cf. 3:5; 19:23) are mapped onto the tabernacle. The theme is pre-empted in the Song of the Sea, which proclaims that Yahweh, 'majestic in holiness', will lead the people to his 'holy dwelling' (15:11, 13). This dwelling, 'made holy by my glory' (29:43 my tr.), is served by holy priests (28:36, 41; 30:30), wearing holy clothes (28:2–4; 29:21; 31:10), who offer holy things (28:38) on a most holy altar (29:37; 40:10).[43] Purity is essential. The altar must be cleansed (*ḥṭ'* piel, 29:36–37) and priests washed before donning their holy garments (29:4–5; 40:12).[44] They must also wash whenever entering the tent or approaching the altar (30:18–21; 40:30–32). The penalty for defiling holy space is stark: death (30:20–21; cf. 28:35, 43). Thus, purity constitutes an inextricable component of the exodus's telos.[45] Yahweh rescues his people from the realm of death and impurity (Egypt), 'cleansing' them in the waters of the Sea, so they can safely approach his holy presence. Construction of a portable shrine in which Yahweh's glory dwells among the people extends the need for purity indefinitely. The implications this has for life in Canaan are teased out in Deuteronomy to Kings.

Deuteronomy

Ritual impurity is a tangential theme in Deuteronomy. Nevertheless, that which is present aligns with Leviticus and Numbers. Sources of impurity include nocturnal emissions (23:11[10]) and death – human (26:14) and animal (14:8, 21). Various creatures are designated either impure or pure (14:3–20). There is also a requirement to separate holy from impure (e.g. 23:11, 15[10, 14]), which has implications for sacrifice and cultic participation (e.g. 26:13–14). While very little is said about remedying ritual impurity, the washing and waiting prescribed in 23:12[11] aligns with expectation.

---

[42] As Frankel 2011: 56 observes, to contaminate land 'would implicitly contravene the very purpose of the exodus from the impure land of Egypt and at least theoretically negate the entire foundation of the relationship between God and Israel.'

[43] Thus, recalling Noah, pure Israelites offer pure animals at a holy high place.

[44] The prohibition against using a 'sword' when constructing stone altars may be to ensure ritual purity (Alexander 2017: 458).

[45] Cf. Frankel 2011: 56.

Deuteronomy displays far greater concern over immoral actions. Bloodshed, sexual immorality and idolatry feature prominently among the behaviours cursed in 27:15–26. These excoriated acts are also understood to defile. The implications of even sanctioned bloodshed upon place are stated in 21:23, which warns that bodies of executed criminals, left hanging overnight, defile (*ṭmʾ* piel) the ground.[46] Deuteronomy 32:43 similarly proclaims Yahweh 'will avenge the blood of his servants; he will take vengeance on his enemies and make atonement for his land' (which had been polluted by shed blood). Prostitution, as well as money earned by such means, is deemed an abomination (23:18–19[17–18]). Any man who remarries his ex-wife after she has been 'defiled' by another in the interim commits an abomination before Yahweh with deleterious effect on the land (24:1–4). Thus, in Deuteronomy, the defilement caused by (at least some) immoral acts displays significant overlap with how moral impurity operates in Leviticus and Numbers. This type of impurity arises from preventable actions and pollutes persons and place.[47]

Concerning these egregious acts, Deuteronomy commands Israel to 'purge the evil from among you' (13:6[5]; 17:7, 12; 19:19;[48] 21:21; 22:21, 22, 24; 24:7).[49] Wickedness is overcome by expunging evildoers from the community. However, in two places, *bʿr* appears with 'blood' as direct object rather than 'evil'. In 19:1–13, cities of refuge are established to prevent blood from being wrongfully spilled upon the land in retaliation for manslaughter (19:10). Murderers, however, must be executed to 'purge (*bʿr*) the innocent blood [of victims] from Israel' (19:13 my tr.). Deuteronomy 21:1–9 addresses cases where the killer remains unknown. In lieu of being able to shed the murderer's blood, atonement is achieved by means of a heifer rite (21:3–6) coupled with a declaration of innocence by the elders of the nearest village (21:7–8).[50] By this means, 'the blood will be atoned (*kpr* niphal) on their behalf' (21:8b) and 'you will purge (*bʿr*) the innocent blood from among you' (21:9 my tr.). Although many English versions supply the word 'guilt' in 19:13 and 21:9 (i.e. 'purge

---

[46] Thus, Josh. 8:29 and 10:26 portray Joshua as not only obedient to Torah, but concerned for guarding Canaan's purity.

[47] Deuteronomy's silence regarding sanctuary defilement may correlate with reluctance to identify 'the place' where Yahweh's name resides.

[48] Deut. 19:19 encompasses bloodshed whenever a capital crime is in view.

[49] Utilizing *bʿr* II ('to purge, remove') in conjunction with *raʿ* ('evil'). 17:12 and 22:22 have 'purge the evil from Israel'.

[50] See Wright 1987a for analysis.

the guilt of innocent blood' ESV; likewise, HCSB, KJV, NIV, NLT; contrast JPS), purification affords a better lens. Affinity with Numbers 35 provides warrant. The context mirrors that of Deuteronomy 19: establishing cities of refuge to protect those who accidently kill another while also demanding capital punishment for premeditated murder. The rationale is maintaining spatial purity. Blood pollutes (*ḥnp*) the land and only the shed blood of the murderer can atone (*kpr*) for defiled land (Num. 35:33). Thus, there is a shared concern in Numbers and Deuteronomy to 'purge'/'atone' land defiled by deliberate bloodshed.

Similarities aside, Deuteronomy also displays variant use of purity terminology. The word *tô ʿēbâ* ('abomination') occurs six times in Leviticus.[51] In 18:22 and 20:13 *tô ʿēbâ* denotes homosexual acts specifically. However, the conclusion to Leviticus 18 utilizes 'abomination' as a catch-all for all prohibited sexual and idolatrous acts (18:26, 27, 29, 30). By 'all these abominations' (*kol-hattô ʿēbōt hā ʾēl*) the Canaanites made themselves and the land impure (18:27 my tr.). Therefore, Israelites and foreign residents must not do 'any of these abominations' (*mikkōl hattô ʿēbōt hā ʾēlleh*) on pain of being cut off (18:26, 29 my tr.). In Deuteronomy, 'abomination' occurs most often in relation to idols and idolatrous practices (7:25–26; 12:31; 13:15[14]; 17:4; 18:9–12; 20:18; 27:15; 32:16). As in Leviticus 18:21, sacrificing children is deemed abominable (Deut. 12:31; 18:10), constituting both idol worship and bloodshed.[52] At the same time, Deuteronomy expands the scope of prohibited activities (esp. 18:9–11). Anything connected to idolatry is an abomination. Moreover, whoever does any of these things *becomes an abomination* to Yahweh (18:12). *Tô ʿēbâ* is also used for sexually immoral acts, albeit less expansively than Leviticus (23:19[18]; 24:4). But Deuteronomy also utilizes *tô ʿēbâ* with a wider field of reference. Banned creatures are an abomination (14:3), as is the sacrifice of a blemished animal (17:1). A woman who dresses as a man, or vice versa, is an abomination to Yahweh (22:5). So are those who use dishonest weights (25:16). It is difficult to ascertain whether these kinds of abomination are assumed to defile in a manner akin to idolatry, sexual immorality and bloodshed. The text simply does not specify. However, the increased scope of 'abomination' opens the potential for

[51] Numbers does not use the term.

[52] The bloodshed implied by offering children is made explicit in Ps. 106:38: 'They shed innocent blood, the blood of their sons and daughters, whom they sacrificed to the idols of Canaan.'

moral impurity to be connected to a wider range of sinful behaviours, a possibility embraced by Second Temple and New Testament literature.

Deuteronomy's use of *šqṣ* ('to detest') also differs. Elsewhere, *šqṣ* appears only in connection with animals deemed unfit for consumption (Lev. 7:21; 11:10, 11[2x], 12, 13[2x], 20, 23, 41, 42, 43; 20:25; Isa. 66:17; Ezek. 8:10).[53] In Deuteronomy, the root is exclusively reserved for idols.[54] Canaanite statues of wood and stone are characterized as 'their detestable things' (*šiqqûṣêhem*, 29:16[17] ESV). Such abominations must be utterly detested (*šaqqēṣ tĕšaqqĕṣennû*, 7:26). In this way, Canaanite religious practice is presented as defiled and loathsome; detestation is the appropriate response. In fact, adopting a term elsewhere linked to distasteful foods exploits notions of physical and psychological queasiness. Idols ought to make one instinctively retch as much as sitting down to a bowl of worms and maggots. Purity connotations thus support the book's polemic against all alternative expressions, modes and sites of worship. The Canaanites' impure forms could never be suitable for worshipping Yahweh. Indeed, their impurity is diametrically opposed to holiness and will, therefore, be consumed by Yahweh's presence. Maintaining purity thus becomes a crucial rationale for expelling the land's pre-Israelite residents (cf. Lev. 18:26–30).

Purity dynamics help clarify other passages. Deuteronomy 12 emphasizes sanctuary centralization. In contrast to 'all the places' (*kol-hammĕqōmôt*, 12:2) utilized by the Canaanites, Yahweh will dictate 'the place' (*hammāqôm*, 12:5) at which sacrifice may be offered.[55] In a context of landed rather than nomadic existence, Deuteronomy 12 makes non-sacred slaughter of livestock permissible 'in any of your towns' (12:15; contrast Lev. 17:3–4). Blood, however, must be poured out on the ground rather than used for cultic ends (12:16, 24). To reinforce the non-sacrificial nature of such slaughter, 12:15 states, 'the impure and the pure may eat it' (my tr.; cf. 15:21–22). Indeed, the impure and pure may eat it 'together' (*yaḥdāw*, 12:22). This would be unthinkable if the meal constituted a

[53] The sole exception is Ps. 22:25[24], which speaks of Yahweh not detesting the afflicted.

[54] This usage accounts for some of the differences between Deut. 14:3–20 and Lev. 11. In Lev. 11 prohibited quadrupeds are 'impure' (*ṭāmēʾ*, 11:4–8), whereas forbidden aquatic and aerial creatures are 'detestable' (*šeqeṣ*, 11:10, 13, 20). Deuteronomy, however, employs *ṭāmēʾ* for all three animal categories (14:7, 8, 10, 19). Direction of dependence between these pericopes has been construed both ways. More recent scholarship envisages a more complex relationship (e.g. Houston 1993: 63–65; Nihan 2007: 284–94).

[55] Not naming 'the place' in Deuteronomy allows for a succession of locales where Yahweh's name may reside, albeit one at a time.

fellowship offering (cf. Lev. 7:20–21; 22:3–7). The settled existence imagined by Deuteronomy also accentuates the twofold mention of 'outside the camp' (*miḥûṣ lammaḥăneh*) in 23:10–15[9–14], a phrase typically found only in Exodus – Numbers in relation to the wilderness experience.[56] The context is vital. Going to war remains the sole situation in which Israelites would again camp in proximity to the ark. This unique situation heightens purity considerations.[57] Hence, utilizing verbal allusions to Leviticus 15:16 and Numbers 5:3,[58] Deuteronomy insists that any man with a nocturnal emission must relocate 'outside the camp' until he washes and evening falls (23:11–12[10–11]).[59] Likewise, defecation must take place 'outside the camp' (23:13[12]). However, this does not mean excrement causes ritual impurity either by touch or proximity;[60] there is no corresponding requirement to wash or wait.[61] Nevertheless, because the camp is 'holy', Yahweh 'must not see the nakedness of a thing among you' (23:15[14] my tr.).[62] The same phrase, 'nakedness of a thing' (*ʿerwat dābār*), occurs in 24:1. In both cases it refers to something unseemly or indecent rather than impure per se. Just as nakedness ought to be hidden, excrement must likewise be covered by dirt rather than left exposed.

In summary, purity in Deuteronomy displays significant continuity with Leviticus and Numbers while also diversifying and expanding the scope of various terms. Benjamin Kilchör's summary is apt: 'it becomes clear that the whole Priestly concept of cleanness and uncleanness was known to the writer of Deuteronomic law. However, it was taken up only selectively, where Deuteronomy has something to say for a new situation and where it is of relevance for the common people.'[63]

---

[56] The only other instance is Josh. 6:23. This section is indebted to Kilchör 2020a: 222–23.

[57] Thus, these instructions do not govern life in the land generally. Num. 5:1–4 provides an analogous situation in which the Israelites travel in Yahweh's war camp on the way to Canaan.

[58] Kilchör 2015: 260.

[59] The phrase 'night accident' (*miqqĕrēh-lāylâ*, 23:11[10] my tr.) is obscure. As women were not present in the war camp, normal intercourse is ruled out – hence, an involuntary 'nocturnal emission' (see McConville 2002: 346). The accidental nature of the emission is nevertheless important as it implies unavoidable ritual impurity rather than moral impurity arising from some immoral act.

[60] Contra McConville 2002: 350. Cf. my discussion of Mark 7 (chapter 7).

[61] Frymer-Kensky 1983: 401.

[62] Exod. 20:26 reveals a similar concern to prevent the (holy) altar being exposed to nakedness.

[63] Kilchör 2020a: 223.

The Former Prophets

The Former Prophets continue to utilize purity for characterization purposes. The presence of Deuteronomy is also felt, especially in the purificatory aims of extinguishing idolatry.

Joshua

Joshua records Israelite entry into and subsequent apportioning of Canaan. Nicholas Lunn notes similarities between the Jericho narratives (2:1–24; 6:1–27) and the legislation in Leviticus 13 – 14 concerning *ṣāra ʿat* (ESV: 'leprous disease').[64] Allusion is a subtle device, often existing on a spectrum of possibility.[65] Nevertheless, an accumulation of shared terms and phrases is a strong indicator that a connection is intended.[66] Parallels between Jericho and a *ṣāra ʿat*-infected house are the clearest.[67] According to Leviticus 14 a priest must 'come' (*bwʾ*) to 'view' (*rʾh*) a suspect house (14:36), whereupon he must order it 'shut up' (*sgr*) 'for seven days' (14:38). Similarly, the men of Jericho deduce that the two Israelites dispatched to 'view' (*rʾh*) the land (2:1) had 'come' (*bwʾ*) as spies (2:2–3). This causes the city to be firmly 'shut up' (*sgr*) as the Israelites march around it for seven days (6:1–4). Jericho's fate also mirrors that of a house defiled by *ṣāra ʿat*: permanent destruction instigated through priestly agency (Lev. 14:40–45; Josh. 6:4–5, 20–21, 24).[68] That Leviticus and Joshua explicitly stipulate the same setting – the land given to Israel as a possession[69] – suggests that preserving the purity of the place where Yahweh resides is the driving concern in both instances. Accordingly, Rahab and her family, former inhabitants of 'impure' Jericho, are initially quartered outside the camp (Josh. 6:23; cf. Lev. 13:46; Num. 5:2–3) before

[64] The connections work irrespective of direction of dependence, which has been construed both ways.

[65] Indeed, one test for establishing allusion is that some readers may miss its presence (Miner 1994: 14).

[66] For the methodological considerations, see Harper 2018: 48–56.

[67] See Lunn 2015: 136–37. Lunn also suggests more tenuous connections to *ṣāra ʿat*-infected people and garments (138–43).

[68] Leviticus orders the removal of materials to an impure location, preventing reuse (14:45); Jericho's ruins receive a curse against rebuilding (6:26) (Lunn 2015: 137).

[69] Compare Lev. 14:34 ('When you enter [*bwʾ*] the land [*ʾereṣ*] of Canaan, which I am giving you [*ʾăšer … nōtēn lākem*] as a possession') with Josh. 1:11 ('you will cross the Jordan here to enter [*bwʾ*] and take possession of the land [*ʾereṣ*] Yahweh your God is giving you [*ʾăšer … nōtēn lākem*] to possess') (Lunn 2015: 138).

being allowed to dwell 'among the Israelites' (Josh. 6:25).[70] Lunn concludes: 'through the subtle use of these allusions the writer of the book of Joshua is portraying the city of Jericho as a leprous house. It has been examined and warrants the dismantling specified by the levitical law.'[71] Establishing Canaan's purity is paramount.

The special status of Canaan is also central in Joshua 22. The passage exposes an immediate obstacle to ongoing fidelity to Yahweh: the potential for geographical separation to instigate religious segregation (22:24–25). The issue turns on underlying tensions between the Western tribes, living in Canaan, and the Reubenites, Gadites and half tribe of Manasseh who were allotted land east of the Jordan (Num. 32; Deut. 3:12–20).[72] Conflict erupts when the Transjordanian tribes construct 'an imposing altar' at the border (22:10). A Western delegation, headed by Phinehas, indicts the Transjordanians for 'treachery' (*maʿal*) and a desire 'to rebel' (*mrd*, 22:16) – loaded terms that recall Achan's disloyalty (Josh. 7:1) and the wilderness revolt (Num. 14:9).[73] Recalling past unfaithfulness continues with reference to the 'sin of Peor' (22:17; cf. Num. 25:1–3), understood as something 'from which even yet we have not cleansed (*ṭhr* hithpael) ourselves' (ESV). Yet there is silence regarding what purification might necessitate. This is consistent with the picture of moral impurity in Leviticus and Numbers. Some egregious sins (bloodshed, immorality and idolatry) produce long-lasting defilement that is not easily expunged.[74] Hence, even though Phinehas's skewering of apostates had stopped the Peor plague (Num. 25:8) and 'made atonement for the Israelites' (Num. 25:13), the people's impurity remained.[75]

But moral defilement also has a deleterious effect on place. This perhaps clarifies the somewhat ambiguous location of the 'imposing altar'.[76]

[70] Lunn 2015: 141. By analogy, the spies who enter Rahab's house and lie down there (Josh. 2:3, 8) become impure according to Lev. 14:46–47. Required washing is perhaps enacted by fording the Jordan en route to the Israelite camp (Josh. 2:23) (Lunn 2015: 138–39).

[71] Lunn 2015: 143.

[72] The convoluted social identities at play in Josh. 22 are traced by Wray Beal 2019: 377–86; Assis 2004.

[73] Wray Beal 2019: 375-76.

[74] *Pace* Butler 1983: 247 who surmises that immoral and idolatrous practices must be ongoing.

[75] This stands in tension with Blenkinsopp 2012: 86 who claims the Peor plague 'marked the final link in a process of purification.' Rather, even though the first generation were eradicated (Num. 26), the polluting effects of their actions persisted.

[76] The altar is constructed 'there', 'at the Jordan', 'opposite the land of Canaan', 'in the region of

The Western tribes consistently show little concern for Transjordanian territories – in their view, they remain distinct from Yahweh's land (22:19). However, an idolatrous altar constructed on the *western* bank of the Jordan would defile Canaan – the place hosting the tabernacle (22:19; cf. Lev. 20:3). That potential best accounts for the Cisjordanians' swift and extreme response (22:11–12; cf. 22:33). Nevertheless, the Western delegation entreats the Transjordanians: 'If the land of your possession is impure (*ṭāmēʾ*), pass over to the land of Yahweh's possession' (22:19 my tr.). Invitation to 'pass over' (*ʿbr*) the Jordan, evoking the initial crossing (*ʿbr*) of the river into Canaan (1:2), is framed as an invitation to join 'us'. From a Cisjordanian perspective the region beyond the Jordan – former Amorite territory (cf. Num. 32:33; Deut. 2:24 – 3:11) – does *not* constitute Israel.[77] Therefore, the Western delegation assumes lands *other than Canaan* could be defiled. Nonetheless, their comment is terse; reason(s) why the Transjordan was considered polluted are left unstated. The likely inference is that the region's former inhabitants defiled their land as the Canaanites had theirs (cf. Exod. 34:15–16; Lev. 18:24–25). It is also possible that the immorality and idolatry of Peor recalled in 22:17 was understood to have irrevocably polluted the region east of the Jordan.

Judges

In Judges, purity terms shape the portrayal of Samson whose birth is uniquely heralded by divine announcement (13:3). The angel of Yahweh insists the boy be set apart as a Nazarite *from birth* (13:5), signifying an entire life dedicated to God at God's behest.[78] Accordingly, Samson's head must remain unshorn (13:5; cf. Num. 6:5). His mother, likewise, must heed Nazarite strictures: avoiding all grape products, wine, strong drink and impure food (13:4, 7, 14; cf. Num. 6:3–4).[79] The sequence ends positively with the boy experiencing Yahweh's blessing and spirit (13:24–25).

Samson's portentous beginnings, however, accentuate his role as literary foil. As the last of the judges, Samson is an anti-hero whose

---

the Jordan', 'on the side of the sons of Israel' (22:10–11 my tr.). Inherent ambiguity means both east and west bank locations have been proposed by commentators.

[77] Moreover, this territory was apportioned by Moses' command, not Yahweh's lot (13:8–33; 22:4; cf. Num. 32:28–29).

[78] Compare the free choice of a man or woman to undertake Nazarite vows in Num. 6:2.

[79] The injunction to avoid impure food is not stated in Num. 6. Nevertheless, it is a logical extension of the holy status of the Nazarite (Num. 6:5) on analogy to priestly diet limitations (e.g. Lev. 22:8).

life fully inverts the paradigm for Israel's deliverers. Disregard for purity enhances the depiction. While journeying to Timnah to marry a Philistine woman, Samson revisits the body of a lion he had slain. In this 'torn', and therefore impure, carcass (14:6; cf. Lev. 11:26–28; 17:15) of an impure animal (Lev. 11:27), a swarm of impure bees (Deut. 14:19; cf. Lev. 11:20) had formed a hive. Samson eats the honey (14:8–9), fully aware of its defiled nature – as later revealed by his determination not to tell his parents the honey he had given them came from a 'lion's carcass' (14:9). Transgression of purity boundaries continues. While Nazarites were to avoid contact with corpses lest they invalidate their vow to Yahweh (Num. 6:6–12), Samson's career is characterized by bloodshed and violence (Judg. 14:19; 15:8, 15–16; 16:30). On one occasion, he even wields the jawbone of an impure donkey as an improvised weapon (15:15; cf. Lev. 11:28). Later, in Gaza, Samson saw a prostitute and 'entered into her' (16:1 my tr.). Climactically, he reveals the secret of his hair to his wife, indicating self-awareness of his Nazarite identity (16:17; cf. 13:5). This explicit reminder of Samson's heritage sharpens the tragic irony of his denouement. Whereas the shaving of a Nazarite's hair at the entrance to the tent of meeting ritually concluded a person's consecration to Yahweh (Num. 6:18), Samson's shaving pre-empts his shameful parade at Dagon's temple (16:23–25). Moreover, Samson's Nazarite separation ends not through contact with one corpse (cf. Num. 6:6–9), but through contact with thousands of dead Philistines (Judg. 16:27–30). Thus, '[t]he whole Samson cycle can be seen as the story of the disintegration of a Nazarite who breaks his vow'.[80]

Cleansing is conspicuously absent – other than that indirectly achieved by the removal of Philistines and Samson from the land. Samson's wanton disregard of ritual and moral purity is emblematic of the nation. The book's conclusion graphically portrays Israel's nadir by characterizing the pre-monarchical tribes as inherently idolatrous, immoral and violent.[81] An aside, mentioning the 'time of the captivity of the land', is ominous (18:30). Ongoing defilement of place, while the 'house of God' *was present at Shiloh* (18:31), has only one assured outcome: exile.

[80] Ashley 2022: 113.

[81] Notions of a slow descent into depravity are disrupted by naming Jonathan, Moses' grandson (18:30), and Phinehas, Aaron's grandson (20:28), in the conclusion. The canaanization of Israel took only a generation (cf. Josh. 24:31, 33; Judg. 2:10). (Thanks to Kit Barker for this observation.)

1 – 2 Samuel

The book of Samuel turns on the reversal of power and position. Yahweh's elevation of the humble and casting down of the proud, pre-empted in Hannah's song (1 Sam. 2:1–10), is realized as Samuel rises to prominence over the house of Eli. Once more, purity themes enhance characterization as alternating episodes develop contrasting portraits of the 'lad' (*na'ar*), Samuel (2:11, 18–21, 26; 3:1–10, 3:15 – 4:1a), and Eli's 'lads' (*nĕ'ārîm*), Hophni and Phineas (2:12–17, 22–25, 27–36; 3:11–14).[82] The narrative setting is the tabernacle, located at Shiloh. There, Samuel, of Levitical heritage (cf. 1 Chr. 6:12–13[6:27–28]), ministers (*šrt*) 'before the face of Yahweh' dressed in a linen 'ephod' (*'ēpōd*, 2:18 my tr.).[83] Additionally, Samuel's mother, portrayed in quasi-Nazarite terms,[84] brings her lad a new 'robe' (*mĕ'îl*) each year (2:19). In Exodus–Leviticus, the *'ēpōd* and *mĕ'îl* are *high*-priestly garments, required whenever Aaron ministered (*šrt*) 'before the face of Yahweh' to prevent his death in 'the holy place' (Exod. 28:35 my tr.).[85] Samuel is, therefore, suitably attired to spend his nights 'lying down in the temple of the LORD, where the ark of God was' (3:3 ESV). In contrast, Hophni and Phineas scorned Yahweh's offerings by demanding the fat that belonged exclusively to God (2:15–17, 29; cf. Lev. 3:16–17), had sex with the women serving at the tabernacle's entrance (2:22; cf. Exod. 38:8), and, by doing so, blasphemed Yahweh (3:13). Samuel acts in accord with proximate holiness, Eli's sons do not. Yahweh's judgment is starkly fitting: the house of Eli would be cut off from the altar (2:33) and its iniquity never atoned by sacrifice or offering (3:14).[86] Concern for purity and holiness depicts Samuel as a faithful priest (2:35; cf. Lev. 10:10).

---

[82] I am indebted to Kit Barker for drawing my attention to this aspect of the narrative.

[83] The shift from Samuel serving 'before the face of Eli the priest' in 2:11 is a further denigration of Eli's house.

[84] Hannah's foreswearing of 'wine and strong drink' (*yayin wĕšēkar*) utilizes the phraseology of priestly prohibition (Lev. 10:9) and Nazarite limitation (Num. 6:3; cf. Judg. 13:4–7, 14). Hannah also promises any son born would be devoted to God and would remain unshorn (1:11; cf. Num. 6:5; LXX adds alcohol avoidance to 1:11). There is, therefore, notable similarity between Hannah and Samson's mother (cf. Judg. 13:4, 7, 14).

[85] For *'ēpōd*, see Exod. 25:7; 28:4, 6, 12, 15, 26, 27, 28, 31; 29:5; 35:9, 27; 39:2, 7, 8, 18, 19, 20, 21, 22; Lev. 8:7. For *mĕ'îl*, see Exod. 28:4, 31, 34; 29:5; 39:22–26; Lev. 8:7. In Samuel, the *'ēpōd* is a typical priestly garment (e.g. 1 Sam. 22:18).

[86] The impossibility of atonement may refer not to forgiveness per se, but to the removal of moral impurity, which would henceforth indelibly stain Eli's lineage.

The dangerous holiness of Yahweh and consequent need for purity continues. The men of Beth-Shemesh vocalize the chief concern: 'Who can stand in the presence of the LORD, this holy God?' (1 Sam. 6:20). Not the house of Eli. Nor Dagon, whose statue fell prostrate before the ark and whose hands and head lay 'cut off' upon the threshold (1 Sam. 5:4 ESV). Nor the men struck dead for peering into the ark (1 Sam. 6:19) or for touching it (2 Sam. 6:6–7). Holiness endangers. Hence, consecration ahead of making sacrifice to Yahweh is crucial (1 Sam. 16:5). For this reason, Saul assumes David's absence from the New Moon sacrifice is because he is 'not pure' (*lōʾ ṭāhôr*, 1 Sam. 20:26). The short-term, remediable nature of minor ritual impurity underlies Saul's consternation when David does not appear the following day (1 Sam. 20:27). Similarly, Ahimelech is willing to allow David's 'lads' (*nĕʿārîm*) to eat the tabernacle's 'holy bread', but only if they have kept themselves from women, with ironic allusion to Eli's 'lads' (1 Sam. 21:5[4] my tr.).[87] Assuring Ahimelech that 'the lads' vessels are holy' (1 Sam. 21:6[5]), they receive the holy bread that had been 'before the face of Yahweh' (1 Sam. 21:7[6], my tr.).

In contrast to his men, David does not keep himself from a woman he spies performing rooftop ablutions. The temporal note, 'When evening time came' (2 Sam. 11:2 my tr.), indicates ritual cleansing. That possibility is corroborated by 11:4, which explains Bathsheba was 'consecrating herself' (*qdš* hithpael) 'from her impurity' (*miṭṭumʾātāh*, my tr.), phrasing that occurs elsewhere only in Leviticus 16:19.[88] If post-menstruation cleansing is intended, there are implications for parsing the illicit liaison between Bathsheba and David.[89] Purification occurred seven days after the first appearance of blood, that is, on day seven of a woman's menstrual cycle. However, ovulation typically occurs on day fourteen. That Bathsheba became pregnant (11:5) implies a time delay between when David saw her and when he slept with her (11:4). If correct, this adds credence to David Firth's contention that David was motivated not by lust, but rather by a desire to remove a rival, namely Uriah.[90] That impulse is seen in David's insistence that Uriah go home to 'wash his feet' (11:8) – a

---

[87] Note: men are the source of sex-impurity (ejaculation of semen) rather than women.

[88] Lunn 2015: 133.

[89] Although Lev. 15 does not stipulate menstruant ablutions, the practice was widespread. Milgrom 1991: 934–35 argues washing is implied on analogy with Lev. 15:16; Num. 19:19.

[90] Firth 2009: 416. Firth notes that David only slept with Bathsheba *after* confirming her identity as Uriah's wife (417).

euphemism for sex. This, however, would make Uriah guilty of violating the purity restrictions pertaining to Israel's war camp (Deut. 23:11[10]).[91] Yet Uriah, with explicit appeal to the ark's presence (11:11), foresees the risk and thereby subverts David's ploy. Nonetheless, this simply instigates a more direct means of ensuring Uriah's demise (11:14–15).

Bloodshed is highly problematic.[92] Wilful killing, especially without cause or in retribution, is reprehensible (1 Sam. 19:5; 25:26–33; 2 Sam. 3:27–28; 4:7–11).[93] Somewhat ironically, David earlier articulates the consequences: 'How much more, when wicked men have killed a righteous man in his own house on his bed, shall I not now require his blood at your hand and destroy you from the earth?' (2 Sam. 4:11 ESV; also 2 Sam. 1:16; 14:6–7). Yahweh's judgment upon David is swift and commensurate (2 Sam. 12:10–12). But bloodshed also raises the spectre of land defilement. That potential is realized in 2 Samuel 21 when Yahweh reveals that a three-year-long famine 'is on account of Saul and his blood-stained house; it is because he put the Gibeonites to death' (2 Sam. 21:1). Saul's unsanctioned bloodshed (21:2) had a lasting and detrimental effect on the land. David therefore canvassed means of making atonement (*kpr*, 21:3). In Numbers 35:33, only the blood of the perpetrator(s) could atone (*kpr*) for land defiled by bloodshed. Yet, Saul was already dead (cf. 1 Sam. 31:4–5). Nevertheless, the legacy of 'bloods' was not Saul's alone, but also of his 'blood-stained house'. Accordingly, seven representatives of his 'house' are selected and executed (21:8–9).[94] However, the famine did not end immediately, presumably because the unburied bodies of the executed (21:10) continued to defile the land, at least from the perspective of Deuteronomy 21:23. Thus, only after atonement is made *and* the remains of the executed are interred (along with the bones of Saul and Jonathan, 21:12–14a) does Yahweh respond on behalf of the land (21:14b).

The resulting portrait of David is complex. Shimei is, at least from one viewpoint, correct: David is a 'man of bloods' (*ʾîš (ha)dāmîm*, 2 Sam. 16:7–8 my tr.).[95] Purity pushes the problem beyond wrongdoing alone to

---

[91] Firth 2009: 418.

[92] Shepherd 2023 analyses the theme of 'blood(s)' in Samuel.

[93] David's imprecation against Joab's house following the murder of Abner desires ongoing ritual defilement by *ṣāraʿat*-infection or genital discharge (2 Sam. 3:29).

[94] The guilt attached to Saul's *house* means the representative executions are perhaps not as unusual as Firth 2009: 506 claims.

[95] David's assertion that Yahweh dealt with him according to the 'cleanness' (*bōr*) of his hands

emphasize the enduring stain of moral pollution and its negative impact on people and land. These intertwined concepts come to a head in 1 – 2 Kings.

1 – 2 Kings

In 1 – 2 Kings purity continues to aid narrative portrayal. In Exodus, *ṭāhôr* repeatedly describes the 'pure gold' (*zāhāb ṭāhôr*) required to construct a suitable habitation for Yahweh. While many English versions use 'pure gold' with respect to Solomon's temple (e.g. 1 Kgs 7:50), the Hebrew clause is different: *zāhāb sāgûr* ('fine gold'[96] or 'solid gold' NLT). Though metallurgic quality is still emphasized, the choice of an alternative lexeme contributes to the narrator's rhetorical intent to subtly diminish the temple vis-à-vis tabernacle.[97] Solomon's construction may be grand(iose), but it is not *ṭāhôr*.

Depicting Gentile concern for purity in 2 Kings 5:1–27 further exposes Israelite negligence. The string of positive attributes that introduces Naaman in 5:1 ('commander,' 'great,' 'highly respected,' 'a mighty man of power') is undone with a single word: *mĕṣōrāʿ* ('he was *ṣāraʿat*-infected', my tr.; NIV: 'he had leprosy'). Yet, on the testimony of a captive Israelite girl, Naaman travels to Samaria to have a prophet 'take him away from his *ṣāraʿat*,' that is, to cure him (my tr.). The king's incredulous outburst indicates the sheer impossibility of Naaman's expectation: 'Am I God? Can I kill and bring back to life? Why does this fellow send someone to me to be cured of his [*ṣāraʿat*]?' (5:7). The reaction is understandable. Leviticus 13 – 14 provides diagnostic criteria and outlines post-remission purification measures – including sprinkling with water seven times (Lev. 14:7) – but proffers no options for curing *ṣāraʿat*.[98] Healing is God's prerogative. The Israelites could address symptoms (ritual impurity), but not the root cause (*ṣāraʿat*). Nevertheless, as the man of God instructed, Naaman immerses seven times in the Jordan and 'his flesh returned to be like the flesh of a young boy' (5:14

(2 Sam. 22:21, 25; cf. 22:27) is limited to the context elaborated in 22:1: David's dealings with Saul (cf. 1 Sam. 24; 26) (Firth 2009: 519).

[96] *HALOT* 2:742.

[97] See Hays 2016: 63–87 who concludes, 'from the very beginning, the temple seems to be tainted with disobedience and unfaithfulness' (87).

[98] In 2 Kgs 7:3, four men with *ṣāraʿat* live outside Samaria (cf. Lev. 13:46). They announce Aramean departure by 'calling out' (*qrʾ*) to the city gatekeepers from afar (7:10), echoing the 'calling out' (*qrʾ*) stipulated by Leviticus 13:45. Similarly, having contracted *ṣāraʿat*, Azariah 'lived in a separate house' (2 Kgs 15:5) and Gehazi 'went out from [Elisha's] presence' (2 Kgs 5:27 my tr.).

my tr.).[99] Yahweh removes Naaman's *ṣāraʿat*, the source of his defilement. Hence, 5:14 concludes, 'Then he became pure' (*wayyiṭhār*, my tr.). This final statement indicates healing is not the sole, or perhaps even ultimate, goal (*ṣāraʿat* is, after all, far from being a life-threatening condition).[100] Rather, eliminating this *particular* disease moves a person from impurity to purity.[101] Only when cleansed does Naaman stand before the face of Elisha (5:15; cf. 5:3).[102] Purified, he returns to Syria intent on building an altar to worship Yahweh.[103] Naaman's Gentile identity is another indicator that defilement and cleansing are human concerns, not just Israelite ones. The narrative anticipates eschatological worship in places beyond the temple and beyond Canaan.[104] While Naaman's devotion incorporates ritual purification, it is Yahweh who removes the root cause of defilement.[105]

Israel and Judah, however, pursue impurity. Rampant idolatry is branded 'a detestable thing' (*šiqquṣ*) and an 'abomination' (*tôʿēbâ*), as in Deuteronomy.[106] Sexually immoral practices are also *tôʿēbâ* (1 Kgs 14:24). The problem of bloodshed, so prominent in 1 – 2 Samuel, continues. Solomon executes Joab for shedding innocent blood in his peacetime killing of Abner and Amasa (1 Kgs 2:5–6, 31). Jehu is appointed to avenge the blood of Yahweh's prophets and servants that had been spilled by Jezebel (2 Kgs 9:7). Jezebel's blood is, subsequently, 'splattered' (*nzh*, 2 Kgs 9:33), a verb consistently used elsewhere in cultic settings, often in purificatory rites. Joram, likewise, dies to fulfil Yahweh's word: 'Yesterday I saw the blood of Naboth and the blood of his sons, declares the LORD, and I will surely make you pay for it on this plot of ground' (2 Kgs 9:26). A connection between bloodshed and land defilement, while not explicit, is implied. The consequences are also consistent with pollution of place: Yahweh vows to banish Judah

---

[99] LXX employs *baptizō* ('to baptise, immerse') for Naaman's cleansing (5:14).

[100] The verb for healing used in 5:3, 6, 7, 11 is also not the common *rp*ʾ, but *ʾsp* (Wray Beal 2014: 333).

[101] For ANE conceptions of *ṣāraʿat*, see Feder 2015.

[102] Wray Beal 2014: 334. Gehazi functions akin to priests in Lev. 14:3: going outside the house/camp to inspect a person ahead of purification from *ṣāraʿat*.

[103] Lovell 2021: 189–91.

[104] Wray Beal 2014: 337.

[105] This is foundational for understanding Jesus' actions in the Gospels (see chapter 7).

[106] For *šiqqûṣ*, see 1 Kgs 11:5, 7; 2 Kgs 23:13, 24; for *tôʿēbâ*, see 1 Kgs 14:23–24; 16:3; 2 Kgs 21:2, 11; 23:13.

because Manasseh spilled blood 'till he had filled Jerusalem' (2 Kgs 21:16; 24:3–4 ESV).

Yet, there are efforts to reverse the trend. The stain of spilled blood is 'removed' (*swr*) through the mechanism of judicial (or extra-judicial) execution (e.g. 1 Kgs 2:31).[107] Various reform movements also highlight removal: of idols (1 Kgs 15:12–13; 2 Kgs 23:11), idolaters (1 Kgs 15:13), sacred items (2 Kgs 18:4; 23:4), pagan altars (2 Kgs 18:22; 23:12, 15) and cultic personnel (1 Kgs 15:12;[108] 18:40; 2 Kgs 23:5, 20). Indeed, a king's success is directly correlated to whether he managed to 'remove' (*swr*) the high places (e.g. 2 Kgs 18:4; 23:19), or not (e.g. 1 Kgs 15:14; 22:43; 2 Kgs 12:4[3]; 14:4; 15:4). Removal ends activities that defile sanctuary and land; namely, sexual immorality, bloodshed and idolatry.[109]

The same end is also achieved through deliberate ritual defilement, a strategy most fully embraced by Josiah in 2 Kings 23.[110] Not only did the young king remove (*swr*) unsanctioned high places and religious relics from Judah and the northern regions, he also enacted a programme of systematically defiling pagan cult centres. The Asherah pole in Yahweh's temple was removed, burned and scattered across the graves of the people (23:6). Other sacred sites were filled with human bones (23:14). Josiah had the high places defiled (*ṭmʾ* piel), from Geba to Beersheba (23:8), including the shrines established by Solomon (23:13). Similarly, Topheth, a sacred site in the Hinnom Valley, was defiled (*ṭmʾ* piel) to ensure it could no longer be used (23:10). Even the altar at Bethel erected by Jeroboam after the division of the kingdom (1 Kgs 12:32–33) is desecrated. Josiah had it torn down and, at his behest, human bones from nearby tombs were burned upon its ruins (23:15–16). Samaria's shrines and high places received similar treatment (23:19). Climactically, Josiah 'sacrificed all the priests of the high places who were there, on the altars, and burned human bones on them' (23:20 ESV). The logic is simple: ritual purity is a prerequisite for cultic operations. Therefore, rendering sacred sites and objects permanently

[107] Similarly, the narrator concludes Yahweh removed (*swr*) both Israel and Judah from his sight because of persistent idolatry and bloodshed (2 Kgs 17:18, 23; 23:27; 24:3).

[108] The idea that 'shrine prostitutes' (1 Kgs 15:12 NIV) operated in Israel has been largely abandoned. See Bird 1995; 2019; Kelle 2005: 123–32.

[109] Desire to preserve the purity of Yahweh's house is evident in Jehoiada's insistence that Athaliah be executed outside the temple precincts (2 Kgs 11:15).

[110] See also 2 Kgs 10:24–27; 11:15–18.

impure removed them from use.[111] For acting this way, in line with Yahweh's command (1 Kgs 13:2; 2 Kgs 23:16–17), Josiah is remembered as Judah's premier king (23:25).[112]

Yet, Josiah's reforms were too little, too late. Consistent failure to 'turn away' (*swr* qal)[113] from false worship provoked Yahweh to 'remove' (*swr* hiphil) his people: 'I will remove (*swr*) Judah also from my presence as I removed (*swr*) Israel, and I will reject Jerusalem, the city I chose, and this temple, about which I said, "My Name shall be there"' (23:27; cf. 2 Kgs 17:18, 23; 24:3). As Frymer-Kensky adduces, 'the microcosm of Israel became so polluted that another cataclysm, the Exile, became necessary to destroy that polluted world.'[114] Nevertheless, like the Genesis flood, exile would not be the final word, but rather a means of purgation ahead of renewal.

Conclusion

Relative to Leviticus and Numbers, the themes of defilement and cleansing are not as prevalent elsewhere in the Pentateuch or in the Former Prophets. Nevertheless, both ritual and moral purity remain important. The sources of ritual defilement itemized in Leviticus and Numbers reappear, requiring similar boundaries between impurity and holiness. Moral impurity, likewise, arises from sexual immorality, idolatry and bloodshed. However, several passages, particularly in Deuteronomy, indicate that moral impurity may also be associated with other transgressions.

Within the narratives, the focus on defilement and cleansing is sometimes made explicit by employing technical terms. Yet, elsewhere, purity remains implicit. In this way, the biblical authors draw on shared cultural understandings to shape portraits of nations (e.g. Egypt in Exodus) and individuals (e.g. Samuel in 1 Samuel). Defilement and cleansing add gravitas to events like the flood and the reforms of Josiah. Ultimately, the themes construct a portrait of true worshippers who reflect Yahweh's holiness and purity. However, precisely because these ideas can operate

[111] Milgrom 1991: 258–59 suggests the resuscitation of pagan worship under Manasseh, following the reforms of Hezekiah, may have provoked the additional measures taken by Josiah.

[112] Wray Beal 2014: 502 notes 2 Kgs 22:1–2 lauds Josiah even above David.

[113] 2 Kgs 3:3; 10:29, 31; 13:2, 6, 11; 14:24; 15:9, 18, 24, 28; 17:22.

[114] Frymer-Kensky 1983: 412.

in the background, interpreters must develop a greater sensitivity to their presence. Otherwise, the richness of the biblical texts can easily be diminished. Nevertheless, many argue it was precisely against these cultic and ritual(istic) concerns of Israelite religion that prophetic voices railed. Thus, we turn now to the Latter Prophets.

4

Defilement and cleansing in the Latter Prophets

There is a long running trend to pitch Israel's prophets against the nation's priests.[1] In this imagined contest, the prophets are the heroes, railing against inflexible cultic and ritual practices, calling Israel instead to embrace emancipated relationship with Yahweh. Here, Wellhausen's shadow looms large. He argued the cult was *das heidnische Element* ('the pagan element') in Israelite religion, which accounts for both prophetic ire and attempts to revive extemporary religious devotion.[2] Of course, the scenario is entirely misconstrued – driven more by Wellhausen's sociocultural context and personal whims than by careful exegesis.[3] Thankfully, recent work on the prophet-priest nexus is more nuanced.[4] This less combative appraisal is germane for my purposes here. Rather than assuming cultic critique a priori, I explore how Israel's writing prophets utilize purity themes. In these books, bloodshed, idolatry and sexual immorality are repeatedly identified as the reason for exile. Yahweh will cleanse his land that has been defiled by these evils, even at significant human cost. Yet, the prophets also foresee a remnant, purified by Yahweh, dwelling in the land once more. Indictment and promise are couched in the language of defilement and cleansing. Thus, the Prophets use and develop purity ideas in ways that become crucial for articulating both Old and New Testament hope. Investigating these books is essential.

[1] Examples are legion; e.g. Bruce 1990: 238; Williams 1991: 129–62; Girard 2005: 43; Hendel 2012.

[2] Wellhausen 1958: 174.

[3] See also Brueggemann and Hankins 2013.

[4] E.g. Klawans 2006: 75–100; Tiemeyer 2009; Eidevall 2012; Glaim 2017.

Isaiah

In Isaiah purity accentuates crucial themes.[5] The book turns on the contrast between the Jerusalem that is and the Jerusalem that will be, and uses this dynamic to emphasize both Yahweh's transformative salvation and his ability to accomplish it. The need for salvation is starkly apparent in the book's opening section, which juxtaposes a litany of Judah's offences with 'the Holy One of Israel' (1:4).[6] Having abandoned Yahweh (1:2–4), the nation's sacrifices are declared worthless (1:11) and their incense an 'abomination' (*tô ʿēbâ*, 1:13; cf. 66:3).[7] Thus, Isaiah premises the efficacy of cultic activity as much on moral purity as ritual. But the people's hands are bloodstained (1:15); the once faithful city has become a 'prostitute' (*zōnâ*), filled with murderers (1:21). A sequence of four imperatives demands change:

> Wash (*rḥṣ*) yourselves!
>   Clean (*zkh*) yourselves!
> Remove your evil deeds from my eyes!
>   Stop doing evil!
> (1:16 my tr.)

Noting that *zkh* is always used in a moral sense in the Old Testament, Lesley DiFransico concludes 1:16 does not command physical ablutions. Instead, the climactic image of hands full of blood in 1:15 functions to 'represent the overall guilt that results from the people's sinful behavior.'[8] Accordingly, 'washing' becomes a metaphor for repentance.[9] However, while DiFransico rightly surmises the metaphorical nature of washing and cleaning, which are equated with ceasing evil (1:16) and practising righteousness (1:17), he does not consider moral impurity as a possible object. Yet, sin – especially bloodshed (1:15) and sexual immorality (1:21)

---

[5] My analysis of the Prophets is based on the received texts. Diachronic and compositional matters, while important, exceed the scope of this study.

[6] Yahweh's designation as 'Holy One' is recurrent (1:4; 5:19, 24; 10:17, 20; 12:6; 17:7; 29:19, 23; 30:11, 12, 15; 31:1; 37:23; 40:25; 41:14, 16, 20; 43:3, 14, 15; 45:11; 47:4; 48:17; 49:7; 54:5; 55:5; 60:9, 14). See also 5:16; 8:13 ('holy God'); 63:10, 11 ('holy spirit'); and 6:3 ('holy, holy, holy').

[7] Regarding how best to understand this dismissal of sacrifice, see my discussion of Jeremiah.

[8] DiFransico 2016: 44.

[9] DiFransico 2016: 45.

– produces a lasting stain. The resulting logic of 1:16–17 coheres with Leviticus and Numbers: one maintains moral purity by eschewing evil. Only by such 'washing' could sins as red as scarlet become white as snow (1:18),[10] enabling life in the land (1:19). Disobedience will, however, incur divine censure (1:20). The inevitability of the latter is indicated by 1:25: 'I will turn my hand against you and will smelt away your dross as with lye and remove all your alloy' (ESV). Yahweh will see his people cleansed, transformed and flourishing in the land, but that will happen through the refining fire of suffering and judgment.

Isaiah 4:2–6 presents a striking vision of what Yahweh will accomplish 'in that day':

> [H]e who is left in Zion and remains in Jerusalem will be called holy … when the Lord shall have washed away the filth (*ṣōʾâ*) of the daughters of Zion and cleansed (*dwḥ*)[11] the bloodstains[12] of Jerusalem from its midst by a spirit of judgment and by a spirit of burning.
> (4:3–4 ESV)

Then, when Jerusalem is cleansed and its people made holy, Yahweh 'will create over the whole site of Mount Zion and over her assemblies a cloud by day, and smoke and the shining of a flaming fire by night' (4:5 ESV). The language recalls the wilderness encampment and the divine presence dwelling within the tabernacle (cf. Exod. 40:34–38; Num. 9:15–16). Yahweh's future cleansing will enable priestlike proximity and intimacy.

The prophet exemplifies the possibility for purification and service in his own experience. In the vision of 6:1–13 Isaiah sees Yahweh seated in his temple, continuously heralded as 'holy, holy, holy' by seraphim who

[10] The wider context of intransigent unrepentance suggests 1:18 ought to be read, not as a promise of forgiveness or atonement, but as an ironic statement. Culver 1969: 140–41 paraphrases accordingly: 'If your sins are as scarlet they will be as white as snow – in court? Of course not! If they are red as crimson cloth they shall be as wool – in court? Of course not! (verse 18). If you expect to enjoy the fruits of righteousness you will have to perform the deeds of righteousness (verses 19 and 20).' Likewise, Lam 2016: 182–83 notes the suitedness of scarlet/crimson for depicting the moral impurity of bloodshed.

[11] In Ezek. 40:38 and 2 Chr. 4:6 'rinsing' (*dwḥ*) is an act of cultic preparation. The only other use of the verb is Jer. 51:34.

[12] DiFransico 2016: 54–56 rejects reading *dam* as 'bloodshed' (NASB) or 'bloodguilt' (HCSB) as it is paralleled with 'filth'. Instead, he reads 'blood' as a metaphor for sin. However, DiFransico ignores the possibility that both 'filth' and 'blood(shed)' indicate the stain of moral impurity that Yahweh will wash and cleanse.

shield themselves from his presence (6:1–3). Finding himself where he ought not to be, the prophet is rightly overcome. His exclamation supposes imminent danger, with word order emphasizing the problem: 'Woe to me! I am cut off! For a man of impure (*ṭāmēʾ*) lips am I, and among a people of impure (*ṭāmēʾ*) lips I live' (6:5 my tr.). The incongruity of the prophet's situation – impurity in proximity to holiness – is the central dilemma that fuels the book's urgent appeal for radical transformation. The prophet's woe is a microcosm of Judah's. Those who ought to represent Yahweh are impure and offensive. Yet, instead of expected banishment (or worse), one of the seraphim touches Isaiah's impure lips with a coal from the altar and declares, 'Behold! This has touched your lips and takes away your iniquity, and your sin is atoned' (6:7 my tr.). The language suggests that impurity in 6:5 is not ritual; in that case, washing and/or waiting would suffice. Instead, 'impure lips' functions synecdochally for moral defilement (cf. 59:3–5).[13] Isaiah in some unstated way shares in the iniquities of the Jerusalemites he lives among. Nevertheless, despite his helplessness, Yahweh removes Isaiah's sin and impurity, opening potential for relationship and service (6:8–9a). Thus, the prophet embodies the transformation the remnant will experience following judgment (cf. 6:11–13).

Isaiah also reveals the cosmic extent of Yahweh's judgment.[14] Beyond Judah and Jerusalem, the nations will likewise be held accountable (esp. 13 – 23). Here, a direct link is made between immoral acts and defilement of place. Because people have disobeyed the laws, violated the statutes and broken the everlasting covenant, 24:5 asserts, 'the earth is polluted (*ḥnp* qal) under its inhabitants' (my tr.).[15] It staggers because 'heavy upon it is the guilt of its rebellion' (24:20). The stain of bloodshed is a recurrent motif.[16] It provokes Yahweh to action: 'the LORD is coming out of his dwelling to punish the people of the earth for their sins. The earth will

[13] Cf. LAE 6:1–3 (first century AD) in which the primordial couple stand neck deep in water because of their impure lips (i.e. their sin).

[14] Judgment extends even to the realm of the dead (14:9–11) and possibly to spiritual beings. Heiser 2015: 83–91, for example, reads 14:12–15 as judgment upon the Gen. 3 serpent.

[15] The noun *ʾereṣ* can be rendered 'earth' or 'land'; translations of Isa. 24 – 27 vary accordingly. Watts 1985: 316, however, notes the close affiliation between 'earth' and 'land' in ancient conception. Regardless of the gloss adopted, Judah and its immediate neighbours are in view.

[16] 1:15; 4:4; 15:9; 26:21; 33:15; 59:2–3, 6–7. Misusing sacrificial blood also frames the book (1:11; 66:3), a matter Lev. 17:4 deems bloodshed. See also the appearance of 'violence' in 59:6; 60:18. Thus, Watts 1985: 317 concludes Isaiah's vision evokes Gen. 1 – 11, especially overcoming violence by means of flood, to emphasize Yahweh's inauguration of a new age.

disclose the blood shed on it; the earth will conceal its slain no longer' (26:21). The portrait of Edom's doom is especially vivid:

> The LORD has a sword; it is sated with blood;
> it is gorged with fat,
> with the blood of lambs and goats,
> with the fat of the kidneys of rams.
> For the LORD has a sacrifice in Bozrah,
> a great slaughter in the land of Edom.
> Wild oxen shall fall with them,
> and young steers with the mighty bulls.
> Their land shall drink its fill of blood,
> and their soil shall be gorged with fat.
> (34:6–7 ESV)

The sacrificial metaphor, while unnerving, accords with Numbers 35:33. Land defiled by bloodshed can only be atoned by shedding the blood of the defiler(s) (see also 14:19–21; cf. Gen. 9:6). Edom's projected judgment is regarded as complete in 63:1–6. A watchman sees someone approaching from Edom, from Bozrah, with garments stained red (63:1). The figure identifies as Yahweh, mighty to save (63:1), returning like a warrior from battle having poured out the lifeblood of his enemies (63:6). The portrayal raises a question: Is Yahweh defiled by the blood with which he is covered? The query is heightened by a recurrent ANE motif in which gods undergo ritual purification following battle.[17] Jason Riley determines that 63:1–6 shares core elements of the motif: a mythological setting, single-handed combat, blood, and the deity becoming both physically filthy and ritually defiled. Ritual defilement is also possibly invoked in 63:3c:

> I have splattered their juice upon my clothes,
> And all my apparel I have stained/defiled (*gʾl* [18]).
> (my tr.)

[17] For the relevant texts, see Riley 2014: 247–56.

[18] *HALOT* lists the verb form as a hiphil/aphel combination, meaning 'to stain' (cf. NIV, ESV). Other traditions (1QIsa.[a], 1QIsa.[b], Syr., Vg.), however, read as piel, 'to pollute, desecrate'. Riley 2014: 260–61 construes the hiphil/aphel with causative force ('I made my garments defiled') with appeal to Lam. 4:14 ('they were so defiled [*gʾl* niphal] with blood that no one was able to touch their garments' [ESV]).

However, defilement by blood in the Old Testament is elsewhere limited to menstruation and childbirth; blood does not defile wholesale.[19] Hence, in battle contexts, pollution is linked to touching corpses or body parts rather than contact with blood (Num. 19:16, 18; Ezek. 39:14–16). Moreover, Isaiah 63 omits any depiction of purification. For Riley, this lacuna indicates a deliberate attempt to employ ANE militaristic imagery, but without conceding Yahweh needed to be purified.[20] This partial use of a widespread ANE motif further accentuates the contrast between Yahweh and other gods.[21]

Cleansing the land of idolatry is also crucial. In addition to usurping witness to Yahweh,[22] idols are an 'abomination' (*tôʿēbâ*, 44:19) and a 'detestable thing' (*šiqquṣ*, 66:3) – as are those who worship them (41:24). Accordingly, the remnant who inhabit Zion will reject their idolatrous ways in response to divine prompting:

> For a people shall dwell in Zion, in Jerusalem … And your ears shall hear a word behind you, saying, 'This is the way, walk in it,' when you turn to the right or when you turn to the left. Then you will defile (*ṭmʾ* piel) your carved idols overlaid with silver and your gold-plated metal images. You will scatter them as unclean things (*dāweh*[23]). You will say to them, 'Be gone!'
> (30:19, 21–22 ESV)

Deliberately desecrating idols renders them unfit for use (cf. 2:20; 2 Kgs 23). Moreover, when the land is no longer defiled by such abominations, it will flourish (30:23–24). Streams of water will flow 'on every high mountain and every lofty hill', replacing the defiling shrines so often found in those locales (30:25; cf. 57:7; 65:7; cf. 2 Kgs 23:13; Jer. 3:6), and sun and moon will shine more brightly (30:26; cf. 60:19–20).

---

[19] Riley 2014: 260, following Milgrom 1991: 403–4, appeals to Lev. 6:20[27] to support impurity conveyed by blood splattering. However, Lev. 6:20[27] is more likely attempting to prevent contagious holiness.

[20] Riley 2014: 262.

[21] One need not conclude with Riley 2014: 263 that Yahweh was once conceived like other gods with the idea only becoming unpalatable by the time of Third Isaiah.

[22] The intersection between Yahweh's image, idolatry, and the Servant is insightfully explored by Batchelder 2023.

[23] *Dāweh* describes feeling faint or unwell (Lam. 1:13; 5:17) and can denote menstruation (Lev. 15:33; 20:18). Hence, NIV 'like a menstrual cloth'.

This cleansed and renewed place – variously construed as restored land (4:2), sacred mountain (11:9; 25:6–8; 27:13; 56:7; 57.13; 65:11; 65:25; 66:20) and (re)new(ed) creation (11:6–9; 65:17; 66:22) – is holy. Therefore, ritual and moral purity become essential: 'a highway will be there; it will be called the Way of Holiness; it will be for those who walk on that Way. The unclean will not journey on it; wicked fools will not go about on it' (35:8). Because the impure will no longer enter Jerusalem, 'the holy city' (48:2; 52:1), a call is issued to God's exiled people:

Turn away! Turn away! Go out from there!
An impure thing (*ṭāmē*ʾ) you must not touch.
Go out from her midst! Purify yourselves (*brr* niphal),
you who carry the vessels of Yahweh.
(52:11 my tr.)

The language alludes to Leviticus 13:45 and reverses the call for impure Jerusalem to 'Turn away' into exile in Lamentations 4:15.[24] The urgent need for purity fits the context of new exodus pilgrimage to the holy place where Yahweh resides. Yahweh is both the people's protection (52:12) and reason for the journey.[25] The ensuing verses connect preparation for Yahweh's presence with the agency of the Servant. The Servant performs a vicarious role: he is pierced for the people's transgressions (53:5), punished for their iniquity (53:6) and cut off because of their rebellion (53:8). Yahweh makes him a restitution offering (53:10), through whom the many are made righteous (53:11). Although implicit, purification is also evoked. Isaiah 53 shares lexical parallels with Leviticus 16, recalling the cleansing achieved on the Day of Atonement.[26] Yahweh also declares that his Servant 'will sprinkle (*yazzeh*) many nations' (52:15). If the reading 'sprinkle' is retained (with MT; also CSB, ESV, NASB), rather than 'startle' (with LXX; also JPS, NRSV, NLT),[27] then *nzh* evokes cultic contexts of

[24] Schnittjer 2021: 241–43.

[25] Watts 1987: 217. Watts, inexplicably, neither translates nor comments on the second half of 52:11.

[26] For details, see Allen 2012 (esp. 180–83), although Allen does not consider the purificatory intent of Yom Kippur.

[27] For the options, see Oswalt 2003: 584.

expiating sin or, more frequently, purging impurity.[28] Its use also extends the Servant's preparatory function beyond Israel.

Regardless of how 52:15 is understood, habitation in future Zion is offered to all:

> Let no foreigner who is bound to the LORD say,
> 'The LORD will surely exclude me from his people.'
> […]
> And foreigners who bind themselves to the LORD
> to minister to him,
> to love the name of the LORD,
> and to be his servants,
> all who keep the Sabbath without desecrating it
> and who hold fast to my covenant –
> these I will bring to my holy mountain
> and give them joy in my house of prayer.
> Their burnt offerings and sacrifices
> will be accepted on my altar;
> for my house will be called
> a house of prayer for all nations.
> (56:3, 6–7)

Cultic and priestly imagery accentuates the location of sacrificial ministry in 'my house' (56:7). Yet, in contrast to the prophet's initial experience of woe when appearing in Yahweh's temple (6:5), these foreigners are joy-filled (cf. 35:10); their purity is assumed (cf. 33:14–16). Thus, in the future Isaiah portrays, the line of separation is constructed around purity, not ethnicity.[29] Whether Israelite or Gentile, the ritually and morally impure are excluded (59:2–8; 65:1–5; 66:15–17, 24). But in that day, out of the Jerusalem and nations of the present, a multi-ethnic Zion will emerge whose populace will be called 'the Holy People' (62:12). Survivors from 'all nations and languages' will be brought to Jerusalem, Yahweh's 'holy mountain', just like offerings are brought to the temple in pure vessels (66:18, 20). Isaiah's 'terminology specifically references the dynamics that

[28] *Nzh* is connected with sin removal in Lev. 4:6, 17, 27; and with impurity removal in Exod. 29:21; Lev. 8:11, 30; 14:7, 16, 27, 51; 16:14(2x), 15, 19; Num. 8:7; 19:4, 18, 19, 21. The remaining uses of the verb in Lev. 6:20[6:27](2x) and 2 Kgs 9:33 reflect the splattering of garments in Isa. 63:3.

[29] This becomes a crucial aspect of Pauline theology. See chapter 8.

underlie every sacrificial ritual as it gradually moves toward the center of holiness at the sanctuary.'[30] And Yahweh will choose some to be priests and Levites (66:19). Thus, 'all mankind will come and bow down before me' (66:23). In all this, God acts for his own sake to preserve his holiness: 'See, I have refined you … For my own sake, for my own sake, I do this. How can I let myself be profaned (*ḥll*)?' (48:10–11 NIV adapted). This is what Yahweh will accomplish (cf. 62:1–4).

The first-person plural voice ('we', 'us') that appears sporadically throughout Isaiah captures the central dynamic. There is frank recognition of current status: 'We have become like an impure thing (*ṭāmē*ʾ) – all of us. And our righteous acts are like a menstrual cloth (*kĕbeged ʿiddîm*)' (64:5[6] my tr.). As in Isaiah 6, this is not detached self-realization, for impurity is threatened by Yahweh's intrinsic nature: 'Who among us can dwell with the consuming fire?' (33:14). Yet, despite this apparent *fait accompli*, a new possibility beckons: 'whoever takes refuge in me will inherit the land and possess my holy mountain' (57:13). There is hope for the future. That hope is premised on purification.

Jeremiah

Determining the structure of Jeremiah is a well-known crux.[31] The book resists linear schemes. Nevertheless, individual pericopes can be read in relation to Yahweh's programmatic intention to 'uproot and tear down, to destroy and overthrow, to build and to plant' (1:10). Passages variously (1) itemize problems in Judah; (2) articulate implications; (3) declare Yahweh's judgment; or (4) envision future restoration. These four categories work heuristically to itemize how the book of Jeremiah appropriates the themes of defilement and cleansing. The appearance of purity language is unsurprising: the book claims Jeremiah's priestly ancestry (1:1). Moreover, Yahweh declares that the prophet's consecration (*qdš* hiphil) precedes birth (1:5), meaning his mandate to censure Judah in a context of looming disaster could not be shirked (1:14–19).

Entrenched idolatry is the core problem. The book's opening speech describes Judah as Yahweh's bride to highlight the incongruity (2:2).

[30] Eberhart 2011: 92.

[31] The problem is accentuated by significant disparity between MT and LXX. Shead 2012: 65–106 surveys the possibilities.

Yahweh reminisces, 'Israel was holy to the LORD' (2:3), planted as 'faithful seed' (2:21 NASB). But Israel abandoned Yahweh: 'long ago I broke your yoke and burst your bonds; but you said, "I will not serve." Yes, on every high hill and under every green tree you bowed down like a whore' (2:20 ESV). The overarching metaphor of betrothal invites a derivative: idolatry is adultery. Purity considerations add rhetorical force to the already confronting sexual imagery. Yahweh inquires, 'How can you say, "I have not defiled myself (*ṭmʾ* niphal); I have not walked after the Baals"?' (2:23 my tr.). Instead, Judah's actions betray self-awareness: 'Though you wash with lye and repeatedly[32] use soap, the stain of your iniquity is before me' (2:22 my tr.). Sin, as DiFransico observes, is a stubborn stain; the people try in vain to remove it.[33] But idolatry, like adultery, also generates moral defilement that is not easily expunged. Jeremiah 2:22 likely encompasses both problems; that is, iniquity (requiring forgiveness) and the residual impurity it generates (requiring purification).[34] And idolatry is not the sole problem. Innocent blood, likewise, stains (2:23; cf. 26:15), and Judah has 'filled this place with the blood of the innocent' (19:4; cf. 22:17). Indeed, the land is full of 'abominations' (*tôʿēbōt*) – immoral deeds (7:9–10)[35] and idols (16:18; 32:35; 44:4, 22; cf. Exod. 34:15–16). And still the people remain intransigent. Twice, Yahweh asks, 'Were they ashamed when they committed abomination?' (6:15; 8:12 ESV). The answer each time is 'No'.

The consequences of Judah's behaviour are inevitable. As in Leviticus and Numbers, moral depravity defiles land. Canaan had been plentiful, filled with good things, Yahweh says, 'But you entered and made my land impure (*ṭmʾ* piel) and made my inheritance an abomination (*tôʿēbâ*)' (2:7 my tr.). Idolatry is singled out as the root cause, again couched as sexual infidelity. The people polluted (*ḥnp* hiphil) the land with their 'prostitution' (*zĕnût*, 3:2). 'On every high hill and under every spreading tree' Israel committed adultery (3:6). Judah did no better: 'she polluted (*ḥnp* qal) the

---

[32] Following Holladay 1986: 99 in reading the root as emphasizing repetition over quantity.

[33] DiFransico 2016: 68; cf. Lam 2016: 179–206.

[34] Some support for this is found in the verb *ktm* ('to stain') which, while a hapax legomenon, is related to a post-biblical noun used to denote menstrual staining on clothing (Holladay 1986: 99–100).

[35] The 'abominations' listed include sins that Leviticus and Numbers associate with moral defilement (murder, adultery, and idolatry), but also stealing and false testimony. Similarly, re-enslavement of people in 34:15–16 profanes Yahweh's name, indicating holiness has relational and ethical entailments operative at a communal level.

land and committed adultery with stone and wood' (3:9 my tr.). Impurity reaches a crescendo in 16:18: 'they have polluted (*ḥll* piel) my land with the carcasses of their detestable idols (*šiqqûṣêhem*), and have filled my inheritance with their abominations (*wĕtô ʿăbôtêhem*)' (ESV). The first-person possessives are important: Yahweh claims Canaan as 'my land' and 'my inheritance' (2:7; 16:18). Because this is Yahweh's dwelling place, pollution must cease. If the people will not return to him, they should expect a certificate of divorce and banishment (3:8). Thus, Jeremiah echoes Pentateuchal concerns to preserve the purity of the place where Yahweh resides (e.g. Lev. 18:24–28; Num. 35:33–34).

Yet Judah defiled not only the land, but also the temple. As in Deuteronomy, Jeremiah 7:30 employs *šiqquṣ* ('detestable thing') as a circumlocution for idols (also 4:1; 16:18; 32:34). By placing 'their detestable things' (*šiqquṣêhem*) in the house that bears Yahweh's name, the people defiled it (*ṭmʾ* piel, 7:30; 32:34 my tr.). Again, this is consistent with moral impurity in the Torah. The infinitive construct in 7:30 and 32:34 (*leṭammĕʾô*, 'to defile it'), perhaps indicates deliberate action; that is, detestable things installed *in order to* defile the temple (see ESV, KJV, NASB). If this is the intended sense, then Yahweh's defiling of Israel's high places falls under the rubric of commensurate action. This is exactly what Jeremiah forecasts as imminent judgment is announced. Calls to (re) turn,[36] to remove detestable things from Yahweh's presence (4:1), and to wash hearts from evil (4:14), prove fruitless. Instead, Judah asserts, 'It's no use! I love foreign gods, and I must go after them' (2:25).

Therefore, Yahweh promises to systematically defile the nation's sacred sites as a necessary precursor to ending its idolatrous ways. In Jeremiah 19 the prophet is ordered to Topheth (lit. 'fireplace') in the Ben Hinnom Valley (19:1–2, 6, 14). Here, Jerusalem's kings and the people of Judah erected high places for foreign gods and offered incense and children to Baal (19:4–5; cf. 7:31). Yahweh, with bitter irony, announces a new name for the site: 'Valley of Slaughter' (19:6; cf. 7:32). The locale stained by innocent blood (19:4) would instead be littered with Jerusalemite corpses (19:7). Topheth would become an overflowing graveyard, rendering it permanently non-sacrosanct (19:11; cf. 7:32; Num. 19). Likewise, Jerusalem's houses which had been used as pagan shrines would be defiled

[36] *Šwb* ('to turn, return') is a *Leitwort* in Jeremiah, which attests the highest number of occurrences in the Old Testament (115x).

(19:13; cf. 32:29) and filled with corpses (33:4–5). In fact, the entire land would be covered by the slain. The bones of Jerusalem's inhabitants, Yahweh announces, will be removed from their graves and spread like dung on the ground (8:1–2). Here too there is a religious motive at work. These impure human remains are to lie exposed before the sun, moon and stars in seeming affront to the celestial bodies venerated by the people (8:2). Land covered by uninterred remains is a frequent motif (8:2; 9:21; 16:4; 25:33), as is the idea of impure birds and animals consuming human corpses (7:33; 15:3; 16:4; 19:7; 34:20).[37] Deliberate desecration echoes the *modus operandi* of reform movements in 2 Kings in which illegitimate sacred sites are deliberately polluted.[38]

Jeremiah also portrays judgment as de-creation. In 4:23 the earth becomes 'formless and empty' (*tōhû wābōhû*), mirroring Genesis 1:2 exactly,[39] and the heavens no longer give light (cf. Gen. 1:3). Moreover, there is no 'man' (*ʾādām*) or bird (4:25; cf. 9:10; 12:4; 33:10, 12) and the fruitful ground becomes desert (4:26). Judah's sin and impurity have environmental consequences, meaning Yahweh is about to uproot 'the whole land' (45:4). The twinned themes of de-creation and systematic defilement echo Yahweh's judgment upon Egypt (see chapter 3). Egypt's fate has become Judah's.

Unrepentant moral deviation also impacts sacrificial performance in Jeremiah (and the other Prophets). For example, 6:20 asserts, 'Your burnt offerings are not acceptable; your sacrifices do not please me' (cf. 7:21; 14:12). The issue is not lack of ritual purity, prerequisite for sacrifice; Jeremiah remains silent on the matter. Nor is it a *carte blanche* rejection of the cult. Instead, Judah's ongoing 'affair' with other deities means the relational dimension of sacrifice is so thoroughly undermined that there is no point in continuing.[40] Göran Eidevall reasons, 'If sacrifices are offered within the framework of a reciprocal human–divine relationship, the sacrificial system will always allow for the possibility that some

[37] Both carnivores and carrion-eaters are impure according to Lev. 11. Judgment is, therefore, commensurate: the impure consume the impure.

[38] Deliberate defilement of pagan shrines indicates a shared worldview regarding corpse-defilement (Thompson 1980: 453)

[39] The phrase occurs only in these two verses.

[40] The relational dimension of sacrifice is crucial for correctly parsing prophetic critique. Lambasting sacrifice in a dysfunctional context is not rejection of sacrifice *in se*. See, further, Harper forthcoming-c.

sacrifices are rejected by the deity.'[41] Rejecting sacrifice is fitting ahead of the imminent judgment announced in Jeremiah. Indeed, for Yahweh to accept offerings at this juncture would portray him as capricious or weak, either unwilling or unable to help Judah despite accepting their gifts.[42] Divine disavowal of sacrifice in this *temporally specific context* reinforces Yahweh's adversarial stance towards his people: '[R]ejection of the cult is part of the punishment.'[43] But, when hostility ends, offerings will resume. Therefore, Jeremiah longs for sacrifice to recommence, properly conducted by morally transformed people when Yahweh restores the nation (17:24–26; 33:10–11, 17–18).[44]

While judgment in Jeremiah may be unavoidable, it is not final.[45] Though Yahweh says, 'I have seen your abominations, your adulteries and neighings, your lewd whorings, on the hills in the field' (13:27 ESV), his subsequent question intimates an alternate future: 'You are not pure – for how long yet?' (my tr.). The Book of Consolation (30:1 – 33:26) forecasts change. Days are coming when 'the whole valley of the corpses and the ashes … will be holy to Yahweh' (31:40) and the land will be restored 'as in the beginning' (33:11 my tr.). Moreover, Yahweh asserts,

> I will cleanse (*ṭhr* piel) them from all their iniquity which they sinned against me. And I will forgive (*slḥ* qal) all their iniquities which they sinned against me.
> (33:8 my tr.)

These lines are not synonymous. Iniquity requires forgiveness, but forgiveness alone is insufficient. Cleansing the stain of moral pollution is also essential. In Jeremiah's anticipated future, Yahweh accomplishes both.[46]

---

[41] Eidevall 2012: 215. Genesis 4:4–5 is paradigmatic: Yahweh favoured Abel's offering, but not Cain's.

[42] Glaim 2017: 126.

[43] Eidevall 2017: 157.

[44] The same sacrificial dimension of future hope is also found in Isa. 56:6–7; 60:7; Ezek. 20:40–44; 43:27; Mal. 3:4. Eidevall 2017: 151–52 proposes a chronological schema to account for this data, which resolves seemingly contradictory prophetic statements: 'Whereas passages denouncing sacrifices always refer to the past, passages promoting sacrifices consistently refer to the future'.

[45] The burning of Jerusalem with fire (e.g. 17:27; 21:10; 32:29; 38:18; cf. 43:12–13) is commensurate with the concepts of purification and refining (cf. 6:27–30; 9:6).

[46] See chapter 8 for how 1 John relates Jer. 33:8 to Jesus.

Ezekiel

The prophet Ezekiel's priestly ancestry (1:3) is evident in the cultic motifs present throughout the book that bears his name.[47] Ezekiel is also saturated with intertextual connections to Leviticus. While the purpose of these connections and their direction of dependence are debated,[48] Ezekiel attests the highest concentration of purity language outside Leviticus and Numbers. Defilement and cleansing are integral to its message. The book divides into two main sections. The first, chapters 1 – 32, judges the past with respect to Judah (1 – 24) and the nations (25 – 32), and the second envisions future restoration (33 – 48). These portraits of past and future shape a message for the author's present. Hearers are not asked to determine their own judgment, but rather to confirm a judgment already made, to identify and side with Yahweh's verdict.[49] Thus, Ezekiel seeks to foster allegiance to the values expressed in Yahweh's acts of judgment and his promises for the future.[50]

Ezekiel presents a damning litany of Judah's offences against Yahweh. Idolatry is pre-eminent. The extent of the problem is shockingly exposed in 8:1–18 as the prophet travels from Babylonian exile to the Jerusalem temple in a vision (8:3; cf. 1:1–3). Ezekiel is summoned as witness (cf. Deut. 19:15). Repeatedly, Yahweh enquires, 'Son of man, do you see?' (8:6, 12, 15, 17).[51] The prophet is shown a series of increasingly 'great abominations' (*tôʿēbôt gĕdōlôt*, 8:6): engravings of creeping things and detestable animals upon the walls (8:10; cf. Lev. 11), idols worshipped with incense in the temple (8:10–11; cf. Lev. 16:12–13), women weeping for Tammuz (8:14), and twenty-five men worshipping the sun with backs turned to Yahweh (8:16). Ezekiel sees the temple defiled by idolatry from within. Moreover, the prophet's guided tour refutes the attestation of Israel's elders: 'The LORD does not see us; the LORD has forsaken the land' (8:12; cf. 9:9). On the contrary, Yahweh is present, and Yahweh

[47] The concluding section (40 – 48), for instance, is an extended vision of a new temple in which sacrifice features prominently (e.g. 40:38–43; 42:13, 18–27; 44:11, 15, 29–30; 45:15–25; 46:2–8, 11–15, 20–24).

[48] See Kohn 2002; Lyons 2009; Kilchör 2020b.

[49] Renz 2002: 57.

[50] Renz 2002: 58.

[51] The thirteenfold use of *rʾh* ('to see') in Ezek. 8 is the highest in the Old Testament.

sees.[52] Therefore, judgment looms (8:17–18) with 5:11 clarifying the causal connection: 'because you have defiled (*ṭmʾ* piel) my sanctuary with all your detestable things (*šiqqûṣayik*) and with all your abominations (*tôʿăbōtāyik*), therefore I will withdraw. My eye will not spare, and I will have no pity' (ESV).[53]

Yahweh's eye will also not spare bloodshed (7:9–11).[54] Both city (7:23) and land (8:17) are filled with violence. Thus, in 22:2, Ezekiel is invited to judge Jerusalem, 'the city of bloods' (my tr.; cf. 24:6, 9), the town that 'sheds blood in her midst … and that makes idols to defile herself (*ṭmʾ* qal)' (22:3 ESV). All within are guilty of shedding blood for dishonest gain – from princes (22:6, 27) to commoners (22:9, 12–13). Therefore, Jerusalem's name is defiled (22:5). Additionally, the priests fail to teach the difference between holy and common, between pure and impure (22:26; cf. Lev. 10:10–11). The resulting conduct is excoriated:

> You have despised my holy things and profaned my Sabbaths. … In you men uncover their fathers' nakedness; in you they violate women who are unclean in their menstrual impurity. One commits abomination with his neighbour's wife; another lewdly defiles his daughter-in-law; another in you violates his sister, his father's daughter.
> (22:8, 10–11 ESV)

Divine reckoning is apropos: 'you have become guilty because of the blood you have shed and have become defiled (*ṭmʾ* qal) by the idols you have made. You have brought your days to a close' (22:4).

Ezekiel 23 reveals the longevity of unfaithfulness by developing an extended allegory of two 'sisters', Oholah and Oholibah, that is, Samaria and Jerusalem (23:4). The passage is saturated with sexual language: the *znh* root ('to fornicate') occurs twenty times;[55] *nʾp* ('to commit adultery')

---

[52] Much modern scholarship echoes the elders' conclusion by supposing that unmitigated impurity forces Yahweh to flee temple and land. I challenge this reading in Harper 2022a.

[53] Ezekiel contains the most occurrences of *šiqqûṣ* (29%) and *tôʿēbâ* (36%) in the Old Testament.

[54] This is also true for the nations (35:5–9).

[55] *Znh* ('to fornicate', 23:3[2x], 5, 19, 30, 43); *taznût* ('fornication', 23:7, 8[2x], 11, 14, 17, 18, 19, 29, 35, 43); *zōnâ* ('prostitute', 23:44); and *zĕnût* ('prostitution', 23:27).

four times; [56] *zimmâ* ('wickedness', often conveying sexual deviance[57]) eight times;[58] and the *ʿgb* root ('to lust') seven times.[59] As in Jeremiah and Hosea, adultery becomes a powerful metaphor. The problem is not political alliances, but spiritual ones, as the repetition of *gillūlîm* ('idols') clarifies (23:7, 30, 37, 39, 49). Lust for foreign gods, beginning in Egypt (23:8), defiled Israel and Judah (23:7, 13, 17[2x], 30, 38). The language is graphic, horrific even. It has earned Ezekiel the moniker 'porno-prophet'.[60] But Yahweh's speech is not gratuitous. It is designed to provoke disgust and abhorrence, a rhetorical aim ably served by impurity motifs (cf. 16:1–63; 20:1–49). Yahweh declares his intent to bring such a horrendous situation to a conclusive end (23:27). The prophet and his hearers are invited to affirm the decision:

> Son of man, will you judge Oholah and Oholibah? Declare to them their abominations (*tôʿăbôtêhen*). For they have committed adultery (*nʾp* piel), and blood is on their hands. With their idols they have committed adultery (*nʾp* piel), and they have even offered up to them for food the children whom they had borne to me. Moreover, this they have done to me: they have defiled (*ṭmʾ* piel) my sanctuary on the same day and profaned (*ḥll* piel) my Sabbaths. For when they had slaughtered their children in sacrifice to their idols, on the same day they came into my sanctuary to profane it (*ḥll* piel). And behold, this is what they did in my house.
> (23:36–39 ESV)

Ezekiel 28 sets Yahweh's judgment against a wider, perhaps even cosmic, tableau. The prophet is commanded to lament for the king of Tyre who once inhabited Eden, the garden of God, the holy mountain of Yahweh (28:13–14). Character and location once correlated ('You were blameless in your ways'), until 'unrighteousness was found in you' (28:15 ESV). Therefore, Yahweh recalls, 'I cast you as a profane thing (*ḥll* piel) from the mountain of God' (28:16 ESV). Irrespective of whether this passage

[56] 23:37(2x), 45(2x).

[57] E.g. Lev. 18:17; 19:29; 20:14(2x); Judg. 20:6; Jer. 13:27.

[58] 23:21, 27, 29, 35, 44, 48(2x), 49.

[59] The verb appears in 23:5, 7, 9, 12, 16, 20; the related noun in 23:11.

[60] Interpretations of Ezekiel's sexualized language are evaluated by Sloane 2008.

denotes Satan's backstory, a matter I will not resolve here,[61] a wider pattern to Yahweh's actions is revealed. Those who render themselves unfit ('profane') to dwell on Yahweh's holy mountain will be expelled. What is true for kings and nations (a similar sequence of events is applied to Assyria and Egypt in 31:1–18), perhaps modelled on primordial events, must assuredly be Judah's fate.

In Ezekiel, moral depravity defiles people, land and temple. Sabbaths are 'profaned' (*ḥll*) by not treating them as holy.[62] Therefore, judgment focuses on eradicating sources of impurity. The remaining populace will be killed or exiled (e.g. 6:7–8; 24:21). The land will be stripped on account of violence done there, becoming a wasteland (12:19–20; 15:8).[63] Judah's altars and shrines will become desolate and will, as in 2 Kings and Jeremiah, be intentionally desecrated: 'I will lay the dead bodies of the people of Israel before their idols, and I will scatter your bones around your altars' (6:5 ESV). Coming 'before Yahweh' to present blood 'all around the altar' is sacrificial language.[64] Here, instead, Israelite corpses are laid 'before their idols' and their impure bones are spread 'around [their] altars'. The rhetoric is biting. More shocking still, the temple is profaned, as it too had become a pagan shrine (cf. 8:5–18). Hence, in Ezekiel 9, after those who grieve the city's abominations are marked (9:4), figures are dispatched to kill everyone else, beginning at the sanctuary (9:6). Desecration is deliberate: 'Defile (*ṭmʾ* piel) the house, and fill the courts with the slain' (9:7 ESV). The land saturated with blood (9:9) is flooded with the blood of perpetrators (cf. Num. 35:33). In all this, Ezekiel and his hearers must not lament: 'I will profane (*ḥll* piel) my sanctuary … you shall not mourn or weep' (24:21, 23 ESV).

Against the backdrop of unrestrained ritual and moral impurity, Ezekiel 1 – 32 decrees death, desolation and defilement. However, these outcomes anticipate restoration. Yahweh will also act to resurrect, re-create and purify. In 37:1–2 the prophet is shown a valley full of unburied bones lying scattered on the ground. These skeletons, which represent the house of Israel, say, 'Our bones are dried up, and our hope is lost; we are

[61] Compare Heiser 2015: 73–82 with Walton and Walton 2019: 212–28.

[62] Ezek. 20:13, 16, 21, 24; 22:8; 23:38; cf. 20:20; 44:24; 46:1–3.

[63] The extent of the exile and associated destruction are debated (see, e.g., Carroll 1992). Nevertheless, and irrespective of historical realities, textual presentations of complete destruction remain rhetorically important.

[64] Exod. 29:16, 20; Lev. 1:5, 11; 3:2, 8, 13; 7:2; 8:15, 19, 24; 9:12, 18; 16:18; Num. 3:26; 4:26.

indeed cut off' (37:11 ESV). Human remains, the most virulent source of ritual impurity, provide an apt conceptualization of a defiled and defiling people. Moreover, the bones are 'very dry' (37:2), implying no one was able to remove impurity by burial (cf. 39:12–16). Nevertheless, into this hopeless situation, Yahweh speaks,

> Thus says the Lord GOD: Behold, I will open your graves and raise you from your graves, O my people. And I will bring you into the land of Israel. And you shall know that I am the LORD, when I open your graves, and raise you from your graves, O my people. And I will put my Spirit within you, and you shall live, and I will place you in your own land. Then you shall know that I am the LORD; I have spoken, and I will do it.
> (Ezek. 37:12–14 ESV)

National death is overcome by resurrection.[65] Defiling bones become living flesh. The land, likewise, will be restored. The people's abominations had defiled it:

> Son of man, when the house of Israel lived in their own land, they defiled (*ṭm'* piel) it by their ways and their deeds. Their ways before me were like the uncleanness of a woman in her menstrual impurity (*kĕṭum'at hanniddâ*). So I poured out my wrath upon them for the blood that they had shed in the land, for the idols with which they had defiled (*ṭm'* piel) it.
> (Ezek. 36:17–18 ESV)

Because it had been defiled by 'abominations', Yahweh made the land desolate (33:28–29).[66] The absence of people and multiplication of wild animals portray a descent into unordered chaos (cf. Jer. 4). Yet, 'the land that was desolate shall be tilled, instead of being the desolation that it was in the sight of all who passed by' (36:34 ESV). That future is wondrously imagined in the vision of 47:1–12 in which waters flowing from the sanctuary bring healing (*rp'*, 47:8, 9, 11, 12) and cause life to flourish (47:9, 12). Defiled land will be re-created.

---

[65] The vision concerns communal, not individual, resurrection.

[66] Cf. 6:14; 12:20; 14:15–16; 15:8.

The people also require transformation. In this respect, Ezekiel poses two significant problems. First, how can past impurity be removed? Unlike ritual impurity, there are no cultic means for cleansing moral defilement. Second, how can the inevitability of future exile(s) be averted? For rebellion will continue to defile people, land and temple and necessitate further banishment from Yahweh's presence. Ezekiel 36 addresses this dual dilemma by declaring what Yahweh will do – for the sake of his own holy name, which Israel profaned among the nations:

> I will sprinkle clean water (*mayim ṭĕhôrîm*) on you, and you shall be clean (*ṭhr* qal) from all your uncleannesses (*ṭum ʾôtêkem*), and from all your idols I will cleanse (*ṭhr* piel) you. And I will give you a new heart, and a new spirit I will put within you. And I will remove the heart of stone from your flesh and give you a heart of flesh. And I will put my Spirit within you, and cause you to walk in my statutes and be careful to obey my rules. You shall dwell in the land that I gave to your fathers, and you shall be my people, and I will be your God.
> (Ezek. 36:25–28 ESV; cf. vv. 21–22)

Yahweh will cleanse his people from their idols (36:25) and from their iniquities (36:33). The emphasis falls on the removal of moral defilement (cf. 37:23). Moreover, God will also dispense his Spirit to make people obedient. Thus, Yahweh addresses both past and future defilement. The people will again dwell in the land that belongs to God, but only by divine agency. The change initiated by the pouring out of Yahweh's Spirit is powerfully conveyed in 39:24, 29:

> I dealt with them according to their uncleanness (*kĕṭum ʾātām*) and their transgressions, and hid my face from them. … I will not hide my face anymore from them, when I pour out my Spirit upon the house of Israel.
> (ESV)

Purification opens new possibilities for relationship and proximity. 'On my holy mountain', declares Yahweh, 'all the house of Israel, all of them, shall serve me in the land' (20:40 ESV). Cultic and priestly resonances continue as Yahweh declares he will accept Israel as a 'pleasing aroma'

(20:41; cf. Lev. 1:9, 13, 17) and be 'proved holy' in their midst in the sight of the nations (20:41; cf. 36:23; 39:27; Lev. 10:3; 22:32). Fittingly, the book ends with a vision of a new city and temple. Both are located on a 'very high mountain' within the land of Israel (40:2), evoking cosmic mountain motifs. The prophet is commanded to 'see' with his eyes and then to declare what he 'sees' to the house of Israel (40:4). The temple architecture (40:5 – 42:20) maps holiness boundaries.[67] The plan reaffirms the separation required between holy and common (40:20), the very thing Israel ignored by setting 'their doorposts beside my doorposts, with only a wall between me and them' (43:8). Now, as the 'glory of Yahweh' again fills the temple (43:2–5; cf. 10:4, 18; Exod. 40:34–35; 1 Kgs 8:10–11), the prophet is told to describe the temple to *shame* Israel (43:10; cf. 20:43). Shame is a prerequisite for heeding the law of the temple: 'All the surrounding area on top of the mountain will be most holy' (43:12). For this reason, the city will henceforth be called *yhwh šāmmâ* ('Yahweh is there'; 48:35 my tr.).

With its pervasive use of purity terminology, Ezekiel is written to inculcate abhorrence of ritual and moral defilement and their sources. All impurity is anathema to God and should be to his people. Thus, Ezekiel cultivates desire for a future, conceptualized as both temple and holy city, where impurity will no longer separate people from God.

The Book of the Twelve

Although not arranged chronologically,[68] the Minor Prophets nevertheless evidence a broad temporal progression from pre-exilic monarchy through the Assyrian and Babylonian crises to post-exilic return to the land.[69] Additionally, when read as a unit as per Hebrew scribal tradition,[70] a broad thematic movement can be discerned: confronting sin; refusal to repent; announcing impending judgment by the nations; judgment of the

[67] The vision is not a blueprint for (re)construction. There are no commands to build the structure and no evidence to show that the post-exilic community attempted to do so (compare Hag. 2:3). Moreover, the temple design provides no vertical dimensions other than for the surrounding wall (40:5). The rhetorical intent of the text lies elsewhere (see Stevenson 1996; Kilchör 2020b).

[68] Joel, for instance, is often regarded as post-exilic and Obadiah belongs to the Babylonian crisis. For manuscript variance, see Fuhr and Yates 2016: 44 n. 7.

[69] Temporal movement is conveyed, in part, by the king lists in Hos. 1:1; Amos 1:1; Mic. 1:1; Zeph. 1:1; Hag. 1:1; Zech. 1:1.

[70] In rabbinic tradition, the Twelve (Minor Prophets) were grouped on one scroll. Recent work has identified numerous literary and rhetorical strategies that traverse the collection (e.g. Redditt 2001; Petterson 2010; Fuhr and Yates 2016: 27–58).

nations, which enables the deliverance of Israel/Judah; and restoration of the nations. Here, I consider how the themes of defilement and cleansing reinforce these larger literary aims.

Hosea opens with the prophet's marriage to a prostitute, a sign-act that graphically illustrates the dynamics of the Yahweh-Israel relationship: 'Go and marry a promiscuous wife and have children of promiscuity, for the land is committing blatant acts of promiscuity by abandoning the LORD' (1:2 HCSB). The ritual (cf. Lev. 15:18) and moral (cf. Lev. 18:24) impurity generated by sexual infidelity increases the effectiveness of adultery as metaphor for spiritual unfaithfulness. Because Israel incessantly chases her 'lovers' (2:7[5], 15[13]), Yahweh declares, 'she is not my wife, and I am not her husband' (2:4[2]). Even Israel's ephemeral desire to return to her 'first husband' (2:9[7] my tr.) would only further defile the land according to Deuteronomy 24:1–4 (cf. Jer. 3:1).[71] The deliberate placement of this poignant suite of images at the beginning of the collection (Amos is chronologically prior) capitalizes on the impact of primacy to affect readers' perceptions. The shocking portrait of Israel's heedless and painful unfaithfulness is designed to provoke disavowal of such behaviours and generate sympathy for Yahweh's indictments.

Divine judgment becomes inevitable as repentance, although invited, is repeatedly eschewed (e.g. Amos 4:1–13). 'The penitential agenda, articulated consistently in the first half of the collection (Hosea–Micah) ultimately fails as the focus shifts from penitence to discipline in Nahum to Habakkuk.'[72] Instead, the Prophets chart an unrestrained slide into sin and impurity. Widespread idolatry pollutes the nation: 'O Ephraim, you have played the whore (*znh* hiphil); Israel is defiled (*ṭmʾ* niphal)' (Hos. 5:3 ESV). The people 'have become detestable things' (*wayyihyû šiqquṣîm*) like the idols they love (Hos. 9:10 my tr.). Sexual immorality is rampant (Hos. 4:13–14;[73] 7:4) and profanes Yahweh's name (Amos 2:7); Nazarites are forced to drink wine, compromising their holy status (Amos 2:12; cf. Num. 6:2–4, 8); bloodshed and violence are endemic (Hos. 1:4; 4:2; 5:2; 6:8; 12:15[14]; Joel 4:21[3:21]; Mic. 3:10; 7:2; Nah. 3:1). Such acts, as

---

[71] Although the respective phrases are different – *ʾîšî hāri ʾšôn* (Hos. 2:9[7]) and *ba ʿlāh hāri ʾšôn* (Deut. 24:2) – 2:18–19[16–17] indicates why Hosea prefers *ʾîš* (Andersen and Freedman 1980: 239).

[72] Boda 2015: 106.

[73] Hosea 4:13–14 could describe actual or metaphorical 'adultery' (or both). See, further, Dearman 2010: 363–68.

expected, have a deleterious effect upon the land (Hos. 4:2–3) and sanctuary (Zeph. 3:1-4; Mal. 2:11).[74]

Incongruity is heightened by the theme of divine holiness. Yahweh is the 'holy one' (Hos. 11:9; Hab. 1:12; 3:3) whose 'holy name' is profaned by his people (Amos 2:7). Yahweh's holiness has implications for the place(s) he resides. He inhabits a 'holy temple' (Jon. 2:5[4], 8[7]; Mic. 1:2; Hab. 2:20; Zeph. 3:4[75]) – that is, Zion, his 'holy mountain' (Joel 2:1; 4:17[3:17]; Obad. 16–17; Zeph. 3:11; Zech. 8:3), his 'holy dwelling' (Zech. 2:17[13]). It is in the 'holy land' (Zech. 2:16[12]) that Yahweh abides in 'holy Jerusalem' (Joel 4:17[3:17]).

A holy God, inhabiting holy space, proves disastrous for defiled and defiling people, despite the sentiment expressed in Micah 3:11.[76] Instead of divine retreat in the face of impurity, Micah proclaims Yahweh's imminent appearance: 'Look! The LORD is coming from his dwelling place; he comes down and treads on the heights of the earth. The mountains melt beneath him' (Mic. 1:3–4; cf. Zech. 2:13). Predictably, judgment involves removal from the land. Hosea anticipates: 'They shall not remain in the land of the LORD, but Ephraim shall return to Egypt, and they shall eat unclean food in Assyria' (9:3 ESV).[77] Micah's opponents are told to depart from the land that is no longer their resting place because they defiled it (Mic. 2:10).[78] Similarly, Amaziah will die in an 'impure land' (*ʾădāmâ ṭĕmēʾâ*) when the nation is exiled (Amos 7:17).[79]

However, divine judgment also falls upon the nations that exile Israel and Judah.[80] Blood defilement provides a rationale. Nineveh is a city of blood which fills lands with corpses without number (Nah. 3:1–3). Babylon shed human blood and did violence upon the earth (Hab. 2:8, 17). Edom's deeds will return upon itself: 'Just as you drank on my holy

[74] As in Exodus and Jeremiah, de-creation motifs portray judgment (e.g. Hos. 4:3; Zeph. 1:2–6) and restoration is imagined as re-creation (e.g. Hos. 2:18).

[75] *Qōdeš* could refer to 'the sanctuary' (so HCSB, NIV, KJV, NASB; cf. Mal. 2:11) or, more generically, to 'that which is holy' (so ESV, JPS).

[76] Yahweh's dwelling with his people is a common motif in the Twelve (Hos. 11:9; Joel 2:27; Amos 5:17; Mic. 3:11; Zeph. 3:5, 15, 17).

[77] The recurrent motif of exile is explored by Petterson 2021.

[78] Allen 1976: 298.

[79] This is another indicator that lands beyond Canaan could become defiled.

[80] Because the world will be filled with Yahweh's glory (2:14) and the earth silent before him in his holy temple (2:20), Habakkuk announces woe upon Babylon for its immorality (2:15–16), violence (2:17), and idolatry (2:18–19). In Mic. 4:11 the nations proclaim their intention to defile Jerusalem.

hill, so all the nations will drink continually' (Obad. 16). The end of Joel is telling:

> Egypt will be desolate,
> Edom a desert waste,
> because of violence done to the people of Judah,
> in whose land they shed innocent blood.
> [...]
> Shall I leave their innocent blood unavenged?
> No, I will not.
> The LORD dwells in Zion!
> (Joel 3:19, 21)

Here, the logic of Numbers 35:33–34 is mapped onto national entities: innocent blood pollutes the land where Yahweh dwells and can only be atoned by shedding the blood of perpetrators.

Yet, judgment is not final. The Twelve anticipates the return of a cleansed and transformed remnant enabled to dwell with Yahweh. Zephaniah captures this dynamic by picturing the coming 'day of Yahweh' as the 'day of Yahweh's sacrifice', to which he invites his consecrated guests (1:7–8 my tr.). Old Jerusalem was rebellious and 'defiled' (*gʾl* niphal) and did 'not draw near to her God' (3:1–2 ESV).[81] But, beyond exile, Yahweh himself will act: 'I will purify the lips of the peoples, that all of them may call on the name of the LORD ... From beyond the rivers of Cush my worshippers, my scattered people, will bring me offerings' (3:9–10; cf. Isa. 6:5–7). Righteousness will allow access to Yahweh's 'holy hill' (3:11–13; Joel 3:16–17).

The post-exilic prophets (Haggai – Malachi) echo these themes, but also extend their scope. Return from exile does not end impurity. As corpse-impurity defiles by contact, '"So it is with this people and this nation in my sight," declares the LORD. "Whatever they do and whatever they offer there is defiled (*ṭāmēʾ*)"' (Hag. 2:13–14). Likewise, Malachi excoriates the priests for offering defiled food (*leḥem mĕgōʾāl*) on the altar, that is, blind, lame, or diseased animals (Mal. 1:6–8, 12–14; cf.

[81] Thus, Zeph. 3:2 reverses the sense of *qrb* ('to draw near') used throughout Leviticus to describe offerers approaching the tabernacle.

Lev. 22:19–22).[82] The abomination of idolatry also persists (Mal. 2:11). Nevertheless, potential for purification is reiterated – graphically illustrated by Joshua's instalment as high priest in Zechariah 3:1–10. Joshua's 'filthy clothes' are removed and replaced (3:3–4). Instead, he is given a 'pure turban' (*ṣānîp ṭāhôr*) to wear (3:5 my tr.). Thus arrayed, Joshua is granted right of access to Yahweh's precincts (3:7). The promise of 3:9, 'I will remove the iniquity of this land in a single day' (ESV), hints at a macrocosmic outworking. Zechariah imagines that future by utilizing water imagery. On that day, a spring will be opened to cleanse 'sin' (*ḥaṭṭā'ṯ*) and 'impurity' (*niddâ*) (13:1); idols will be no more (13:2); Yahweh will remove 'the spirit of impurity' (*rûaḥ haṭṭum'â*) from the land (13:2); and 'living waters' (*mayim-ḥayyîm*) will flow from Jerusalem, thereby facilitating widespread holiness (14:8, 20–21 my tr.).[83] In Malachi, the 'messenger of the covenant' prepares for Yahweh's arrival by 'purifying' (*ṭhr* piel) the Levites (3:1–3). Then, 'the offerings of Judah and Jerusalem will be acceptable to the LORD, as in days gone by, as in former years' (3:4). Amazingly, the transformation and purification required to present offerings is extended to the nations. Blood and abominations are removed (Zech. 9:7) and many peoples approach Jerusalem, Yahweh's 'holy mountain' (Zech. 8:3, 22; cf. 2:14–16[10–12]). Malachi's vision is global:

> from the rising of the sun to its setting my name will be great among the nations, and in every place incense will be offered to my name, and a pure offering (*ûminḥâ ṭĕhôrâ*). For my name will be great among the nations, says the LORD of hosts.
> (Mal. 1:11 ESV)

Excursus: defilement and cleansing of land

Purity dynamics in the Pentateuch and Prophets help to clarify the concept of land defilement.[84] Humans are consistently portrayed as

[82] This contributes to Malachi's wider rhetorical purpose to ironically reverse the priestly blessing of Num. 6:23–27 (see Schnittjer 2021: 463–66).

[83] 'Living waters' echoes ritual purification rites for major impurity in Lev. 14:5, 50; Num. 19:17. Yahweh as 'fountain of living waters' appears twice in Jeremiah (2:13; 17:13). For the appropriation of Zechariah's vision in the Gospels, see chapter 7.

[84] This excursus summarizes Harper 2025.

placed creatures; personhood and geography remain inextricably linked.[85] However, the relationship between humans and their environment is not always harmonious. The Prophets echo Leviticus and Numbers to reaffirm that egregious moral sins defile both perpetrators *and* land. This raises a crucial question: can human defilement of land be remedied? Is it possible to cleanse place? In the Old Testament, those questions primarily relate to Canaan. This territory is, at least in some traditions, sacrosanct – the place where Yahweh resides (e.g. Exod. 15:17; Num. 35:34).[86] Yet, as Gordon McConville recognizes, 'ability to turn the specific into paradigm is completely central to the Old Testament imagination.'[87] Israel's life in Canaan becomes a microcosm with wider ramifications.

Leviticus and Numbers itemize three categories of sin that generate geospatial impurity. Sexual immorality and idolatrous practices pollute: 'all these things were done by the people who lived in the land before you, and the land became defiled' (Lev. 18:27). Likewise, 'Bloodshed pollutes the land' (Num. 35:33). As noted earlier, these conceptions are reflected in other traditions. Deuteronomy 24:1–4 (and its echo in Jer. 3:1) connects sexual misconduct to land pollution. Deuteronomy 21:22–23 extends the defiling potential of bloodshed to sanctioned killing. Hence, even though David conducted war at Yahweh's behest (e.g. 1 Chr. 14:8–10), bloodshed (and its implied defilement) meant David was permanently prevented from constructing a sacred dwelling for Yahweh (1 Chr. 22:8). The polluting force of idolatry reaches its zenith in the Prophets.[88] In Jeremiah 3, Yahweh inveighs, 'You have polluted (*ḥnp*) the land with your vile whoredom. … Because [Israel] took her whoredom lightly, she polluted (*ḥnp*) the land, committing adultery with stone and tree' (3:2, 9 ESV). Ezekiel 36:17–18, likewise, connects idolatry to land pollution. This discrete set of moral transgressions defiles place. The resulting impurity is extensive; consistently, it is 'the land' that is defiled, not a localized portion or region. Moreover, defilement is indefinite. Even though defiled land does not convey secondary pollution to people or objects, the lack of purification rites is problematic. As Leviticus and Numbers clarify, Yahweh's

[85] On human situatedness, see Relph 1976; Bartholomew 2011.

[86] Differing Old Testament land ideologies are explored by Brueggemann 1977; Habel 1995; Frankel 2011.

[87] McConville 2016: 85.

[88] Milgrom 2000b: 1575 argues that connecting idolatry to land defilement was an innovation of the seventh-century prophets.

dwelling must be separated from impurity. He will not tolerate a defiled abode. Accordingly, there are hints that Yahweh will purify polluted land. Although cleansing land is not formally part of the cultic system, ritual purification provides heuristic categories to conceptualize God's actions.

First, washing commonly ameliorates impurity (e.g. Lev. 15:12, 18). Interesting in this respect are several interpretive traditions that understand the flood as an act of purification. For instance, in 1 Enoch the deluge functioned to 'cleanse the earth from all injustice, and from all defilement,' so that, 'the earth shall be cleansed from all pollution, and from all sin' (10:20, 22; see, similarly, 4Q422; 1 Pet. 3:20–21; *Mos.* 2.64).[89] Sin and impurity remain distinct categories; the flood addresses both. Thus, 'the flood not only stymied endemic antediluvian violence (Gen 6:11, 13) but also cleansed the earth from defilement due to bloodshed and sexual immorality (compare with Gen 6:1–4).'[90] Purification, however, is catastrophic for humans.

Second, sources of impurity can be removed (e.g. Lev. 13:45–46; Num. 5:1–3). This motif is vividly employed in Leviticus 18 as Yahweh declares the land will vomit out sources of defilement. In context, this indicates expulsion of the land's inhabitants – Canaanite or Israelite – who defile habitat through immorality and idolatry (18:24–25). Threatened ejection intersects neatly with the wider theme of exile.

Third, waiting addresses some forms of impurity (e.g. Lev. 15:16; Num. 19:11). By analogy, removing the source of land defilement (i.e. morally corrupt inhabitants) through the mechanism of exile (vomiting out) enables temporal remediation of impurity. The idea is present in 2 Chronicles 36. As soon as seventy years of exile are complete, Yahweh causes Cyrus to order the rebuilding of the formerly defiled Jerusalem temple (2 Chron. 36:22–23; cf. Ezek. 9:7–10; Dan. 9:1–2). Canaan, now cleansed, is once more fit for the divine abode.

Fourth, and perhaps most arresting, sacrifice removes land impurity. Blood sacrifice commonly mitigates major defilement (e.g. Lev. 12:6–7; 14:9; 15:13–15; Num. 19:2–9). Against that backdrop, Numbers 35:33 is striking: 'land upon which blood has been poured out cannot be atoned except by the blood of the one who poured it out' (my tr.). If blood atonement is avoided, then the land where Yahweh dwells would remain defiled

[89] Text cited from Charlesworth 1983–1985.

[90] Harper 2025: 233–34.

(Num. 35:34). This explains the non-negotiability of capital punishment in murder cases (Num. 35:16–21, 30–31; cf. 2 Sam. 4:11). Land defiled by bloodshed must be purified, but purification comes at the cost of the defiler's life (cf. Deut. 32:43).

What emerges from these observations is that Yahweh acts not so much to cleanse impure land, but to extinguish the source of its ongoing defilement.[91] However, because people are the sole source of land defilement, amelioration entails significant human cost: banishment or death. As I surmise elsewhere,

> A tension thereby arises: YHWH, it seems, can have either a land to dwell in or a people to dwell with, but not both. Interestingly, in this apparently zero-sum game, it is the land that is consistently privileged. Canaan is YHWH's abode; its purity will be preserved. Therefore, the violent, the immoral, and the idolatrous must be executed, vomited out, or scattered among the nations. There is hope for the land. But what hope remains for people?[92]

The Prophets answer that question by anticipating a future work of God in which he radically transforms people. Ezekiel's stunning vision is worth repeating:

> I will sprinkle clean water on you, and you shall be clean from all your uncleannesses, and from all your idols I will cleanse you. And I will give you a new heart, and a new spirit I will put within you. And I will remove the heart of stone from your flesh and give you a heart of flesh. And I will put my Spirit within you, and cause you to walk in my statutes and be careful to obey my rules. You shall dwell in the land that I gave to your fathers, and you shall be my people, and I will be your God. And I will deliver you from all your uncleannesses.
> (36:25–29 ESV)

---

[91] Cf. my discussion of Samson in chapter 3. Samson's death (and that of the Philistines), at minimum, removes a source of defilement from the land. But it may also function as blood poured out to atone for land defiled by bloodshed (cf. Num 35:33), even though Judges does not explicitly say so. If this is the way to understand Samson's death, then it adds another dimension to Yahweh's promise to deliver Israel through him (Judg. 13:5).

[92] Harper 2025: 237.

People-cleansing leads to a transformed relationship with place (cf. Ezek. 36:35; Jub. 50:5). In the Old Testament, therefore, '[t]here is hope for the world but ultimately that hope lies not in remedying what people have done, but in remedying people.'[93]

Conclusion

Despite diversity in content, style and provenance, defilement and cleansing are important themes in the Prophets. These books do not attempt to establish or explain a purity system, but rather to capitalize on a pre-existing matrix of beliefs and practices for rhetorical ends.[94] Ritual purity remains a constant concern. It is prerequisite for sacrifice and entry to sacred locales. Sex, corpses, certain foods, and menstruation are assumed to be defiling.[95] Nevertheless, ritual impurity is not irredeemably problematic; cultic measures provide sufficient cleansing. Instead, the Prophets display far greater concern with moral impurity. This makes sense. Exile, whether imminent, current or recently experienced, is a ubiquitous motif. National banishment is repeatedly tied to transgressions that generate an unwashable moral impurity that pollutes people, temple and land. In the absence of possible purification, attention shifts from human agency towards a deeper, inner work of transformation and cleansing that Yahweh will enact through the outpouring of his Spirit – upon both Israel/Judah *and* the nations. This becomes a central tenet of prophetic, and biblical, hope: when sin and impurity are vanquished, people will be able to dwell permanently with God in his holy place. Anticipation of this coming reality directly shapes Second Temple and New Testament expectations. Before engaging those texts, however, the third section of the Hebrew canon, the Writings, has its own unique contribution to make.

[93] Harper 2025: 239.

[94] Ezekiel 40 – 48 is, perhaps, the exception.

[95] *Ṣāraʿat* does not feature in the Prophets.

5

Defilement and cleansing in the Writings

The third major division of the Hebrew canon is the Writings.[1] This is an eclectic corpus, which displays considerable generic and historic diversity. Even though containing older material, these books are substantially products of the post-exilic era. Many were composed in this period (e.g. Ezra-Nehemiah, Chronicles, Daniel); others were edited into their current form (e.g. the Psalter, Proverbs). Therefore, although precise dating remains contentious, the Writings contains the latest Old Testament texts. For this reason, charting the development of defilement and cleansing ideas in these books is crucial ahead of investigating Second Temple and New Testament literature. In the Writings, purity themes from the Pentateuch and Prophets are reiterated. Moreover, concerns about ritual and moral purity not only continue into the post-exilic era, in some cases, they actively increase. In Ezra-Nehemiah and Chronicles, for instance, clarifying the purity implications of being God's holy people becomes a defining social question. Here we also begin to see divergence from Leviticus and Numbers as latent ideas are extrapolated for new contexts.

Psalms

Psalms 1 and 2 are programmatic for reading the Psalter.[2] Psalm 1 establishes a binary between the righteous, imaged as a tree (trans)planted by streams of water, and the wicked who are like wind-dispersed chaff. The

[1] In this chapter I proceed according to Hebrew canonical order while also grouping some books together for ease of discussion (i.e. the wisdom literature and *Megilloth*).

[2] The point is widely noted (e.g. Cole 2013).

righteous are blessed as they 'murmur' (*hgh*) Yahweh's Torah (1:2 my tr.), in contrast to those who 'murmur' (*hgh*) against Yahweh and his anointed one (2:1–2 my tr.). This anointed son, to whom Yahweh has become father (2:7), is central to Psalm 2. But so too is the place from which he reigns: 'I have installed my king on Zion, my holy mountain' (2:6). Psalms 1 and 2 thus create a web of interconnected themes that becomes foundational for reading the Psalter: Zion is the cosmic mountain,[3] the sacred locale where Yahweh reigns with and through his appointed king, and where the righteous gather and experience blessing.[4]

Righteousness is required to approach Yahweh's sacred dwelling. The question posed in Psalm 15:1, 'Who may dwell on your holy mountain?' (my tr.), is given a qualified answer: only the one who walks blamelessly and does what is right (15:2). Such a person, like the tree of Psalm 1, 'shall never be moved' (15:5 ESV). While right action incorporates ritual fidelity, the behaviours and attitudes listed in 15:2–5a emphasize the moral conduct befitting those who desire access to God's presence. Psalm 24 reiterates:

> Who shall ascend the hill of the LORD?
> And who shall stand in his holy place?
> He who has clean (*nāqî*) hands and a pure (*bar*) heart,
> who does not lift up his soul to what is false
> and does not swear deceitfully.
> (24:3–4 ESV)

'Clean' or 'innocent' hands are hands not covered in blood (cf. Exod. 21:28; Josh. 2:17–20).[5] A 'pure heart' signals inner integrity. Therefore, both outward action and internal disposition – towards people and God – must display righteousness.[6] Psalms 15 and 24 insist moral purity is

---

[3] Cosmic mountain ideology is prevalent in ANE and Old Testament texts (see Lundquist 1984; 1994; Levenson 1985; Morales 2012; 2014).

[4] This theological collocation becomes the basis for pilgrimage to Jerusalem in the Psalms of Ascent (Pss. 120 – 134).

[5] Goldingay 2006: 359.

[6] Similarly, in Psalms 94:21 and 18:21[20], 25[24], *nāqî* and *bar* parallel *ṣaddîq* and *ṣedeq* ('righteous') respectively. Congruence between God and worshipper is captured in 18:27[26]: 'to the pure (*brr* niphal) you show yourself pure (*brr* hithpael)'. Moreover, because Yahweh's commands are 'pure' (*bar* 19:9[8]; cf. 12:7[6]), a person may keep their way pure (*zkh* piel) by heeding them (119:9; cf. 19:10[9]).

essential for accessing Yahweh's holy hill. Ethical conduct has spatial consequences (cf. Lev. 18:24–30).[7] A similar dynamic is evident in Psalm 73 as the psalmist, dismayed by the prosperous wicked (73:3–12), declares, 'Surely in vain I have kept my heart pure and have washed my hands in innocence' (73:13). Nevertheless, a pure heart allows the psalmist access to the sanctuary, which prompts needed perspective regarding the destiny of the ungodly (73:17). The psalm's conclusion is dominated by a sense of the psalmist's nearness to God (73:23–28), unlike the wicked who perish far from him (73:27). Thus, the psalm's opening statement is confirmed: Yahweh is indeed good 'to those pure in heart' (*lĕbārê lēbāb*, 73:1 my tr.).

The implications of conduct for proximity to sacred space influence the Psalter's rationale for exile. Psalm 37:29 proves ominous: 'The righteous will inherit the land and dwell in it forever'; the wicked, however, will be 'cut off' (*krt* 37:9, 22, 28, 34, 38; cf. 101:6–8).[8] Psalm 106 inhabits that potential as the psalmist speaks from exile to recall Israel's long rebellion (106:47). He remembers how even in the beginning the people 'joined themselves to Baal Peor and ate sacrifices of the dead' (106:28 my tr.; cf. Num. 25). Protracted idolatry had cumulative results:

> They served their idols,
>   which became a snare to them.
> They sacrificed their sons
>   and their daughters to the demons;
> they poured out innocent blood,
>   the blood of their sons and daughters,
> whom they sacrificed to the idols of Canaan,
>   and the land was polluted (*ḥnp* qal) with blood.
> Thus they became unclean (*ṭmʾ* qal) by their acts,
>   and played the whore (*znh* qal) in their deeds.
> (106:36–39 ESV)

Idolatry and associated bloodshed, conceptualized as fornication, pollute the land. Yahweh therefore gave the people into the hands of the nations (106:41).

---

[7] Cf. Ps. 26:6.

[8] That cutting off is synonymous with removal is indicated by the parallelism in 37:9, 22.

However, the burning and profaning of Yahweh's dwelling (74:7) opens new possibilities for the future. Psalm 79 appeals directly to defilement of temple and city to provoke Yahweh's intervention:

O God, the nations have come into your inheritance;
  they have defiled (*ṭm'* piel) your holy temple;
  they have laid Jerusalem in ruins.
They have given the bodies of your servants
  to the birds of the heavens for food,
  the flesh of your faithful to the beasts of the earth.
They have poured out their blood like water
  all around Jerusalem,
  and there was no one to bury them.
(79:1–3 ESV)

Although Israel's misdeeds inevitably pollute land and sanctuary, the psalmist recognizes the inappropriateness of defilement becoming permanent. He therefore petitions Yahweh to atone (*kpr*) the sins of the people (79:9) and to avenge the 'poured out blood of your servants' (79:10 my tr.).

That Yahweh might overcome egregious sin and its resulting impurity is intrinsic to Psalm 51. The superscription invites readers to hear the poem as David's supplication following his wrongdoing against Bathsheba and Uriah. Hence, adultery/rape and murder are foregrounded (cf. 51:16[14]; 2 Sam. 11 – 12).[9] The defiling nature of these acts, coupled with human inability to remove pollution, is recognized in the poem's petitions:

Wash (*kbs* piel) me thoroughly from my iniquity,
  and cleanse (*ṭhr* piel) me from my sin!
[…]
Purge (*ḥṭ'* piel) me with hyssop, and I shall be clean (*ṭhr* qal);
  wash (*kbs* piel) me, and I shall be whiter than snow.
  […]
Hide your face from my sins,
  and blot out all my iniquities.

[9] See chapter 3.

Create in me a clean (*ṭāhôr*) heart, O God,
 and renew a right spirit within me.
(51:4[2], 9[7], 11–12[9–10] ESV)

The implications of moral failure for dwelling with God are also understood:

Cast me not away from your presence,
 and take not your Holy Spirit from me.
(Ps. 51:13[11] ESV)

The psalmist's insistence that Yahweh does not desire sacrifice is unsurprising (51:18[16]). Deliberate rebellion rendered sacrificial devotion (temporarily) inappropriate (see 51:21[19]). Moreover, the cult had no sacrificial means to effect either forgiveness or purification for high-handed sins such as adultery and bloodshed.[10] The only recourse, as modelled by the psalm, is appeal to divine mercy (51:3[1]).[11] Nevertheless, the language of the plea is unusual; the motif of washing away sin, as opposed to impurity, is uncommon in the Old Testament.[12] However, rather than disregarding purity categories, Psalm 51 instead appropriates ritual concepts to express hope that Yahweh might be able to eliminate the stain of sin and its defilement as easily as ritual impurity is removed.[13] The psalmist expects God can do what humans cannot.

Proverbs and Job

In Proverbs, purity is exclusively a moral, rather than ritual, concern and is ultimately tied to the virtue of possessing wisdom (itself an ethical category).[14] Defilement and cleansing accentuate the contrast between the righteous and wicked intrinsic to wisdom texts.[15]

[10] The Day of Atonement mitigated the impact of such deeds upon the sanctuary and community, not the perpetrator(s).

[11] Moses' repeated intercessions regarding Israel's rebellion likewise make no appeal to sacrifice (e.g. Exod. 32:11–14; Num. 14:11–20).

[12] Only, elsewhere, Isa. 1, 4; Jer. 2, 4 (DiFransico 2016: 24).

[13] Klawans 2000: 36. Verses 20–21[18–19] shift the focus from individual to nation.

[14] The *ṭm'* root ('to be impure') does not appear in Proverbs. Perhaps the universal purview of wisdom literature partly explains the focus, although Gentiles are also susceptible to ritual impurity (see chapters 2 and 6).

[15] The focus on moral purity explains the paucity of purification language in Proverbs, which

Proverbs labels a range of evils 'abominations' (*tôʿēbōt*): dishonest scales (11:1; 20:10, 23), lying lips (12:22), wicked deeds (16:12), acquitting the guilty (17:15) and condemning the righteous (17:15). Indeed, there 'are six things that the LORD hates, seven that are an abomination to him': haughty eyes, a lying tongue, hands that shed blood, a heart that plans wickedness, feet that run into evil, a false witness breathing lies, and one who sows discord (6:16–19 ESV).[16] Naming body parts that participate in evil (eyes, tongue, hands, heart, feet) collapses the distance between action and actor (cf. 26:25). Therefore, the perverse person is also 'an abomination to Yahweh' (3:32 my tr.; cf. 11:20; 15:9, 26; 16:5; 24:9). While individuals may consider themselves 'pure' (*zak*), ultimately it is Yahweh who evaluates motives (16:2). Even a whole generation may be 'pure' (*ṭāhôr*) in its own eyes and yet remain unwashed from its 'filth' (*ṣōʾâ*) (30:12 my tr.; cf. Isa. 4:4). Thus, as in the Prophets and Psalms, the unpalatability of the morally filthy has cultic implications:

> The sacrifice of the wicked is an abomination to the LORD.
> (15:8 ESV; also 21:27; cf. Sir. 34:21–23)

> If one turns away his ear from hearing the law,
> even his prayer is an abomination.
> (28:9 ESV)[17]

Evil deeds also have consequences for longevity in the land. Whereas the righteous will never be removed, the wicked will not dwell there, but will be cut off and rooted out (2:21–22; 10:30–31). Hence, although not explicitly utilizing the language of pollution, the logic is compatible with the wider Old Testament understanding that (at least some) evil deeds generate a moral defilement that negatively impacts geographical locale.[18]

---

references cleansing only twice. Prov. 20:9 asks (with implied negative answer): 'Who can say, "I have kept my heart pure (*zkh* piel); I am cleansed (*ṭhr* qal) from my sin"?' (HCSB). Prov. 20:30 adapts ritual terminology for blows that 'scour away' (*mrq*) evil (cf. Lev. 6:21[28]; elsewhere, *mrq* means 'to polish' [Jer. 46:4; 2 Chr. 4:16]).

[16] Thus, contra Klawans 2000: 90, Proverbs broadens the scope of moral defilement. For Klawans, only sexual immorality, idolatry, and bloodshed morally defile in the Old Testament; expansion is credited to the Qumran community. However, Prov. 6:16–19 indicates expansion was already underway before then (Klawans' engagement with wisdom literature is slight).

[17] Job's insistence that his prayer is 'pure' (*zak*, 16:17) bolsters his claim to righteousness.

[18] See the excursus in chapter 4.

On the other hand, righteousness and moral purity are synonymous. 'The conduct of the pure (*zak*) is upright' (21:8 ESV). 'Even a young man is known by his actions – if his behaviour is pure (*zak*) and upright' (20:11 HCSB). Likewise, pleasant words are 'pure' (*ṭāhôr*, 15:26), and the king will be a friend to the one who loves a 'pure heart' (*ṭĕhôr-lēb*, 22:11 *qere*). Accordingly, the righteous shun abomination (8:7) and so stand diametrically opposed to the wicked:

> An unjust man is an abomination to the righteous,
> but one whose way is straight is an abomination to the wicked.
> (29:27 ESV; cf. Wis. 2:16)

Purity terms awaken feelings of desire and disgust, which serve to promote moral virtue:

> Those of crooked heart are an abomination to the LORD,
> but those of blameless ways are his delight.
> (11:20 ESV)

Ultimately, purity and impurity become, respectively, expressions of wisdom and foolishness. The fool regards turning from evil an abomination (13:19). This undivided focus on moral purity in Proverbs does not negate ritual concerns.[19] Rather, the singular emphasis serves the purpose of the book: to school readers in wisdom (1:1–7). Wisdom, in the purview of Proverbs, is the summary descriptor of all who live morally upright lives in fear of Yahweh.

The book of Job, likewise, primarily utilizes purity terminology to designate moral actions.[20] Each of Job's interlocutors appeals to purity in their opening speech. Eliphaz asks, 'Can a person be more righteous than God, or a man more pure than his Maker?' (4:17 HCSB). The parallel lines equate 'being pure' (*ṭhr* qal) with 'being righteous' (*ṣdq* qal) and support Eliphaz's attempt to prompt Job to confess hidden sin. Bildad, similarly, opines, 'if you are pure (*zak*) and upright, even now he will rouse himself

[19] The portrayal of Woman Folly in Prov. 1 – 9 frequently incorporates death and Sheol, which (implicitly) raise notions of ritual impurity and compound the need to avoid her abode (e.g. 2:18; 5:5; 7:27; 9:18; cf. 8:36).

[20] Physical purity also appears: 'pure gold' (*ketem ṭāhôr* 28:19) and a sky 'cleansed' (*ṭhr* piel) by the wind (37:21).

on your behalf and restore you to your prosperous state' (8:6). Zophar raises the stakes as he expresses frustration at Job's refusal to recant: 'For you say, "My doctrine is pure (*zak*), and I am clean (*bar*) in God's eyes"' (11:4 ESV).[21] Zophar's own verdict asserts the opposite: 'God has even forgotten some of your sin' (11:6). Elihu echoes Zophar in his attempt to expose Job's perceived overreach:

> But you have said in my hearing –
> I heard the very words –
> 'I am pure (*zak*), I have done no wrong;
> I am clean (*ḥap*[22]) and free from sin.
> Yet God has found fault with me'
> [...]
> But I tell you, in this you are not right.
> (33:8–10, 12)

However, Job's claims to be blameless (e.g. 9:21) are not protestations of sinlessness. In 14:4, contemplating human transience and weakness, he asserts, 'Who can bring what is pure (*ṭāhôr*) from the impure (*ṭāmēʾ*)? No one!' Accordingly, Job desires that God would not keep track of his sin, but instead cover it (14:16–17), including the sins of his youth (13:26). Rather, Job's distress derives from incommensurate suffering (13:21–23). God's agency in piercing Job's kidneys and spilling his gall upon the ground (16:13) is deemed unjust because he is innocent of violence (16:17). Hence, Job exclaims, 'Earth, do not cover my blood; may my cry never be laid to rest' (16:18; cf. Gen. 4:10). Similarly, Job's final speech surveys serious moral infractions he is *not* guilty of – including sexual immorality (31:1–4, 9–12), idolatry (31:24–28) and violence (31:29–30) that would have made his land cry out against him (31:38).[23]

Nevertheless, operating with the same understanding of proportional punishment, Job's interlocutors become increasingly convinced that

---

[21] Zophar proceeds to insist that if Job turns from sin he will be 'without blemish' (11:15). While *mûm* ('blemish') primarily occurs in relation to cultic unsuitability (Lev. 21:17, 18, 21, 23; 22:20, 21, 25; Num. 19:2; Deut. 15:21; 17:21), in Deut. 32:5 the term has a moral sense: 'they are blemished; they are a crooked and twisted generation' (ESV).

[22] *ḥap* is a hapax, which *HALOT* 1:339 glosses as '(morally) clean'.

[23] If land crying out is understood to result from sexual immorality, idolatry, or violence, then the other transgressions listed (falsehood, injustice, inhospitality) are likewise deemed to negatively impact place.

suffering is caused by intransigence and unrepentance. Their rhetoric stiffens. Eliphaz asks, incredulously, 'What are mortals, that they could be pure (*zkh* qal), or those born of woman, that they could be righteous?' (15:14). If even the heavens are not pure (*zkk* qal) in God's eyes, how much less a man like Job who drinks unrighteousness like water (15:15–16). That Job's hands are clean (*bōr*) remains only a hypothetical potential on the other side of repentance (22:30). Bildad's final riposte echoes Eliphaz:

> How then can a mortal be righteous before God?
>   How can one born of woman be pure (*zkh* qal)?
> If even the moon is not bright
>   and the stars are not pure (*zkk* qal) in his eyes,
> how much less a mortal, who is but a maggot –
>   a human being, who is only a worm!
> (25:4–6)[24]

Megilloth: The five Scrolls

The five books known as the Scrolls (Hebr. *Megilloth*) have long been used as lectionary readings for the major Jewish festivals: Song of Songs (Passover), Ruth (Feast of Weeks), Lamentations (Ninth of Ab), Ecclesiastes (Tabernacles) and Esther (Purim).[25] However, the grouping is functional and does not indicate these books ought to be considered a collection, let alone a redacted composition (contrast the Book of the Twelve). The Scrolls are not always contiguous in the various manuscript traditions, nor in the same order.[26] My analysis, therefore, does not assume any close connection between the texts.

Although not prominent, purity motifs are present.[27] Contemplating

---

[24] Whether intentional or not, the metaphorical equation of Job with *impure* swarming creatures (maggots, worms) adds to Bildad's contention that Job cannot be pure (cf. Lev. 11; Deut. 14).

[25] For an introductory survey, see Webb 2000.

[26] Compare LXX (contiguous: Song, Ruth, Lam., Eccl., Est.) with Codex Vaticanus (non-contiguous: Ruth, Eccl., Song, Est., Lam.).

[27] The books of Ruth and Esther do not utilize purity lexemes, although there is an interesting verbal correspondence between Ruth 'washing' (*rḥṣ*), 'anointing' (*swk*), and donning a 'cloak' (*śimlâ*) in preparation to visit Boaz (3:3), and David 'washing' (*rḥṣ*), 'anointing' (*swk*), and changing his 'cloak' (*śimlâ*) to enter the house of Yahweh (2 Sam. 12:20).

the inevitability of death, Ecclesiastes 9:2 asserts, 'All share a common destiny – the righteous and the wicked, the good and the bad, the pure (*ṭāhôr*) and the impure (*ṭāmēʾ*), those who offer sacrifices and those who do not' (NIV adapted). Although offering sacrifice requires ritual purity, the preceding pairs (righteous-wicked, good-bad) suggest reading 'morally pure' and 'morally impure'. Either way, the resulting binary view of the world is typical of wisdom literature: righteous, good, pure, and sacrifice-making belong together conceptually and are set against those who are wicked, bad, impure and non-sacrifice-making.[28] Purity also describes physical attributes. In Song 6:9, the beloved is 'pure [*bārâ*] to her who bore her' (ESV).[29] The term could imply integrity of character along with *tammātî* ('my perfect one') in the previous clause (cf. 'pure [*bar*] in heart', Pss. 24:4; 73:1). However, the use of *bārâ* again in 6:10 ('pure as the sun', my tr.) suggests that incomparable form is meant.[30] This better fits the context of the poem and its extolling of bodily attributes. Similarly, Lamentations 4:7–8 recalls that while '[Zion's] princes were purer (*zkk*) than snow … [and] the beauty of their form was like sapphire' (ESV), their skin is now shrivelled and black. Employing purity terms to mark physical quality is consistent with wider usage (e.g. 'pure gold', Exod. 25:11).

The most sustained use of purity themes occurs in Lamentations. The book personifies Jerusalem as a widow bereft of her children and exploits this motif to explore the affective impact of divine judgment. The opening acrostic begins,

> How deserted lies the city,
>   once so full of people!
> How like a widow is she,
>   who once was great among the nations!
> […]
> Bitterly she weeps at night,
>   tears are on her cheeks.

[28] That the 'good' and 'pure' make offerings corrects reductionistic understandings of sacrifice as mere problem fixing with respect to either sin or impurity.

[29] LXX, Syr., and Vg. translate *bārâ* as 'chosen' or 'select' (cf. NIV 'favourite'; Hess 2005: 194 'special').

[30] Hence, Provan 2001: 339 n. 14 renders *bārâ* in 6:9 as 'a shining light' (based on 6:10 and parallels with Ps. 19).

Among all her lovers
  there is no one to comfort her.
(Lam. 1:1–2)

In similar manner to Jeremiah, with which Lamentations is traditionally linked, allegiance to idols and associated nations is portrayed in sexualized terms ('lovers') as infidelity against Yahweh (cf. 1:19). Such sin defiles: 'Jerusalem sinned greatly; thus, she became an impure thing (*nîdâ*)' (Lam. 1:8 my tr.).[31] 'Her impurity was in her skirts' (*ṭum᾿ātāh bĕšûlêhā*, 1:9 my tr.).[32] With nakedness exposed (1:8), she saw nations enter her sanctuary (1:10; cf. Ps. 74:4–8).[33] The poem concludes, 'Jerusalem has become something impure [*niddâ*]' (Lam. 1:17 HCSB).

Pollution instigates divine action. The intentional defilement evident in the Prophets is close to the surface in the lament of 2:20–21:

Look, O LORD, and see!
  With whom have you dealt thus?
Should women eat the fruit of their womb,
  the children of their tender care?
Should priest and prophet be killed
  in the sanctuary of the Lord?
In the dust of the streets
  lie the young and the old;
my young women and my young men
  have fallen by the sword;
you have killed them in the day of your anger,
  slaughtering without pity.
(ESV)

For this reason, 2:4 bemoans the death of all 'in the Daughter of Zion's tent' (my tr.). This unusual use of 'tent' to denote the city perhaps evokes

[31] The hapax *nîdâ* is usually translated as 'unclean thing' (with Syr.; e.g. NASB) or 'object of head-shaking' (e.g. Hillers 1992: 70). Even if the second option is preferable, there may be an intended pun with *niddâ* (Hillers 1992: 85).

[32] The reference could either be to menstrual blood (Longman 2008: 347) or to blood stemming from sexual violence (Dobbs-Allsopp 2002: 63–65).

[33] Temple desecration (entering) likely has sexual overtones in context.

the ritual impurity generated by corpses lying within a 'tent' (Num. 19:14). Filled with the slain, morally impure Jerusalem becomes ritually defiled.

Lamentations 4:11–16 combines ritual and moral impurity to justify the severity of Jerusalem's censure. Yahweh gave full vent to his wrath (4:11) because prophets and priests shed 'the blood of the righteous (*dam ṣaddîqîm*)' within the city (4:13).[34] In fact, they became so 'defiled with blood (*nĕgō'ălû baddām*)' no one would touch their clothing (4:14).[35] Instead, echoing Leviticus 13:45, the people cried, 'Turn away! Impure!' (4:15 my tr.). The sequence is unusual in that moral impurity (shedding innocent blood) invokes ritual consequences (untouchable clothing and social exclusion). Yet, the conflation is rhetorically powerful. Just as one would instinctively cry, 'Turn away! Impure!', if approached by a *ṣāra'at*-infected person, moral impurity should likewise provoke intense aversion. Jerusalem's destruction and the banishment of its populace is not only warranted, it is desirable. Lamentations 4:16 simply states, 'Yahweh's presence [lit. 'face'] scattered them' (my tr.).

Daniel

The book of Daniel is set within the Babylonian exile.[36] It is somewhat surprising that a portrait of exilic experience has so little to say about matters of ritual and moral purity, especially when migrant experience often heightens socioreligious concerns (contrast Ezekiel). Instead, the idiolect of Daniel centres on sin, transgression, rebellion and disobedience, even when considering reasons for exile (esp. 9:1–19).[37]

Nevertheless, the narrator's comment in 1:8 regarding impurity avoidance is well known: 'Daniel resolved not to defile himself (*g'l* hithpael) with the royal food and wine, and he asked the chief official for permission not to defile himself (*g'l* hithpael) in this way.' Daniel's refusal is often interpreted against Leviticus 11 (par. Deut. 14:1–21) to emphasize Torah observance at great personal risk. However, that conclusion is premature.

[34] This may be literal bloodshed or failure to correct the nation, which led to Babylonian invasion (Longman 2008: 384).

[35] The causal connection between shedding righteous blood and the destruction of Jerusalem is appropriated in Matthew to articulate the consequences of shedding Jesus' blood (see chapter 7).

[36] Narrative setting and date of composition are not the same thing. Lucas 2002: 306–16 provides a useful summary of the key issues.

[37] Regarding the borrowing of Pentateuchal formulations in Daniel's prayer, see Harper 2015.

First, Daniel's resolution includes 'wine', which neither Leviticus 11 nor Deuteronomy 14 forbids. Second, the noun *mišteh* in the phrase *ûbyên mištāyw* ('or with the wine that he drank' ESV) usually denotes a banquet or feast (e.g. Gen. 19:3; Judg. 14:12; Esth. 5:4–6; 7:2). Daniel avoids not drinking wine per se, but *celebratory* drinking. Third, Daniel's resolution is time limited. Daniel 10:3 indicates that Daniel regularly partook of 'choice food', 'meat' and 'wine' in the context of the Babylonian court except, as per 10:2–3, during specific times of mourning. This normal mode of conduct must shape interpretation of abstinence in 1:8. Fourth, 1:8 employs *gʾl* rather than the *ṭmʾ* root used in Leviticus 11. Although the terminological shift is typical of post-exilic literature, Daniel displays close lexical and thematic correspondence with Leviticus elsewhere.[38] Considering these features, kosher concerns do not seem primary. Rather, in a context of recent military defeat (1:1–2a), transfer of temple treasures to Babylonian shrines (1:2b) and theophoric renaming of captives to honour pagan deities (1:7), Daniel refuses to partake in the accompanying feasting with its honorific associations vis-à-vis the Babylonian pantheon (1:8). Food becomes a means of resisting a totalitarian regime.[39] Daniel's concern lies more with avoiding the moral impurity connected to idol worship than the ritual impurity of forbidden food.[40]

Irrespective of the precise source of defilement in 1:8, resistance functions narratively to separate Daniel and his companions from the remainder of Nebuchadnezzar's captives who assimilated wholesale (1:6 'among those').[41] This theme of purity as social boundary becomes especially prominent in the post-exilic books. It resurfaces in Daniel's final chapters. Chapter 11 sketches key events between the seer's present (the first year of Darius, 11:1) and the time of the end. The final king of the North (i.e. Antiochus IV) would set himself against the holy covenant (11:28, 30). His forces would desecrate (*ḥll* piel) the temple and abolish

[38] See Harper 2015. Elsewhere, *gʾl* can denote ritual (e.g. Mal. 1:7, 12), moral (e.g. Lam. 4:14), or genealogical impurity (e.g. Ezra 2:62; Neh. 7:64). LXX translates *gʾl* in 1:8 with *alisgeō* ('to pollute'), a root that occurs once in the New Testament: 'abstain from food polluted by idols' (Acts 15:20).

[39] Resistance is conveyed through root play involving *śym* ('to set, place'). Nebuchadnezzar's chief official 'placed' names on the young men and 'placed' Belteshazzar upon Daniel (1:7), so Daniel, in response, 'placed' it upon his heart not to defile himself with the king's food and drink (1:8). For analysis of 'soft' resistance, see Dreher 2020.

[40] Although assuming a different basis (loyalty to a foreign king), Baldwin 1978: 83 concurs that moral rather than ritual concerns dominate. My suggestion also differs from those who argue the problem is food sacrificed to idols. For evaluation of the options, see Goldingay 1989: 18–19.

[41] Towner 1984: 26.

daily sacrifice (11:31; cf. 1 Macc. 1:41–64). Moreover, they would set up the *haššiqqûṣ měšômēm*, 'the detestable thing which makes desolate' (11:31 my tr.; cf. 9:27;[42] 12:11). The referent of this enigmatic phrase is debated; suggestions range from a sacrificed pig to Jesus' crucifixion. However, considering the widespread use of *šiqqûṣ* ('detestable thing') as a circumlocution for idols throughout the Old Testament,[43] 11:31 most probably pictures the instalment of an idol within the temple as part of the intentional desecration of Jerusalem's most holy site.[44] This climactic act of defilement epitomizes the godlessness of Israel's oppressor. Nevertheless, this troubled time will also see the wise emerge, those who are refined (*ṣrp*), purified (*brr*) and made white (*lbn*) (11:35). These roots reappear in 12:10 to exhort active virtue while awaiting the end (cf. 12:9): 'Many shall purify themselves (*brr* hithpael) and make themselves white (*lbn* hithpael) and be refined (*ṣrp* niphal), but the wicked shall act wickedly' (ESV). Those who are 'wise' will understand this (12:10) and, when they awake at the end of the age (12:2), 'will shine like the brightness of the heavens' (12:3).

Ezra-Nehemiah

The books of Ezra and Nehemiah, originally one composition, were separated in Christian tradition in the third century AD (by Origen) and in Jewish tradition in 1448. Hence, although the combined 'book' contains odd features – abrupt shifts from third- to first-person, two protagonists (Ezra and Nehemiah), non-chronological alignment,[45] and two languages (Hebrew and Aramaic[46]) – it is best approached as a rhetorical unit.[47] Tamara Eskenazi, following Claude Bremond, argues Ezra-Nehemiah in its final form is primarily concerned with building Yahweh's house. The fourfold use of *bayit* ('house') in the book's opening section (Ezra 1:1–4)

[42] 9:27 is plural: 'detestable things'.

[43] Deut. 29:16[17]; 1 Kgs 11:5, 7; 2 Kgs 23:13, 24; Jer. 4:1; 7:30; 16:18; 32:34; Ezek. 7:20; 20:7–8, 30; 37:23; Hos. 9:10; 2 Chr. 15:8.

[44] See, further, chapter 6.

[45] Hence, Williamson 1985: xlviii 'although the books have an initial appearance of straightforward historical narrative, they do not regard chronology in the same rigid manner we do.'

[46] The Aramaic passages are Ezra 4:8–24; 5:1–17; 6:1–18; 7:12–26.

[47] Childs 1979: 635 cautions: 'the usual critical move which disregards the present form of the tradition and seeks to reconstruct a more historical sequence on the basis of literary and historical criteria runs the risk of failing to understand the theological concerns which are reflected through the canonical process'. See also Escott 2019.

signals the interest.[48] She observes, however, that 'house' incorporates not only altar and temple (Ezra 1:5 – 6:22), but also community (Ezra 7:1 – 10:44) and city walls (Neh. 1:1 – 7:73).[49] Accordingly, the book moves to celebration only when all constituent elements are 'built' (Neh. 8:1 – 13:31).[50] Extending the scope of 'house' in this way has implications for how Ezra-Nehemiah construes purity. However, while the 'law' or 'book' of Moses is repeatedly invoked (Ezra 3:2; 6:18; 7:6; Neh. 8:1; 13:1; cf. Neh. 1:7–8; 8:14; 9:14; 10:30[29]),[51] the book's relationship to the Pentateuch is not straightforward. Ezra-Nehemiah innovates even as it reiterates.[52]

In Ezra-Nehemiah, the temple is holy even though it is not explicitly described that way. Nehemiah acknowledges the boundary between sacred and mundane when he responds, having been urged to hide in the temple precincts, 'And what man such as I could go into the temple and live? I will not go in' (Neh. 6:11 ESV). Instead, the book acknowledges priests as 'holy to Yahweh' (Ezra 6:28 my tr.) in addition to items used in the temple (Ezra 6:28), offerings (Ezra 3:5; Neh. 10:34[33]; cf. Neh. 12:47) and the 'most holy' food derived therefrom (Ezra 2:63; Neh. 7:65). Yet, in line with the extension of 'house' noted above, the city gates and walls are also consecrated as holy (Neh. 3:1) and Jerusalem is labelled 'the holy city' (*ʿîr haqqōdeš*, Neh. 11:1, 18).

Expanding holiness parameters heightens purity concerns. In Ezra 6:20 the priests and Levites 'purified themselves' (*ṭhr* hithpael) so they would be 'pure' (*ṭāhôr*) ahead of slaughtering Passover lambs on behalf of returned exiles (cf. Num. 9:6–11; 2 Chr. 30:3). The returnees ate with 'all those who had separated themselves (*bdl* niphal) from the impurity of the nations of the land (*miṭṭum ʾat gôyē-hā ʾāreṣ*) to join them' (Ezra 6:21 NASB). The implication is that all non-returnees are considered impure by default, with implications for socioreligious boundaries (see below). 'Within the ideological framework of EN, in which holiness and purity are paramount to reconstituted Israel, this syncretistic group would have

---

[48] *Bayit* occurs a further seventy-eight times in Ezra-Nehemiah.

[49] Eskenazi 1988: 39-40.

[50] Eskenazi 1988: 38. Eskenazi's analysis, however, does not sufficiently acknowledge the anti-climactic nature of Neh. 13 or consider this pericope's role within the rhetoric of the whole. There are also elements of celebration prior to Neh. 8:1 (notably Ezra 6:16).

[51] *Tôrâ* ('law, instruction'), used twenty-five times, is an important *Leitwort* (only the Psalter has more occurrences). In addition, *dāt* ('law') occurs six times in the Aramaic sections.

[52] See, e.g., the reception of Passover traditions assessed by Lau 2009.

been anathema.'[53] Accordingly, only those willing to devote themselves to Yahweh could celebrate Passover.[54] In Nehemiah 12:30 the priests and Levities purify themselves (*ṭhr* hithpael), but also the people, gates and city walls – performing the 'service of purification' (*mišmeret haṭṭāhărâ*, 12:45; cf. 1 Chr. 23:28). This cleansing of the entire 'house' facilitates celebratory sacrifice and is encapsulated in the expansive phrase, 'the joy *of Jerusalem*' (Neh. 12:43 ESV, emphasis mine).[55] Climactically, the final chapter re-emphasizes purity and place. Nehemiah removes Tobiah from his room in the 'house of God', which had to be cleansed (*ṭhr* piel) before it could accommodate sancta and offerings (13:7–9). He also commands the Levites to purify themselves (*ṭhr* hithpael) in preparation for guarding the gates consecrated in 3:1, to prevent continued profanation of the Sabbath (Neh. 13:22; cf. 13:17–18; 9:14). Thus, Levitical appointment to guard the sacred space of the tabernacle (Num. 18:2–5) finds an analogy in relation to the city. Jerusalem's holy boundary must be similarly safeguarded. The book ends with Nehemiah asking God to remember those responsible for 'defiling' (*gō ʾal*) the priesthood in contrast to his own efforts to establish the priests and Levites and to cleanse (*ṭhr* piel) them from everything foreign (Neh. 13:29–30).[56] In this way, primacy (the 'house of Yahweh' in Ezra 1:1–4) and recency (emphasizing defilement and cleansing in Neh. 13) reinforce the importance of purity within the book's rhetoric.[57]

The association of defilement with foreignness in Nehemiah 13:30 is indicative of a wider theme. As noted, Jerusalem is understood as a holy enclave (cf. Ezra 9:8). This, however, raises questions about how Canaan (or, more properly, Yehud) is perceived. The appropriation of exodus motifs in the prayer of Ezra 9:6–15 is telling (cf. Neh. 9:9–25). Returnees had experienced captivity (9:7) and slavery (9:8–9), and although God extended love to them (9:9), they forsook his commandments (9:10), especially the prohibition against intermarrying when they took possession of

---

[53] Lau 2009: 369.

[54] Lau 2009: 364–65. Because Ezra-Nehemiah denies the legitimacy of any Jews outside the returnee group, those who join are best regarded as Gentiles who are included based on prior Passover admittance of foreigners (Williamson 1985: 85; Lau 2009: 365). Ezra-Nehemiah, however, remains silent on the matter of circumcision (cf. Exod. 12:43–49).

[55] Note the explicit inclusion of 'women and children' (Neh. 12:43).

[56] Hayes 2002: 27–28 notes a shift of terminology from exogamy 'profaning' (*ḥll*) the priestly line in Lev. 21:15 to 'defiling' (*gʾl*) it in Neh. 13:29. Hence, removal of foreign persons is described as 'purification' (Neh. 13:30).

[57] Cf. Rimmon-Kenan 2002: 121–23.

the land (9:11–12). That territory is regarded as defiled by its inhabitants, just like the prior pollution of Canaan by its pre-Israelite peoples (cf. Lev. 18:24–28): 'The land that you are entering, to take possession of it, is a land impure (*niddâ*) with the impurity (*bĕniddat*) of the peoples of the lands, with their abominations (*bĕtô ʿăbôtêhem*) that have filled it from end to end with their uncleanness (*beṭum ʾātām*)' (Ezra 9:11 ESV).[58] In these ways, Ezra-Nehemiah presents the exiles' return to Yehud as a recapitulation of the exodus. Those already living in situ, regardless of religious or ethnic affiliation, are correspondingly branded 'Canaanite'.

The resultant calls for separation bequeath a xenophobic tenor to the book. Neighbouring groups are prohibited from assisting temple reconstruction and are regarded as 'adversaries' (*ṣar*) even though claiming to worship God (Ezra 4:1–3). Intermarrying with these 'peoples of the lands' (ESV) is deemed a sin requiring confession (Ezra 9:1–15). Hence, returnees who had acquired 'foreign wives' are commanded to separate from them (Ezra 10:11), which they do with accompanying guilt offering (Ezra 10:19).[59] Nehemiah pushes further: 'As soon as the people heard the law, they separated from Israel all those of foreign descent' (Neh. 13:3 ESV). Nehemiah 9:2 makes the ethnic distinction explicit: 'The seed of Israel separated themselves from all the sons of foreignness' (my tr.). The Torah's partial ban against intermarriage becomes universal as Ezra-Nehemiah draws a tight ethnoreligious line around two distinct humanities: the community of returned exiles, and everyone else.

This separatist rationale prompts Christine Hayes to adopt Michael Fishbane's category of 'genealogical impurity'.[60] Distinct from ritual or moral purity, genealogical purity is indexed to biological descent. The idea is latent in Leviticus in its concern to preserve Aaron's descendants from marital threat (Lev. 21:7, 9), especially the high priest who must not 'profane his seed' (Lev. 21:15 my tr.; cf. 21:13–14). Ezra-Nehemiah echoes this impulse to guard the holy status of priests (cf. Lev. 21:6). Those unable to prove priestly ancestry are 'excluded from the priesthood as unclean' and are barred from the 'most holy food' (Ezra 2:62–63; Neh. 7:64-65 ESV). However, Ezra-Nehemiah goes further: 'Ezra's innovation is to apply the

---

[58] Thus, contra Alon 1977: 183–86, territories, whether Gentile or otherwise, are not intrinsically impure, but are polluted by morally defiling acts.

[59] A list of the guilty is preserved in Ezra 10:20–44.

[60] Hayes 2002: 7; Fishbane 1988: 120; similarly, Lau 2009: 370; Furstenberg 2023: 37–38.

concept of genealogical purity to lay Israelites as well as to priests.'[61] This is accomplished by designating Israel as 'holy seed' (*zeraʿ haqqōdeš*, Ezra 9:2 my tr.). Therefore, 'just as the priest's holy seed is preserved by means of certain marriage restrictions, so also marriage restrictions are needed to preserve the holy seed of the ordinary Israelite.'[62] Genealogical purity created a less permeable boundary around the community of returnees than could either ritual impurity (easily addressed by cultic means) or moral impurity (which could be ameliorated through avoidance or reformation).[63] Ezra-Nehemiah thus justifies more extreme prohibitions against Gentile intermarriage and assimilation than do the Torah or Former Prophets.[64]

However, it is vital to note that the boundary between insider and outsider in Ezra-Nehemiah remains porous in some respects.[65] Although exogamous marriage is prohibited, inclusion within the community is not. In Ezra 6:21 those who separated themselves from the impurity of the peoples of the land *joined* the community of returnees. Thus, Gentiles are not deemed intrinsically impure, either ritually or morally.[66] Instead, those who eschew moral impurity, and presumably avoid ritual impurity,[67] eat Passover on equal footing with returned exiles. This complex boundary between Israelite and Gentile establishes important context for both late Second Temple and New Testament boundary markers.

1 – 2 Chronicles

As it closes the Hebrew canon, 1 – 2 Chronicles does not merely reiterate 1 – 2 Kings. Instead, the book articulates a distinctive message for its

---

[61] Hayes 2002: 28.

[62] Hayes 2002: 28. Hayes is careful to qualify that Ezra does not consider Gentiles to be genealogically defiled (30–32).

[63] Hayes 2002: 32–33.

[64] Hayes 2002: 28 also finds evidence of this shift in Ezek. 44 and Mal. 2:11–12. In contrast, Torah prohibits intermarriage only with *certain* tribes based on moral considerations (e.g. immorality in Num. 25 or idolatry in Deut. 7; cf. Ezra 9:14). Hence, the Former Prophets record the inclusion of Gentiles such as Rahab and the exclusion of Israelites like Achan based on (in)fidelity to Yahweh.

[65] Likewise, Escott 2019: 271–76. Lau 2009: 372 finds the 'almost impenetrable boundary for gentiles' mitigated by the religious grounds of membership evident in Ezra 6:21; Neh. 10:29[28].

[66] Hayes 2002: 35, following Klawans 1995: 292, concludes Gentiles are intrinsically *profane* (rather than impure), which accounts for their limited access to *holy* places. However, as Klawans himself admits, Gentiles are never described this way in the biblical texts (292 n. 34).

[67] Regarding Gentile susceptibility to ritual impurity, see chapters 2 and 6.

post-exilic audience. The figures of David (1 Chr. 11 – 29) and Solomon (2 Chr. 1 – 9) dominate, but their accounts are shaped to emphasize temple themes.[68] Solomon establishes the house of Yahweh for which David had meticulously planned and prepared (1 Chr. 28:10–21). Narrative contours reveal rhetorical purpose. As Hugh Williamson surmises, it is 'difficult to avoid the impression that the Chronicler is presenting David's reign as a paradigm for his own readers.'[69] David, however, is more than just the model king; he demonstrates what it means for a person to seek Yahweh.[70] The extended genealogies with which the book opens (1 Chr. 1 – 9) further connect the post-exilic community to their pre-exilic forebears and invite a family resemblance among the faithful.[71]

An essential component of that portrait is one's attitude towards the holiness and purity of the temple cult. Chronicles regards the temple as permanently holy to God (2 Chr. 7:16) and therefore suitable to house both the ark and Yahweh's 'sacred articles' (1 Chr. 22:19; cf. 1 Chr. 23:25–26).[72] Likewise, Aaron's line is permanently, and uniquely, set apart as holy to serve Yahweh (1 Chr. 23:13; cf. 2 Chr. 13:8–12).[73] The priests offer daily sacrifice and set out bread on the 'pure table' (2 Chr. 13:11 my tr.). The Levites' attendant role includes 'purification of all the holy things' (1 Chr. 23:28–32 ESV; cf. Neh. 12:45).

As Yahweh's dwelling is holy, purity boundaries are essential. Consecration and washing are necessary before the priests contact holy objects (1 Chr. 15:12–14) or enter holy places (2 Chr. 4:6; 5:11). Solomon removes his wife, the daughter of Pharaoh, from the city of David 'because the places the ark of the LORD has entered are holy' (2 Chr.

---

[68] David, for instance, brings the ark to Jerusalem (1 Chr. 15 – 16), dedicates the spoils of war to temple building (1 Chr. 18 – 20), locates the site for the temple (1 Chr. 21:28 – 22:1), plans its construction (1 Chr. 22; 28 – 29), and establishes cultic offices (1 Chr. 16:4–7; 23 – 26). This theme continues with other kings. Hezekiah, for example, is remembered for his wholehearted work in service of God's temple (2 Chr. 31:21).

[69] Williamson 1997: 469–70.

[70] Duke 1990: 63.

[71] Childs 1979: 655; also Hill 2003: 46.

[72] Suitability is accentuated by the presence of 'pure gold' (*zāhāb ṭāhôr*, 1 Chr. 28:17; 2 Chr. 3:4; 9:17; cf. *zāhāb sāgûr* ['fine gold'], 2 Chr. 4:20, 22; 9:20).

[73] Nevertheless, the portrait of David in 1 Chr. 15:27 – 16:3 is intriguing. He dresses in priestly attire (15:27), actively participates in cultic procession (15:29), offers sacrifice (16:2), blesses the people in a manner akin to the high priest (16:2; cf. Lev. 9:22), and distributes sacrificial portions (16:2–3; cf. 2 Chr. 31:19).

8:11).[74] Maintaining purity is also why Solomon, rather than David, is appointed to build the temple. Although David desired to construct a house for Yahweh's name (1 Chr. 22:7), he was forbidden from doing so. Yahweh's reasoning turns on the logic of defilement: 'You have shed much blood and have fought many wars. You are not to build a house for my Name, because you have shed much blood on the earth in my sight' (1 Chr. 22:8; cf. 1 Chr. 28:2–3). Despite David's battles being fought at God's behest, bloodshed nonetheless generates a long-lasting pollution. Therefore, Solomon, whose reign was characterized by 'rest' and 'peace' instead of violence, would build Yahweh's house (1 Chr. 22:9–10, 18–19).

Purity remains important in the divided monarchy (2 Chr. 10 – 36). In the coup d'état against Athaliah (2 Chr. 23:1–21), Jehoiada instigates a priest-led rebellion to install the rightful king (23:1–2). Because only priests and Levites were holy and could enter the house of Yahweh (23:6), the temple precincts become a covert staging post (23:7–10). Concern for temple purity also informs Jehoiada's command regarding Athaliah, 'Do not put her to death at the temple of the LORD' (23:14). That logic is inverted with respect to Mattan, the priest of Baal, who is executed before the altars at the house of Baal, presumably to deliberately defile the shrine (23:17). With Athaliah deposed, Jehoiada appoints the Levites as gatekeepers to ensure nothing 'impure' (*ṭāmēʾ*) could enter the temple. The logic intrinsic to the Athaliah account explains 2 Chronicles 26:16–23. King Uzziah's desire to impinge upon priestly duties is considered unfaithful and motivated by pride (26:16). Indeed, priestly censure only enrages the king (26:17–19). Yet, recalcitrance is overcome when Uzziah is struck with *ṣāraʿat* (NIV: 'leprosy') 'in the house of the LORD' (26:19; cf. Num. 12:10–11), provoking instant and unanimous desire to remove the ritually defiled monarch from sacred space (26:20). *Ṣāraʿat*-afflicted for the rest of his days, Uzziah remains permanently excluded from Yahweh's house (26:21) and is separated from kin in both life (26:21) and death (26:23).

Uzziah's disregard of the temple's holiness and purity is emblematic of a wider pattern. Jehoram murdered his brothers and caused Judah to prostitute (*znh* hiphil) itself to idols (1 Chr. 21:13). Under Joash the people abandoned the house of Yahweh and turned to idols (2 Chr.

---

[74] Although 1 Kgs 9:24 also records the relocation, only the Chronicler provides a reason. Dillard 1987: 65 determines that gender is the driving concern, not Gentile identity, and wonders if this might be to validate segregation in Second Temple worship.

24:17–18). When rebuked by Zechariah, Joash ordered him to be stoned in the temple courts (24:21), provoking the priest's appeal for divine vengeance (24:22; cf. 24:25). Ahaz (2 Chr. 28:3) and Manasseh (2 Chr. 33:2) embraced the 'abominations of the nations' (*tôʿăbôt haggôyim*), as did Jehoiakim (2 Chr. 36:8).

As in Kings, various reforms attempt to reverse the trend. Asa removed 'the detestable things' (*haššiqqûṣîm*) from the land of Judah (2 Chr. 15:8 my tr.), including the 'repulsive image' his mother had made (15:16). Hezekiah's likeness to David is illustrated with respect to the temple (2 Chr. 29). He orders the priests to consecrate themselves and the temple, and to 'remove all defilement (*niddâ*) from the sanctuary' (29:5). So, the priests 'cleanse' (*ṭhr* piel) Yahweh's house by removing 'all the impurity (*ṭumʾâ*) which they found in the temple' (29:15–16 my tr.). Cleansing temple, altar and utensils allows sacrificial worship to recommence (29:18, 21–24, 31). When the king also commands Passover observance (2 Chr. 30), the Levites slaughter lambs for everyone who was 'not pure' (*lōʾ ṭāhôr*, 30:17 my tr.). Indeed, because the people had not purified themselves (*ṭhr* hithpael), Hezekiah intercedes on their behalf for not acting in accord with the sanctuary's purity (30:18–19). That Yahweh heard and *healed the people* suggests enacted judgment for ritual transgression (30:20; cf. 2 Chr. 7:14).[75] Likewise, the celebration of Passover in Josiah's day (2 Chr. 35:1–19), remembered as the greatest since the days of Samuel (35:18), culminates the king's efforts to purge Judah of high places and idols (2 Chr. 34:3–4a, 6–7, 33), to desecrate pagan shrines (2 Chr. 34:4b–5) and to cleanse both temple and land (2 Chr. 34:8). Nevertheless, and despite prophetic warning (2 Chr. 24:19; 36:15), the Chronicler records reckless defilement: 'All the officers of the priests and the people likewise were exceedingly unfaithful, following all the abominations (*tôʿēbōt*) of the nations. And they polluted (*ṭmʾ* piel) the house of the LORD that he had made holy in Jerusalem' (2 Chr. 36:14 ESV). Banishment and destruction become inevitable (36:16–20).

Yet, exile opens new possibilities. The removal of the populace because of their defiling deeds (cf. 1 Chr. 5:25–26) means the land, no longer polluted by its inhabitants, could enjoy Sabbath rest (2 Chr. 36:21). Cleansing of place sets the immediate context for Cyrus's decree to return and rebuild: 'The LORD, the God of heaven, has given me all the kingdoms of the earth, and he has charged me to build him a house at Jerusalem, which

[75] Dillard 1987: 76-81 distils the Chronicler's theology of immediate divine retribution.

is in Judah. Whoever is among you of all his people, may the LORD his God be with him. Let him go up' (2 Chr. 36:23 ESV). The jussive verb with which the Old Testament concludes ('Let him go up') sounds a perpetual invitation to all God's people, in every time and place, to follow David's example by establishing and preserving the dwelling place of Yahweh among his people.[76] The Chronicler's appeal to positive and negative examples from the past generates a lingering question with respect to the holiness and purity of God's temple: 'What course, then, will you choose?'[77]

Conclusion

The themes of defilement and cleansing remain important in the Writings as the corpus variously employs the language of physical, ritual and moral purity. The sources of ritual impurity adumbrated by Leviticus and Numbers are assumed. Likewise, idolatry, bloodshed and sexual immorality are understood to defile and are, as in the Prophets, repeatedly identified as the reasons for exile. Yet, there is also modification. Lexically, the *gʾl* ('to defile') and *brr* ('to purify') roots increasingly appear as synonyms for *ṭmʾ* ('to be impure') and *ṭhr* ('to be pure') respectively. An expanded list of evils is designated *tôʿēbâ* ('abomination'), continuing a trend already initiated in Deuteronomy and underway in the Prophets (see chapter 4). Furthermore, Ezra-Nehemiah instigates the notion of genetic or genealogical purity. This, likewise, develops ideas latent in the Pentateuch (esp. priestly stipulations in Leviticus) and constitutes an attempt by the post-exilic community to grapple with being God's holy people in a context of external threat and 'group identity liminality'.[78] In these ways, Torah is adapted for new situations. Therefore, rather than indicating a diminished (or diminishing) focus on purity in the post-exilic era, the data from the Writings reveal the opposite. This trend towards increased focus on the causes and amelioration of defilement, especially with respect to social boundaries and concern for the temple's sanctity, sets the trajectory and immediate context for the late Second Temple and New Testament periods.

---

[76] David's example includes his repentance in 1 Chr. 21 (Knoppers 1995: 469). The account of Manasseh (2 Chr. 33:10–17) is also striking in this regard.

[77] Duke 1990: 104.

[78] Lau 2009: 369–70.

6

Defilement and cleansing in Second Temple literature

The body of extra-biblical texts produced between the reconstruction of the temple (c. 516 BC) and the second century AD is collated under the rubric 'Second Temple literature'. While the nomenclature suggests 'collection' or 'corpus', the material is widely divergent in language, genre, theology and geographical origin.[1] Functioning as an umbrella category, Second Temple literature includes the apocrypha (deuterocanonical works), Old Testament pseudepigrapha and Dead Sea Scrolls, as well as authors contemporaneous with early Christianity, such as Philo and Josephus. Although largely deemed non-canonical by later Jewish and Christian traditions,[2] this material nevertheless grants crucial insight into how Old Testament themes were adopted and adapted by subsequent interpretative communities. Grappling with these texts thus clarifies the immediate background of the New Testament and begins to account for points of divergence from the Hebrew Scriptures. Hence, while perhaps unfamiliar to some readers, gaining even a little understanding of this literature pays dividends.

Accordingly, I survey Second Temple texts with respect to defilement and cleansing.[3] However, several caveats are required. First, there are

[1] Hence, Hayes 2002: 46 notes, 'these texts are collated simply by virtue of what they are *not* ... they are neither biblical nor (canonically) rabbinic'. For an overview of texts, provenance, and subsequent transmission, see Collins 2002.

[2] The Roman Catholic canon incorporates Tobit, Judith, 1 – 2 Maccabees, Wisdom of Solomon, Ecclesiasticus, and Baruch; Orthodox Bibles include 1 Esdras, Tobit, Judith, 1 – 3 Maccabees, Wisdom of Solomon, Sirach, Baruch, and the Epistle of Jeremiah. Both also include the additions to Esther and Daniel found in LXX. Kruger 2012 surveys the processes that shaped canon formation.

[3] The appropriation of purity in post-biblical rabbinic and Christian theology is beyond the scope of this volume. Extensive treatment can be found in Neusner 1973; 1994; Klawans 2000; Hayes 2002; Latz and Ermakov 2014; Balberg 2014; Bildstein 2017; Furstenberg 2023.

already many fine analyses of purity in this literature; my goal is not to add to these in any substantive way.[4] Instead, I utilize existing studies to chart how defilement and cleansing were understood in this period. Thus, second, I make no pretence of being exhaustive. In what follows, I present examples and illustrations of purity concepts, not a comprehensive account. Third, regarding methodology, I do not attempt to construct an overall conception of purity or propose a developmental schema. The heterogenous nature of Second Temple texts must be recognized. While significant similarities are evident, stemming from a shared Old Testament heritage, there is nevertheless a risk of marginalizing counter-evidence in the pursuit of synthesis. Accordingly, I remain content to tease out differing conceptions of defilement and cleansing without seeking to reconcile them into a neat framework.[5] This fits the evidence of distinct communities, which utilized purity conceptions in different, sometimes mutually exclusive, ways. Still, identification of broad trends proves useful for assessing purity in the New Testament. Fourth, there are multiple ways to arrange the data: by date of composition, text type, community of origin, theological outlook, and so on. Each has its merits. I have chosen to proceed thematically to better highlight points of continuity and discontinuity with the analysis of defilement and cleansing in previous chapters.

Ritual purity in Second Temple literature

The destruction of the temple by the Romans in AD 70 was a watershed moment for Judaism. The cult, which had hitherto heightened the immediacy and social relevance of ritual purity laws, became non-functional.[6] Until this point, the importance of ritual purity was simply assumed:

> Every important sect had to define its relationship to the Temple, and one predominant question concerned actually keeping or not keeping the purity laws, making them into a metaphor for the ethical life, or otherwise reinterpreting them. The only thing no one could do was ignore them.[7]

[4] In addition to the previous footnote, see Sanders 1992; Harrington 1993; Werrett 2007; Haber 2008; Magness 2011; Kazen 2010; 2021.

[5] Similar approaches are adopted by Hayes 2002: 46–47; Klawans 2006: 145–47.

[6] Neusner 1973: 32.

[7] Neusner 1973: 33.

The wider point is well made even though Jacob Neusner's limitation of purity concerns to cultic contexts has been rightly challenged.[8] Irrespective, ritual defilement and cleansing permeate Second Temple literature.[9] Moreover, the portrayal is largely unexceptional: 'purity and impurity occur in routine ways and entirely within the interpretative framework set forth in the Hebrew Scriptures'.[10] The sources of ritual defilement enumerated in Leviticus and Numbers, and reiterated across the Old Testament – food, childbirth, *ṣāra ʿat* (ESV: 'leprous disease'), sex, bodily fluids and corpses – are taken for granted.

Ritual purity is frequently discussed in relation to sacred space. Second Maccabees (second century BC) remembers the deliberate pollution of the sanctuary under Antiochus IV who ordered sexual intercourse within the temple precincts (6:4) and the sacrifice of 'abominable offerings' on the altar (6:5 RSV; cf. 1 Macc. 1:45–47; contrast T. Levi 9:13).[11] Eleazar, a man in his nineties, refused to eat pig-flesh from such sacrifices, accepting martyrdom instead of defiling his old age (6:18–31; 4 Macc. 5:1 – 6:30; cf. Jdt. 12:2).[12] The implications of ritual impurity for holy places are also recognized in the Psalms of Solomon (first century BC), which admonishes those who,

> walked on the place of sacrifice of the Lord,
> (coming) from all kinds of uncleanness;
> and (coming) with menstrual blood (on them), they defiled the sacrifices
> as if they were common meat.
> (8:12)[13]

[8] E.g. Poirier 2003: 265 'The notion that the ritual purity laws of Second Temple Judaism existed solely for the sake of the temple is a scholarly construct with little basis in reality.' Kazen 2021: 278 concurs: 'scholarly tendency to limit purity practices to the cult reflects an anachronistically modern and secular understanding of religion as separate from life at large.' Indeed, Kazen and Furstenberg find that the temple's destruction had little immediate impact on ritual purification, at least until the Bar Kokhba revolt (Kazen 2021: 283; Furstenberg 2023: 143–44). See also Alon 1977; Alder 2011: 71–72; Kazen 2016: 127.

[9] Klawans 2000: 63 observes that no one disputes the point.

[10] Neusner 1973: 33, who notes Jubilees as a particular exception.

[11] Gentile defilement of sacred precincts is also present in Jdt. 9:8.

[12] Williams 2017 assesses the belief that martyrdom atoned for the nation.

[13] Unless otherwise noted, all translations of Second Temple texts are from Charlesworth 1983–1985.

Indeed, the Epistle of Jeremiah (third century BC) argues that, because idol sacrifices are touched by women who are menstruating or giving birth, one can know for certain that idols are not true gods (29). Relatedly, Josephus (b. AD 37) asserts the importance of preventing those with 'leprosy' (i.e. *ṣāraʿat*) from entering Jerusalem and of keeping post-partum women, menstruants and impure men away from temple and sacrifices (*J.W.* 5.5.6 §227; cf. *Ant.* 3.11.3–5 §§261–69).

Accordingly, ritual cleansing ahead of approaching sacred locales is commonplace. In the Testaments of the Twelve Patriarchs (second century BC), Levi is anointed with 'pure water' (T. Levi 8:5) and told, 'Before you enter the sanctuary, bathe; while you are sacrificing, wash; and again when the sacrifice is concluded, wash' (T. Levi 9:11; similarly, Jub. 21:16). Josephus, writing from a priestly perspective, states, 'Now the law has appointed several purifications at our sacrifices, whereby we are cleansed after a funeral, after what sometimes happens to us in bed, and after accompanying with our wives, and upon many other occasions' (*Ag. Ap.* 2.24 §198).[14] He also acknowledges the need to purify the temple following Pompey's invasion and the slaying of priests as they went about their duties (*J.W.* 1.7.5 §150). His comment, however, is terse and sheds little light on process: 'he commanded the ministers about the temple, the very next day after he had taken it, to cleanse it' (*J.W.* 1.7.6 §153). The book of Jubilees (second century BC) regards the Garden of Eden as 'more holy than any land' (3:12). Thus, based on the timeframes for childbirth impurity in Leviticus 12:2–5, the author determines that Adam was brought into the Garden only after forty days and Eve after eighty (3:8–12).[15]

In the above texts, it is proximity to the temple (or the Garden sanctuary in Jubilees) that problematizes impurity. Yet, concern for ritual cleansing also appears in non-cultic contexts. Judith, for instance, washes daily at a spring in preparation for prayer and so returns to her tent 'clean' (Jdt. 12:7–9 RSV; cf. Let. Aris. 305–6). Josephus notes concern about corpse-impurity in relation to building Tiberias on a gravesite (*Ant.* 18.2.3 §§36–38). Tobit purifies himself from corpse-impurity before eating at home (Tob. 2:5). In addition, commonly held purity beliefs could be used

[14] All quotations of Josephus are from Josephus 1987.

[15] In this way, Jubilees regards ritual impurity as intrinsic to humanity, even at creation (Philip 2006: 117).

for rhetorical ends. Sirach 34:25–26 reflects on cleansing corpse-impurity to construct a moral lesson: 'If a man washes after touching a dead body, and touches it again, what has he gained by his washing? So if a man fasts for his sins, and goes again and does the same things, who will listen to his prayer?' (RSV).

There is also a tendency in some texts to regard ritual impurity as a metaphor or allegory for ethical matters.[16] Testament of Asher 4:5 compares unorthodox persons, who nevertheless abstain from what God hates, to gazelles and stags: 'In appearance they seem wild and unclean, but as a whole they are clean' (cf. Deut. 14:5).[17] This allegorizing trend is especially apparent in communities that were separated from the Jerusalem temple, whether geographically or theologically. Philo, born in Alexandria c. 20 BC, is perhaps the pre-eminent exemplar of the former. At times, Philo simply lists or acknowledges ritual purity laws (e.g. *Spec.* 1.24.117–19; 1.48.261). Frequently, however, he engages in figural readings of Old Testament ritual legislation. Regarding the high priestly ban on entering a house containing a 'dead soul' (*napšōt mēt*, Lev. 21:11), Philo ruminates, 'But the death of the soul is a life according to wickedness; so that he must never touch any pollution such as folly is fond of dealing with' (*Flight* 21.113).[18] Similarly, laws concerning *ṣāra'at* are deemed to use 'symbolical expression' to convey that 'intentional offences, even if they do not extend over a wide surface … are rightly accounted unholy, and polluted, and impure' (*Unchange.* 27.128; cf. Lev. 13:11). Indeed, in Philo's estimation, the disease 'is an emblem of a life unsteady and tossed about in any direction' (*Dreams* 1.34.202).

Theologically motivated distancing from the temple is best exemplified by the Qumran community who considered the Jerusalem cult defiled. Instead, the community fashioned a self-understanding that appropriated temple ideology. In 1QS 8:5–6, a council of twelve men and three priests is termed a 'holy of holies for Aaron',[19] with corresponding purity implications (cf. 1QS 9:3–11).[20] A heightened concern for purity is borne out

[16] See also 4 Macc. 8:1, 12; T. Iss. 4:4. This trajectory continues in early Christian texts, e.g., Ep. Barn. (c. AD 100).

[17] Cf. Acts 9:36–37 where Tabitha means 'gazelle'.

[18] All quotations of Philo are from Philo 1993.

[19] Unless otherwise stated, translations of DSS are from García Martínez 1996.

[20] Whether or not the Qumran community understood itself as a new temple is debated. Hultgren 2007: 309 concludes, 'the community-as-temple concept was already present at the founding of the community as a refuge from impurity.' Klawans 2006: 168 is more cautious: '[the]

archaeologically. The quantity and location of water cisterns at Qumran suggests their probable function as *miqwāʾôt* (ritual baths).[21] Textual evidence confirms the importance of ritual purity. Hannah Harrington concludes, 'a quick survey of the legal texts found at Qumran yields a preponderance of laws centred around purity issues'.[22] Klawans concurs.[23] Continuity with Old Testament purity practices is widespread, including the need to bathe or wash clothes (e.g. 4Q274 1:1–4; 4Q514 1:1–6; 11Q19 45:15–16) and to avoid impure foods (e.g. 11Q19 48:1–7). Yet, there is also noticeable discontinuity. Old Testament legislation is frequently intensified. According to Leviticus 15:16–18, emission of semen makes a man impure 'till evening'. 11Q19 45:7–12, however, stipulates a three-day impurity. Similarly, 4QMMT 16–19 deems those who slaughter the red heifer to be impure even though Numbers 19 remains silent on the matter. Innovation is also present. Certain disabilities are deemed defiling, with 11Q19 45:12–14 ascribing lifelong impurity to blind people, thus barring them from the temple lest they defile Yahweh's dwelling.[24] Extra protections around cultic activities are stipulated, including preventing (impure) dogs from entering the holy camp lest they eat bones from the temple sacrifices (4QMMT 61–62). There is also a redefinition of what constitutes cultic activity. Meals, for example, take on added significance in some texts, with 1QS 5:13 requiring all to wash before eating the 'pure food of the men of holiness'.[25]

---

sectarians saw their community as a provisional replacement for a temple, even though their provisional replacement fails by comparison to the temple itself. … the texts themselves do not assert that the community is better than or even as good as a temple would be'. Either way, impurity concerns are heightened, even if there are limits to the community-as-temple metaphor (cf. Newton 1985: 10–51; Wassén 2013: 58–62, 69–73).

[21] 'Unless we imagine that the sectarians were constructing luxurious swimming pools, or assume a vastly overdesigned system or a much larger population than the evidence indicates, we must conclude that the stepped cisterns were used for religious rites' (Wood 1984: 58). See also Hidiroglou 2000; DiFransico 2016: 161–69.

[22] Harrington 2000: 78.

[23] Klawans 2010: 381.

[24] Klawans 2006: 154 suggests this may not indicate innate impurity, but rather that blindness may result in inadvertent defilement. In 4Q266 the rationale for excluding the disabled is premised on angels being in the midst of the community (Barton 2014: 192 n. 19).

[25] Harrington 2000: 79. This remains the case despite Wassén's qualification regarding eating at Qumran: 'that complete purity was required at all meals should be replaced by a more nuanced reconstruction involving distinct purity requirements for different kinds of meals' (Wassén 2016a: 109). Neusner proposed a similar trend in Pharisaism: 'The Pharisees saw eating as a cultic act and transferred to the home and table many of the laws that had originally applied to the Temple and altar. … They therefore held one must eat his secular food, that is, ordinary, everyday meals, in a

As this brief overview indicates, ritual impurity remains an important consideration in Second Temple literature. At the same time, the evidence demonstrates that not all communities had the same outlook or priorities when it came to matters of ritual defilement. Appropriation of Old Testament beliefs and practices is uneven. Some, like the Qumran community, actively *increased* expectations around ritual purity and extended its purview beyond the confines of the Jerusalem temple. Yet others, like the Zealots portrayed by Josephus (see *J.W.* 4.3.13 §215; 5.1.1–3 §§1–20; cf. *Ant.* 20.8.5 §165), were either indifferent to ritual impurity or minimized its relative importance.

Moral purity in Second Temple literature

Second Temple literature also acknowledges impurity caused by moral vices. As might be expected (in line with Old Testament conceptions), idolatry, bloodshed and sexual immorality feature prominently and are understood to pollute people, sanctuary and land.

In a context of post-diluvian conflict, Jubilees records the making of 'graven images and polluted likenesses' by which 'cruel spirits' led the people astray into sin and transgression, even to pouring out blood upon the earth (11:4–5). Thus, Abraham warns his sons against the defilement connected to idols (20:7). The Testament of Moses (first century AD) connects Israel pursuing foreign gods to pollution of the house of worship (5:2). Equating idolatry with sanctuary defilement is especially prominent in Maccabees where the cultural genocide enacted by Antiochus IV, designed to eradicate Torah observance, hinged on broad-spectrum desecration of the temple. At Antiochus's decree, idol sacrifice commenced in Jerusalem and in all the cities of Judah, precipitating a crisis for the faithful (1 Macc. 1:41–52). Jarvis Williams highlights what was at stake: 'Antiochus's desecration of the temple ended Jewish particularity and identity as they knew it (i.e., their religious life as they practiced it in compliance with the torah in distinction from the nations).'[26] A defiled temple was unusable. Thus, its subsequent restoration and purification by

state of purity *as if one were a Temple priest*' (Neusner 1973: 56, 65). Neusner's conclusion has been strongly challenged, most recently by Furstenberg 2023.

[26] Williams 2017: 243.

Judas Maccabaeus in 164 BC was immortalized in the annual festival of Hanukkah (1 Macc. 4:36–59).[27]

Bloodshed also defiles. In Jubilees, Noah worries that demons are misleading his sons and will cause them to shed blood upon the earth (7:27). Echoing Numbers 35:33, Noah warns, 'the land will not be cleansed of the blood which is poured out upon it, because by the blood of one who poured it out will the land be cleansed in all of its generations' (7:33; also 21:19). His warning takes on added urgency after the flood, which God used to purify the earth from injustice and violence (7:21–25). The temple is similarly polluted by bloodshed. First Maccabees recalls, in relation to Antiochus IV, 'On every side of the sanctuary they shed innocent blood; they even defiled the sanctuary' (1:37 RSV). Hence, Judas appeals to blood-pollution to urge God to act (2 Macc. 8:2–4). Josephus articulates the same defiling effect of bloodshed in the context of Roman invasion, especially the blood of non-combatants (*J.W.* 1.7.5–6 §§150–53). The problem is exacerbated by murder in the temple courts (*Ant.* 20.8.5 §165). Thus, Josephus reasons, 'God had doomed this city to destruction, as a polluted city, and was resolved to purge his sanctuary by fire' (*J.W.* 4.5.2 §323; cf. *Ant.* 20.8.5 §166). Elsewhere, Josephus connects pollution to the bodies of the slain piled up in the temple precincts (*J.W.* 6.2.1 §110).[28] In this way, bloodshed and corpse-impurity combine to contaminate the temple and instigate divine purging 'by fire'.

Like bloodshed, sexual sin is understood to generate significant pollution. It leaves a (permanent) stain upon people (Tob. 3:14–15). Consequently, Jubilees 33:7, elaborating on Reuben taking his father's concubine in Genesis 35:22, has Bilhah say to Jacob, 'I am not clean for you since I have become polluted for you because Reuben has defiled me and lay with me at night.' Subsequent evocation of Leviticus 18:8 and 20:11 indicates that moral rather than ritual defilement is intended (33:10). Consequently, in line with Leviticus 18:24–25, Reuben and Bilhah are understood to 'have made a defilement on the earth' (33:10).[29] Jacob, therefore, subsequently avoided Bilhah (33:9). Thus, for the author

[27] Similarly, at Qumran, the 'sons of truth' are marked by 'magnificent purity which detests all unclean idols' (1QS 4:5).

[28] See also *J.W.* 6.2.3 §121: 'all the space round about within the temple might be compared to a burying ground, so great was the number of the dead bodies therein.'

[29] This remains the case even though the text acknowledges Bilhah's innocence and subsequent lament (33:3–7).

of Jubilees, immorality is the most egregious sin: 'For defiled, and an abomination, and blemished, and polluted are all who do them upon the earth before our God. And there is no sin greater' (33:19–20). The same concern is evident in the Psalms of Solomon as the daughters of Jerusalem 'defiled themselves with improper intercourse' (2:13). Moreover, in 8:9–12, the impurity from sexual sin (parent-child incest and adultery) defiles temple[30] and sacrifices. By such deeds, 'they defiled Jerusalem and the things that had been consecrated to the name of God' (8:22).

The polluting effect of immorality upon the temple is also important in the Testament of Levi. The patriarch warns his children about a future 'uncleanness' by which the sanctuary will become desolate and they will go into exile (T. Levi 15:1). The source of impurity is explicitly sexual: sharing sacrificial food with prostitutes, profaning married women, sleeping with prostitutes and adulteresses, taking Gentile women as wives, and having sexual relations in the manner of Sodom and Gomorrah (T. Levi 14:5–6). Accordingly, Levi asserts, 'for seventy weeks you shall wander astray and profane the priesthood and defile the sacrificial altars. … You shall have no place that is clean' (T. Levi 16:1, 5). A rationale for banishment is conveyed in T. Joseph 4:4–5, which avers that adultery defiles the heart, making a person unfit for the divine presence. In this passage, Potiphar's wife promises Joseph she will live in the presence of his God if he sleeps with her. The patriarch, however, recalls, 'I kept telling her that the Lord did not want worshipers who come by means of uncleanness', for he is pleased with those who are 'pure in heart and undefiled in speech'.

The link between sexual immorality and defilement of place can have cosmic consequences. Both 1 Enoch and Jubilees interpret Genesis 6:2 as angels taking human wives (1 En. 6:1–2; Jub. 5:1). Enoch classifies the union as adultery, which defiles both human and spiritual participants (10:9, 11; 12:4), and which requires the deluge to cleanse the earth from its resultant pollution (10:20, 22). Jubilees terms the act 'fornication' and the 'beginning of impurity' and lists it as one of the three reasons the flood came (7:21).[31] Likewise, because Sodom and Gomorrah polluted the earth with sexual immorality, God declares he will punish other societies that 'act according to the pollution of Sodom' (Jub. 16:5–6; cf. 20:5–6; 2

[30] Reading 8:12 with Syr.

[31] The other two are 'injustice' (i.e. violence) and 'pollution' (7:20).

Pet. 2:6; Jude 7–8).[32] Recalling the flood and Sodom indicates that moral impurity was understood to have implications beyond the borders of Israel.

In addition to idolatry, bloodshed and sexual immorality, other evils defile. In the 1 Enoch passage examined above, the deluge cleanses the earth from injustice and defilement. Yet, the flood also ends 'all oppression', 'all sin' and 'all iniquity' (10:20; cf. 10:22). The categories imply a more expansive list of deeds that pollute the earth. Similar expansion is evident in Jubilees 22:21–23 where Abraham instructs Isaac:

> I see, my son,
> every deed of mankind, that (they are) sins and evils;
> and all of their deeds are defilement and corruption and
>   contamination;
> [...]
> Turn yourself aside from all their deeds and from all their
>   defilement;
> and keep the commands of God Most High.

Abraham's exhortation to Jacob proceeds along similar lines:

> Separate yourself from the gentiles,
> and do not eat with them,
> and do not perform deeds like theirs.
> And do not become associates of theirs.
> Because their deeds are defiled,
> and all of their ways are contaminated, and despicable, and
>   abominable.
> (Jub. 22:16)[33]

Jubilees 23:21 also speaks of a future generation who will engage in deceit and wealth acquisition and so 'pollute the holy of holies with their pollution'.

[32] The fire and brimstone used to destroy Sodom are typically cleansing agents (Walton and Walton 2017: 130).

[33] Although subsequent verses can be broadly collated under idolatrous practices (22:17–19, 22) and concerns about intermarriage (22:20–21), the phrase 'all of their ways' suggests a broader scope.

In the Qumran literature a wide range of moral faults defile.[34] The use of bribery or judicial deceit 'defiles the House with the wickedness of sin' (11QT[a] 51:11–15). In 4QPseudo-Moses Apocalypse[e] God declares that financial domineering, stealing and persecuting one's neighbour 'will defile my temple' (frag. 2, 1:8–9). The wicked priest in 1QpHab defiles the sanctuary of God by violence, but also by oppressing and plundering the poor (12:1–10). Similarly, because 'wicked wealth' defiles, the faithful must separate themselves from it, along with stealing from the poor and widows, and murdering orphans (CD 6:14–17). 11QT[a] 52:17–18 commands that the slaughter of blemished animals occur more than thirty stadia from the temple because 'it is abominable flesh'.[35]

Regarding the impetus for enlarging the domain of moral impurity, Klawans notes that while 'abomination' (*tô ʿēbâ*) in Deuteronomy frequently refers to idolatry, sexual sin and murder, it also has wider referents, including greed (Deut. 25:16). He suggests, 'Perhaps for earlier ancient Jews too – as for the later rabbis – the Deuteronomic reference to avarice as abomination led to the idea that this sort of behavior could defile the sanctuary.'[36] Klawans' contention finds support in the Old Testament texts surveyed in chapters 3 – 5 in which the language of 'abomination' increasingly becomes an umbrella designation for a host of moral evils. The Second Temple texts sampled above develop what is already latent in the Old Testament Scriptures.

Although Second Temple texts are circumspect about cleansing moral impurity, some entertain the possibility. As discussed above, 1 Enoch 10:20–22 understands the flood as a divine act of purging the earth. A similar dynamic, but premised on human agency, is evident in Josephus. He notes that Judas Maccabeus cast Judah's 'enemies out of the country, and put those of their own country to death who had transgressed its laws, and purified the land of all the pollutions that were in it' (*Ant.* 12.6.4 §286). The means by which purification is achieved are ambiguous, but the implication is that removing the (human) sources of impurity, whether by exile or execution, stymies land pollution. Josephus applies

[34] I am indebted to Klawans 2006: 147–48 for this paragraph. See also, Klawans 2000: 75–91.

[35] This implies defilement of the temple from afar. Klawans 2006: 293, however, argues that the litmus test of defilement at a distance is not applicable in this case as sacrifice is only performed at the temple. The 11QT[a] passage, however, addresses *non-sacrificial* slaughter of blemished animals (see 52:9–11).

[36] Klawans 2006: 150.

the same logic to his own day, holding that the Romans came 'to purify' Jerusalem, which, on account of its defiled nature, 'couldst be no longer a place fit for God' (*J.W.* 5.1.3 §19; cf. *J.W.* 6.2.1 §110).[37] In each of these examples, impurity is mitigated by cessation rather than purging rites.[38]

Other texts hold open the possibility of active purification procedures. Jubilees records Noah offering sacrifice following the deluge (cf. Gen. 8:20) and determines, 'he made atonement for the land. And he took the kid of a goat, and he made atonement with its blood for all the sins of the land' (6:2).[39] The Qumran community, likewise, prescribed purification for moral violations.[40] Various infractions necessitated a period of separation from the pure food of the Many: one year for lying, for responding brusquely, for speaking angrily, or defaming another; six months for deception; three months for negligence or for walking around naked without cause; thirty days for the one who 'giggles inanely'; and ten days for 'talking in the middle of the words of his fellow' (1QS 6:24 – 7:18). Ablutions also feature. In 1QS 2:25 – 3:12, washing and sprinkling with water form part of the cleansing process for a wayward initiate. Wickedness is conceptualized as 'slime', which leaves 'stains on his conversion' (3:2–3).[41] Ongoing recalcitrance prohibits purification: 'He will not become clean by the acts of atonement, nor shall he be purified by the cleansing waters, nor shall he be made holy by the seas or rivers, nor shall he be purified by all the water of the ablutions. Defiled, defiled shall he be all the days he spurns the decrees of God' (3:4–6; cf. 5:13–14). Through humility, however, 'his flesh is cleansed by being sprinkled[42] with cleansing waters and [by] being made holy with the waters of repentance' (3:8–9). DiFransico concludes, 'the willing and humble individual is both cleansed spiritually by his right behavior and is also cleansed

[37] Josephus attributes defilement to the 'blood of all sorts of dead carcasses [which] stood in lakes in the holy courts themselves' (*J.W.* 5.1.3 §18). He also portrays Titus entreating Jerusalem's defenders to move away from the temple complex so the ensuing battle would not defile the sanctuary, so preserving its holiness (*J.W.* 6.2.4 §§124–128).

[38] See, similarly, 1QS 5:13–14, which equates cleansing with turning from wickedness and 1QH[a] 8:18, which connects purifying hands to detesting sin.

[39] The sins in view are immorality and violence (5:1–2).

[40] Following Neusner 1973: 54.

[41] Here, *g'l* is used to conceptualize moral transgression as a 'stain' (DiFransico 2016: 180 n. 12).

[42] Use of *nzh* evokes Num. 19 where corpse-defiled persons are 'sprinkled' to purify them (DiFransico 2016: 181 n. 19).

via purification with water.'[43] While DiFransico understands physical washing as targeting sin, it is possible that ablutions were understood to remove the moral pollution that arises from transgression. Nevertheless, DiFransico highlights the relative rarity of the idea:

> In the sectarian literature, the concept of washing away sin comes to be expressed as a real practice wherein members of the community wash in water as a solution to both impurity and sin, but even this actual practice only finds occasional mention in the texts.[44]

Nonetheless, the point remains: in at least some texts, moral impurity could be ameliorated by human means. Other passages utilize 'washing' to evoke the agency of God's Spirit in cleansing sin and impurity. 1QS 4:20–22 asserts:

> God will refine, with his truth, all man's deeds, and will purify for himself the configuration of man, ripping out all spirit of deceit from the innermost part of his flesh, and cleansing him with the spirit of holiness from every irreverent deed. He will sprinkle over him the spirit of truth like lustral water (in order to cleanse him) from all the abhorrences of deceit and from the defilement of the unclean spirit.

The connection between human ablutions and washing by God's Spirit is left unstated.[45] 1QH^a 8:20 is more direct as it asks God 'to purify me with your holy spirit.' By such means, removing moral impurity is deemed possible. Neusner agrees:

> Now what makes this view of impurity other than metaphorical is the provision of both a specific disability consequent on sin-impurity and a rite of purification – whatever it may be. This means the impurity is regarded as affective, the man is really impure and

[43] DiFransico 2016: 185.

[44] DiFransico 2016: 197.

[45] The possibilities this raises for understanding the actions of John the Immerser are explored in chapter 7.

> requires cleansing from impurity before he may have contact with the pure objects of the community.[46]

These observations raise questions about the perceived relationship between ritual and moral impurity in Second Temple communities. The data from Leviticus and Numbers elaborates two related, but distinct conceptions of purity that operated in biblical Israel. For the most part, the above survey indicates that distinguishing ritual from moral impurity continued in Second Temple texts. Klawans reaches the same conclusion:

> None confuses or integrates ritual and moral impurity in any way. Just as in the book of Leviticus itself, in each of these texts, if both types of impurity are discussed, they are juxtaposed without any attempt to integrate them.[47]

The Qumran literature, however, is different. Neusner argues strongly for conflation: 'For the *yaḥad*, one cannot distinguish between cultic and moral impurity. In themselves and in their consequences they are identical.'[48] Klawans concurs: 'At Qumran the once distinct concepts of ritual and moral impurity were merged into a single conception of defilement.'[49] This, he says, is evident in five ways: (1) all sins are described as impurities; (2) sinners outside the community are deemed ritually impure; (3) community members who sin are considered defiling; (4) initiation involves repentance and ritual cleansing; and (5) certain ritual defilements are understood to stem from sin.[50] Klawans' observations, however, must be qualified. As he himself recognizes, the Qumranic literature evinces a spectrum of approaches to purity: some texts conflate ritual and moral impurity (e.g. 1QS) while others maintain a distinction (e.g. the Temple Scroll).[51] Additionally, Cecilia Wassén cautions against

---

[46] Neusner 1973: 54. Neusner regards the notion that moral impurity caused actual, rather than metaphorical, defilement to be a Qumranic innovation. In chapter 2, I explain why I reject this claim.

[47] Klawans 2000: 60. His conclusion is made in relation to Ezra-Nehemiah, 4Q381, 1 Enoch, Jubilees, the Temple Scroll, the Damascus Document, the Testament of Levi, and the Psalms of Solomon.

[48] Neusner 1973: 54; similarly, Harrington 2011: 126; DiFransico 2016: 198.

[49] Klawans 2000: 75.

[50] Klawans 2000: 75–88.

[51] Klawans 2000: 90. Klawans, accordingly, advocates a diachronic approach to the data (91). See also the cautions voiced by Hayes 2002: 65–66.

overstating the symmetry: while it is clear that sinners were regarded as defiled, ritually impure people were not therefore regarded as sinners (with the possible exception of *ṣāraʿat*-infected people in 4Q274 1:1–4).[52] Kazen's conclusion is more cautious in proposing '*some* sort of interaction or link between sin and bodily impurity both in popular belief and among Essenes as well as among Pharisees.'[53] Once again, there is not a singular conception of purity in the surviving texts. Rather, divergence indicates that purity was a somewhat fluid category that was understood differently by diverse communities and, perhaps, even over time within the same community.[54]

Gentile impurity, genealogical impurity and the question of intermarriage

The viewpoint expressed in some Qumranic texts regarding the ritually and morally defiled status of outsiders raises larger questions about how Gentiles are perceived in Second Temple literature. In what ways, if at all, are defilement and cleansing applied to non-Jews?

There is a widespread assumption among scholars that Gentiles, and possibly their lands, were understood as *intrinsically* impure in biblical times.[55] Gedaliah Alon, for instance, regards Gentiles as permanently defiled by virtue of being Gentile, a pollution he links to the ritual impurity of idols.[56] Saul Olyan, likewise, claims foreigners were considered categorically impure.[57] However, these conclusions are overstated. Divine–human intimacy in Genesis 1 – 2, acceptance of Gentile sacrifice (e.g. Gen. 8:20–21; Lev. 17:8–9; Num. 15:14–16), and having non-Jews enter sacred precincts (e.g. Isa. 56:3–7), excludes notions of ontological impurity.[58] Similarly, in the New Testament era, Paul addresses synagogue audiences comprising Jews *and Greeks* (Acts 14:1; 17:1–4).[59] Instead, Gentile *susceptibility* to impurity aligns better with the biblical evidence. This is patently

[52] Wassén 2013: 68 n. 61.

[53] Kazen 2002: 219.

[54] For diachronic analysis of ritual purity in the late Second Temple era, see Furstenberg 2023.

[55] E.g. Dunn 1990: 142; Neyrey 1986: 108.

[56] Alon 1977: 147–48, 87.

[57] Olyan 2000: 83–84.

[58] Hayes 2002: 20–22.

[59] Klawans 1995: 302; Hayes 2002: 50.

clear for moral impurity, which affects Israelite and 'foreign resident' (*gēr*) equally (e.g. Gen. 6 – 9; Lev. 18:24–30). Abhorrent deeds make any person impure (cf. Mark 7:20–23; Acts 15:19–20; b. Sanh. 74a).[60] Thus, neither Israelite nor non-Israelite is inherently polluted. Accordingly, foreigners could join the community of Israel (e.g. Josh. 6:22–25; 2 Sam. 15:17–22; Ruth 4:13–22).[61]

Determining Gentile susceptibility to ritual impurity is more contentious, especially regarding extent. Emil Schürer championed a widespread application of ritual impurity to Gentiles premised on their failure to adhere to Torah purity instructions.[62] Hayes, however, qualifies susceptibility based on her understanding that holiness and purity are covenantal notions not applicable to Gentiles. Thus, Leviticus 12 – 15 applies to Israelites alone; Gentiles remain impervious to ritual defilement.[63] She concedes, however, that there are exceptions. In Numbers 19 and 31 non-Israelites are polluted by corpse-contact and, in turn, defile when dead.[64] Similarly, Leviticus 17:15–16 applies ritual impurity from eating animal carcasses to non-Israelites.[65] Hayes deals with these exceptions by advocating a conceptual parallel with Noahic covenant prohibitions against murder and consuming blood (Gen. 9:3–6). Leviticus 17 and Numbers 19 thus represent 'the logical and consistent extension of principles implicit in [Gen. 9].'[66] However, it is unlikely that non-Israelite menstruants or foreigners with genital discharges were permitted to enter sacred precincts to offer sacrifice (this is explicitly disavowed in Ep. Jer. 29). Moreover, the narrative account of Naaman in 2 Kings 5 turns on removing *ṣāraʿat*-infection as a prelude to the worship of Yahweh, opening the possibility that Leviticus 12 – 15 might apply more universally.[67] Either way, the Old Testament avers that Gentiles could *become* ritually impure to at least some degree. The corollary is important to state: Gentiles are not ritually impure by default. Klawans is correct: 'it is an error to assume that

[60] Maccoby 1999: 199, noting that the flood generation, Sodom, and Nineveh earn divine censure, concludes that 'certain things are wrong even if the Land is not involved.'

[61] Regarding Rahab's temporary exclusion from the Israelite camp, see chapter 3.

[62] Schürer 1891: 2:54.

[63] Hayes 2002: 20-21.

[64] Hayes 2002: 37–39; contra Büchler 1928: 2; Klawans 1995: 290.

[65] Noted by Klawans 1995: 290 n. 26 despite his later conclusion, 'no biblical text considers Gentiles to be ritually impure' (291).

[66] Hayes 2002: 39.

[67] See chapter 3.

Jews in ancient times generally considered Gentiles to be ritually defiling, and it is even more of an error to assume that such a conception would have been an impediment to Jewish–Gentile interaction.'[68] For Jews and Gentiles alike, becoming morally or ritually impure was a real possibility. On the other hand, maintaining purity was also possible. Accordingly, the key concern in Second Temple literature regarding Gentile interactions is avoiding moral and religious impurity, not Gentiles per se.

Second Temple texts thus advocate measured distancing from non-Israelites. Third Maccabees 3:3–10 (first century BC) records separation with respect to worship and food, but it also describes Jewish involvement in 'community life' (3:5) in which Gentiles were regarded as 'neighbors and friends and business associates' (3:10). Similarly, Josephus promulgates an openness to cultivating 'friendship' with non-Jews, albeit premised on shared ethical standards ('those that would live after the same manner with us', *Ag. Ap.* 2.29 §§209–10). According to the Letter of Aristeas (150–100 BC), ritual purity laws serve to dissuade moral assimilation with Gentiles: 'to prevent our being perverted by contact with others or by mixing with bad influences, [God] hedged us in on all sides with strict observances connected with meat and drink and touch and hearing and sight' (142). Accordingly, 'Second Temple sources are unanimous in the opinion that the laws regulating and restricting Jewish–Gentile interaction are not based on a desire to avoid a ritual defilement communicated by impure Gentiles … On the contrary, the deleterious moral and religious effect of intimate contacts are cited as the basis for various laws that promote social *amixia*.'[69]

Maintaining purity in situations of intimate contact becomes more pressing in relation to Jew–Gentile marriage.[70] Hence, Second Temple texts frequently appeal to purity concerns to prohibit exogamous unions, although they do so according to differing rationales. Correctly distinguishing conceptions of Gentile impurity and their resulting social implications becomes crucial. As Hayes demonstrates, ritual purity is not the driving concern. Instead, in line with Old Testament prohibitions, Second Temple texts proscribe interethnic unions to preserve either

[68] Klawans 1995: 288.

[69] Hayes 2002: 49.

[70] Hayes 2002 provides the most comprehensive treatment to date. This section is indebted to her analysis.

moral (cf. Deut. 7:1–4) or genetic (cf. Ezra 9:1–2) purity.[71] The former rationale is the more prevalent. Constructing a moral-religious boundary between Jews and Gentiles established an impermanent line of separation; that is, a non-Jewish person could assimilate into the Jewish community if they turned from idolatry and immorality (cf. *Sifre Deut.* 213–14).[72] The dynamic nature of moral purity made intermarriage possible, premised upon repentance and conversion (e.g. *Ant.* 20.7.1 §§137–40). Other texts, however, labelled 'an extremist trend' by Cana Werman, categorically ban exogamous relations in order to preserve genealogical purity.[73] Hayes attributes this idea to Ezra 9:1–2 and charts its subsequent development in Jubilees and 4QMMT.[74] In these works, interracial marriage is classified as sexual sin.[75] Jubilees, for instance, defines exogamous unions as impure and an abomination on par with incest and bestiality.[76] Accordingly, offenders attract extreme, even capital, punishment (Jub. 30:7–15). Priestly requirements for endogamous marriage (Lev. 21:7, 14–15) provide a biblical basis for protecting genealogical purity. The democratization of these strictures, premised on Israel's status as a holy nation, meant even lay Israelites could profane or defile the holy seed through intermarriage and create a permanent impurity in their line of descent.[77] In these texts, 'Intermarriage with any Gentile – converted or unconverted – becomes an impossibility'.[78] In contrast to morality, equating purity with race forms an impermeable barrier between two different lines of 'seed' – one Jewish and the other Gentile.[79] Conversion, therefore, is impossible. At one level, these post-exilic developments can be understood as responses to the identity crisis provoked by diaspora communities. With Jewish people living outside the land, non-geographic social markers were required. Asserting that the people of Israel, wherever

[71] Hayes 2002: 68–70.

[72] Hayes 2002: 193.

[73] Werman 1997: 22.

[74] See Hayes 2002: 27–33, 73–89; also Milgrom 1993: 281–83; Werman 1997: 6–17.

[75] Hayes 2002: 194.

[76] Kugel 1996: 25; Werman 1997: 12–14.

[77] Milgrom 1993: 281; Hayes 2002: 69, 193.

[78] Hayes 2002: 68; also Lau 2009.

[79] Werman 1997: 14 n. 60 identifies the underlying logic: 'Gentiles constitute an entity basically different from Israel; while the former are under the influence of the defiling spirits who descended from the Watchers and human women (Jub. 11.5; 15.30–32), the latter are under the supervision and rule of God.'

located, were ontologically different to the rest of humanity provided one such boundary.[80]

The related issues of Gentile purity, conversion and intermarriage had a significant social impact in the Second Temple period and beyond:

> Diverse understandings of the nature of Jewish 'holiness-purity' as opposed to Gentile 'profaneness-impurity' led different groups to construct more or less permeable boundaries between Jews and Gentiles. Disagreements over group boundaries contributed significantly to Second Temple sectarianism and, ultimately, to the separation of Christianity and Judaism in the first few centuries of the common era.[81]

Whereas Jewish communities could claim a foundational genetic heritage, no matter how theologically or socially unorthodox they appeared to one another, this was not so for the emerging Christian sect. This increasingly Gentile community 'met *none* of the requirements of Jewish identity: neither the sufficient condition of genealogical filiation nor the condition of moral-religious conversion as signalled by circumcision and observance of Jewish law. By no definition, then, could such persons lay claim to Jewish identity.'[82]

Conclusion

Hayes aptly summarizes the findings of this chapter: 'There is a fundamental continuity between biblical texts and Second Temple Jewish writings in the details and dynamics of the various purity systems and the place of Gentiles within them.'[83] Continuity does not, however, mean exact correspondence. The value of this chapter's survey, therefore, is in elucidating the nuances. Old Testament purity legislation was appropriated by Second Temple communities in different ways and to different degrees; it was not considered fixed and unchanging. There is innovation as well as imitation. Some texts, such as those from Qumran, expand the

[80] Kugel 1996: 28.

[81] Hayes 2002: 196; also Furstenberg 2023.

[82] Hayes 2002: 198.

[83] Hayes 2002: 45.

sources and effects of ritual and moral impurity. Other writings reveal conflicting opinions regarding the purity status of Gentiles and the degree to which they could (or could not) be incorporated into Jewish corporate life. Some documents raise the possibility of washing away sin or cleansing the stain of moral impurity. Others look to God's Spirit to enact purification. Yet, despite the diversity, one thing is clear: defilement and cleansing remain essential. Although Second Temple communities understood the categories in dissimilar ways, the only thing no one did was ignore them.[84] '[T]he questions of who are the pure, from whom and what they should separate, and what sets of beliefs and practices are material to this status permeated intersectarian discourse, thereby defining both religious ideologies and group identities within the Second Temple period.'[85] Unsurprisingly, therefore, all the same concerns re-emerge in the New Testament.

[84] Cf. Neusner 1973: 33.

[85] Furstenberg 2023: viii.

7

Defilement and cleansing in the Gospels and Acts

The presentation of Jesus in the Gospels and Acts is dependent on the witness of the Old Testament. Israel's Scriptures and their articulation of the *Missio Dei* were appropriated to make sense of Jesus' life and ministry. There is a notable polemic at work. As James Sanders recognizes, 'The problem of the first century, and hence of the NT, was whether the NT was biblical.'[1] Validating apostolic witness to Christ explains why the New Testament is saturated with citations, allusions and echoes of Old Testament texts and structures.[2] The rhetorical aim is transparent: Jesus is the fulfilment of scriptural anticipation, not an unexpected or failed deviation. The complex web of Old Testament themes and motifs, including purity, centres on him. Careful exploration of the Gospels and Acts thus provides crucial data for constructing a biblical theology of defilement and cleansing.

However, the relationship between Jesus and Israel/Judaism's purity system is contested. Should Jesus be understood *within* first-century Judaism or set *against* it? Did he 'cut himself off from the community of Judaism',[3] or was Jesus a fully observant Jew?[4] Both options, and a range of mediating positions, have enjoyed their heyday. The various 'Quests' for the historical Jesus over the past two-and-a-half centuries illustrate

[1] Sanders 1976: 552. Likewise, Goldingay 2015: 172 'The question [the first-century faith community] had to handle was not whether the [OT] Scriptures fitted with Christian faith but whether Christian faith fitted with the [OT] Scriptures.'

[2] For exploration of connections and their function, see Hays 1993; 2015; Beale and Carson 2007; Henze and Lincicum 2023.

[3] Käsemann 1964: 37.

[4] As argued by Levine 2006: 17–52; Wassén 2016b: 31.

the vacillation within New Testament scholarship.[5] One hallmark of the Second Quest was its anti-Semitism. Reflecting wider trends in late nineteenth and early twentieth-century European academia, 'many scholars wanted to make Jesus look as little like a typical first-century Jew as they could.'[6] This trajectory reached its nadir in the construction of an Aryan Jesus stripped of even his Middle Eastern heritage.[7] The Third Quest, however, was more willing to situate Jesus in his Jewish milieu,[8] including reconsideration of his stance towards purity.[9] However, Wassén determines that many scholars continue to claim Jesus dismissed the Jewish purity system.[10] Thiessen pushes the point further:

> When it comes to the question of Jesus and the Jewish law, particularly aspects of it such as ritual purity, commentators through the centuries have almost universally misconstrued the Gospel writers' portrayals.[11]

While significant disagreement continues, the data surveyed in chapters 1 – 6 enable a more sensitive reading of the Gospels. Regarding what we can expect to derive from these accounts, John Meier draws a useful distinction between searching for the real Jesus (everything he was in actual life), the historical Jesus (what can be reconstructed using historical tools alone) and the canonical Jesus (that which can be discerned from the biblical texts).[12] The first category is unknowable (cf. John 21:25) and the second varies drastically depending on the criteria employed and one's underlying presuppositions. My approach best approximates Meier's third option: understanding the portrait of the canonical Jesus as revealed in the Scriptures. While, in my view, this canonical portrait faithfully preserves things Jesus did and said, heeding his literary depiction focuses attention on what the Gospel writers were concerned to highlight, with

---

[5] The Quests are charted, most recently, by Brown and Evans 2022; Blomberg 2023: 1–221.

[6] Blomberg 2023: 36.

[7] Bergen 1996: 155 concludes regarding 1930s Germany, 'German Christians resolved the problem posed for them by Jesus' ancestry in a straightforward way: they denied that he was Jewish.' See also Heschel 2008.

[8] Holmén 2001: 143; Blomberg 2023: 102.

[9] Blomberg 2023: 89 regards Fredriksen 1999 as the seminal work.

[10] Wassén 2016b: 12. Blomberg 2023: 333 agrees: 'For much of church history, it was taken as granted that Jesus abolished the laws of ritual purity.'

[11] Thiessen 2020: xii.

[12] Meier 1991: 1:21–55.

resulting implications for faith and practice.[13] Their combined testimony is crystal clear: Jesus is the purifier par excellence.

Mark

Many scholars believe Mark's Gospel addresses a (predominantly) Gentile audience.[14] Thus, whenever crucial to meaning, the author explains Jewish purity rites for a readership unfamiliar with the details (e.g. 7:2–4).[15] At other times, purity issues remain unexplained because the primary interest lies elsewhere (e.g. highlighting Jesus' *power to heal* the haemorrhaging woman in 5:25–34 based on her *faith*).[16] Nonetheless, defilement and cleansing influence Mark's portrait of Jesus in important ways. Some use this to set Jesus against Judaism.[17] Indeed, Craig Blomberg argues that Markan priority, a view not widely held throughout church history, supported a Protestant agenda to make Jesus less Jewish, thereby freeing Protestants from Jewish and Catholic concerns.[18] A more careful reading of purity motifs in Mark's Gospel, however, leads in a different direction.

Mark's 'good news about Jesus' (1:1) begins with John who 'came baptizing in the wilderness and preaching a baptism of repentance for the forgiveness of sins' (1:4 CSB; cf. Isa. 40:3). As I discuss more fully in relation to the Fourth Gospel, John's baptism would have been interpreted as ritual immersion. Yet, ablutions performed by John also foreshadow someone more powerful who would baptize with the Holy Spirit (1:7–8),[19] presumably to enact a more profound cleansing. In 1:10, the Holy Spirit descends on Jesus following immersion by John. The coincidence is not

[13] Hence, I engage historical reconstructions only whenever they become especially pertinent.

[14] E.g. Lane 1974: 12–17; Crossley 2004: 200; Kazen 2021: 246–49.

[15] Explanations are also provided for cultic matters (e.g. 7:11) and Aramaic transliterations (e.g. 5:41; 7:34; 15:34).

[16] See Haber 2008: 136; cf. Wassén 2016b: 26.

[17] E.g. Loader 2002: 62 'the Jesus of Mark no longer operates on the assumption that clean-unclean boundaries … have validity.' Similarly, Selvidge 1990; Borg 1998: 15; Chilton 2000: 89–90.

[18] Blomberg 2023: 8, 14, 16–17. The logic assumes Mark's Jesus stood against Judaism. Thus, the (presumed) earliest and most historically reliable Gospel reveals an anti-Judaic and anti-ritualistic Jesus.

[19] Matthew 3:11 adds 'and fire' (also Luke 3:16). While fire as judgment is foregrounded in Matt. 3:10–12, it is nevertheless connected to cleansing: 'he will clean out (*diakathariei*) his threshing floor' (3:12 my tr.). Removal of evil through divine judgment, recalling Isaiah, leaves a purified people (cf. France 2007: 115).

arbitrary: ritual purification is prerequisite for encountering the holy. Although Mark provides no comment regarding whether Jesus required purification, the Synoptic tradition is unanimous in connecting the Holy Spirit to Jesus at this juncture (cf. Matt. 3:16; Luke 3:21–22).

The presence of the Holy Spirit in Jesus accentuates his confrontation with a man possessed by an 'impure spirit' (*pneumati akathartō*) in 1:21–28 (par. Luke 4:31–37). 'Impure' rather than 'evil' (contra NIV84) is the Gospels' preferred adjective for describing malevolent spiritual beings.[20] As 'the Holy One of God', Jesus threatens *impure* spirits by his very presence.[21] This use of a divine epithet ('Holy One') evokes the characterization of Yahweh in the Prophets (esp. Isaiah) and heightens the dangerousness of the encounter. That threat extends to more than the impure spirit; the first-person plural pronoun, 'Have you come to destroy *us*?' (1:24), merges man and demon into a single endangered entity. Yet, Jesus banishes the impure spirit while simultaneously restoring the man (1:25–26).[22] Jesus' mission is redemptive. This recalls Zechariah's prophecy that when Yahweh cleansed the inhabitants of Jerusalem from sin and impurity he would also remove 'the spirit of impurity' (*rûaḥ haṭṭumʾâ*) from the land (Zech. 13:1–2). Exorcism, conceptualized as purging the land of impure spirits,[23] becomes a noted hallmark of Jesus' ministry (1:27–28, 32–34, 39; 3:11, 22–27; 5:2–20; 7:25–30; 9:17–29). It also encapsulates his disciples' core commission: 'Calling the Twelve to him, he … gave them authority over impure spirits' (6:7; cf. 3:14–15; 6:13). This explains the severity of Jesus' indictment against some teachers of the law who suppose he is possessed by Beelzebul (3:22), claiming, 'He has an impure spirit' (3:30; pars. Matt. 12:24–32; Luke 11:15–22). Labelling the spirit in Jesus 'impure' is not just a category error, it constitutes blasphemy against the *Holy* Spirit – a sin, Jesus says, that cannot be forgiven (3:29). Misconstruing purity categories can have eternal ramifications.

[20] Luke makes the connection explicit in 4:33 by adding *daimoniou* ('demon'). 'Evil spirit' occurs in Luke 7:21; 8:2; cf. Matt. 12:45; Luke 11:26; Acts 19:12–16. The biblical and extra-biblical background is explored in Colpe 2003: 316–26; Heiser 2015; Walton and Walton 2019; Thiessen 2020: 123–39.

[21] Contra Thiessen 2020: 141 'When the impure comes into contact with the holy, it is customary for the holy to withdraw.' For evaluation of this common (mis)conception of the holiness-impurity dynamic, see Harper 2022a.

[22] Thiessen 2020: 141–42; cf. France 2002: 229-30.

[23] Contra Paschen 1970: 36. This does not negate other entailments such as Jesus' *power* over the demonic (e.g. 3:22–27; Luke 11:21–22). On exorcism in Jewish eschatology, see Evans 2005.

In 1:40–45 (pars. Matt. 8:2–4; Luke 5:12–14) Jesus encounters another source of impurity: 'A *lepros* came to him' (1:40 my tr.).[24] The typical rendering 'leper' (e.g. ESV, NASB, KJV; cf. NIV: 'man with leprosy') is problematic. The prevalence of Hansen's Disease (i.e. leprosy) in the first century is debated.[25] Moreover, Greek had a technical term for the disease – *elephantiasis* – which is not used here.[26] 'Leper' also suggests the man's condition was life-threatening (or at least debilitating), thereby emphasizing deliverance from a critical condition (cf. CSB 'serious skin disease'). Instead, *lepros* indicates the man had the condition outlined in Leviticus 13 – 14 (i.e. *ṣāraʿat/lepra*). The disease was not dangerous, but it was defiling. This explains the man's appeal for purification, not healing (contra NLT): 'If you are willing, you are able to cleanse (*katharisai*) me' (1:40 my tr.). Jesus' response is striking. First, he *touched* the man, a surprising action considering the severe nature of the impurity (cf. Lev. 13:45–46), before declaring, 'I am willing. Be clean!' (1:41 my tr.).[27] Immediately, the *lepra* dissipated and 'he was cleansed' (*ekatharisthē*, 1:42). But even more unexpectedly, Jesus was 'indignant' (*orgistheis*) as he healed him. Although the textual variant *splanchnistheis* ('moved with compassion') is better attested,[28] 'indignant' or 'deeply angered' is preferable as the harder reading (with NIV).[29] Verse 43 only heightens Jesus' annoyance: 'and having scolded him, [Jesus] immediately cast him out' (*kai embrimēsamenos auto euthys exebalen auton*, my tr.).[30]

Why was Jesus so angry? Some suggest Jesus' ire was provoked either by the Jewish purity system and its exclusionary policies or by the concept

[24] The intervening episode (1:29–34; pars. Matt. 8:14–17; Luke 4:38–39) records Jesus curing Simon's mother-in-law of fever that, while not in itself defiling, signalled the encroachment of death. Matthew's quotation of Isa. 53:4 in this context ('He took up our infirmities and bore our diseases', 8:17) raises the possibility that Jesus bore people's impurities. Hence, Furstenberg 2023: 57 reasons Jesus 'was willing to defile himself to help the ill and impure.'

[25] For an overview, see Thiessen 2020: 43–49.

[26] E.g. Plutarch, *Moralia* 731A–B; Celsus, *On Medicine* 3.25.1.

[27] Although Blomberg 2023: 342 claims Jesus touched the man to demonstrate imperviousness to defilement, it is difficult to see how those present would perceive this. Opinion is divided regarding whether Jesus could (e.g. Trummer 1991: 85; Bird 2008: 16; Wassén 2016b: 26; Kaplan 2022: 88; Moffitt 2022: 114) or could not (e.g. Pagola 2009: 195; Smith 2018: 98–100; Thiessen 2020: 96; Scarlata 2021: 109) become ritually defiled. See also chapter 9.

[28] Cf. NASB, CSB, NLT. *Orgistheis* occurs only in D, three Old Latin manuscripts, and the Diatessaron.

[29] Also France 2002: 115. That neither Matthew nor Luke mention Jesus' anger or compassion further implies *orgistheis* is original (Thiessen 2020: 55–57).

[30] Casting the man out recalls Jesus 'casting out' (*ekballō*) impure spirits (1:34, 39).

of impurity itself.[31] However, these conclusions are undermined by Jesus addressing the source of defilement (rather than dismissing the problem as irrelevant), and, in 1:44, by commanding the man to enact the cleansing rituals prescribed by Leviticus 14:2–20 (presumably because ritual impurity is a real condition requiring removal).[32] Instead, Jesus' anger seems directed at the man's flippant attitude towards purity boundaries (cf. Lev. 13:45–46; Num. 5:2–3) and his initial question.[33] The *lepros* confidently declares, 'you are able to cleanse me' (*dynasai me katharisai*, 1:41), but questions Jesus' willingness ('If you are willing' [*ean thelēs*]). Irrespective of the man's reasons for doubt, Jesus' words ('Be clean!') and subsequent instruction to enact sacrificial cleansing (1:44) signal his upholding of ritual categories. Therefore, the episode does not indicate a reversal of defilement, with Jesus purifying the *lepros* by touch.[34] If that were the case, there would be no need for priestly purification rites. Instead, the passage reveals Jesus doing what Israel's priests could not: healing *ṣāraʿat*/*lepra*.[35] Jesus overcomes the *source* of impurity, preventing re-pollution.[36]

Mark 5 (pars. Matt. 8:28–34; 9:18–26; Luke 8:26–56) recounts Jesus' interactions with a demon-possessed man (Matt. 8:28: 'men'), a haemorrhaging woman and a dead girl. Ritual impurity is implicit throughout. Jesus and his disciples travel to the predominantly Gentile area east of Lake Galilee (5:1). There, in a region regarded by many Jews as defiled, a demoniac confronts Jesus (5:2).[37] The man comes 'out of the tombs' (*ek tōn mnēmeiōn*) in which he lived (5:2–3 my tr.).[38] Habitual contact with

[31] E.g. France 2002: 117–18.

[32] Thus, Jesus' command, 'Be clean!' (1:41), does not purify the man but rather stops recurrent pollution by healing the disease (1:42).

[33] Regarding the separation of the *lepra*-infected in the late Second Temple period, see Kazen 2021: 251–75. Proximity is compounded in Luke's account where 'a man full of *lepra*' appears 'in one of the towns' (5:12 my tr.).

[34] Contra Bird 2008: 24; Beck 2012: 30. The pericope is, therefore, problematic for what Fletcher-Louis 2007: 65 deems an 'emerging consensus' of those who advocate Jesus' contagious purity.

[35] This constitutes the 'testimony' of 1:44.

[36] A similar emphasis is conveyed by the designation 'Simon the *lepros*' (14:3; par. Matt. 26:6). Although Shinall 2018: 932 concludes Simon's *lepra* was current, Bradford's contention that the genitive epithet references Simon's *prior* condition is more likely given the concern for ritual purity elsewhere in the Gospels. Simon's moniker acknowledges the significance of healing for his ongoing identity (Bradford 2025: 88; cf. Nolland 2005: 1051).

[37] Regarding Israelite/Jewish conceptions of impure Gentile territories, see chapters 2 – 5.

[38] Luke is explicit: 'For a long time this man had not … lived in a house, but had lived in the tombs' (8:27).

graves and bone fragments rendered him impure according to Numbers 19:16. Moreover, his antisocial and violent behaviour (5:3b–4) would have made cleansing rites impossible, resulting in him being 'cut off' from God (cf. Num. 19:13, 20).[39] Instead, day and night, likely naked as he roamed among the tombs (cf. 5:15; Luke 8:27), he cut himself with stones (5:5; cf. Lev. 19:28). For the man was possessed by not just one 'impure spirit' (5:1), but by a legion of impure spirits (5:9). Resisting banishment, the demons plead to be dispatched into a herd of (impure) pigs (5:10–12; cf. Lev. 11:7). The swine, plunging into the lake, fill it with defiling carcasses (5:13; cf. Lev. 11:26). It would be difficult to construct a more comprehensive picture of ritual impurity and its implications than this man cut off from God and people and inhabited by the denizens of hell. Moreover, Mark does not indicate how the man became possessed; culpability is muted. Sin is not the only separator of persons from God. Yet, Jesus reverses the man's plight: demons are banished and the man is found 'sitting there, dressed and in his right mind' (5:15). A commission to tell of the Lord's mercy (5:19) means, in this case, to testify to Jesus' power over impurity and its sources, both natural and supernatural.

Back on the other side of the lake, Jesus' journey to Jairus's house to heal a dying daughter is interrupted by an unnamed woman (5:21–25). She, we are informed, had been bleeding for twelve years (5:25). Whether continuous or sporadically recurring, the abnormal nature of the discharge is indicated by the woman's repeated seeking of medical intervention (5:26). While Mark emphasizes healing and faith (5:34), not purification, the woman's condition nevertheless rendered her impure and contagious to others according to Leviticus 15:25–27.[40] She would therefore have been excluded from temple entry and participation in sacrifice (cf. Lev. 7:20–21; 12:4; 15:31; *J.W.* 5.5.6 §227; *Ant.* 3.11.3 §261; m. Kelim 1:6–8). Her desire for a different reality is poignantly indicated in 5:26: 'She had suffered a great deal under the care of many doctors and had spent all she had'. Desperation motivates her to seek Jesus (5:28). Willingness to be present in a crowd and to touch Jesus (5:24b, 27) need not indicate indifference to ritual impurity – the woman touches only his clothing and

[39] Num. 19:10 applies corpse-impurity to Israelites and Gentiles.

[40] The lexical correspondence with Leviticus is itemized by Kazen 2013a: 112 n. 2; Thiessen 2020: 83.

may not have been currently bleeding (although 5:29 implies otherwise).[41] Either way, the encounter draws forth power to heal (5:29–30; cf. 6:56), releasing her from suffering (5:29, 34) – primarily the woman's physical symptoms, but also temple exclusion. The delay, however, means Jesus does not arrive before Jairus's daughter expires (5:35). The house is already filled with mourners, now defiled by the presence of a corpse (5:38–39; cf. Num. 19:14). Nevertheless, Jesus, taking three disciples and the girl's parents, approaches the body (5:40), indicating that becoming ritually impure was not sinful.[42] Touching the girl's corpse by the hand, Jesus raises her to life (5:41–42). While Mark's focus lies elsewhere, all three episodes involve major impurity, beyond human power to prevent (5:3–4, 23, 26). Yet, Jesus overcomes each source as demons are exorcised, abnormal haemorrhaging is stopped, and a twelve-year-old daughter is restored to life.[43] In each instance, the protagonists model the appropriate response by falling at Jesus' feet (5:6, 22, 33).

The interaction between Jesus and religious leaders in Mark 7:1–23 (par. Matt. 15:1–20) has generated a massive body of literature. Important historical questions arise: How, when and why did handwashing emerge in Judaism?[44] Did the Pharisees embrace a quasi-priestly identity?[45] Is the phrase 'all the Jews' (7:3) a statement of fact regarding halakic practice or Markan hyperbole? Hermeneutical considerations include appropriation of Old Testament texts,[46] identifying the 'tradition of the elders' (7:3, 5; cf. 7:8, 9, 13) and clarifying the relationship between biblical and rabbinic purity legislation.[47] This is not the place to resolve these issues. More important is the supposition that 7:1–23 indicates (1) dismissal of the ritual purity system; (2) an overturning of Torah food prohibitions; and

---

[41] Whether a *zābâ* was able to wash her hands to prevent cross-contamination as per the *zāb* (Lev. 15:11) is debated. Haber 2008: 128 concludes she could; Kazen 2015a: 174–75 asserts the converse (cf. m. Kelim 1:4).

[42] Although Matt. 9:25 has Jesus enter alone, the account emphasizes physical contact with both woman and girl (9:18, 20, 21, 25). That Jairus petitions Jesus to touch his already dead girl (9:18) indicates that becoming ritually defiled was socially acceptable in certain circumstances. Matthew remains silent regarding the effect (if any) upon Jesus.

[43] There is here, perhaps, a hint that resurrection (*egeire*, ['Rise!'], 5:41) is an important mechanism for overcoming corpse-impurity.

[44] See Sanders 1990: 131–254; Crossley 2004: 183–205; Kazen 2013a: 124–27; 2015a: 175–87.

[45] Neusner 1973: 64–70 argues the affirmative. His view is strongly challenged by, among others, Sanders 1990: 173–76; Kazen 2015a: 178–81; Furstenberg 2023.

[46] These include Isa. 29:13 in 7:6–7; Exod. 20:12, 17 in 7:10; Lev. 11 and Deut. 14 in 7:19.

[47] See Klawans 2000; Furstenberg 2023.

(3) the prioritizing of ethics over ritual. Ultimately, all three issues are intertwined.

Tension arises when those gathered around Jesus 'saw some of his disciples eating food with hands that were defiled (*koinais*), that is, unwashed (*aniptois*)' (7:2). That handwashing provokes debate rather than Torah observance indicates that the food in question is permitted (as per Lev. 11; Deut. 14:3–21). This is telling: the disciples, and presumably Jesus, are portrayed as observing a kosher diet. However, Jesus' disciples were eating with unwashed hands. Even though ritual handwashing is rare in the Old Testament, the practice had become widespread by the first century.[48] Nevertheless, all parties in Mark 7 recognize the extra-canonical status of handwashing before meals: it is classified as 'tradition' (*paradosin*) by both the religious leaders (7:5) and Jesus (7:8). This evokes Jesus' exhortation to prioritize the 'commands of God' over 'human traditions' (7:8), illustrated by discussion of *qorban* (7:9–13).

Jesus then adjures the crowd: 'There is nothing outside of a person that, entering them, is able to defile (*koinōsai*) them, but the things coming out of a person are the things which defile (*ta koinounta*) the person' (7:15 my tr.).[49] When later asked by the disciples to explain this 'parable' (7:17), Jesus attends to both halves of 7:15 in order.

First, vv. 18–19 address things that enter a person. In context, 'things' primarily refers to kosher foodstuffs eaten with unwashed hands (cf. 7:1–5). Jesus declares that such items cannot defile a person; for, as he explains, they enter the stomach, not the heart, and are subsequently excreted (7:19). Verse 19 concludes with the enigmatic phrase, 'cleansing all the foods' (*katharizōn panta ta brōmata*, my tr.).[50] The antecedent of the masculine participle *katharizōn* ('cleansing') is left unspecified. Typically, Jesus is made the implied subject (e.g. NIV: 'Jesus declared all foods clean').[51] Although this rendering has often been understood as Jesus

---

[48] See Exod. 30:20–21; 40:30–31; Lev. 15:11. While washing implements is more commonly attested (e.g. Lev. 11:32), this removed known, rather than potential, defilement. Furstenberg 2008: 192–98 proposes that handwashing before meals was an innovation based on Greco-Roman practice.

[49] Matt. 15:11 adds 'mouth' to explicitly restrict the issue to handwashing (Crossley 2004: 200–2, 208). This offends the Pharisees (15:12) as it categorizes the false honour of their lips (15:8) as a (morally) defiling overflow of the heart (15:18).

[50] Because Matthew does not include the phrase, Kazen 2013a: 129 suspects he may be correcting misinterpretations of Mark 7:19c which advocated ignoring dietary laws.

[51] Likewise, CSB, ESV, NASB; France 2002: 291.

dismissing Torah food prohibitions wholesale,[52] several considerations mitigate against that reading.[53] First, as noted, the debate concerns permitted foods, not food in general.[54] Second, dietary laws are not 'human tradition', but they represent the 'commands of God' (cf. Lev. 11:1–2). It would be odd to have Jesus strenuously defend Torah obedience in 7:9 only then to undermine the practice in 7:18–19. Third, the disciples are later portrayed as observing kosher practice (e.g. Peter in Acts 10:14: 'I have never eaten anything impure or unclean') and prohibitions against consuming blood are reiterated for Gentile converts (Acts 15:20, 29; cf. Gen. 9:3–4; 17:10). Instead, taken as an editorial comment, but constrained by the limitations listed above, Mark understands Jesus as pronouncing the inability of defiled food to pollute persons; he is, in that sense 'cleansing all foods'. Both NA[28] and UBS[5], however, include 7:19c as part of Jesus' question and not as an editorial comment (see also KJV). Accordingly, Logan Williams proposes that *anthrōpos* ('person') in 7:18 is the more likely antecedent.[55] On this reading, even if defiled food is ingested, Jesus assumes a person's stomach acts as a purifying agent, 'cleansing all foods' through the digestive process.[56] Either way, the statement in 7:19c reinforces the central conclusion: handwashing is unnecessary.

Jesus, therefore, does not dismiss the reality of defilement, but instead, he clarifies direction. The threat is not external things entering a person (as per the Pharisees); rather, 'the things coming out of a person are the things which defile (*ta koinounta*)' (7:15 my tr.). This accords with Old Testament belief that *humans* are the source of impurity. Various bodily secretions ('things coming out') ritually defile (e.g. vaginal blood and semen). Other emissions ritually pollute without having entered a person (e.g. corpse-impurity and *ṣāraʿat*).[57] Thus, Jesus resists expanding the scope or direction of impurity beyond the teaching of Scripture (cf.

---

[52] E.g. Grindheim 2020: 62: 'Jesus dismissed the value of the Mosaic food laws'.

[53] See, similarly, Kazen 2013b: 182; Strahan 2024; Williams 2024.

[54] Crossley 2004: 192, 208 uses a similar conclusion to argue Mark was written before conflict arose over Christians not observing food laws.

[55] Williams 2024: 383.

[56] Williams 2024: 384–86 notes how this understanding aligns with widespread Jewish beliefs that excrement is pure. Thus, whatever the purity status of ingested food, it is purified en route through the stomach and emerges cleansed.

[57] Kazen 2013a: 134 suggests that corpse-impurity ('death ooze') and *ṣāraʿat* ('"leprosy-stuff" breaching the body envelope') could also be construed as 'things coming out'.

7:9–13).[58] Moreover, humans are also the source of moral impurity, a fact Jesus highlights in vv. 20–23. Several of the listed vices are explicitly said to defile in the Old Testament (sexual immorality, murder and adultery) or are linked with the language of 'abomination'.[59] The remainder echo the expansionist trend in Second Temple literature regarding sources of moral pollution. Thus, Jesus indicates that moral defilement as a category continues. Therefore, although 7:1–23 has sometimes been taken as indicating Jesus' dismissal of, or indifference towards, impurity, that is a misreading. Instead, Jesus assumes the legitimacy of both ritual and moral defilement. While moral impurity, stemming from 'evils' within (7:23), is more serious – an idea commensurate with Old Testament belief – that does not make ritual impurity a non-issue.[60]

The block of material immediately following 7:1–23 highlights Jesus' power to heal (7:24–37) and to provide (8:1–10). Yet, Mark emphasizes not only what happened, but where and to whom. Contact with Gentiles predominates as Jesus travels to Tyre (7:24[61]), Sidon and the Decapolis (7:31), and Dalmanutha (8:10). Again, Jesus expels an impure spirit – this time from a Syro-Phoenician girl (7:25–26, 29–30; par. Matt. 15:21–28). Between motherly plea and exorcism, however, lies a curt exchange initiated by Jesus: 'First let the children eat all they want … for it is not right to take the children's bread and toss it to the dogs' (7:27). The commonly utilized slur is derogatory; dogs were impure (Lev. 11:27).[62] Nevertheless, the woman responds, 'even the dogs under the table eat the children's crumbs' (7:28). While there is more to the exchange, the theme of eating so prominent in 7:1–23 reappears. In fact, making the woman's Gentile heritage explicit ('The woman was a Greek, born in Syrian Phoenicia', 7:26; Matt. 15:22: 'Canaanite') forces the issue regarding interpretation of 7:19c ('cleansing all the foods'). Are Jewish food prohibitions invalidated by Jesus? Intriguingly, the woman's response envisions the 'dogs' eating the *same* food as the 'children'. Similarly, in 8:1–9, Jesus miraculously

---

[58] The biblical concern is to prevent one's impurity from contaminating surroundings. The Pharisees reversed this dynamic to one of protecting their own (presumed) purity from external defilement (Furstenberg 2023: 74).

[59] Lev. 18:16 also lies behind John's censure of Herod's marriage in 6:17–18.

[60] Likewise, Kazen 2016: 136.

[61] Many early MSS have 'Tyre and Sidon' (see ESV; cf. Matt. 15:21).

[62] That Jesus repeats a common slur (cf. 2 Sam. 16:9; Ps. 22:17[16]; Phil. 3:2) does not indicate acceptance of Jewish exclusivism. If Jesus had an exclusionary agenda, why travel to Tyre in the first place?

feeds a Gentile crowd[63] by providing the *same* food – fish and bread (6:41; 8:6–7) – that he had in a Jewish setting (6:35–44). Although subtle, positioning Gentile eating scenes immediately after 7:1–23 further cautions against treating 7:19c as a sweeping verdict.

Purity may also subtly influence Jesus' response to the Sadducees regarding marriage at the resurrection. His statement, 'when they rise from the dead, they neither marry nor are given in marriage, but are like angels in heaven' (Mark 12:25 ESV; pars. Matt. 22:30; Luke 20:35–36), has been variously understood. However, in Second Temple literature, angels are frequently ascribed a priestly role in the heavenly sanctuary.[64] If becoming 'like angels in heaven' relates to function, rather than ontology, then heightened purity requirements explain the absence of marriage in the eschaton as well as Luke's addition, 'they can no longer die' (20:36).[65] Because death and sexual intercourse defile they are inappropriate for those serving in God's sanctuary (cf. 1 En. 15:7; b. Ber. 17a).[66]

Jesus' announcement in 1:15 is programmatic for Mark's Gospel: 'The time is fulfilled, and the kingdom of God has come near. Repent and believe in the good news!' (CSB). Yet, while the arrival of God's kingdom necessitates repentance, belief and forgiveness, purity is also required. This is conveyed, in part, by the prominence granted to defilement and cleansing in Mark 1 – 8. The full range of Old Testament ritual impurities is evoked: food (7:1–19), *ṣāra ʿat* (1:40–45), discharges (5:25–34), and death (1:29–34; 5:2–5, 21–24, 35–43).[67] Although often implicit, purity themes become Christologically significant as Jesus overcomes impurity's sources. Thus, Mark presents Jesus as the comprehensive means of preparing people for the arrival of God's kingdom in all its eschatological fullness.

The salvation wrought by Jesus ultimately centres on his death and resurrection. In Mark, as in the other Gospels, the cross looms large. Readers are primed to grasp the significance of this event through prior

[63] The implied setting is the Decapolis (7:31; note the change of scene in 8:10).

[64] The texts are surveyed in Klawans 2006: 111–44.

[65] Regarding humanity's priestly identity in biblical anthropology, including its forecasted replacement of angelic service, see Malone 2017; Klawans 2006; Moffitt 2022: 117–34.

[66] Explicit recall of the burning bush in 12:26 (cf. Exod. 3:6) further invokes the purity required by proximate holiness and the priestly commission of God's people (see also chapters 3 and 8).

[67] Impure demons (1:27–28, 32–34, 39; 3:11, 22–27; 5:6–13; 7:25–30; 9:17–29), moral defilement (6:17–18; 7:20–23), and perceptions of Gentile pollution (7:24–8:10) also feature.

narrative cues.[68] Jesus tells his disciples he will give his life as a 'ransom for many' (10:45). His will be a 'place-taking' death, one that Mark links with overcoming sin, death, the devil and God's wrath.[69] Moreover, Jesus' 'blood … poured out for many' (14:24), evokes not only covenant ratification (cf. Exod. 24; Jer. 31:31–34), and possibly the vicarious death of Isaiah's Servant (Isa. 53:12), but also sacrificial atonement.[70] This suggests Jesus' death secures both forgiveness and purification. Furthermore, by foregoing wine until the kingdom comes (14:25), Jesus indicates that his impending death will be the means of realizing Isaiah's vision of the messianic banquet (cf. Isa. 25:6–8),[71] implicitly evoking the purification of God's people anticipated on that day (see chapter 4). On the other hand, Gentile destruction of Jesus' body-as-temple (see 14:58; 15:29; cf. John 2:21) recalls the desecration of the Jerusalem sanctuary by Nebuchadnezzar (587 BC) and by Antiochus IV (169 BC) and makes the cross an act of sacrilege.[72] Matthew more fully develops the implications for Jesus' protagonists (see below). In all these ways, the cross is crucial. Nevertheless, to claim that Jesus' 'death was the last necessary event before the coming of the kingdom' downplays both the resurrection and the instrumental role of the Holy Spirit in purifying God's people,[73] a point developed in John's Gospel (see below).

Matthew

Throughout Matthew, Jesus' teaching frequently reveals shared purity assumptions.[74] He declares the 'pure in heart' (*katharoi tē kardia*) blessed because they will see God (5:8), revoicing the correlation between moral uprightness and proximity to Yahweh found in the Psalms.[75] Similarly, 7:6

[68] Consult Bolt 2004.

[69] Bolt 2004: 73–75, 105. Cole (2009: 67–84), similarly, connects Jesus' death to deliverance from sin, wrath, judgment, broken relationships, evil powers, and cosmic decay. Neither, however, links Jesus' death to purification.

[70] Evans 2001: 394; Bolt 2004: 105.

[71] Bolt 2004: 106.

[72] Bolt 2004: 101.

[73] Quoting Bolt 2004: 79. Bolt, however, later deems the resurrection also essential for kingdom inauguration (117, n. 4).

[74] This and the following sections examine passages not already discussed in relation to Mark.

[75] Similarly, 5:5 quotes Ps. 37:11 to connect righteousness with land possession (cf. Ps. 37:3, 22, 29, 34).

derives additional impetus from its juxtaposition of holiness and impurity: 'Do not give what is holy to dogs nor throw your pearls before pigs' (my tr.; cf. 24:28).[76] Later, in 12:43 (par. Luke 11:24–26), Jesus' comment that an impure spirit passes through waterless places when exorcised contrasts the frequent association of water with purity. Moreover, that a person 'swept clean' might become re-defiled by seven more evil spirits assumes purity is dynamic (12:44–45).[77]

Matthew, like Mark, also remembers cleansing as an integral dimension of Jesus' activity. A message sent to the imprisoned and doubting John testifies, '[T]he blind receive sight, the lame walk, those with *lepra* are cleansed (*leproi katharizontai*), the deaf hear, the dead are raised, and the good news is proclaimed to the poor' (11:5 NIV adapted; cf. 11:2–3). The list recalls Elisha's miracles, miracles that surpassed those of Elijah, just as Jesus would supersede John (understood as 'Elijah' in 11:14).[78] But Jesus also invites emulation as he grants his disciples authority to cast out 'impure spirits' (10:1) and commands them to 'Heal the sick! Raise the dead! Cleanse *leproi*! Cast out demons!' (10:8 my tr.). Vanquishing sources of defilement explicitly becomes a task for Jesus' followers. By healing, raising, cleansing and exorcising, the disciples further Jesus' purifying work as they proclaim the coming kingdom (10:7). The prospect of God's immanent arrival makes purity essential.

Matthew's most sustained use of purity terms appears in Jesus' pronouncements against the teachers of the law and Pharisees (23:1–39). The leaders' rejection of the kingdom of heaven (23:13) correlates with their myopia regarding impurity. They strain out gnats, Jesus says, but swallow a camel (23:24; cf. Lev. 11:4, 20). Moreover, they 'clean the outside of the cup and dish, but inside they are full of greed and self-indulgence' (23:25). These sayings indicate Jesus (and his audience) distinguished between ritually pure and impure animals and vessels.[79] Notably, Jesus does not dismiss straining out gnats or cleansing cups and dishes (cf. 23:23 'without neglecting the former'); rather, he excoriates his addressees for

[76] 'Their feet' (7:6b) also evokes the primary physical trait used to distinguish impure quadrupeds (Lev. 11:7, 26–27). Cf. the portrayal of religious leaders as (impure) snakes (3:7; 23:33).

[77] Cf. France 2007: 494. That impure spirits are considered evil (*ponēros*, 12:45) indicates demonic impurity is moral rather than ritual.

[78] The fulfilment of Elisha's 'double portion' (2 Kgs 2:9) is conveyed narratively by ascribing fourteen miracles to him compared to Elijah's seven.

[79] Wassén 2016b: 31; Bockmuehl 2000: 10.

ignoring the more important moral purity God also requires. This ought to be of primary importance (23:26).[80] The following woe escalates the rhetoric as Jesus paints the leaders as 'whitewashed tombs' (23:27). Their external façade may be spotless, but 'within they are filled with the bones of the dead and all impurity' (23:27 my tr.). The jibe would lose its force if Jesus and his protagonists did not share the belief that corpse-impurity is a major pollution. However, as in the previous woe, ritual impurity is utilized to expose moral bankruptcy: 'on the outside you appear to people as righteous but on the inside you are full of hypocrisy and wickedness' (23:28). Jesus makes the leaders' ritual fastidiousness a lesson concerning ethical matters they should not have neglected (cf. 23:23).

The final woe reaches a crescendo as Jesus evokes the moral pollution of bloodshed. He draws a direct line between those who murdered prophets and Judea's contemporary religious leadership (23:30–31). Genetic similarity is evidenced by shared traits: the prophets Jesus sends will similarly be killed, crucified, flogged and pursued (23:34). Therefore, Jesus declares, 'upon you will come all the righteous blood that has been shed on earth, from the blood of righteous Abel to the blood of Zechariah son of Berekiah, whom you murdered between the temple and the altar' (23:35). Consequently, Jerusalem's 'house' will become desolate (23:37–38) – most likely a reference to the temple, which 23:39 implies will be abandoned by God (cf. 27:51).[81] David Moffitt observes that *haima dikaion* ('righteous blood') used in conjunction with *ekcheō* ('to shed, pour out', 23:35) also occurs in LXX Lamentations 4:13.[82] There, shedding of 'righteous blood' by the religious establishment is singled out as the reason for Babylonian destruction of Jerusalem.[83] Tellingly, allusion to Lamentations 4:13 is immediately followed by Jesus pronouncing Jerusalem's imminent demise (24:2). This focus on 'righteous blood' is recalled in Matthew 27 as Pilate's wife urges him to have nothing to do with 'that righteous man' (27:19 ESV), as the crowd declares, 'his blood be on us' (27:25), and as Pilate

[80] The causal relationship between inner and outer cleansing aligns with the portrait of the Holy Spirit's transformative work in the Fourth Gospel to enact purification in both physical (ritual) and spiritual (moral) spheres (see below).

[81] Jesus subsequently embodies divine departure in 24:1 (Howell 1990: 153), thus re-enacting the departure of Yahweh's glory from temple to the Mount of Olives in Ezek. 11:23 (cf. Matt. 24:3).

[82] Moffitt 2022: 211. Elsewhere, the collocation occurs only in Joel 4:19.

[83] Moffitt 2022: 212.

claims, 'I am innocent of the blood of this man' (27:24 my tr.).[84] Moffitt concludes,

> allusions to Lamentations function as scriptural warrant for interpreting certain historical events theologically and polemically – namely, for understanding Jesus's crucifixion as the act of righteous bloodshed par excellence that directly results in the destruction of Jerusalem and the temple.[85]

While Moffitt rightly notes the judgment occasioned by shedding Jesus' blood, he does not tease out the purity implications. Yet, as the Old Testament maintains, shedding innocent blood defiles the land. Thus, while punishment is apropos, purification is also required. However, according to Numbers 35:33, only shedding the blood of wrongdoers atones defiled land.[86] Thus, while the destruction of the temple and the religious establishment is conceived as divine judgment, it also achieves purificatory ends.

John

Although purity is not a major theme in the Fourth Gospel it remains important. As in the Synoptics, John the Immerser is significant in Jesus' early career.[87] As those immersed by John were Jews, washing does not indicate conversion to Judaism.[88] Rather, Old Testament and Second Temple practices, coupled with the ubiquity of *miqwāʾôt* (ritual baths) in first-century Israel,[89] meant submersion in water would have been imme-

[84] Moffitt 2022: 214–15. Similarly, Judas confesses betrayal of 'innocent blood' (*haima athōon*) before hanging himself (27:4–8). The returned 'blood money' (*timē haimatos*) was used to buy a burial plot that became known as 'Field of Blood' (*agros haimatos*) (cf. Acts 1:18–19).

[85] Moffitt 2022: 226.

[86] Cf. discussion of Josephus in chapter 6.

[87] John's spoken testimony is crucial (1:6–7, 15, 19–36), indicating he did not view baptism alone as sufficient to remove sin (Harrington 2011: 129). Michaels 2010: 110 correlates John's moniker, 'lamb of God' (1:29), with purity: 'the One who purifies the world is himself pure'.

[88] The occurrence of proselyte baptism in the first century is debated. Compare Keener 2003: 1:444–47 with Webb 1991: 122–30; Harrington 2011: 123 n. 15; Kazen 2021: 17.

[89] For the archaeological evidence, see Zissu and Amit 2008; Zangenberg 2013; Miller 2015; DiFransico 2016: 161–69. *Miqwāʾôt* were not a feature of diaspora communities (Kazen 2021: 284 n. 26).

diately perceived as a purification rite.[90] This is corroborated in 3:23–26 where, in the context of John and Jesus baptizing, a debate arose 'concerning purification' (*peri katharismou*, 3:25 my tr.). Marianne Thompson therefore concludes that John was providing ritual cleansing for Israel, a practice commensurate with purity norms governing human–divine encounter.[91] The importance of such procedures lies behind the Pharisees' question in 1:25, 'Why then do you baptize if you are not the Messiah, nor Elijah, nor the Prophet?' Unperturbed, John contrasts his washing ('I baptize with water', 1:26) with the greater immersion enacted by 'one who will baptize with the Holy Spirit' (1:33). The correlation between immersions, albeit asymmetric, suggests baptism with/in (*en*) the Holy Spirit in the Fourth Gospel is conceptualized as an act of cleansing.[92] The purificatory dimension of John's baptism also serves Christological ends. As ritual cleansing was preparatory for divine revelation in the Old Testament, so 'Israel must be ritually pure to be able to perceive who Jesus is.'[93] This sharpens questions regarding Jesus' identity: who is this mortal who requires ritual purification ahead of his arrival?[94]

Cleansing resurfaces in connection with the first of Jesus' 'signs' (2:1–11). In the socially humiliating situation of wedding guests sans refreshment, Jesus' mother comments, 'They have no more wine' (2:3), before instructing the servants, 'Do whatever he tells you' (2:5). The narrator continues, 'Now six stone water jars had been set there for Jewish purification' (2:6 CSB). In a laconic account, which does not even narrate the actual miracle, the details of 2:6 stand out.[95] 'Stone water jars' (*lithinai hydriai*) used for 'purification' (*katharismon*) make sense considering Leviticus 11; unlike clay vessels, which had to be broken when defiled (Lev. 11:33–35; cf. Num. 31:22–23), stone was considered impervious to ritual

---

[90] So also Chilton 1997; Taylor 1997; Harrington 2011; Blomberg 2023: 340–41; Furstenberg 2023: 53; Rogan 2023: 43. For a qualified position, see Regev 2016.

[91] Thompson 2017.

[92] Similarly, Harrington 2011: 119 'for many Jews in the late Second Temple era, purification in water preceded and anticipated the work of the Spirit to generate life, provide atonement, bring divine revelation, and usher in the eschaton.'

[93] Rogan 2023: 29. Rogan locates the conceptual background in Old Testament (and Second Temple) instances of washing ahead of theophanic revelation (33–59). Thus, ritual purification positively prepares one to receive from God what comes from God (43).

[94] Rogan 2023: 49.

[95] Blomberg 2023: 237. 2:9 simply mentions the water that had already been turned into wine in a subordinate clause.

impurity.[96] The significant volume of water (and wine!), approximately 450 to 690 litres, demonstrates ritual purification was taken seriously by at least some in first-century Israel, even when geographically distant from the temple.[97] The 'sign' serves the author's point that, as John testified (1:26–34), something greater had arrived in Jesus. Thus, water formerly required for ritual purification could now become wine – hinting at both a new and better source of cleansing instigated by Jesus and the resultant joy it should elicit, with all its rich Old Testament resonances (e.g. Isa. 25:6–8; Jer. 31:11–13; Joel 3:18; Ps. 104:15). Although the Cana incident has been read as evidence of Jesus' stance against Jewish purification,[98] the author's point is more subtle. Jesus does not dismiss ritual cleansing, but rather *transforms* it into something greater.[99]

The so-called temple cleansing episode, which follows in 2:12–25, has provoked considerable debate, especially regarding whether this is the same event narrated in the Synoptics (Matt. 21:12–16; Mark 11:15–17; Luke 19:45–46) or a second, prior, occasion.[100] Either way, there are subtle purity implications in play. Although some regard 2:21 as dismissal of the temple due to its replacement by Jesus and/or the church,[101] Boris Paschke correctly observes that zeal to expel animals and traders alike (2:16–17) instead reveals Jesus' *high* view of the earthly sanctuary as sacred space.[102] Thus, while a rubric of judgment fits the Synoptic portrayal of temple-clearing at the end of Jesus' ministry, the episode's early appearance in the Fourth Gospel accentuates (hoped-for) restoration.[103]

Jesus' concern to preserve holiness affects his stance towards ritual purity. Verse 13 records him travelling to Jerusalem because 'the Passover of the Jews was near' (*engys ēn to pascha tōn Ioudaiōn*, my tr.). While festal pilgrimage was expected of all Jewish men (cf. Deut. 16:16),[104] arrival in Jerusalem *ahead* of Passover ('was near') had become common practice

[96] Although Kazen 2021: 286 n. 29 concedes this is an inference from silence.

[97] See Poirier 2003; Kazen 2021: 277–302.

[98] E.g. Barrett 1955: 160; Brown 2003: 305 (also n. 11).

[99] Jobes 2021: 60; Thompson 2001: 217–20; Blomberg 2023: 239, 57. The contrast is between good wine and best wine (Rogan 2023: 56).

[100] For evaluation, see Morris 1995: 166–69; Carson 1991: 177–78.

[101] E.g. Lightfoot 2015: 123; Talbert 1992: 92–93.

[102] Paschke 2018: 283–84.

[103] Cf. Klawans 2006: 213–45.

[104] This expectation did not thereby exclude women (cf. Mary's pilgrimage habits in Luke 2:41), but rather freed them from *obligation* to attend (cf. 1 Sam. 1:21–22).

to facilitate purification (cf. Num. 9:6–14). Josephus and Philo record pilgrims arriving about a week beforehand for the necessary rites (*J.W.* 6.5.3 §290; *Spec.* 1.261).[105] John 11:55 makes the logic explicit: 'The Passover of the Jews was near (*engys*), and many went up to Jerusalem from the countryside, before Passover (*pro tou pascha*), to purify themselves (*hagnisōsin heautous*)' (my tr.). Intriguingly, 11:56 notes that these early-bird Passover attendees kept looking for Jesus, indicating that he was well known for attending purification rites preceding a festival. Thus, while the author stops short of saying that Jesus also purified himself during such times, Blomberg concludes, 'Here is one of the clearest indications that Jesus still practiced the purity laws.'[106] Pre-Passover purification potentially also influences the following episode. In 12:1–8, six days before Passover, Jesus arrives in Bethany. There, while reclining at dinner, Mary pours a bottle of 'pure nard' (*nardou pistikēs*) over him (12:2–3). Jesus links Mary's act to his immanent burial (12:7). Both the timing (approximately one week before Passover) and the evocation of corpse-impurity suggest the anointing could be understood as a quasi-purification rite (perhaps, in this climactic instance, substituting for the more normal purification procedures ahead of eating Passover).[107]

Themes of water and spirit reappear in Jesus' interactions with Nicodemus and a woman from Samira. Both dialogues are cryptic. Nicodemus's confusion over being born 'again'/'from above' (*anōthen*, 3:3–4) is clarified by Jesus as being born 'of water and spirit' (*ex hydatos kai pneumatos*, 3:5 my tr.). The phrase is best understood as alluding to Ezekiel 36:25–27.[108] Thus, new birth equates to the cleansing and renewal hoped for in the Prophets.[109] Jesus declares that such Spirit-effected purification is the entry point to the kingdom (3:5; cf. 1:33).[110] The narrative in

[105] See also Sanders 1992: 132–35; Kazen 2015a: 167; Blomberg 2023: 288 n. 90.

[106] Blomberg 2023: 288 (emphasis removed). Similarly, Fredriksen 1999: 200–7 argues we should assume the historical Jesus performed purificatory processes.

[107] So Blomberg 2023: 294–95. The passage becomes ironic considering Numbers' portrayal of Israelites unable to celebrate Passover due to corpse-impurity (9:6–11).

[108] See Belleville 1980 and Carson 1991: 191–96 who provide extended consideration of the possibilities. A primary background in Ezek. 36:25–27 is also preferred by Köstenberger 2007: 434; Blomberg 2023: 245–46.

[109] Carson 1991: 195. Rogan 2023: 88–89 suggests new birth results from the purifying ablutions of John (water) and Jesus (spirit).

[110] I am indebted to Blomberg 2023: 246 for highlighting the importance of 3:5. That the 'children of God' are born 'not of blood … but of God' (1:12–13 ESV) may imply that new birth avoids all association with childbirth impurity (cf. Lev. 12).

John 4 likewise exploits *double entendre*. Responding to bemusement that he would ask a Samaritan woman for a drink (4:9), Jesus claims his prerogative to dispense the 'gift of God', that is, 'living water' (4:10). 'Living water' (*hydōr zōn*) is a Semitic idiom for 'running' or 'fresh' water. Here, however, the phrase takes on additional meaning. Whoever drinks the 'living water' Jesus distributes will not thirst again (4:14a). 'Indeed', Jesus says, 'the water I give them will become in them a spring of water welling up to eternal life' (4:14b; cf. Jer. 2:13; 17:13). The language evokes purification. Springs were resistant to defilement (Lev. 11:36). Moreover, 'living water' was essential for cleansing major ritual impurity (Lev. 14:5–6, 50–52; 15:13; Num. 19:17). Thus, an internal spring of 'living water', gifted by Jesus, hints at continuous cleansing. Such cleansing becomes a prerequisite for worshipping the Father in spirit and truth (4:23–24), no longer constrained by the parameters and procedures of sacred locales (4:21).[111] As in John 2, purity concerns are not summarily dismissed. Rather, they are transposed by Jesus who regards himself the purveyor of a more extensive, permanent, cleansing.

'Living water' appears again in 7:38 in the context of the Feast of Tabernacles, a seven-day event concluded by a special assembly on day eight (cf. Lev. 23:33–43; Num. 29:12–39; m. Sukkah 5:6). Each day, water was carried from the Pool of Siloam, a public *miqweh* south of the sanctuary, to the temple where it was poured out at the base of the altar (m. Sukkah 4:1, 9–10).[112] Although not prescribed in the Old Testament, these water rites drew on the well-established trope of water/living water symbolizing eschatological cleansing and restoration (e.g. Isa. 12:3; 44:2–3; Ezek. 36:25–26; 47:1–11; Joel 3:18; Zech. 13:1; 14:8; Neh. 9:20). This entire matrix of scriptural expectations became associated with Tabernacles – and was deliberately evoked by Jesus.[113] On the last, climactic, day of the feast, having taught 'in the temple courts' throughout the week (7:28; cf. 7:14),[114] Jesus declares, 'Let anyone who is thirsty come to me and drink. Whoever believes in me, as Scripture has said, rivers of living water

[111] M. Nid. 4:1, perhaps reflecting first-century beliefs, regards Samaritan women as being menstruants from birth and, hence, ritually impure. Moreover, the woman's moral status in John 4 is, at minimum, ambiguous (4:16–18). In context, therefore, 'living water' conceivably has potential for both ritual and moral purification.

[112] Blomberg 2023: 273.

[113] Köstenberger 2007: 454. See also Carson 1991: 325–28.

[114] The 'greatest day' (7:37) could be either the seventh (Burge 2000: 227) or eighth (Carson 1991: 321).

(*potamoi … hydatos zōntos*) will flow from within them' (7:37–38). From a later vantagepoint, the narrator surmises: 'By this he meant the Spirit' (7:39). The variegated Old Testament background evokes not just water generally, but *lustral* waters.[115] Accordingly, the 'living water' of the Holy Spirit, continually welling up in God's people like a spring or fountain, enables continuous purification, fulfilling prophetic anticipation of the day Yahweh would save his people from their impurities (esp. Ezek. 36:25–29). Ultimately, purification makes God's people fit to receive the *Holy* Spirit and so usher in the new age (cf. 7:39; 20:22).[116]

The dawning of a new era is further indicated by Jesus' declaration to be 'the resurrection and the life' (11:25). His power to reverse death (11:25), displayed in calling Lazarus forth from the grave (11:43–44), simultaneously overcomes corpse-impurity, the most virulent form of ritual defilement. Lazarus is not only raised by Jesus, he is purified. The resurrection age announced (11:23–26) and inaugurated by Jesus' own resurrection (20:13–18) anticipates the permanent end of death and its defilement. '[R]esurrection to eternal life with a transformed body is the ultimate in making a person pure again.'[117] In this way, the Fourth Gospel makes Jesus the central pivot between death/impurity and life/purity.[118]

While purity themes are less prominent in 12 – 21, they are still present. In 13:3–11, as Passover began,[119] Jesus washes his disciples' feet. Attempts to bathe Peter's feet, however, provoke a strong negative reaction: 'you shall never wash my feet' (13:8). Jesus' retort, that the unwashed have no part with him, elicits a corresponding request to wash feet, hands and head (13:9). Peter's desire to be washed entire, however, is met with Jesus' assertion: 'The one who has bathed does not need to wash, except for his feet, but is completely clean. And you are clean, but not every one of you' (13:10 ESV). Footwashing was primarily pragmatic:

---

[115] See discussion of the key passages in chapters 3 – 5.

[116] Jesus' self-identification as 'temple' (*naos*) in 2:19–21 follows the Holy Spirit's descent (1:32–33) after the purification of his baptism (cf. 1:31).

[117] Blomberg 2023: 325.

[118] Corpse-impurity lies behind several other episodes. Desire to avoid defilement in 18:28 may be due to the unresolved corpse-impurity of a Gentile building associated with torture and execution. There is also concern to remove corpses before the Sabbath (19:31), presumably to prevent land pollution (cf. Deut. 21:23). In 19:38–42, Joseph and Nicodemus expose themselves to defilement by preparing Jesus' body for burial. Nonetheless, this intentional pollution is portrayed as virtuous. Avoiding contamination may also explain the 'other' disciple's reticence to enter Jesus' tomb although arriving before Peter (20:4–5).

[119] For identifying the 'evening meal' (13:2) as Passover, see Blomberg 2023: 297–98.

the removal of dust and animal faeces before entering a house. It was a dirty task, reserved for the lowest ranked servants. Jesus therefore models the upside-down values of God's kingdom in which the greater serves the lesser (13:13–14). Yet, the pericope extends beyond hygiene. The terms for washing (*niptō*, 13:5, 6, 8[2x], 10, 12, 14[2x]) and cleanness (*katharos*, 13:10[2x], 11) are commonly associated with ritual bathing.[120] Moreover, reference to 'one who has bathed' (*ho leloumenos*) may recall immersion by John (or Jesus) along with its ritual overtones (cf. 1:26, 33; 3:22–23). But the statement that not all the disciples were 'clean' (*katharoi*, 13:10b) – referencing Judas's planned betrayal (13:2, 11) and theft (12:6) – expands purity to the moral sphere. Rogan concludes, 'Those who do not receive God's purifying work in Jesus will be unable to perceive and enter the life of God that Jesus mediates.'[121]

Cleansing also appears in 15:2–3. Conceptualizing the Father as vine-dresser, Jesus says, 'Every branch in me that does not produce fruit he removes (*airei*), and every [branch] that does produce fruit he cleanses (*kathairei*) so that it produces more fruit' (15:2 my tr.). Root play between *airei* and *kathairei* emphasizes the contrast between branches that are 'cut off' and those that are 'cut back' (lit. 'cleansed'; NIV 'prunes').[122] In addition to the role of the Spirit in cleansing God's people (see above), Jesus adds the agency of his word: 'You are already clean (*katharoi*) because of the word I have spoken to you' (15:3). As in 13:3–11, *katharos* signals moral purity. Hearing and acting upon Jesus' word cleanses (cf. 14:15, 21; 15:10, 14) – perhaps insofar as it prohibits deeds that generate moral defilement.[123] Cleansing also connects to the emphasis on the Spirit in 14 – 16. The Spirit who already 'lives *with* you', Jesus says, soon 'will be *in* you' (14:17, emphasis mine). The shift in pronoun is important. Blomberg reasons that if the Holy Spirit comes to dwell in believers, that can only help increase their holiness.[124] While true, there is a more fundamental logic: the Holy Spirit living in believers requires their prior purification. Thus, the Spirit becomes both the agent of, and reason for, purifying God's people.

---

[120] Blomberg 2023: 299.

[121] Rogan 2023: 151.

[122] Cf. Blomberg 2023: 309.

[123] The collocation of Jesus making people pure and commanding love (13:1–38; 15:1–17) leads Rogan 2023: 108 to infer that moral purification achieves both moral quality and moral capacity.

[124] Blomberg 2023: 311.

Defilement and cleansing are important in the Fourth Gospel. Blomberg, following David deSilva, asserts the author remaps purity along ethical lines, as indicated by a relative shift in emphasis from ritual cleansing to spiritual sanctification in 12 – 21.[125] However, moral (ethical) purity is a consistent concern throughout the Old Testament, indeed, the primary concern considering the lack of purification procedures and more dire consequences.[126] Thus, 'remap' claims too much. Instead, rather than dismissing ritual impurity or making it only symbolic of spiritual realities,[127] the author highlights the role of Jesus and the Spirit as agents of cleansing with respect to *both* ritual and moral defilement. The Fourth Gospel envisions the total and permanent cleansing of God's people, fulfilling Old Testament expectation. Wai-Yee Ng's verdict is more nuanced: it is a case of 'anticipation and fulfillment rather than renouncement and replacement.'[128]

Luke-Acts

Luke-Acts provides further insight into how Jesus and the early church engaged with purity.[129] In John's birth narrative, the angel who tells Zechariah that Elizabeth would bear him a son insists, 'he must not drink wine or strong drink, and he will be filled with the Holy Spirit, even from his mother's womb' (Luke 1:15 ESV). Prohibiting 'wine and strong drink' (*oinon kai sikera*) recalls Numbers 6:3 (cf. Judg. 13:4, 7, 14), leading some to conceptualize John as a Nazarite.[130] Nazarite vows enabled 'a man or woman' (Num. 6:2) to attain quasi-priestly holiness, with corresponding purity implications. However, John was from a *priestly* family (Luke 1:5) and it is not clear that priests ever took Nazarite vows. Leviticus 10:9 is perhaps a more likely background: 'Drink no wine or strong drink (*oinon*

[125] Blomberg 2023: 291–332, 366; cf. deSilva 2013: 147. Thus, for Blomberg, ritual washing merely symbolizes spiritual realities (302), meaning, in time, ritual impurity would become 'moot' (304).

[126] Contra Arnold 2010: 387 who supposes the New Testament replaces outward cleansing with a concern for inward purity.

[127] This would, of course, raise questions about the need for addressing ritual impurity at all, esp. considering the pervasive focus on ethical matters in both Testaments.

[128] Ng 2001: 69.

[129] Regardless of whether 'Luke-Acts' or 'Luke and Acts' is preferable, the books are clearly meant to be read in conjunction.

[130] E.g. Leaney 1958: 41; Fitzmyer 1981: 326.

kai sikera) … when you go into the tent of meeting, lest you die' (ESV).[131] If this is the intended backdrop, then the parallel suggests a correlation between priests approaching Yahweh's tabernacle presence (Lev. 10:9) and John being filled with the Holy Spirit (Luke 1:15). Continual exposure to God's indwelling Holy Spirit ('filled … from his mother's womb') would require commensurate carefulness (cf. Luke 7:33; Lev. 10:1–2; Eph. 5:18).[132]

Purity considerations are also raised as John and Jesus are circumcised and named on the eighth day (Luke 1:59; 2:21; cf. Lev. 12:3). That Elizabeth's relatives come to her for the ceremony (1:58–59) indicates both her ongoing impurity (cf. Lev. 12:2–4) and that being ritually impure did not always necessitate social exclusion. Mary, likewise, is portrayed as impure following birth. Accordingly, she and Joseph travel to the temple to perform the stipulated sacrifices, 'when the days of their purification according to the law of Moses were finished' (Luke 2:22 CSB; cf. 2:24; Lev. 12:4, 6). Intriguingly, Luke's language is plural: 'their purification' (*tou katharismou autōn*).[133] Darrell Bock argues that *autōn* ('their') refers to Mary and Joseph, with Joseph's impurity stemming from aiding with the birth.[134] However, secondary defilement in this case would last only one day and, more importantly, did not require sacrifice (Lev. 12:2; cf. 15:19). Moreover, Jesus' delivery was at least forty days prior (cf. Lev. 12:2–4; Luke 2:22). Another option is that 'their' refers to Mary and Jesus. Although only mothers became impure following birth, the communicable nature of impurity invariably affected the child. Read this way, 2:22 assumes that Jesus' incarnation rendered him susceptible to ritual impurity.[135] Either option remains tentative.

In his public ministry, Jesus' interactions with various forms of impurity align with Mark and Matthew.[136] Jesus' physical contact with the

[131] Although Bock 1994: 85, following Marshall 1978b: 57, asserts 1 Sam. 1:11 is the 'strongest OT parallel to the wording', that passage utilizes *methysma*, not *sikera*, for 'strong drink'.

[132] Priestly abstinence (Lev. 10:9), demanded immediately after the deaths of Nadab and Abihu (Lev. 10:1–2), inspired rabbinic conclusions that drunken (mis)behaviour led to their demise. Ephesians 5:18 is conceptually similar: the debauched acts that drunkenness emboldens are contrasted with being Spirit filled.

[133] Although textual variants are attested – *autēs* ('her'; 76 Vg; cf. KJV) and *autou* ('his'; D 2174*) – *autōn* ('their') is the more difficult reading and enjoys the best external evidence. See, further, Marshall 1978b: 116; Bock 1994: 235.

[134] Bock 1994: 236–37.

[135] If this option is preferred, then a question arises regarding when Jesus' susceptibility to impurity ceased. The most likely possibilities are (1) his baptism and filling with the Holy Spirit; (2) his resurrection; or (3) his ascension.

[136] Jesus encounters people with *lepra* (5:12–16; 7:22; 17:11–19; cf. 4:27), genital discharges

impure is frequently emphasized (5:13; 6:18–19; 7:14, 39; 8:44–47, 54). On approach to Nain, and moved by compassion, Jesus touches the passing funeral bier of a widow's only son (7:11–13). The pallbearers stop still, perhaps surprised at the intentional defilement (7:14a). Nevertheless, Jesus commands the dead man to rise, overcoming the source of impurity (7:14b–15). Other interactions proceed without contact. In 17:11–19 ten men with *lepra* approach Jesus. As stipulated in Leviticus 13:45–46, they maintain their distance while pleading for pity (17:12–13). Jesus instructs the men to show themselves to the priests (cf. Lev. 14:2–3), as he did with the man in 5:14. En route, 'they were cleansed' (*ekatharisthēsan*, 17:14). Verse 15, however, clarifies that Jesus enabled their *healing*. While this prevented further defilement (cf. 17:17), the passage distinguishes between ability to cure *lepra* (Jesus) and enacting ritual purification for having had *lepra* (the priests).

Purity themes also feature in Jesus' teaching. Ritual defilement is important in the so-called 'Parable of the Good Samaritan' (Luke 10:25–37). In the parable, a man, assailed while going down from Jerusalem to Jericho, is left naked and half dead (10:30). Spying his body, a priest and a Levite pass by 'on the other side' (10:31–32). The likely motivation is avoiding corpse-impurity. However, Luke records that the priest was 'going down' the road – that is, *away from* Jerusalem (10:31) – and, 'likewise', the Levite (10:32). Thus, the potentially laudable motivation of protecting temple sancta from defilement is undermined. Instead, the parable exposes a lack of compassion either in not assisting a person close to death or ensuring proper burial (contrast the Samaritan in 10:33–34). Jesus tells the story to extol loving one's neighbour above any (potential) risk of becoming ritually impure (10:27, 36–37; cf. Lev. 19:18). Doing so is commensurate with loving God (10:27; Deut. 6:5).

The six woes pronounced by Jesus against the Pharisees in 11:37–54 overlap with Matthew 23:1–39, albeit with differences. The Lucan setting is a meal at which the host, a Pharisee, is surprised that Jesus did not wash before eating (11:37–38). As discussed above, handwashing had become increasingly widespread in the late Second Temple period. Yet, for Jesus not to wash constituted a break with tradition, not Scripture (cf. Matt. 15:1–2; Mark 7:1–5). As in Matthew, Jesus proceeds to use

(8:43–48), and impure spirits (4:31–37; 6:18; 8:26–39; 9:37–43; 11:14–15, 24–26), as well as dead bodies (7:11–15, 22; 8:49–56).

accepted ritual categories to expose moral vices. The Pharisees clean the outside of the cup, but they are full of greed and wickedness (11:39); they are like unmarked graves, which people walk over without knowing (11:44), thereby making others impure (cf. Num. 19:16). Moreover, the teachers of the law and their generation would 'be held responsible for the blood of all the prophets that has been shed since the beginning of the world' (11:50). Again, Jesus does not dismiss ritual purity (cf. 11:42), but emphasizes the indispensability of inner, moral purity: 'Did not the one who made the outside make the inside also?' (11:40). Instead, Jesus says, 'give as alms those things that are within, and behold, everything is clean (*kathara*) for you' (11:41).

The book of Acts, as part two of an 'orderly account' (Luke 1:3; cf. Acts 1:1), establishes a strong continuity between Jesus' earthly deeds and his continuing activity as risen Lord, through his disciples, by the power of the Spirit.[137] That ministry is echoed in the banishment of impure spirits and diseases (5:15–16; 8:7). Moreover, Jesus' positive stance towards purity is reflected in nascent Christian practice. When Tabitha (Dorcas), a disciple in Joppa, dies, her body is washed before being placed in an upstairs room (9:36–37; cf. m. Šabb 23:5). While the subsequent summoning of Peter and his command that Tabitha rise (9:38–40) recall Jesus and Jairus's daughter (Luke 8:49–56), Peter notably touches the woman's body only *after* she is made alive (contrast Jesus touching the girl beforehand in Luke 8:54).[138]

Other episodes provide glimpses of the ongoing importance of temple purification rites. In 18:18, Paul 'had his hair cut off at Cenchreae because of a vow he had taken.' The combination of vow-making and shaving indicates Paul was most likely concluding a period of Nazarite separation (cf. Num. 6:5, 18). The statement is terse, however; nothing is said about making the prescribed sacrifices (cf. Num. 6:14–15).[139] A similar episode in 21:17–30 is more explicit. The scene turns on concern that Jerusalemite Jews would hear Paul had returned to the city (21:22). Knowing he had a reputation (deserved or otherwise) for dismissing Moses (21:21), the elders entreat him to join four men who were concluding their time as

---

[137] The author regards his 'former book' (i.e. Luke) as detailing what Jesus *began* to do and teach (Acts 1:1). See, further, Thompson 2011.

[138] Although this may serve to highlight the efficacy of prayer over innate power (Bock 2007: 378).

[139] M. Naz. 3:6; 5:4 permits haircutting before making sacrifice (Bock 2007: 585–86).

Nazarites.[140] They suggest a public display of conformity: 'purify yourself (*hagnisthēti*) along with them and pay their expenses, so that they may shave their heads. Thus all will know that ... you yourself also live in observance of the law' (21:24 ESV). Paul assents. 'The next day Paul took the men and purified himself along with them (*syn autois hagnistheis*). Then he went to the temple to give notice of the date when the days of purification (*tōn hēmerōn tou hagnismou*) would end and the offering (*hē prosphora*) would be made for each of them' (21:26). Paul – and the other believers with him – reveal no qualms about performing purification rites, including making sacrifice at the temple.[141] Indeed, reflecting on this event before Felix, Paul refutes an accusation of temple desecration by challenging his prosecutors to prove any violation (24:6, 11–13; cf. 21:28). Instead, Paul insists he came to Jerusalem to 'present offerings' and was already ritually purified (*hēgnismenon*) when found in the temple precincts (24:17–18). Thus, the presentation of Paul's innocence in Acts includes him upholding purity conventions with respect to the temple and its sacrificial processes (cf. 1 Cor. 9:20–21).[142]

Purity motifs are vital in two other key episodes; namely, Peter's vision in 10:1 – 11:18 and the Jerusalem Council in 15:1–35. Both directly address the pressing question of Gentile inclusion in a predominantly Jewish church.

In 10:11–13, Peter sees a vision of a sheet containing all manner of animals and hears a command to kill and eat. The creatures, which include species prohibited by Leviticus (cf. Acts 11:6), provoke an expected response: 'Certainly not, Lord, because I have never eaten anything common (*koinon*) and impure (*akatharton*)' (10:14 my tr.; cf. 11:8; Ezek. 4:14).[143] Despite Peter defending his unswerving commitment to a kosher diet, the voice continues, 'What God has cleansed (*ekatharisen*), you must

[140] Note the same combination of vow-making and shaving (21:23–24) coupled with a seven-day process (21:27) aimed to ameliorate corpse-impurity following overseas travel (cf. Furstenberg 2023: 29).

[141] While Blomberg 2023: 368 views Paul's participation as 'steps taken backward' in wrestling with purity, Peterson 2009: 588 is closer in observing that reiteration of the Jerusalem Council's verdict (21:25) functions to distinguish Jewish-Christian and Gentile-Christian obligations.

[142] This observation must qualify conclusions that Luke-Acts regards the temple as dismissed or superseded.

[143] *Koinon* and *akatharton* are often read as synonyms. Furstenberg 2023: 211 n. 25, however, suggests *koinon* may distinguish what has been made impure by something else from that which is innately impure. Either way, the verse is another indicator that the disciples did not understand Jesus to have dismissed dietary restrictions.

not declare common (*mē koinou*)' (10:15 my tr.; cf. 11:9). While often understood as overturning Leviticus 11, the meaning of the vision instead lies elsewhere, as Peter realizes after some initial perplexity: 'God has shown me to call no person common (*koinon*) or impure (*akatharton*)' (10:28 my tr.; cf. 10:17).[144] The vision addresses the purity of *people*, not animals.[145] This is the arena in which 'making no distinction' applies (11:12 ESV; cf. 15:9). As Peter summarizes, 'I now realise how true it is that God does not show favouritism but accepts from every nation the one who fears him and does what is right' (10:34–35). The lesson is this: Gentiles are not, by nature, ritually impure. Moreover, they can avoid moral impurity by fearing God and doing what is right.[146] Thus, if God acts to cleanse Gentiles, they must not be considered common or impure (cf. 10:15). God's intent is conclusively demonstrated when the Holy Spirit comes upon Cornelius and companions (stated three times in 10:44–47), indicating that non-Jews could also become fit dwellings (cf. 11:16–17). Later, in 15:8–9, Peter reiterates this connection between God giving the Holy Spirit to Gentiles and cleansing their hearts by faith (*tē pistei katharisas tas kardias autōn*).

In Acts 15, the Jerusalem Council advises Gentiles 'to keep away from food sacrificed to idols and blood and strangled things and sexual immorality' (15:29 my tr.; cf. 15:20; 21:25). Many read the prohibitions against a Greco-Roman background as banning participation in pagan temple worship.[147] However, the list strongly resonates with Old Testament purity concerns.[148] Indeed, the same vices occur in Leviticus 17 – 18 in the same order: idol food (17:3–4a, 5, 7), blood (17:4b, 10–12), undrained (i.e. strangled) animals (17:15; cf. 17:13–14) and sexual immorality (18:6–30). Such things defile, ritually and morally (17:15; 18:24–30), and would make Yahweh set his face against the culprit (17:10), resulting in them

[144] The extent of, and basis for, Jew-Gentile separation in 10:28 is debated (see Bock 2007: 393–94). Klawans 1995: 301 notes that Peter regards contact as 'unlawful', not defiling. Second Temple texts reveal a spectrum of responses to the question (see chapter 6).

[145] Peter does not eat any of the animals (even within the vision) and presumably continues his kosher diet. Cf. my discussion of Rom. 14 in chapter 8.

[146] This does not obviate the need for faith (10:43; 11:17), forgiveness (10:43), repentance (11:18), or divine agency (10:45; 11:17–18).

[147] Seminally, Witherington 1998; followed by Bock 2007: 505–6; Thompson 2011: 182–87. Butova 2018 reaches a similar conclusion, but based on a natural law reading of Gen. 1 – 3.

[148] Barrett 1998: 735–36 notes that while early MSS combined ritual and moral demands, later traditions revised the requirements in an ethical direction. Butova 2018: 1–39 attributes this change to anti-Jewish polemics in the first to fourth centuries AD.

being cut off (17:4, 9, 10, 14; 18:29) or even vomited from the land (18:25, 28). In Leviticus, these prohibitions explicitly apply to Israelites *and non-Israelites* alike (esp. 17:8, 10, 13, 15; 18:3, 24, 26, 27). Furthermore, if 'blood' includes its extended meaning of 'bloodshed' (as in Lev. 17:4b), then Acts 15:29 highlights those sins – idolatry, bloodshed and sexual immorality – that defile not only people (whether Jew or Gentile), but also land.[149] The universal applicability and severe consequences of these evils in the Old Testament make good sense of the Council's resolutions. Avoiding impurity remains an ongoing concern for God's multi-ethnic people.[150]

Conclusion

The Gospels and Acts provide crucial insights for constructing a biblical theology of defilement and cleansing. Karl Barth summarizes their testimony:

> The Word did not simply become any 'flesh,' … It became Jewish flesh. … The pronouncements of New Testament Christology … relate always to a man who is seen to be not a man in general, a neutral man, but the conclusion and sum of the history of God with the people of Israel, the One who fulfills the covenant made by God with his people.[151]

Despite claims to the contrary, the canonical Jesus fits within his first-century milieu. The forms and effects of impurity found in the Old Testament, and reiterated in Second Temple literature, continue, and are taken seriously by Jesus – a trend that extends into the early Christian period. At the same time, Jesus is portrayed as having unique ability to overcome sources of defilement, whether *lepra*, discharges, death or the demonic. This reiterates not only the reality of impurity and the barrier it presents to communion with God, but also God's commitment to remove

[149] The problem of blood(shed) occurs elsewhere in Acts. The egregious nature of killing the author of life is remembered in 3:13–15. This provokes a response from the religious leaders in 5:28: 'you … are determined to make us guilty of this man's blood.' Twice, Paul declares he is 'clean' (*katharos*) from blood, that is, 'innocent' (18:6; 20:26).

[150] This paragraph summarizes Harper 2024.

[151] Barth 1985: 166.

every hindrance. That commitment comes into sharpest focus in the cross of Christ, which becomes the central mechanism for preparing people for the immanent fullness of God's kingdom. Jesus' place-taking death secures the final victory over the devil and impure spirits; it opens the door to resurrection and freedom from death; it deals with divine wrath; and, conceptualized as sacrificial atonement, it expiates sin and purges defilement.[152]

Yet purification in the Gospels remains triune. A rich collocation of motifs – water, life, cleansing – emphasizes the agency of the Holy Spirit as an all-sufficient and inexhaustible source of purification, fulfilling the hopes of Israel's prophets. The themes of defilement and cleansing thus underline the importance of holistic purification ahead of God's dawning kingdom and the end of the age. As William Witt and Joel Scandrett state, 'The fallen human situation requires transformation from within. What is needed is not enlightenment and pardon alone but re-creation and transformation, an undoing of evil itself.'[153] Absolution is necessary, but so too is purification, new birth and resurrection. The Jesus who says, 'your sins are forgiven' (Mark 2:5), also declares, 'I am willing … Be clean!' (Mark 1:41). Thus, defilement and cleansing accentuate aspects of Jesus' ministry that sometimes go unnoticed. Blomberg is correct: purity in the Gospels is a topic to which we should have devoted more attention.[154]

[152] See my discussion of atonement in Leviticus (chapter 1).

[153] Witt and Scandrett 2022: 224. See also deSilva 2014.

[154] Blomberg 2023: 378. Likewise, Fredriksen 2021: 2 remarks: 'The quarrels with "Pharisees," "scribes," and others that the gospels narrate concern *how*, not *whether*, to construe purity. If the issue itself – ritual purity – were not important to all of the narrative contestants *and to their evangelical authors*, we would not be reading about these encounters at all.'

8
Defilement and cleansing in the epistles

The New Testament epistles are occasional documents, written to distinct audiences and situations. This does not rule out applicability to other recipients (Col. 4:16; Rev. 3:22) or undermine theological utility (2 Pet. 3:15–16), but it does urge caution. These letters are not treatises, let alone systematized theologies. Coverage of topics is ad hoc, partial and rhetorically geared for specific contexts. Gaps abound. Nevertheless, the textual data provide glimpses, however incomplete, of the authors' respective belief systems. These bear the unmistakable imprint of both the Old Testament Scriptures and the variegated Judaisms of the late Second Temple period. Hence, because purity constitutes such an important dimension of that cultural heritage, defilement and cleansing appear throughout the epistles, albeit in sporadic fashion.

In these documents, defilement and cleansing are appropriated primarily for Christological, sacerdotal and eschatological ends. These topics, vital to New Testament theology, are illuminated to the degree that readers appreciate the underlying purity concerns. God's purity and holiness, as well as that of his coming kingdom, are repeated refrains. Consequently, avoiding defilement informs social and ethical boundaries and drives exhortation for transformation.

Nevertheless, determining the epistles' stance towards Judaism is contested. The degree to which variant purity beliefs in Second Temple communities are reflected in these texts is also an open question. The biblical and extra-biblical issues are complex; scholarly dialogue is correspondingly fractious.[1] My own approach is to assume continuity until otherwise demonstrated. That decision is not simply arbitrary or

[1] See, e.g., Borgen and Giversen 1997; Klawans 2000: 136–57; Tomson 2001; Nanos and Zetterholm 2015; Culpepper and Anderson 2017; deSilva 2022.

pragmatic. The latent bias towards reading the New Testament through an early Christian lens instead of (or in conjunction with) a first-century Jewish one has been deservedly criticized – along with the evolutionary assumptions that often undergird such approaches.[2] Instead, the evident high regard for Israel's Scriptures, coupled with the Jewish heritage of most New Testament authors, suggests perceived dissimilarity should be carefully weighed against what is often substantial similarity. 'Intramural debate' may be the best heuristic label. Furthermore, the literary positioning of Acts is crucial as it influences readers' perceptions of Paul and other key figures before encountering the letters they penned.[3] In Acts, John respects temple practices (3:1); Peter observes a kosher diet (10:14); James advises Gentile avoidance of land-defiling moral evils (15:29); and cultic fidelity vindicates Paul against rumours that he dismissed Torah (21:20–26).

The Pauline epistles

Purity and community identity

Paul's conception of the Christian community-as-temple grounds his use of purity concepts for identity formation and ethical instruction. As Micheal Newton concludes, '[m]uch of Paul's use of purity terminology centres upon his view that the believers constitute the temple of God and as such enjoy the presence of God in their midst.'[4] Although the metaphor is not unique to Paul, he utilizes it in distinctive ways.[5] In Ephesians 2, Christ not only makes once-excluded Gentiles 'fellow citizens' and 'members of God's household' (2:19; cf. 2:11–12), he builds Jews and Gentiles together into a 'holy temple … in which God lives by his Spirit' (2:21–22; cf. Rom. 8:9, 11). The corporate implications focus on ending Jew–Gentile tensions within the Ephesian community (2:14–16) by establishing a shared holy status (2:21), which provides equal access to God (2:18). A similar impetus lies behind 1 Corinthians 3:16–17: 'Don't you know that you yourselves are God's temple and that God's Spirit

[2] E.g. Klawans 2006; Bird 2008; Thiessen 2023.

[3] Thiessen 2023: 28.

[4] Newton 1985: 52. Newton's analysis has influenced the arrangement of the following sections.

[5] See chapter 6. See also Gärtner 1965; Newton 1985.

dwells in your midst? If anyone destroys God's temple, God will destroy that person; for God's temple is sacred, and you together are that temple.' While destroying God's temple refers in the first instance to the factions undermining Corinthian unity (e.g. 1 Cor. 1:10–13; 3:2–4; 6:1–8), the image also invokes the desecration and eventual razing of Solomon's temple as a direct consequence of unrestrained sin and resultant defilement – a dynamic I return to when considering Paul's ethical exhortations.

The base metaphor of community-as-temple allows multiple extensions. Paul's consistent description of believers as *naos* (the inner sanctum) rather than *hieros* (the entire temple complex) substantially increases purity expectations.[6] Fittingly, Paul appropriates cultic terms to describe his ministry. Romans 15:16 recalls his commission 'to be a minister of Christ Jesus to the Gentiles, serving as a priest of God's good news … that the offering of the Gentiles may be acceptable, sanctified by the Holy Spirit' (HCSB). Paul's priestly vocation also includes self-offering. Twice, he terms himself a 'drink offering' – complementing the Philippians' sacrifice and service (Phil. 2:17), and to summarize his life's ministry (2 Tim. 4:6). Furthermore, Paul acknowledges his right to draw wages from the work of the gospel on analogy to priests who share in offerings made at the altar (1 Cor. 9:13–14). In Weiss's striking turn of phrase, Paul is 'Priest of the Christian cult-community'.[7]

Paul's self-conception as priest and sacrifice extends to his addressees. The Gentiles are a sacrifice Paul offers to God (Rom. 15:16).[8] Philippian monetary gifts are 'a fragrant offering, an acceptable sacrifice, pleasing to God' (Phil. 4:18). Moreover, cultic purity terms – *amemptos* ('blameless'), *akepaios* ('unmixed') and *amōmos* ('unblemished') – describe the believer's entire life in Christ (Phil. 2:15).[9] Similarly, Roman readers are urged to present their bodies as living sacrifices, holy and pleasing to God (12:1), demanding the ongoing purity of offerers-as-offerings (cf. Lev. 22:3–9; 19–20; 26:31).[10] Priestly analogy may also influence Paul's explanation for why believers should not divorce unbelieving spouses:

[6] See 1 Cor. 3:16–17; 6:19; 2 Cor. 6:16; Eph. 2:21; Newton 1985: 54.

[7] 'Priester der christlichen Kultgemeinde' (Weiss 1954: 355).

[8] Cf. Moo 1996: 890.

[9] Newton 1985: 84-86.

[10] The reverse is amply illustrated in prophetic decrial of offerings made while simultaneously rebelling against God (see chapter 4).

> For the unbelieving husband is made holy (*hēgiastai*) because of his wife, and the unbelieving wife is made holy (*hēgiastai*) because of her husband. Otherwise your children would be unclean (*akatharta*), but as it is, they are holy (*hagia*).
> (1 Cor. 7:14 ESV)

The argument and language are unusual for Paul.[11] Holiness in 7:14 denotes a status, not an ethical evaluation (the unbeliever is not vicariously made righteous through their spouse). Leviticus 21:10–15 provides a possible conceptual background. The passage stipulates that the high priest, sanctified by anointing, must protect his holiness by marrying a virgin, undefiled by sex, 'so that he will not profane his offspring among his people' (my tr.). At stake in 7:14, then, is Paul's understanding that 'Holy bodies, individual or corporate, must be protected from unions with impure bodies' (cf. 5:9–13; 6:12–20; 2 Cor. 6:14–7:1).[12] Sexual intercourse, which makes parties 'one flesh' (1 Cor. 6:16), is especially problematic. However, for mixed-faith marriages Paul prioritizes preservation over separation wherever possible (7:12–13, 15). Any children are deemed holy (by virtue of the believing spouse), not impure (by virtue of the non-believing spouse). Thus, sex with a person outside the Christian community is not inherently defiling. Sexual immorality, however, always defiles, whether with insiders (1 Cor. 5:1) or outsiders (1 Cor. 6:15). First Corinthians 7:14 thus constitutes an important exception regarding pre-existing marriages with unbelievers.[13]

Purity and community membership

Entry to a community conceptualized as temple and priesthood has two basic requirements according to Old Testament precedent: purification and consecration. In several passages, therefore, Paul interweaves both processes to conceptualize what God accomplished through Jesus.[14] First Corinthians 6:9–10 lists ten (representative) evils that bar practitioners from inheriting the kingdom of God. Yet, although these behaviours

---

[11] Fee 1987: 299. Interpretations are correspondingly legion; the main options are outlined by Adewuya 2011: 139 n. 45.

[12] Hayes 2002: 97. Hayes coins the phrase 'carnal impurity' to categorize Paul's logic (96).

[13] Hayes 2002: 94.

[14] Paul also employs other salvific conceptions, including justification (Rom. 3:24), redemption (Tit. 2:14), reconciliation (Eph. 2:16), and adoption (Gal. 4:5).

once categorized the Corinthians, 6:11 states, 'But you were washed, you were sanctified, you were justified in the name of the Lord Jesus Christ and by the Spirit of our God'. Separation from God is overcome by a trinitarian work of salvation that renders the formerly wicked pure ('washed'), holy ('sanctified') and righteous ('justified').[15] These are not synonymous outcomes; rather, they mark distinct, albeit related, salvific benefits.[16] Likewise, in Ephesians, Paul declares that the blood of Christ brings people near to God (2:13). He later expands on how proximity is enabled. As Saviour (5:23), Christ gave himself for the church 'to make it holy, cleansing (*katharisas*) it by the washing (*loutrō*) of water by the word' (5:26 my tr.). Christ's purpose was to present the church to himself without 'stain or wrinkle', 'holy and unblemished' (5:27 my tr.). Accordingly, in addition to redeeming from wickedness, Titus 2:14 concludes that Jesus acted 'to purify (*katharisē*) for himself a people'. Purification is linked to regeneration: 'He saved us through the washing (*loutrou*) of rebirth and renewal by the Holy Spirit' (3:5).[17] Similarly, in Romans 6, baptism into Christ Jesus (v. 3) marks the transition to a new life (v. 4), which means believers are henceforth dead to sin (v. 11). With this constellation of overlapping images, Paul extends Christ's salvific work to encompass the purification and consecration achieved through the agency of word and Spirit.[18] Indeed, making people holy is deemed God's purpose in election (Eph. 1:4; Col. 3:12; 2 Tim. 1:9). Hence, *hagiois* ('saints' or 'holy ones') becomes a foundational epithet for God's people throughout Paul's letters as he appropriates a rich Old Testament terminological heritage (e.g., LXX Exod. 22:30; Num. 16:5; Isa. 62:12; Dan. 7:27).[19] While *hagiois* incorporates ethical quality, holiness defines a broader suitedness for God's realm.[20] Thus, God's work in Christ to purify and

[15] While Paul's argument in Rom. 3:21–26 primarily focuses on justification, the use of *hilastērion* ('sacrifice of atonement') in 3:25 evokes the frequent use of the root in LXX Leviticus (49x) in connection with removing both sin and impurity.

[16] 1 Cor. 6:11 also echoes the typical order of Old Testament sacrifice in its movement from purification offering, to ascension offering, to fellowship offering (e.g. Lev. 9:22).

[17] *Loutron* ('washing') occurs only here and in Eph. 5:26.

[18] Cf. John 15:3, 'You are already clean because of the word I have spoken to you.'

[19] See Rom. 1:7; 8:27; 12:13; 15:25, 26, 31; 16:2, 15; 1 Cor. 1:2; 6:1, 2; 14:33; 16:1, 15; 2 Cor. 1:1; 8:4; 9:1, 12; 13:12; Eph. 1:1, 15, 18; 2:19; 3:8, 18; 4:12; 5:3; 6:18; Phil. 1:1; 4:21, 22; Col. 1:2, 4, 12, 26; 3:12; 1 Thess. 3:13; 2 Thess. 1:10; 1 Tim. 5:10; Phlm. 5, 7.

[20] Despite an initial claim by Porter 1993: 397 that Paul's use of holiness terminology is decidedly non-cultic, he nevertheless proceeds to note multiple 'cultic overtones' throughout the corpus. See also my discussion of holiness in chapter 2.

consecrate enables access to his presence that now indwells the *naos* of the believing community.

Purity and community ethics

Because God presently dwells with his people, anticipating eschatological fullness (cf. 1 Cor. 13:12), the purity of Christian communities becomes paramount. This explains the copious admonitions throughout Paul's letters to reject sources of impurity and embrace that which is pure. Second Timothy 2:20–21 contrasts gold and silver vessels with those made of wood and clay. When defiled, the former materials could be cleansed (Num. 31:22–23); the latter, understood as being more susceptible, were typically destroyed (Lev. 11:33).[21] Thus, Paul enjoins Timothy: 'if anyone purifies himself (*ekkatharē heauton*) from these, he will be a vessel for honour, made holy (*hēgiasmenon*), and useful to the master, prepared for every good work' (my tr.; cf. Rom. 9:21–24). The following verses indicate that purification is accomplished by fleeing evil and pursuing the righteousness, faith, love and peace that proceed from a 'pure heart' (*katharas kardias*, 2:22). First Timothy 1:5 similarly understands love to flow from a 'pure heart'.[22] That good deeds proceed from pure hearts (cf. Ps. 24:4) demonstrates Paul's understanding that Jesus' purificatory work effects a fundamental realignment that awakens a moral capacity that is expressed in changed behaviour.[23] This connection is made explicit in the Titus 2 passage examined above. Those whom Jesus purifies become 'eager to do what is good' (2:14; cf. Rom. 6:1–4). This reiterates the tenor of Titus 1:15:

> To the pure (*katharois*), all things are pure (*kathara*), but to the defiled (*memiammenois*) and unbelieving, nothing is pure (*katharon*); but both their minds and their consciences are defiled (*memiantai*). (ESV)

[21] Cf. Paul's 'jars of clay' metaphor in 2 Cor. 4:7 (cf. Gen. 2:7; 3:19; Jer. 18:1–10) – susceptible to impurity but nevertheless containing great treasure. For Paul, physical limitation is temporary. In the next chapter he anticipates mortality being swallowed up by life (5:4b); that is, the transformation of earthly physicality into heavenly physicality (5:1–4a), so that believers might reside with the Lord (5:6–8) – an outcome guaranteed by the already indwelling Spirit (5:5).

[22] Similarly, in John 13:1–38; 15:1–17 Jesus makes his disciples pure before commanding them to love one another (cf. Rogan 2023: 108).

[23] Compare my discussion of the Fourth Gospel (chapter 7).

The running contrast between righteous and unrighteous behaviours in 1:5–14 indicates that moral purity is in view. Hence, to the *morally* pure, all things are pure. William Mounce renders the second clause, 'all things are (ritually) pure'.[24] However, the depiction of the morally defiled and unbelieving, for whom nothing is pure, acting in denial of God and thereby becoming 'detestable' (*bdelyktoi*, 1:16), suggests 'all things are pure' is better understood as including moral behaviours. This does not imply purity of life is automatic. Paul prays that the Philippian church might properly discern what is best so they might be 'pure (*eilikrineis*) and blameless for the day of Christ' (1:9–10),[25] setting their minds on 'whatever is pure' (*hosa hagna*, 4:8). Similarly, Timothy is urged to set an example for the believers in speech, life, love, faith and purity (*en hagneia*, 1 Tim. 4:12; cf. 5:2, 22; Tit. 2:5) and 'to keep the commandment unstained (*aspilon*) ... until the appearing of our Lord Jesus Christ' (6:14 ESV).

Maintaining purity also means removing sources of defilement. Accordingly, Paul confronts a sexually immoral relationship between a man and his father's wife (1 Cor. 5:1–13). The act is not only proscribed by Leviticus 18:8 (which Paul deems applicable to a predominantly Gentile community living outside the borders of Israel),[26] it also generates moral impurity that, left unaddressed, will permeate 'the whole batch of dough' (5:6).[27] Paul therefore orders: 'Cleanse out (*ekkatharate*) the old leaven' (5:7); 'Purge the evil person from among you' (5:13 ESV).[28] Excommunication (5:2, 5; cf. 1 Tim. 1:20) is purificatory and approximates the Levitical penalty of 'cutting off'.[29] Moreover, the man becomes an exemplar of a wider pattern: 'you must not associate with anyone who claims to be a brother or sister but is sexually immoral or greedy, an idolater or slanderer, a drunkard or swindler. Do not even eat with

[24] Mounce 2000: 401. His conclusion is premised, in part, on the supposition that 'ritual purity is inconsequential'; indeed, 'Ritual is wrong' (401–2).

[25] *Eilikrinēs* indicates purity of thought (BDAG 282: 'without hidden motives'; cf. 2 Pet. 3:1) which, here, results in blameless behaviour.

[26] This has positive implications for Christian application of Lev. 18 despite claims the legislation is limited to either Canaan/Palestine (e.g. Milgrom 2000b: 1786–88) or to ancient Israelites (e.g. Hollier 2019: 84–102).

[27] Paul's logic is not that moral impurity is contagious, but rather that unsanctioned sexual sin may inspire similar misconduct.

[28] Cf. *exairō* ('to purge') in LXX Deut. 19:19; 21:21; 22:24; 24:7 (Newton 1985: 96).

[29] Thus, Paul demonstrates the ongoing utility of the so-called 'civil law' for dictating church practice.

such people' (5:11).[30] Because, '[h]oliness, for Paul, is in its essence social holiness',[31] moral defilement has corporate implications.

Separation along purity lines appears again in 2 Corinthians 6:14 – 7:1. The opening imperative not to be yoked with unbelievers (6:14) recalls Deuteronomy 22:10 and its prohibition against ploughing with an ox and donkey together (cf. Lev. 19:19). Whatever pragmatic concerns lie behind Deuteronomy's instruction, the rationale turns on purity: oxen were pure, donkeys were impure. Paul continues to distinguish pure from impure in a series of binaries that contrast righteousness-light-Christ-believer with lawlessness-darkness-Belial-unbeliever (6:14–15). The sequence climaxes, with appeal to Leviticus 26:12, by identifying the Corinthians as God's temple and posing the resulting question: 'What agreement is there between the temple of God and idols?' (6:16). Purity and impurity are incompatible. Intimacy with God demands separation.[32] Accordingly, Paul appropriates Isaiah 52:11 and Ezekiel 20:34 as the Lord's commands to the Corinthians: 'Therefore, come out from their midst and be separate … And do not touch what is unclean; And I will welcome you' (6:17 NASB; cf. Rev. 18:4). Paul's concluding exhortation indicates that avoiding impurity is not merely a spiritual exercise: 'let us cleanse ourselves (*katharisōmen heautous*) from every defilement (*pantos molysmou*[33]) of body and spirit, bringing holiness to completion in the fear of God' (7:1 ESV). Maintaining purity of body and spirit highlights Paul's holistic anthropology. There are things that defile inwardly ('spirit') and there are things that defile outwardly ('body'). For Paul, both must be avoided.

Purity and the embodied community

One of the elements that emerges from consideration of defilement and cleansing in the Pauline epistles is the importance of the physical body. Holiness for believers is not merely spiritual, but includes one's corporeal self. Holistic consecration makes inward and outward purity essential. Thus, in the passage just examined, Paul urges the Corinthians to cleanse themselves 'from every defilement of *body and spirit*' (2 Cor. 7:1 ESV emphasis mine). Likewise, he wants the Thessalonians to be *entirely* (*holoteleis*) made

[30] Table fellowship is banned as it implies kinship and peaceful relations.

[31] Adewuya 2011: 196.

[32] Guthrie 2015: 347.

[33] *Molysmos* appears three times in LXX (Guthrie 2015: 360), two of which concern land defilement (Jer. 23:16; 1 Esd. 8:80).

holy, in 'spirit and soul and body' (1 Thess. 5:23 NASB). Regarding bodily purity, Paul places particular emphasis on sex, food and resurrection.

Sex

In the Pauline epistles the noun *akatharsia* ('impurity') appears nine times. Eight occurrences reference, or at least include, prohibited sexual activity.[34] Romans 1:18–32 outlines human wickedness that arouses divine wrath. The fundamental issue is deliberate suppression of the truth about God, expressed as idolatry (1:18–23). Because of this, God hands idolaters over 'to impurity' (*eis akatharsian*), that is, to dishonouring their bodies through unnatural sexual relations (1:24, 26–27). Later, Paul reminds the Romans of how they formerly presented their bodies as 'slaves to impurity' (*doula tē akatharsia*, 6:19). Ephesians 4:19 similarly decries Gentiles who give themselves over to sensuality and 'every kind of impurity (*akatharsias pasēs*)' (ESV; cf. 4:17). Within the churches, Paul laments he may have to deal with those refusing to repent of 'impurity (*akatharsia*) and sexual immorality and debauchery' (2 Cor. 12:21 my tr.). In the vice lists that punctuate the Pauline material, *akatharsia* always appears alongside *porneia* – an umbrella term for various forms of prohibited sexual activity. In Galatians 5:19, *akatharsia* comes between 'sexual immorality' (*porneia*) and 'debauchery' (*aselgeia*).[35] The sins the Colossians must mortify begin with 'sexual immorality, impurity (*akatharsian*), lust, evil desires' (3:5). Likewise, in Ephesians 5:3, 'sexual immorality and all impurity' (*porneia de kai akatharsia pasa*) head the series.[36] Such sexual sin must be avoided, according to 1 Thessalonians 4:7, because 'God has not called us for impurity (*epi akatharsia*), but in holiness' (ESV; cf. 4:3–6). Similar use is evident with the adjective *akathartos* ('impure'). Besides 1 Corinthians 7:14 (discussed earlier) and 2 Corinthians 6:17 (which quotes Isa. 52:11), *akathartos* occurs alongside *pornos* to describe those who have no inheritance in God's kingdom (Eph. 5:5; cf. 1 Cor. 6:9–10; Gal. 5:21).

In the LXX, *akatharsia* primarily denotes ritual impurity (e.g. Lev. 15:24–26; Num. 19:13; Judg. 13:7; 2 Sam. 11:4).[37] Yet it also conveys moral

[34] The ninth indicates Paul's denial of 'impure motives' (1 Thess. 2:3).

[35] *Aselgeia* especially denotes sexual excesses (BDAG 141). The Byzantine text tradition adds *moicheia* ('adultery') (cf. KJV).

[36] *Porneia* and *akatharsia* are linked with *kai* ('and') whereas the next item, 'covetousness', follows *ē* ('or').

[37] Similarly, *akathartos* (e.g. Lev. 11:24; 12:2; Num. 5:2).

defilement (e.g. translating *tô ʿēbâ* ['abomination'] in Prov. 6:16; 24:9 ESV). This latter sense is foremost for Paul for whom *akatharsia* frequently functions as an umbrella label for sexual sins, akin to the *porneia* word-group. This does not ignore the ritual impurity generated by sexual acts (see below), but it does signal a predominant focus on moral pollution. Such impurity had more serious ramifications and applied equally to Jews and Gentiles.[38] Because moral defilement is improper for God's 'holy ones' (Eph. 5:3), and unsafe because it provokes divine wrath (Col. 3:6), avoiding acts that pollute the body is crucial.[39]

These themes coalesce in 1 Corinthians 6:12–20. Paul confronts sexual immorality tolerated within the church under the auspices of the slogan, 'I have the right to do anything' (6:12), supported, in turn, by an underlying cultural ambivalence towards the physical body.[40] However, anticipating 15:1–58, Paul states that the body does matter because God will raise it (6:14).[41] Indeed, one's physical self already belongs to the Lord (6:13) and is conceived as part of Christ's body (6:15). The question follows, 'Shall I then take the members of Christ and unite them with a prostitute?' (6:15). Paul appeals to the 'one flesh' logic of Genesis 2:24 (6:16), but also, implicitly, to purity mores. While sexual intercourse ritually defiles (Lev. 15:18), sexual immorality generates moral pollution (Lev. 18:24–30). Thus, for believers to become 'one flesh' with a prostitute would, by the same act, defile Christ of whom the believer is a part (6:17).[42] Such outrageous incongruity fuels Paul's exhortation. Being 'in Christ' has physical implications. Moreover, because moral pollution also affects the sanctuary (cf. Lev. 20:3; Ezek. 23:37–39), Paul continues to contrast impurity with holiness by asking, 'do you not know that your body is a temple of the Holy Spirit within you?' (6:19 ESV). Although 6:19 is often understood individually, Paul frequently uses *sōma* ('body') corporately (e.g. 1 Cor. 10:17; 12:12–27). The blending of individual and corporate matches the logic of moral impurity in which private deviance has communal

[38] See my discussion in chapters 2 and 6.

[39] This logic informs 2 Cor. 11:2–4 where Paul appropriates sexual faithfulness as a metaphor to urge theological fidelity. He desires to present the Corinthians as a 'pure virgin' to one husband, Christ (11:2), but worries other suitors might weaken their 'pure devotion' (11:3–4).

[40] See Wright 2003: 32–84.

[41] The topics of sex and food in 6:13 are similarly expanded in 7:1–40 and 8 – 10 respectively.

[42] Likewise, Hayes 2002: 93. Note: 6:16 assumes sexual intercourse produces 'one flesh', not marriage.

implications, a concern supported in context by Paul's command to avoid immoral 'brothers' lest their influence spread like yeast (5:6–11).

Food

In the first century, food and table fellowship significantly impacted Jew-Gentile social relations.[43] So too in the early churches (cf. Acts 10:28; Gal. 2:12–14). In Romans 14, Paul tackles ethnic tensions by reframing divisive cultural-religious practices.[44] Opinions about permitted foods (14:2–3, 6b) and observance of special days (14:5–6a) are deemed 'disputable matters' (14:1). They are further minimized by emphasizing God's verdict upon one's life (14:7–8, 10–12). Consequently, Paul concludes, 'let us stop passing judgment on one another' (14:13). The non-mention of *eidōlothytos* makes it unlikely that 'food sacrificed to idols' is the issue (cf. Acts 15:29; 1 Cor. 8:1).[45] Instead, Mosaic stipulations are a likely dividing point between the 'weak' and the 'strong'.[46] The following verse legitimizes individual conviction: 'I know and have been persuaded by the Lord Jesus that nothing is impure (*koinon*) in itself,[47] but to the one who reckons something to be impure (*koinon*), it is impure (*koinon*) to that person' (14:14 my tr.).[48] Alternate diet does not legitimize discrimination. 'Do not, for the sake of food, destroy the work of God. Everything is indeed clean (*kathara*), but it is wrong for anyone to make another stumble by what he eats' (14:20 ESV). Thus, Paul does not universalize the dietary laws of Leviticus 11 (par. Deut. 14:3–20). Instead, highlighting individual conscience (cf. 14:22), he permits separate Jewish and Gentile culinary practices while also exhorting unity (cf. 15:1–13).[49]

---

[43] For the background, see Blomberg 2005: 65–96; Furstenberg 2023: 84–110.

[44] This remains the case irrespective of whether Paul has a specific Roman dispute in mind or is making a more general exhortation (perhaps based on 1 Cor. 8 – 10).

[45] Moo 1996: 830. In 1 Cor. 8:7 Paul says a person's conscience is 'defiled' (*molynetai*) if they eat believing the food has really been offered to an idol.

[46] The point is contested. Reasoner 1999 evaluates the options.

[47] Leviticus 11, similarly, does not suppose innate animal impurity; rather, prohibited species are deemed 'impure for you' (11:8 my tr.), that is, for Israel, which Yahweh set apart from the nations (Lev. 20:25–26).

[48] *Koinon* (lit. 'common') parallels *akathartos* ('impure') in Mark 7:2; Acts 10:14, 28 and was increasingly used to denote ritually defiled food. Cf. Furstenberg 2023: 211 n. 25.

[49] Romans 14 is the clearest indicator in the New Testament that Lev. 11 restrictions do not apply to Gentiles. Likewise, 1 Tim. 4:4–5 asserts everything (in context, food included) is made holy by the word of God and prayer. For consideration of Mark 7:19 and Acts 10:13–15, see chapter 7.

Resurrection

While the Pauline epistles emphasize moral impurity and its effects on body and spirit, ritual impurity remains an important consideration. It too inhibits access to sacred places. Even if geographic distance from the temple lessened the immediacy for ritual purification in diaspora or Gentile communities, this could only ever be an interim solution. The reason is straightforward. Paul's eschatology (mirroring that of the wider Scriptures) envisions a future in which God dwells with his people in unrestricted holiness. Yet, because ritual pollution arises from uncontrollable bodily processes, it remains beyond the reach of willpower to rectify. How then can permanent dwelling with God be secured?

Paul addresses the issue by forecasting the transformation of human physicality. The idea appears in Philippians 3:20–21, which states that because believers' citizenship is in heaven, Christ 'will transform our lowly bodies so that they will be like his glorious body'. The implication is that 'lowly bodies' are unsuited for heavenly habitation (cf. 2 Cor. 5:1–8). Change is required. Christ's glorious body, which already exists in heaven (3:20), becomes the template for remodelling. This notion is developed further in 1 Corinthians 15 as Paul defends the indispensability of bodily resurrection for a community that doubted either its feasibility or necessity (or both).[50] Yet, if Jesus was raised, as the preaching of eyewitnesses claimed (15:5–8, 11–12), then bodily resurrection is possible (15:12–20). Furthermore, Paul asserts, Jesus is the 'firstfruits' of resurrection (15:20, 23). This means those who belong to him will also be raised bodily (15:22–23); in addition, they will receive the same kind of body Christ received (15:49). All flesh is not the same; different kinds of flesh are required to inhabit different realms (15:39–41). Resurrection accomplishes the requisite transformation. The 'natural body' (*sōma psychikon*), classed as perishable, dishonourable and weak, becomes a 'spiritual body' (*sōma pneumatikon*), which is imperishable, glorious and powerful (15:42–44).[51] In this way, believers will bear the image of the heavenly man (15:49). Verse 50 provides the rationale: because flesh and blood cannot inherit the kingdom of God, nor the perishable the imperishable, the dead will be raised imperishable (15:52). The crucial issue is not mere

[50] Wright 2003: 312–74.

[51] 'Spiritual body' does not mean non-material (see Thiessen 2023: 105–11).

resuscitation, but the transformation of all who are destined to inherit the kingdom. For this reason, Paul concludes,

> We will not all sleep, but *we will all be changed* – in a flash, in the twinkling of an eye, at the last trumpet. For the trumpet will sound, the dead will be raised imperishable, and *we will be changed*. For the perishable must clothe itself with the imperishable, and the mortal with immortality.
> (15:51–53, emphasis mine)

Reversal of death and physical transformation are the mechanisms by which bodily sources of ritual defilement are definitively overcome.[52] This, coupled with inability to sin (*non posse peccare*), enables permanent *physical* dwelling with God.

Conclusion

Paul's extant discourse on purity remains incomplete, shaped by the needs of his addressees. We might wish he had said more. Nonetheless, what is present provides invaluable insight into Paul's theological world-view, which (unsurprisingly) fits within the spectrum of Second Temple Judaism. In accord with that tradition, the impurity that arises from immoral behaviours is understood as a universal, human problem. Thus, the mixed Jewish-Gentile communities to which Paul writes are commanded, en masse, to avoid impurity and to pursue what is pure. The crucial motivator for this impetus is Christ's work of purification, which not only addresses the stain of prior moral pollution, but empowers moral capacity. Fundamentally, that capacity is expressed in obedience enabled by the agency of the Holy Spirit whom God has placed in believers. Indeed, believers corporately constitute a holy temple in which God dwells by his Spirit. While these realities operate spiritually, holiness and purity continue to have physical entailments.[53] This anticipates the need for a radical reconfiguration of human bodies at the eschaton, a transformation Paul locates in resurrection from the dead.

---

[52] Thus, 2 Cor. 5:17 ('The old has gone, the new is here!') must also be situated within Paul's already-but-not-yet eschatological framework.

[53] The presence of the Spirit in bodily experience is God's affirmation of the body (Fee 1987: 264).

The non-Pauline epistles

The Christological, sacerdotal and eschatological uses of defilement and cleansing in Paul's letters find analogues in the remaining New Testament documents. Taken together, a richer composite picture emerges.

Hebrews

Hebrews opens with a statement of Jesus' pre-eminence. Whereas God formerly spoke through the prophets (1:1), divine revelation climaxes with the son who is 'the radiance of God's glory and the exact representation of his being' (1:2–3). Verse 3b summarizes the son's accomplishments: 'after making purification for sins (*katharismon tōn hamartiōn poiēsamenos*), he sat down at the right hand of the Majesty on high' (ESV). Purification becomes the author's primary vehicle for conceptualizing Christ's work.

Establishing Jesus' high priestly function is central to that presentation. Several strands of Second Temple literature regard angels as 'priests' of the heavenly temple.[54] Hebrews assumes this role in its cultic description of angels as 'ministering spirits' (*leitourgika pneumata*, 1:14).[55] Yet, while 'ministering spirits' serve God's people (1:14) and speak God's word (2:2), they cannot deal categorically with human sin.[56] Jesus, however, is superior to the angels in his ability to provide purification (1:3–4) and, by becoming high priest, to atone sins (2:17). For this reason, Jesus is also superior to the Aaronic priesthood. Although, as a Judahite, Jesus could not be a priest on earth (7:13–14; 8:4), Hebrews establishes an alternate dynasty and arena of service. Utilizing Psalm 110:4, the author positions Jesus as high priest in the order of Melchizedek (5:5–6; cf. 5:10; 7:1–17) based on his indestructible life (7:3, 16).[57] Because Jesus lives forever, his priesthood is permanent (7:24). Moreover, as holy, innocent and undefiled (*amiantos*, 7:26),[58] Jesus is qualified to serve as high priest in the heavenly tabernacle, of which the earthly tent was but a copy (8:1–2, 5;

[54] See Klawans 2006: 111–44.

[55] Ellingworth 1993: 132–33; Moffitt 2011: 204.

[56] Contra T. Levi 3:5 in which (arch)angels make propitiation.

[57] Attridge 1989: 199; Moffitt 2022: 83–84.

[58] If 'undefiled' includes Jesus' physical body, now resurrected and ascended ('exalted above the heavens'), then Hebrews also highlights the importance of resurrection for overcoming physical impurity. Moffitt 2022: 143 n. 19 concurs: 'By virtue of his resurrection the morally pure Jesus, who was without sin (Heb 4:15), now has ritually pure humanity.'

9:11; cf. Exod. 25:8–9). It is in relation to this sanctuary that Jesus enacts purification.

Hebrews 9 – 10 utilizes Yom Kippur to explicate that cleansing. On this day, Israel's high priests entered the most holy place – a dangerous exercise (Lev. 16:2, 13; cf. Lev. 10:1–2) that required careful ritual preparation, including washing and blood sacrifice (Lev. 16:3–6; Heb. 9:7). The ritual cleansed the tabernacle, altar and people from the effects of sin and impurity.[59] Jesus performs analogous rites in relation to the heavenly tabernacle:[60]

> when Christ appeared as a high priest of the good things that have come, then through the greater and more perfect tent (not made with hands, that is, not of this creation) he entered once for all into the holy places, not by means of the blood of goats and calves but by means of his own blood.
> (9:11–12 ESV)

By entering the heavenly most holy place, offering his own blood instead of animal blood, Jesus secures eternal redemption (9:12) and cleanses both believers' consciences (9:14) and the heavenly tabernacle (9:23–24).[61] Jesus therefore accomplishes what the Old Testament cult could not.[62] The Levitical system was effective, but only within certain limitations: cleansing impurity and securing forgiveness for inadvertent and minor sins (e.g. Lev. 4:22–26; 12:6–7; cf. Heb. 9:7, 13, 22). It could not (nor was it intended to) deal with 'high-handed' sins. Nor could it overcome the source of sin. Leviticus and Numbers provide measures to deal with effects, not root causes (as with ritual impurity). This is why sacrifices continued: people kept sinning (Heb. 8:8a; 10:1–4). Jesus, however, in a climactic act that removes sin once for all (9:26), inaugurates the reconstitution of God's people anticipated by the prophets (cf. the use of

[59] See chapter 1.

[60] Here I substantially agree with Moffitt 2022: 117–34 who appropriates categories from Soskice 1985 to argue that Hebrews presents a homeomorphic rather than paramorphic model of the earthly tabernacle. That is, the earthly tabernacle is the same kind of thing as the heavenly sanctuary. Thus, analogy rather than metaphor best describes the relationship.

[61] This need not indicate actual impurity in heaven, but is a necessary component of explaining Christ's priestly mediation against the backdrop of Yom Kippur (Schenck 2007: 168).

[62] It is essential to rightly qualify the (in)effectiveness of the Levitical cult. See Harper forthcoming-c.

Jer. 31:31–34 in Heb. 8:8–12; 10:15–18). This is what being made perfect (10:14; 12:23) and having one's conscience cleansed (9:9, 14; 10:2, 22) signifies: not the removal of guilty feelings,[63] but overcoming propensity to sin.[64]

Accordingly, because Jesus overcame sin and impurity, believers can serve the living God (9:14). That service is cast in priestly terms – including entry to the heavenly tabernacle. Purification is still essential, but now premised on the work of Christ. Against the backdrop of Yom Kippur, 10:19–22 is striking:

> since we have confidence to enter the Most Holy Place by the blood of Jesus, by a new and living way opened for us through the curtain, that is, his body, and since we have a great priest over the house of God, let us draw near to God with a sincere heart and with the full assurance that faith brings, having our hearts sprinkled to cleanse us from a guilty conscience and having our bodies washed with pure water.

The effectiveness of Christ's ritual agency, which secures inner ('hearts') and outer ('body') purification, grants every believer entry to the heavenly most holy place. However, entering sacred space (within the world of the Yom Kippur analogy) has ethical implications for Christian conduct. Positively, all God's people receive a priestly vocation to express thanks and worship (12:28) and to continually offer sacrifices of praise and good works (13:15–16). Negatively, they must avoid evil, especially acts that contaminate – like the bitter root that defiles (12:15)[65] and sexual immorality (12:16; 13:4). This dynamic explains the stark *a fortiori* rhetoric of the epistle's warning passages. If Moses was rightly terrified at Mt. Sinai, then how much more those who come to Mt. Zion (12:21–22)? 'For if they did not escape when they refused him who warned them on earth, much less will we escape if we reject him who warns from heaven' (12:25 ESV). For, 'our God is a consuming fire' (12:29; cf. Lev. 10:1–2; Isa. 33:14). Thus, as elsewhere in the epistles, the purification God secures for his people through the life, death, resurrection, ascension and ongoing priestly

[63] Contra Kistemaker 1984: 273; Pierce 2020: 133.

[64] See, further, Harper forthcoming-c.

[65] The phrase is borrowed from Deut. 29:18 where Moses warns against idolatry (Bruce 1990: 349).

ministry of Jesus should lead not to passivity, but to active striving for purity. Doing otherwise designates one unfit for sacred space and at odds with God's purposes for his people.

James

There is an evident affinity between James and Old Testament wisdom traditions.[66] One vestige of that correspondence is the frequent use of contrast (including pure-impure distinctions) throughout the epistle to drive moral exhortation. In 1:21, *rhyparia*, primarily meaning 'dirt' (cf. *rhypara esthēti* ['dirty clothing'], 2:2 my tr.), is used figuratively alongside *kakia* ('evil') to denote the moral filthiness that must be avoided to pursue the righteous life God desires (1:20). Instead, one must 'accept' (1:21) and 'do' (1:22; cf. 1:25) the word. The result is 'religion that is pure (*kathara*) and undefiled (*amiantos*) before God', evidenced by constrained speech, aiding the helpless and keeping oneself 'unstained' (*aspilon*) by the world (1:26–27 ESV).[67]

Remaining 'unstained' is further developed in 3:1–12 and 4:1–10.[68] Purity terms resurface. In 3:6, the tongue is labelled a 'world of unrighteousness' (*ho kosmos tēs adikias*) and 'the defiler' (*hē spilousa*) of the whole body, able to propel a person towards hellfire (3:6 my tr.). Accordingly, those who avoid stumbling in speech are considered 'perfect' (*teleios*), capable of controlling the body (3:2). Outward conduct thus reveals whether one's life is a manifestation of earthly wisdom (3:13–16) or of the heavenly wisdom that is 'pure' (*hagnē* 3:17). The necessity of attaining purity is conveyed in 4:8:

> Draw near to God, and he will draw near to you. Cleanse (*katharisate*) your hands, you sinners, and purify (*hagnisate*) your hearts, you double-minded.
> (ESV)

The idiom of drawing near (*engizō*) to God evokes cultic settings (cf. LXX Exod. 19:22; 24:2) and serves as a reminder that divine proximity problematizes impurity. Commands to cleanse deeds ('hands') and purify

[66] See Bauckham 1999; Morgan 2010.

[67] Moo 2000: 95 argues that 1:26–27 'set[s] the agenda for the rest of the letter'.

[68] Morales 2018: 103.

thoughts ('hearts') recall the stipulation in Psalm 24:3–4 (LXX 23:3–4) that anyone desiring to approach Yahweh's holy place must be 'guiltless in hand and clean in heart' (NETS). James 4:9–10 implies purification is accomplished through contrition and repentance. This is not initial conversion, but rather the renouncing of evil practices by those already considered believers.[69] Purity becomes an ongoing Christian pursuit that is achieved by turning away from, or avoiding outright (cf. 4:1–4, 11), sins that defile. This reflects depictions of eschewing moral impurity in Old Testament and Second Temple texts (e.g. Isa. 1:16; Ps. 51:4[2]).

1 – 2 Peter

Purity and priesthood are important concepts in 1 Peter and aid the letter's purpose to urge steadfastness in faith (5:12). Through the consecrating work of the Spirit, those chosen by God are inducted into the realm of the holy 'for obedience and for sprinkling with the blood of Jesus' (1:2 HCSB; cf. 1:14–16).[70] The collocation of terms likely recalls ratification of the Mosaic covenant during which the Israelites swore obedience (Exod. 24:3, 7) and were sprinkled with blood (Exod. 24:8).[71] There may also be an allusion to the consecration of Israel's priests.[72] Either way, God's commission is conceptualized as new birth into an inheritance that is 'imperishable, undefiled, and unfading' (1:3–4 ESV). New birth and future inheritance frame 1 Peter's eschatology and carry ethical entailments.[73] Because that inheritance is imperishable, kept in heaven until the coming of salvation (1:4–5), God's people must undergo transformation to possess it. Thus, 1:23 affirms, 'you have been born again, not of perishable seed, but of imperishable, through the living and enduring word of God' (cf. 1 Cor. 15:42–55). Likewise, because the inheritance is 'undefiled' (*amianton*), purity is essential. While cleansing is achieved by the agency of the divine word, inner purity must be reflected in outward conduct: 'Having purified (*hēgnikotes*) your souls by your obedience to the truth

[69] Martin 1988: 153.

[70] Goppelt 1993: 73–74.

[71] Jobes 2005: 72.

[72] In Lev. 8:30 sprinkling with blood is enacted in obedience to Yahweh's prior command (cf. Exod. 29:21).

[73] Jobes 2005: 49.

for a sincere brotherly love, love one another earnestly from a pure heart (*katharas kardias*)' (1:22 ESV; cf. 2:1–2; 3:1–2; 1 Tim. 1:5; 2 Tim 2:22).[74]

The purity required of God's people is commensurate with their priestly identity. That vocation is corporate.[75] Thus, Israel's call to '[B]e holy, because I am holy' is reiterated for Peter's recipients (1:15–16; cf. Lev. 11:44–45; 19:2; 20:7, 26). The wording reflects Leviticus 19:2 verbatim. This appropriates the wider concern of Leviticus 17 – 27 that holiness (and purity) characterize the entire nation, including non-Israelites, to support Peter's exhortation to readers to live in reverent fear 'as foreigners' (1:17).[76] For although they are scattered among the nations (1:2), God's elect are nevertheless, like living stones, 'being built into a spiritual house to be a holy priesthood, offering spiritual sacrifices acceptable to God through Jesus Christ' (2:5). Accordingly, terms applied to Israel at Sinai are reappropriated for this dispersed Christian community: 'you are a chosen race, a royal priesthood, a holy nation, a people for his own possession' (2:9 ESV; cf. Exod. 19:5–6).[77] The linked ideas of purity, holiness and priesthood bolster the ethical demands of the letter.

The warnings in 2 Peter are comparable. Through the promises of God, believers 'may participate in the divine nature, having escaped the corruption in the world caused by evil desires' (1:4). Worldly corruption is exemplified by recalling fallen angels, the flood generation, and Sodom and Gomorrah (2:4–9; cf. Jude 6–7). Implicit in each case is the moral pollution that stems from unrestrained sexual immorality and violence (see chapter 3). These historic examples of what befalls the ungodly confirm the certainty of divine censure for all who similarly 'follow the polluting desires (*epithymia miasmou*) of the flesh' (2:10 CSB). The letter's opponents, who fall into this category, are accordingly deemed 'stains and blemishes' (*spiloi kai mōmoi*, 2:13 NASB). Moreover, by appealing to fleshly desires (2:18), these false teachers entice others who were escaping the 'defilements of the world' (*ta miasmata tou kosmou*, 2:20 ESV), causing them to turn away from the holy command like a dog returns to vomit or

[74] Cf. Rogan 2023: 108. Jobes 2005: 251–56 adduces a similar sense in 3:21: baptism does not remove moral filth once-for-all but is a pledge to live righteously before God.

[75] See Malone 2017: 147–78.

[76] The 'foreign resident' (*gēr*) occupies a prominent place within the instruction of Lev. 17–27 (17:8, 10, 12, 13, 15; 18:26; 19:10, 33, 34[2x]; 20:2; 22:18; 23:22; 24:16, 22; 25:23, 35, 47[3x]).

[77] This assumes, with current consensus, that the letter's primary audience was Gentile. See Jobes 2005: 5–41.

a washed pig to mud (2:21–22; cf. Prov. 26:11). Moral pollution, like its ritual counterpart, spreads if left unchecked and leads away from holiness. Therefore, because the believer's destiny is a new heaven and earth,[78] the home of righteousness (3:13), the letter concludes with an exhortation to be found 'unstained and unblemished' (*aspiloi kai amōmētoi*, 3:14 my tr.; cf. 2:13).

1 – 3 John

In the Johannine epistles, cleansing describes the purging of sin and sin's effects by means of Jesus' blood:

> The blood of Jesus, his son, cleanses (*katharizei*) us from every sin … If we confess our sins, he is faithful and righteous, and he will forgive (*aphē*) us our sins and he will cleanse (*katharisē*) us from every unrighteous thing.
> (1 John 1:7, 9 my tr.)

The language recalls LXX Jeremiah 40:8 where Yahweh promises to cleanse injustice and to forget sin,[79] two distinct actions that together enable restoration of people and land (40:7, 10–11). Likewise, 1 John 1:9 distinguishes two acts of God on behalf of the penitent 'us': forgiveness (*aphē*) and cleansing (*katharisē*).[80] Each is required to address the sin and impurity that inhibit relationship with God. While Leviticus prescribes blood atonement for purifying major ritual impurity (e.g. Lev. 14:10–20) and facilitating forgiveness for confessed inadvertent and minor sins (e.g. Lev. 4:22–26), 1 John is more expansive. The blood of Jesus cleanses from 'every sin' (*pasēs hamartias*, 1:7) and 'every unrighteous thing' (*pasēs adikias*, 1:9). Fulfilling Jeremiah's promise, Jesus' blood cleanses even those defiled by wilful transgressions – something Israel's cult could not achieve.[81] For this reason, Jesus is described as the 'atoning sacrifice'

---

[78] Whether the current earth is purified or is destroyed and recreated is debated. Second Peter 3:10–12 has been understood both ways. Bauckham 1996: 314–21 and Beale 1999: 1039–43 assess the options.

[79] 'I will cleanse them from all their injustices which they sinned against me, and I will not remember their sins which they sinned' (NETS) (EVV Jer. 33:8).

[80] While Marshall 1978a: 114 acknowledges the terms may not be synonymous, he nevertheless suggests purification removes guilt and sin's power.

[81] See chapter 1.

(*hilasmos*) for sins (2:2), a term that evokes the frequent use of the root in LXX Leviticus in connection with expiating sin and purging impurity.[82]

In 1 John 3, cleansing is cast in preventative terms; that is, moral purification is achieved by avoiding acts that defile.[83] Because the children of God 'know that when he appears we shall be like him' (3:2 ESV), readers are exhorted to increasingly conform to that future reality. Transformation is described as purification: 'All who have this hope in him purify themselves (*hagnizei*), just as he is pure (*hagnos*)' (3:3). That 3:3 concerns moral purification is clarified by the repetition of *kathōs* and *estin*. Because believers will become 'just as he is' (*kathōs estin*, 3:2), they must purify themselves 'just as he is pure' (*kathōs ekeinos hagnos estin*, 3:3) by doing righteousness 'just as he is righteous' (*kathōs ekeinos dikaios estin*, 3:7).[84] Thus, 1 John connects both purification from past sins and ongoing purity of life to the person and work of Jesus.

Jude

Jude is an exhortation to contend for the faith against 'ungodly' adversaries who 'pervert the grace of … God into a license for immorality' (vv. 3–4). The author invokes past precedent by recalling Genesis 6:1–4 (v. 6) and Sodom and Gomorrah (v. 7).[85] These episodes serve as premier exemplars of the divine judgment aroused by 'sexual immorality and perversion' (v. 7). The defilement produced by such deeds, whether by angels or humans, is explicitly applied to the current situation: 'these dreamers likewise defile their flesh (*sarka … miainousin*)' (v. 8 HCSB; cf. 1 En. 9:8; 10:11; 12:4). Moral defilement is further intimated as Cain (bloodshed) and Balaam (sexual immorality and idolatry) are recalled in v. 11.[86] Pollution in these instances had long-lasting effects: banishment (Gen. 4:13–16) and ongoing defilement (Josh. 22:17), respectively. Likewise,

[82] This opens new possibilities for understanding how Jesus' atoning sacrifice is for the 'whole world' (2:2). Although often assessed only in relation to forgiveness (and the extent of [the] atonement), the removal of moral impurity with consequent benefit for the *land* (cf. LXX Jer. 40) suggests 2:2 may be operating with a broader conception of Christ's achievement.

[83] Cf. Marshall 1978a: 114 n. 14.

[84] The collocation occurs elsewhere in the Johannine epistles only in 1 John 4:17 where to become 'just as he is' (*kathōs ekeinos estiv*) in relation to love gives one confidence on the day of judgment.

[85] These examples are widely recalled as proverbial warnings in the late Second Temple period (e.g. Wis. 10:7; Jub. 16:5–6; 3 Macc. 2:5; T. Levi 14:6; Luke 17:26–30; 2 Pet. 2:4–6).

[86] With Korah, the focus shifts from sins committed to punishment received, accounting for the non-chronological arrangement (Bauckham 1996: 84).

the opponents are metaphorically termed *spilades* (v. 12). The feminine noun has two meanings: 'a rocky hazard hidden by waves' (cf. CSB, ESV, NASB, NLT) or 'that which soils or discolors' (cf. KJV, NIV).[87] Both options work in context, as indicated by variance in the versions. However, the running theme of moral pollution suggests the second – 'blemish' (NIV) or 'spot' (KJV) – may be more likely.[88] This sense is reinforced by 2 Peter 2:13, which uses the masculine form *spilos* ('stain, spot') along with *mōmos* ('defect, blemish') as metaphorical appellatives for the sexually immoral. Unimpeded following of 'natural instincts' sets Jude's opponents against God's Spirit (v. 19) and renders them liable to judgment when the Lord appears with his holy ones (vv. 14–15). Accordingly, readers are urged to 'save others by snatching them out of the fire' while 'hating even the garment stained by the flesh' (v. 23 ESV). Showing mercy and abhorring sin are not mutually exclusive. Seeing an allusion to Zechariah 3, Richard Bauckham suggests the image of garments soiled by the body ('flesh') is intentionally unpleasant, but nevertheless hopeful as Joshua's dirtied garments are replaced by clean ones, indicating purification by God (Zech. 3:4–5).[89]

Revelation

Revelation utilizes Old Testament echoes and allusions more than any other New Testament book.[90] Correctly negotiating these parallels is essential for discerning the book's message. Indeed, misreadings of Revelation (and there are many) frequently go awry at precisely this point. Recognizing how Revelation appropriates the categories of priesthood, sacrifice and temple is vital for understanding the book's purity dynamics.

Revelation 1 draws extensively on Daniel 7 to visualize Jesus. Like a son of man, he comes with the clouds of heaven (1:7, 13; cf. Dan. 7:13). His description evokes physical purity: 'The hair on his head was white like wool, as white as snow, and his eyes were like blazing fire' (1:14; cf. Dan. 7:9; 10:6),[91] and 'his face was like the sun shining in all its brilliance'

---

[87] BDAG 938.

[88] The possibilities are surveyed by Bauckham 1996: 85–86 who prefers 'rock'.

[89] Bauckham 1996: 116–17.

[90] Numerous studies explore the complex web of intertexts (e.g. Beale and Carson 2007: 1081–1161; Henze and Lincicum 2023: 555–76).

[91] Revelation draws on variant Gk. textual traditions (LXX and θ) to adopt Daniel's description of the Ancient of Days for Jesus.

(1:16). More subtly, Jesus is depicted in high priestly attire.[92] This fits his spatial location walking 'among the lampstands' (1:13; cf. Lev. 24:3–4), that is, in the temple's holy place. However, identifying these 'lampstands' as the seven churches to whom John writes (1:4, 20) also conceptualizes Christian communities within the temple's holy precincts. Thus, description as God's 'holy ones' (5:8; 8:3, 4; 11:18; 13:7, 10; 14:12; 16:6; 17:6; 18:20, 24; 19:8; 20:6, 9) who serve as 'priests' (1:6; 5:10; 20:6) is fitting. The removal of sin required for instalment is accomplished by Jesus' blood (1:5; cf. Lev. 8:14–30). Similar themes emerge in the description of the great multitude standing before God in 7:9. The crowd wears white robes (7:9, 13), emblematic of the purification required to approach God's throne: 'they have washed their robes and made them white in the blood of the Lamb. Therefore, they are before the throne of God and serve him day and night in his temple' (7:14–15).

Portrayal as holy priests, serving God in his temple, sharpens the disjuncture of moral impurity within the communities addressed by the letter. Accordingly, the 'teaching of Balaam' and 'that woman Jezebel' are excoriated for inciting sexual immorality and idolatry (2:14, 20). Instead, the one who persists in righteousness is promised sustenance from the tree that is in the paradise of God (2:7; cf. 22:19), evoking primordial access to the divine presence in the Garden. Like the Sardisians who did not defile (*ouk emolunan*) their clothes (3:4–5), overcomers will be dressed in white, the colour of heaven (cf. 2:17; 4:4; 6:11; 7:9, 13; 14:14; 19:11, 14; 20:11; similarly, 19:8). Indeed, they will become pillars in God's temple, never to depart (3:12). Present and future situatedness within sacred space demands commensurate conduct. The Laodiceans are therefore urged to purchase white clothes to cover their nakedness (3:18).

This ethical imperative is ultimately a call to renounce Babylon and its manifold impurities.[93] Already in the Old Testament, 'Babylon' takes on symbolic resonance beyond the historic city-empire, becoming a cipher for opposition to God. Throughout Revelation, Babylon is epitomized by defiling sins, particularly sexual immorality, idolatry and bloodshed. The city is a 'prostitute' (17:1, 5, 15, 16; 19:2) who seduces kings and peoples

[92] See Winkle 2017: 339–46; Beale 1999: 208–9.

[93] The potential is embodied in the 144,000 male virgins who did not defile themselves with women (14:4; cf. 7:3–4). Irrespective of exact identification, a long-debated topic, moral and maybe also ritual purity is emphasized and befits those who accompany the Lamb 'wherever he goes' (cf. Deut. 23:9–14).

into committing fornication (14:8; 17:2; 18:3, 9; 19:2). She carries a cup 'filled with abominations (*bdelygmatōn*) and the impurities (*ta akatharta*) of her sexual immorality' (17:4 my tr.). Indeed, she 'is mother of prostitutes and of earth's abominations (*tōn bdelygmatōn tēs gēs*)' (17:5 ESV). Babylon is 'a home for demons and a prison for every impure spirit and a prison for every impure bird and a prison for every impure and hateful beast' (18:2 my tr.) – a veritable menagerie of impurity.[94] Bloodshed also looms large. The city that freely trades in human souls (18:13) is drunk with the blood of the saints (17:6). 'In her was found the blood of prophets and of God's holy people, of all who have been slaughtered on the earth' (18:24; cf. Jer. 51:49). For this reason, the righteous slain cry out, 'How long, Sovereign Lord, holy and true, until you judge the inhabitants of the earth and avenge our blood?' (6:10).

The various judgment sequences depicted throughout the book recall the plagues against Egypt. This time, the scale is global. Creation is undone (6:12–14; 8:7–12; 16:1–12; cf. 11:18) and systematically defiled:[95] waters turn to blood (8:8; 11:6; 16:2, 4; cf. Exod. 7:19), plagues and sicknesses are unleashed (11:6; 16:2; cf. Exod. 9:3, 9), impure frog-demons traverse the world (16:13–14; cf. Exod. 8:2[6]), and land and seas are filled with the slain (11:8–9; 16:3; 19:17–18, 21; cf. Exod. 9:19; 14:28–30). Such overwhelming judgment is nevertheless commensurate ('they have shed the blood of your holy people and your prophets, and you have given them blood to drink as they deserve' [16:6]). It also satisfies the petition of 6:10 ('He has avenged on her the blood of his servants' [19:2]).

Avenging bloodshed not only extirpates perpetrators, it mitigates land defilement (cf. Num. 35:33). The spatial cleansing made possible by Babylon's judgment is realized in the book's climactic vision. John sees 'a new heaven and a new earth' (21:1; cf. Isa. 65:17; 66:22), figured as 'the Holy City, the new Jerusalem, coming down out of heaven from God' (21:2).[96] The city's cubic dimensions and construction from 'pure gold' (21:16, 18, 21) evoke the temple's most holy place (cf. 1 Kgs 6:20), a cultic resonance underlined by incorporating Garden of Eden imagery in 22:2–3. Furthermore, the city

---

[94] *Phylakē*, meaning 'prison' or 'prison house', is an unusual word for 'haunt' (NIV, ESV). The term implies the *deliberate* retention of impure creatures, natural and supernatural. Text critical issues in 18:2b are discussed by Beale 1999: 895; Osborne 2002: 636 n. 4.

[95] See my discussion of Exodus in chapter 3.

[96] Whether new Jerusalem is coterminous with the new earth or is situated within it, the images are closely aligned.

is served by a 'river of living water' (22:1 my tr.; cf. 7:17; 21:6; 22:17; Ezek. 47:1–9; Zech. 14:8), invoking notions of purity and cleansing.[97] These ideas combine to frame a central truth: 'Look! God's dwelling place is now among the people, and he will dwell with them. They will be his people, and God himself will be with them and be their God' (21:3). In this most sacred place, God's people behold his face as they serve him (22:3–4). Defilement is banished: death ends (21:4); those who morally pollute are excluded (21:8; 22:15); and 'everything impure' (*pan koinon*) and all 'doers of abomination' (*poiōn bdelygma*) are forbidden entry (21:27 my tr.).

Purity themes enhance Revelation's call to faithful discipleship.[98] The eschatological portrait of purity shapes imagination and informs present conduct, exhorting believers vis-à-vis Babylon, '"Come out of her, my people," so that you will not share in her sins, so that you will not receive any of her plagues' (18:4; cf. Isa. 52:11; Jer. 51:45).[99] Urgency is enhanced by establishing correspondence between sin in the churches and the depiction of Babylon.[100] Therefore,

> Blessed are those who wash their robes, that they may have the right to the tree of life and may go through the gates into the city. Outside are the dogs, those who practise magic arts, the sexually immoral, the murderers, the idolaters and everyone who loves and practises falsehood.
> (22:14–15)

The unshielded holiness of God's eschatological presence leads to a necessary correlate: in the end, everything is pure, and purity is everything.

Conclusion

With respect to Palestinian Jews of the Second Temple period, Yair Furstenberg observes that, 'minute differences in purity practices created

[97] The connection is made explicit in the minority reading 'pure river' (*potamon katharon*; only 051ˢ 2030 2377 M^A). See also my discussion of 'living water' in chapter 7.

[98] Cf. Stephens 2011.

[99] The defiling nature of Babylon's sins (esp. idolatry) is reinforced by the Isa. 52:11 parallel and the threefold use of *akathartos* ('impure') in 18:2 (Beale 1999: 898).

[100] E.g. the verb *porneuō* ('to fornicate') only appears with respect to Babylon (17:2; 18:3, 9) and the churches (2:14, 20). Likewise, *porneia* ('fornication') is identified in the churches (2:21), Babylon (14:8; 17:2, 4; 18:3; 19:2), and among the people of Babylon (9:21).

a rich taxonomy of social boundaries and religious ideologies.'[101] That rich diversity is reflected in the New Testament letters. Although sporadic, purity is marshalled to promote Christological, sacerdotal and eschatological ends. Jesus is God's ultimate means of purification. In priestlike manner, Jesus provides washing and cleansing for the defiled who, because of their pollution, are necessarily separated from God. He accomplishes this by virtue of his own blood, shed at the cross, which not only purges sin and impurity, but inaugurates the reconstitution of God's people, fulfilling Old Testament prophetic hopes. This has significant implications for identity formation as communities of believers are variously described as temple, priesthood and sacrifice. Thus, purity constitutes more than simply a preliminary status; it becomes an ongoing and active requirement. Sources of defilement must be avoided and removed. Instead, believers must cultivate the pure conduct that arises from purified hearts. Nothing less will suffice ahead of the dawning eschatological age when God dwells with his people in absolute purity and holiness.

[101] Furstenberg 2023: 10–11.

9

A biblical theology of defilement and cleansing

In this final chapter I sketch a biblical theology of defilement and cleansing. This is an important point of synthesis as I assemble the variegated data from the biblical and extra-biblical texts into a cohesive whole, which capitalizes on the insights made possible by a canonical survey. David Starling articulates the potential:

> While Christian theology and hermeneutics rightly speak of Scripture as a unity, it is a weighty, complex, multilayered unity. The Bible did not fall from the sky like a single snowflake; it rolled down the hill of salvation history, adding layers as it went. Each new layer of the accumulating collection presupposes what comes before and wraps itself around it; in so doing it offers direction in how to read it and asks, in turn, to be interpreted in light of it.[1]

Although systematization is always a reductionist exercise, I trust the preceding chapters suffice as exegetical warrant for conclusions drawn here. Then, to ground initial theologizing still further, I explore some implications for thinking about the incarnation, atonement and global missions. While the findings of this volume invite integration with a wider range of biblical, theological and practical ministry topics, all I can do here is offer something of a primer.

[1] Starling 2016: 14.

Toward a biblical theology of defilement and cleansing

Purity and impurity are powerful conceptual and hermeneutical tools through which ideas about self and other can be manifested.[2] The concepts are malleable. Purity encompasses the physical quality of gold, the ritual status of people and objects, the moral uprightness of those who shun evil, and the genealogical integrity of returnees in Ezra-Nehemiah. Yet purity is also dynamic; it can be undone. Metals become tarnished, people are polluted by bodily processes and egregious sins, and lineages succumb to corruption. Remedial processes are therefore required to refine, to cleanse and to preserve. The use of shared terminology across disparate categories offers the biblical authors rich potential for metaphorical extensions which they exploit with aplomb. The resulting composite is complex.[3] Nevertheless, emplotting defilement and cleansing within the Bible's overarching narrative affords unique insights.

Nevertheless, care is needed. Canonical progression could be misconstrued as development from ritual (Leviticus and Numbers) to moral purity (the Prophets and epistles). That potential is made more likely in the Protestant canon, which places the Prophets immediately before the New Testament. However, presumed advancement cannot support evolutionary schemas in which moral purity trumps ritual, thereby making ritual redundant. On the contrary, concern for moral purity is already firmly entrenched in books supposedly dominated by ritual (e.g. Lev. 18 – 20), and the Gospels reveal a Jesus who consistently affirms the importance of ritual as well as moral purity. In fact, recognizing the interplay between different forms of purity is often crucial. Barton is therefore right to challenge the false dichotomizing that is endemic to modern Western consciousness. Ultimately, both ritual and moral purity are ethical and are *together* essential for communion with God.[4]

In biblical anthropology, impurity is overwhelmingly linked to human causes. It is not simply an inherent feature of creation.[5] Moreover, the

[2] Balberg 2014: 2.

[3] As Lam 2016 demonstrates, metaphor often operates alongside literal meanings. The potential for *double entendre* complicates matters further.

[4] Barton 2014: 185–210.

[5] The overemphasis on 'fallen' creation in Western theology is challenged by Garvey 2019; Collins 2018: 238.

Old Testament breaks with the ANE pattern of ascribing impurity to the demonic.[6] Even in the New Testament, which typically terms demons 'impure spirits', no direct lines of causation are established. Demons possess, afflict, and even harm, but they are never directly said to defile. Instead, impurity, in two major forms, arises from people. A discrete set of bodily processes pollutes: *ṣāraʿat* (ESV: 'leprous disease'), genital discharges and corpses. Although usually short term and unavoidable, the resulting impurity requires separation from the holy and is, in fact, endangered by holiness. Physical distancing becomes essential. Moreover, impurity of this sort could be contagious, spreading to others by contact with communal ramifications. A second form of impurity arises from evil acts: prototypically, bloodshed, idolatry and sexual immorality, but also a wider range of egregious activities. The resulting impurity is long term and affects not only the perpetrator(s), but also sanctuary and land. Therefore, while not transmissible by contact, this kind of impurity has serious social and ecological consequences.

The machinations of human impurity directly affect the earth. In biblical purview, land is more than mere stage. There is a real cause and effect relationship between habitat and inhabitants. Sins pollute land. The resulting antagonism between people and place is graphically captured by the image of land vomiting out defiling inhabitants (Lev. 18:25). Such deleterious impact upon geographical space cannot and will not be left unaddressed, for God desires a place to dwell *in* as much as a people to dwell *with*.[7] Thus, at various points (think: Noah, Sodom, or sixth-century Judah), God cleanses defiled land. Yet, the means of purification – flood, destruction and exile – are catastrophic for humans. Thus, prophetic and apostolic hope for the land/earth is projected onto the future transformation of people who will no longer defile the places they inhabit (cf. Ezek. 36:24–35; Rom. 8:19–21). Only this can secure God's permanent dwelling with people in a physical locale.

Ultimately, the themes of defilement and cleansing clarify aspects of God's self-revelation. He is consistently correlated with all that is physically, ritually and morally pure. Indeed, it is God's intrinsic holiness that problematizes and endangers impurity. The correlation between God and purity validates all commensurate states and behaviours and becomes

[6] Milgrom 1991: 50.

[7] Indeed, as I demonstrate elsewhere (Harper 2025), God often prioritizes land over people.

socially formative by establishing boundaries around acceptable practice. In contrast, the association of impurity with visceral disgust (encouraged by connection to dirt, decay and detergent-resistant stain) utilizes psychological and physiological reflexes to underline the divine-human schism. God rightly and repeatedly bars the impure from temple and land and invites analogous exclusion from Christian communities. The eschatological orientation of the Scriptures projects these partial realizations onto a universal future conceived as God's presence filling everything in every way (e.g. Hab. 2:14; 1 Cor. 15:28).

Yet God acts. Anticipating eschatological purity and demonstrating his commitment to Israel and to creation, God itemizes sources of ritual impurity, instigates cleansing processes, and warns against evils that generate moral defilement. Inscripturated, the concepts of defilement and cleansing become powerful rhetorical tools. Unlike deliberative modes of ethical reasoning, impurity-disgust works at a non-rational level to compel hearers to embrace moral standards.[8] God's purificatory agenda reaches its crescendo in Jesus. The preparatory and purificatory nature of John's baptism underlines the significance of Jesus' appearance. In his ministry, Jesus reiterates warnings against moral pollution while demonstrating a unique ability to overcome ritual impurity by extinguishing its very sources: disease, discharges, even death. The shedding of his blood on the cross is the superlative act of atonement that conclusively purges the stain of sin and impurity and leads to the transformation of God's people. Jesus makes his followers morally pure through the agency of his word. Fulfilling prophetic hope, the resurrected Christ pours out the Holy Spirit who, like living water, wells up to effect continuous cleansing within the lives of those baptized into him. Yet, in cleansing a people for himself, Jesus also empowers moral capacity and commands his people to live in purity by performing Spirit-enabled works of righteousness that flow from pure hearts. Then finally, reconstituted by resurrection at the last day, believers' bodies will, like Christ's glorious body, become fit for divine proximity. This suite of gracious divine interventions makes holistically purified people possible. No longer defiled or defiling, in body or spirit, God's people will boldly enter God's sanctuary to serve him face-to-face. Indeed, a rich seam of cultic language, stretching from the prototypical Garden sanctuary to Revelation's eschatological vision

[8] Lam 2016: 206.

of world-as-temple, indicates that a priestly vocation lies at the centre of human purpose and identity.[9] *Endzeit* reflects *Urzeit*.[10] In the wake of Genesis 3, however, teleology is premised on profound transformation.[11] This, God ultimately accomplishes through Christ. The destiny of all who belong to him is comprehensive purity.

Purification is not simply another way to parse forgiveness, justification or even sanctification. Rather, in Old and New Testament alike, purity sits alongside these other themes as they mutually inform the necessity and scope of the *Missio Dei* and its ultimate realization in and through Jesus. As Jesus and the apostles taught, evil continues to defile both people and place as internal desires are expressed in outward physical acts. Our not-yet-perfected bodies also await final reconstitution. Until then, the indwelling Holy Spirit provides continual 'living water' to effect cleansing and guides believers towards purity of life as they are fashioned into a temple made fit for God's presence. Understanding defilement and cleansing, therefore, ought to evoke increased appreciation of, and thankfulness for, the triune God's salvific kindness, which meets the entirety of creation's need.

Thinking about the incarnation

At the beginning of this book, I posed the following questions: Was Jesus ever impure? Did he ever require cleansing? These queries get to the heart of what it meant for the second Person of the Trinity to take on human form. Nevertheless, the widely divergent and often incompatible answers given to these questions indicate the difficulty of forming definitive conclusions. While some things can be asserted with confidence, others remain (perhaps, frustratingly) less clear. Moreover, while various proposals, like the flat denial of Jesus' Jewish ancestry in 1930s Germany, can be ruled out on other grounds, the textual data permit a range of legitimate options, each influenced by one's prior theological commitments. All this to say: others will assemble the pieces differently to what I propose here.

[9] See Beale 2004; Malone 2017.

[10] This is correspondence in kind, not in magnitude; the end does not simply recapitulate the beginning.

[11] Cf. deSilva 2014.

A careful reading of the biblical texts reveals distinct, albeit overlapping, forms of purity that must not be conflated.[12] Hebrews 4:15 affirms that Jesus, although tempted in every way, did not sin. Hence, I take it he never became morally impure. Furthermore, because moral defilement arises only from the commission of morally reprehensible acts, it is not communicated to persons by virtue of an originating sin or by possession of corrupted human nature. Thus even if, as some argue, Jesus' incarnation included him taking on sinful flesh,[13] this does not require that he thereby became morally impure.

Whether Jesus was ever ritually impure is more difficult to ascertain. The Gospel accounts remain circumspect, and the epistles never discuss the matter.[14] Nevertheless, the texts indicate he underwent ritual purification rites: possibly as a baby with his mother (Luke 2:22), at his immersion by John (Mark 1:9 and pars.) and, as was seemingly his custom, ahead of pilgrim feasts (John 2:13; 11:55–56). Yet, these recollections stop short of asserting that Jesus *required* purification. Although he may have submitted to various ritual demands and expectations, were these necessary in his case?

Here, we are forced to extrapolate beyond what is explicit. One common proposal maintains Jesus did not require purification. Instead, identification as the 'Holy one of God' (Mark 1:24; John 6:69) is used to support the idea of intrinsic purity and contagious holiness.[15] Hence, instead of touch defiling Jesus as might be expected, the dynamic is reversed: purity flows from Jesus to the defiled. However, on several occasions the Gospels carefully distinguish between Jesus healing sources of defilement and the purification subsequently achieved through other means. Regarding the *lepros* in Mark 1:40, for instance, miraculous cure following physical touch (by Jesus) enables purification (by the priests) in line with scriptural mandate (1:44; cf. Lev. 14:2–20). On these occasions, healing prevents re-defilement; it does not purify per se. This raises questions about the plausibility of contagious purity.

---

[12] Here I omit both physical and genealogical purity.

[13] Bello 2020 surveys the historical and theological issues.

[14] Related matters also remain opaque. For instance, did Jesus ever participate in temple sacrifice?

[15] E.g. Fletcher-Louis 2007: 63; Bird 2008: 24; Beck 2012: 30; with respect to moral purity, Blomberg 2005: 137. This view is also, at times, premised on the notion that impurity threatens holiness (e.g. Thiessen 2020: 141).

Another possibility is that the incarnate Jesus took on fallen human physicality. Thus, like every other Jewish man and woman (and, perhaps, every person), he became subject to ritual impurity. Ritual purification enacted by his mother when he was a child was therefore both required and effectual. Likewise, ritual immersion by John prepared Jesus to be filled with the Holy Spirit. While this creates an inescapable tension – proximity to the indwelling Holy Spirit coupled with ongoing susceptibility to impurity[16] – perhaps this further indicates the purificatory role of the Spirit as internalized 'living water'. Henceforth, indwelt by God's Spirit, Jesus was rightly called God's holy one. His presence therefore endangered impure spirits. It also posed a threat to impure people. Accordingly, when Jesus encountered, or was encountered by, defiled persons (especially those with major impurity: disease, discharges and death), he graciously removed the cause of defilement. Thus, as when a haemorrhaging woman touched him, it was not purity that flowed from Jesus, but power to heal (Mark 5:30). Perhaps Matthew intimates, by quoting Isaiah 53:4 (Matt. 8:17), that Jesus took on the impurities of his people as he also bore their sickness, sin, shame and separation from God.[17] Yet, resurrection from the dead effects a fundamental physical reconstitution. As the New Testament affirms, Jesus' raised body is glorious, no longer subject to death and defilement, and therefore fit for heaven (Phil. 3:21). In all these ways, Jesus is paradigmatic. In solidarity with his people, he entered fully into their lowly estate and walked the path towards ultimate transformation ahead of them (cf. Phil. 2:5–8; Heb. 2:5–18). Now raised and ascended, Jesus serves as high priest in the heavenly tabernacle and ministers on his people's behalf until the day when they, likewise transformed, enter the holy of holies to serve God face-to-face.

In the end, both the contagious-purity and subject-to-defilement conceptions of Jesus' incarnation are plausible based on the available data. On balance, I favour the second, however tentatively. Not only does it attend more closely to subtleties in the Gospel accounts, it highlights yet another way that the second Person of the Trinity forsook transcendent glory to purify a people for himself.

---

[16] The same tension is evident for Israel's priests who could simultaneously be holy and impure.

[17] If correct, then the separation so poignantly evident at the cross ('why have you forsaken me?') is already realized, in part, throughout Jesus' life.

Thinking about (the) atonement

Atonement is complicated.[18] The breadth of material in Old and New Testaments, coupled with two thousand years of post-biblical reflection, guarantees as much. This explains why various conceptualizations of (the) atonement have emerged through the centuries. Each sets out to articulate the mechanism by which humans are reconciled to God. However, the resulting models are necessarily reductionistic in their attempts to synthesize the otherwise unsystematized biblical data. They also bear the hallmarks of the historical contexts from which they emerged. Nonetheless, each articulation provides crucial insights into Christ's salvific work; the composite picture is correspondingly rich. The major models include, with historic exemplars, Ransom (Origen), Recapitulation (Irenaeus), Incarnation (Athanasius), Satisfaction (Anselm), Divine Love (Abelard), Governmental Theory (Grotius), Penal Substitution (Calvin), Moral Example (Rashdall) and Christus Victor (Aulén).[19]

What is striking about the various syntheses, however, is a complete absence of purification. Despite the frequent, perhaps primary, use of atonement lexemes (esp. *kpr*) in purificatory contexts (see chapter 1),[20] and the Gospels' presentation of Jesus as the purifier par excellence (see chapter 7), none of the frameworks surveyed above considers Christ's work in terms of removing impurity.[21] In fact, a restricted understanding is often intentionally embraced. While Oliver Crisp, for instance, affirms Colin Gunton's sweeping definition of atonement as 'reconciliation between God and the world', he pursues 'a narrower working definition of atonement … that focuses on human beings'.[22] Moreover, Crisp restricts

[18] For the sake of argument, I use the gloss 'atonement' (coined by William Tyndale in 1526) even though it does not adequately translate the Hebrew verb *kpr*.

[19] For surveys, see Grudem 1994: 579–82; Berkhof 1996: 384–91; Erickson 1998: 798–840; Beilby and Eddy 2006; Pugh 2014; Witt and Scandrett 2022. Vaughn 2022: 11 notes that the various models are often simply granted an assumed validity. Accordingly, disagreement tends to concern which model is primary or should be considered the 'centre'.

[20] If, as I argue in chapter 1, Yom Kippur primarily achieves purification, not forgiveness, then 28/49 occurrences of *kpr* in Leviticus explicitly address impurity (compared with 13/49 occurrences which explicitly facilitate forgiveness of sin). Whether these outcomes can be neatly distinguished is debated (see Sklar 2005; Greenberg 2019).

[21] While Green makes some preliminary remarks in Beilby and Eddy 2006: 172–79, they remain underdeveloped. Other treatments which utilize purification language tend to make it synonymous with forgiveness (e.g. Cole 2009: 164–66; Crisp 2022: 203).

[22] Crisp 2022: 16; citing Gunton 1989: 2.

Christ's atoning work to only 'dealing with human sin'.[23] Limiting scope is not inherently wrong, and discerning the mechanism by which Jesus deals with human sin is paramount. Yet, deliberately excluding significant aspects of the biblical witness renders any conclusions drawn about atonement tentative by virtue of being incomplete. As McKnight rightly recognizes, 'We cannot discuss atonement until we define the problem that atonement remedies.'[24]

This study helps to clarify the scope of the problem. Human sin, as the models listed above acknowledge, presents a fundamental barrier to communion with God. Sacrificial atonement, as conceptualized in Leviticus and climactically enacted through the death of Jesus, provides necessary expiation (e.g. Lev. 17:11; Heb. 9:28; 1 John 1:7). Yet the Scriptures also reveal impurity as a distinct, albeit related, barrier between people and God. Ritual impurities, produced by bodily processes, require physical separation from God's presence.[25] Moral impurity, arising from evil behaviours, produces a stain that is more problematic still. It defiles people, sanctuary and place, leading to extirpation and exile in the Old Testament, excommunication in the New. Moreover, the problems of defiled sanctuary and polluted land extend the need for atonement beyond the human realm, a matter simply ignored when atonement is limited to cancellation of sin and its penalty (as per Crisp).

The severity of the problem posed by impurity is accentuated by eschatological realities. The picture of the end is one of proximate holiness, which requires a purified world inhabited by purified people who no longer defile place or one another. Impurity in all its various manifestations is incommensurate with creation's telos and must be eradicated. Accordingly, as this volume demonstrates, the New Testament draws on a rich scriptural heritage to locate the ultimate means of atoning purification in the life, death, resurrection and ascension of Jesus.[26] He is simultaneously the priest who makes atonement (Heb. 2:17), the

[23] Crisp 2022: 16. Likewise, while Craig 2020: 2-3, 22 recognizes that *kpr* takes both sin and impurity as object, he assesses atonement only through the lens of sin removal. He also deliberately sets aside bloodless sacrifice even though non-blood (Lev. 5:11–13) and non-sacrificial (Num. 17:12[16:47]) rites atone (20 n. 13).

[24] McKnight 2007: 23.

[25] Although atonement is not required for minor ritual impurity, it is for major impurities (see chapter 1).

[26] While forgiveness and justification are also essential for reconciliation with God, they do not remove impurity.

atoning sacrifice (1 John 2:2), and the place of atonement (Rom. 3:25). His blood purifies people (Tit. 2:14), the heavenly sanctuary (Heb. 9:23–24), and, depending on how 1 John 2:2 is read, the world. Hence, while Witt and Scandrett do not consider purification in their analysis of atonement, they rightly identify its eschatological and cosmic trajectory:

> atonement has a teleological dimension. The doctrine of atonement does not simply look back to Jesus Christ's once-for-all death on the cross but looks forward to the eschatological acquittal and renewal of all creation: the vision of and full sharing in the mutual knowledge and love of the Father, Son, and Holy Spirit, when we shall see the triune God face to face and know fully as we are fully known.[27]

Clarifying the cruciality of purgation does not diminish atonement's expiatory function. These outcomes are complementary.[28] Neither does atonement as purgation require construction of a new model. Instead, increased sensitivity to the biblical themes of defilement and cleansing can enrich existing frameworks.[29] While space does not permit doing that work here,[30] the benefits are clear: a more holistic conception of what Christ has achieved and, by also including atonement of place, one that prevents anthropological reductionism.

Thinking about global mission

While the biblical concept of purity has exerted influence on some church practices,[31] it remains of marginal significance for many Western Christians. The lacuna is tangible when it comes to explications of the gospel message that typically resort to legal metaphors: we have

[27] Witt and Scandrett 2022: 226.

[28] See Sklar 2005.

[29] For example, Christus Victor emphasizes Christ's defeat of Satan and the forces of darkness, but this is also a victory over *impure* spirits and a means of *purifying* the world (see chapter 7).

[30] For a recent attempt to include purification as a constituent aspect of atonement, see Vaughn 2022.

[31] E.g. Gregory the Great's instruction that 'a man after sleeping with his own wife ought not to enter the church unless washed with water' appropriates Lev. 15:16 (*NPNF*², 13:78–79); menstruating women do not usually partake of the Eucharist in Orthodox churches (Dale 2018: 29); and Roman Catholicism makes provision for 'churching' new mothers based on Lev. 12 (Kaplan 2022: 100–1).

transgressed God's *law*, but, although God's *verdict* declares us *guilty*, he *judges* Jesus instead, *punishing* him that we might go *free*. On the one hand, this is understandable: legal terminology is used throughout the Bible to articulate both human predicament and God's salvific action. But this is not the sole mode of explanation. Sin is more often a burden that God lifts, an accounting ledger that is cleared, a path one turns from, or a stain that is removed.[32] Salvation is conceptualized as reconciliation, redemption, re-covenanting, reconfiguration, removing shame and, as this volume details, restoring purity. Each articulation is necessary, but not by itself sufficient. Soteriology is irreducibly rich.

The importance of cultivating competency in different modes of gospel presentation becomes apparent when engaging people from different cultural backgrounds.[33] The person and work of Jesus are appreciated most when received as God's solution to life's greatest concerns. Yet, felt needs differ significantly from people group to people group (and often within people groups). For many communities today, as in antiquity, purity is a crucial aspect of daily life and profoundly shapes practice and belief. Yet Christians accustomed to thinking only in terms of wrongdoing as (legal) impediment to communion with God may run into difficulties. As Barton illustrates:

> Jews, for whom the idea of impurity from the wrong food is entirely current and comprehensible … share with Muslims an abhorrence of eating pork (for example) that is visceral, and that is perceived as the transgression of a rule just as 'ethical' as the prohibition of theft or adultery. There may be a sliding scale of severity in the breach of the various commandments, but there is no difference in *kind* such as Christians tend to perceive.[34]

Accordingly, Bruce Thomas concludes, 'perhaps the greatest need felt by … Muslim people is not for assurance of salvation but for deliverance from the tyranny of being in a near constant state of defilement.'[35] Moyra

[32] See Lam 2016.

[33] This, as Chan 2018 demonstrates, is also true for many Western subcultures.

[34] Barton 2014: 193.

[35] Thomas 1994: 287.

Dale, who spent many years working in Muslim contexts, poses the resulting questions:

> How then do we respond to our Muslim friends when they discuss questions of ritual purity and its implications in daily life and pious practices? When their whole life has been defined by practices of purity in approaching God, are we to say that it no longer matters: purity is only concerned with the heart and not with bodily rituals?[36]

The answer, of course, is robust engagement with what the Bible has to say about defilement and cleansing. Sin is not the only barrier that separates persons from God. Nor is forgiveness all that people need. Purification, too, is essential. On that front, and irrespective of intrinsic complexities and gaps in our understanding, the canonical testimony is strikingly clear: climactically in Jesus, God has acted to purify men and women, in body and spirit, so they can boldly approach his presence and there experience joy now and forevermore. Put most simply: Jesus can make you pure.

This profound truth has considerable traction in explaining the good news about Jesus in contexts that operate according to different theological anthropologies. Badru Kateregga and David Shenk make the point with respect to Islam:

> Islam does not identify with the Christian conviction that man [sic.] needs to be redeemed. The Christian belief in the redemptive sacrificial death of Christ does not fit the Islamic view that man [sic.] has always been fundamentally good, and that God loves and forgives those who obey his will.[37]

For this reason, Hibbert suggests framing the gospel in terms of pollution and purity: 'One possibility is to highlight Christ, the Pure One, coming to make us pure by becoming defiled instead of us and, so, taking away our impurity.'[38] Christians can affirm that purity of body and spirit matters, recognize the impossibility of effecting self-purification, and then point to the one who cleanses people. To the person who says, 'If you are

---

[36] Dale 2018: 30.

[37] Kateregga and Shenk 1997: 175.

[38] Hibbert 2008: 352.

willing, you are able to cleanse me', Jesus responds, 'I am willing. Be clean!' (Mark 1:40–41 my tr.). There is provision here in abundance.

Final words

Here, at the end, it is perhaps fitting to return to where exploration began. That is, after all, so often the pattern of biblical theology in which past informs future and future grants new insight into past. Teleology is already operative in Leviticus, which, in profound ways, is an eschatological text. The book portrays as-yet unrealized possibilities as it seeks to shape the imagination of hearers and invite them to participate in the community of Yahweh worshippers.[39] Potential becomes promise fulfilled as the blessedness of life with God is increasingly experienced. And it is God who secures that blessing. Thus, the title of this book, drawn from Leviticus 16:30, encapsulates the hope of God's people in every era who await a fuller realization: 'You shall be clean.'

[39] See Harper 2018: 84–88.

Bibliography

Adewuya, J. Ayodeji. 2011. *Holiness and Community in 2 Cor 6:14-7:1: Paul's View of Communal Holiness in the Corinthian Correspondence.* Eugene: Wipf & Stock.

Alder, Yonatan. 2011. *The Archaeology of Purity: Archaeological Evidence for the Observance of Ritual Purity in Ereẓ-Israel from the Hasmonean Period until the End of the Talmudic Era (164 BCE–400 CE) [Hebrew].* Ramat-Gan: Bar-Ilan University Press.

Alexander, T. Desmond. 2017. *Exodus.* AOTC 2. London: Apollos.

Allen, David L. 2012. 'Substitutionary Atonement and Cultic Terminology in Isaiah 53'. In Darrell L. Bock and Mitch Glaser (eds.), *The Gospel According to Isaiah 53: Encountering the Suffering Servant in Jewish and Christian Theology.* Grand Rapids: Kregal, 171–189.

Allen, Leslie C. 1976. *The Books of Joel, Obadiah, Jonah and Micah.* NICOT. Grand Rapids: Eerdmans.

Alon, Gedaliah. 1977. *Jews, Judaism and the Classical World: Studies in Jewish History in the Times of the Second Temple and Talmud.* Translated by Israel Abrahams. Jerusalem: Magnes.

Alter, Robert. 2004. *The Five Books of Moses: A Translation with Commentary.* New York: Norton & Co.

Andersen, Francis I., and David Noel Freedman. 1980. *Hosea: A New Translation with Introduction and Commentary.* AB 24. Garden City: Doubleday.

Arnold, Clinton E. 2010. *Ephesians.* ZECOT. Grand Rapids: Zondervan.

Ashley, Timothy R. 2022. *The Book of Numbers.* NICOT. 2nd edn. Grand Rapids: Eerdmans.

Assis, Elie. 2004. '"For It Shall Be a Witness between Us": A Literary Reading of Josh 22'. *SJOT* 18: 208–31.

Assmann, Jan. 2003. *Mort et au-delà dans l'Egypte ancienne.* Monaco: Éditions du Rocher.

Attridge, Harold W. 1989. *The Epistle to the Hebrews: A Commentary on the Epistle to the Hebrews.* Hermenia. Philadelphia: Fortress.

Averbeck, Richard E. 1997. 'Clean and Unclean.' In *NIDOTTE* 4:477–86.

Awabdy, Mark A., and Tobias Häner. 2022. 'Sacrificial Fathers and the Death of Their Children: How the Story of Job Challenges the Priestly Tradition'. *HTR* 115: 149–70.

Balberg, Mira. 2014. *Purity, Body, and Self in Early Rabbinic Literature*. Berkeley: University of California Press.

Baldwin, Joyce G. 1978. *Daniel: An Introduction and Commentary*. TOTC. Leicester: IVP.

Barker, Kit. 2016. *Imprecation as Divine Discourse: Speech Act Theory, Dual Authorship and Theological Interpretation*. JTISup 16. Winona Lake: Eisenbrauns.

Barr, James. 1961. *The Semantics of Biblical Language*. Oxford: Oxford University Press.

Barrett, C. K. 1955. *The Gospel According to St John: An Introduction with Commentary and Notes on the Greek Text*. London: SPCK.

———. 1998. *A Critical and Exegetical Commentary on the Acts of the Apostles. Volume 2: Introduction and Commentary on Acts XV–XXVIII*. ICC. Edinburgh: T&T Clark.

Barth, Karl. 1985. *Church Dogmatics. Volume IV: The Doctrine of Reconciliation. Part 1*. Edinburgh: T&T Clark.

Bartholomew, Craig G. 2011. *Where Mortals Dwell: A Christian View of Place for Today*. Grand Rapids: Baker.

Barton, John. 2014. *Ethics in Ancient Israel*. Oxford: Oxford University Press.

Batchelder, Caroline. 2023. *Charged with the Glory of God: Yahweh, the Servant, and the Earth in Isaiah 40–55*. Bellingham: Lexham.

Bauckham, Richard J. 1996. *Jude, 2 Peter*. WBC 50. Nashville: Thomas Nelson.

———. 1999. *James: Wisdom of James, Disciple of Jesus the Sage*. London: Routledge.

Beale, G. K. 1999. *The Book of Revelation: A Commentary on the Greek Text*. NIGTC. Grand Rapids: Eerdmans.

———. 2004. *The Temple and the Church's Mission: A Biblical Theology of the Dwelling Place of God*. NSBT 17. Leicester: Apollos.

Beale, G. K., and D. A. Carson. 2007. *Commentary on the New Testament Use of the Old Testament*. Grand Rapids: Baker.

Beck, Richard. 2012. *Unclean: Meditations on Purity, Hospitality and Mortality*. Cambridge: Lutterworth.

Beilby, James K., and Paul R. Eddy (eds.). 2006. *The Nature of the Atonement: Four Views*. Downers Grove: IVP.

Belleville, Linda L. 1980. '"Born of Water and Spirit": John 3:5'. *TrinJ* 1: 125–41.

Bello, Rafael N. 2020. *Sinless Flesh: A Critique of Karl Barth's Fallen Christ*. Bellingham: Lexham.

Bergen, Doris L. 1996. *Twisted Cross: The German Christian Movement in the Third Reich*. Chapel Hill: University of North Carolina Press.

Berkhof, Louis. 1996. *Systematic Theology*. New Combined ed. Grand Rapids: Eerdmans.

Bildstein, Moshe. 2017. *Purity, Community, and Ritual in Early Christian Literature*. Oxford: Oxford University Press.

Bird, Michael F. 2008. 'Jesus as Law Breaker.' In Scot McKnight and Joseph B. Modica (eds.), *Who Do My Opponents Say That I Am? An Investigation of the Accusations against the Historical Jesus*. LNTS 327. London: T&T Clark, 3–26.

Bird, Phyllis A. 1995. 'The End of the Male Cult Prostitute: A Literary-Historical and Sociological Analysis of Hebrew *Qādēš-Qĕdēšîm*.' In J. A. Emerton (ed.), *Congress Volume Cambridge 1995*. VTSup 66. Leiden: Brill, 37–80.

———. 2019. *Harlot or Holy Woman? A Study of Hebrew Qedešah*. University Park: Eisenbrauns.

Blenkinsopp, Joseph. 2012. 'The Baal Peor Episode Revisited (Num 25, 1–18)'. *Biblica* 93: 86–97.

Blomberg, Craig L. 2005. *Contagious Holiness: Jesus' Meals with Sinners*. NSBT 19. Downers Grove: IVP.

———. 2023. *Jesus the Purifier: John's Gospel and the Fourth Quest for the Historical Jesus*. Grand Rapids: Baker.

Bock, Darrell L. 1994. *Luke 1:1–9:50*. BECNT. Grand Rapids: Baker.

———. 2007. *Acts*. BECNT. Grand Rapids: Baker.

Bockmuehl, Markus. 2000. *Jewish Law in Gentile Churches: Halakhah and the Beginning of Christian Public Ethics*. Edinburgh: T&T Clark.

Boda, Mark J. 2009. *A Severe Mercy: Sin and Its Remedy in the Old Testament*. Siph. 1. Winona Lake: Eisenbrauns.

———. 2015. *'Return to Me': A Biblical Theology of Repentance*. NSBT 35. Downers Grove: IVP.

Bolt, Peter G. 2004. *The Cross from a Distance: Atonement in Mark's Gospel*. NSBT 18. Downers Grove: IVP.

Boorer, Suzanne. 2016. *The Vision of the Priestly Narrative: Its Genre and Hermeneutics of Time*. AIL 27. Atlanta: SBL.

Borg, Marcus J. 1998. *Conflict, Holiness and Politics in the Teachings of Jesus*. Harrisburg: Trinity.

Borgen, Peder, and Soren Giversen (eds.). 1997. *The New Testament and Hellenistic Judaism*. Peabody: Hendrickson.

Bradford, Timothy P. 2025. 'Restoring and Revealing the Human Condition: Matthew's Servant and the Establishment of מִשְׁפָּט / κρίσις on the Earth.' In Peter G. Bolt (ed.), *God beyond Ideology: Rediscovering Theology through Narrative*. Norwest: SCD Press, 75–96.

Brown, Colin, and Craig A. Evans. 2022. *A History of the Quests for the Historical Jesus*. Grand Rapids: Zondervan.

Brown, Raymond E. 2003. *An Introduction to the Gospel of John*. ABRL. New York: Doubleday.

Bruce, F. F. 1990. *The Epistle to the Hebrews*. NICNT. Grand Rapids: Eerdmans.

Brueggemann, Walter. 1977. *The Land: Place as Gift, Promise, and Challenge in Biblical Faith*. OBT 1. Philadelphia: Fortress.

Brueggemann, Walter, and Davis Hankins. 2013. 'The Invention and Persistence of Wellhausen's World.' *CBQ* 75: 15–31.

Bruno, Chris, Jared Compton, and Kevin McFadden. 2020. *Biblical Theology According to the Apostles: How the Earliest Christians Told the Story of Israel*. NSBT 52. London: Apollos.

Büchler, Adolph. 1928. *Studies in Sin and Atonement in the Rabbinic Literature of the First Century*. London: Oxford University Press.

Burge, Gary M. 2000. *John*. NIVAC. Grand Rapids: Zondervan.

Butler, Trent C. 1983. *Joshua*. WBC 7. Waco: Word.

Butova, Elena. 2018. *The Four Prohibitions of Acts 15 and Their Common Background in Genesis 1–3*. Eugene: Wipf & Stock.

Carr, David M. 2005. *Writing on the Tablet of the Heart: Origins of Scripture and Literature*. Oxford: Oxford University Press.

Carroll, Robert P. 1992. 'The Myth of the Empty Land'. *Semeia* 59: 79–93.

Carson, D. A. 1991. *The Gospel According to John*. PNTC. Eerdmans: Grand Rapids.

Chan, Sam. 2018. *Evangelism in a Sceptical World: How to Make the Unbelievable News About Jesus More Believable*. Grand Rapids: Zondervan.

Charlesworth, James H. (ed.). 1983–1985. *The Old Testament Pseudepigrapha*. New York: Doubleday.

Childs, Brevard S. 1979. *Introduction to the Old Testament as Scripture*. London: SCM.

Chilton, Bruce D. 1997. 'John the Purifier.' In Bruce D. Chilton and Craig A. Evans (eds.), *Jesus in Context: Temple, Purity, and Restoration*. AGJU 39. Leiden: Brill, 203–20.

———. 2000. *Rabbi Jesus: An Intimate Biography*. New York: Doubleday.

Cole, Graham A. 2009. *God the Peacemaker: How Atonement Brings Shalom*. NSBT 25. Downers Grove: IVP.

Cole, Robert L. 2013. 'Psalms 1 and 2: The Psalter's Introduction.' In Andrew J. Schmutzer and David M. Howard (eds.), *The Psalms: Language for All Seasons of the Soul*. Chicago: Moody, 183–95.

Collins, C. John. 2018. *Reading Genesis Well: Navigating History, Poetry, Science, and Truth in Genesis 1–11*. Grand Rapids: Zondervan.

Collins, John J. 2002. 'The Literature of the Second Temple Period.' In Martin Goodman (ed.), *The Oxford Handbook of Jewish Studies*. Oxford: Oxford University Press, 53–78.

Colpe, Carsten. 2003. *Iranier – Aramäer – Hebräer – Hellenen: Iranische Religionen und ihre Westbeziehungen. Einzelstudien und Versuch einer Zusammenschau*. WUNT 154. Tübingen: Mohr Siebeck.

Cox, Jennifer A. 2011. 'Disability as an Enacted Parable.' *JRDH* 15: 241–53.

Craig, William Lane. 2020. *Atonement and the Death of Christ: An Exegetical, Historical, and Philosophical Exploration*. Waco: Baylor University Press.

Craigie, Peter C. 1976. *The Book of Deuteronomy*. NICOT. Grand Rapids: Eerdmans.

Cranz, Isabel. 2017. *Atonement and Purification: Priestly and Assyro-Babylonian Perspectives on Sin and Its Consequences* FAT 2/92. Tübingen: Mohr Siebeck.

Crisp, Oliver D. 2022. *Participation and Atonement: An Analytic and Constructive Account*. Grand Rapids: Baker.

Crossley, James G. 2004. *The Date of Mark's Gospel: Insight from the Law in Earliest Christianity*. JSNTSup 266. London: T&T Clark.

Culpepper, R. Alan, and Paul N. Anderson (eds.). 2017. *John and Judaism: A Contested Relationship in Context*. RBS 87. Atlanta: SBL.

Culver, Robert D. 1969. 'Isaiah 1:18: Declaration, Exclamation, or Interrogation?' *JETS* 12: 133–41.

Dale, Moyra. 2018. 'Ritual Purity and Defilement: What Place Does It Have?' *WWS* 2: 6–36.

Davies, G. Henton. 1962. 'Leviticus.' In *IDB* 3:117–22.

Dearman, J. Andrew. 2010. *The Book of Hosea*. NICOT. Grand Rapids: Eerdmans.

DeLapp, Nevada L. 2018. *Theophanic 'Type-Scenes' in the Pentateuch: Visions of YHWH*. LHBOTS 660. London: T&T Clark.

deSilva, David A. 2013. 'Clean and Unclean'. In Joel B. Green, Jeannine K. Brown and Nicholas Perrin (eds.), *Dictionary of Jesus and the Gospels*. Downers Grove: IVP, 142–49.

———. 2014. *Transformation: The Heart of Paul's Gospel*. Bellingham: Lexham.

———. 2022. *Honor, Patronage, Kinship, and Purity: Unlocking New Testament Culture*. 2nd edn. Downers Grove: IVP.

DiFransico, Lesley. 2016. *Washing away Sin: An Analysis of the Metaphor in the Hebrew Bible and Its Influence*. BTS 23. Leuven: Peeters.

Dillard, Raymond B. 1987. *2 Chronicles*. WBC 15. Waco: Word.

Dobbs-Allsopp, F. W. 2002. *Lamentations: Interpretation: A Bible Commentary for Teaching and Preaching*. Louisville: John Knox.

Douglas, Mary. 1966. *Purity and Danger: An Analysis of the Concept of Pollution and Taboo*. London: Routledge.

———.1973. 'Critique and Commentary'. In Jacob Neusner, *The Idea of Purity in Ancient Judaism: The Haskell Lectures, 1972–1973*. Leiden: Brill, 137–42.

———. 1993a. 'The Forbidden Animals in Leviticus'. *JSOT* 59: 3–23.

———. 1993b. *In the Wilderness: The Doctrine of Defilement in the Book of Numbers*. JSOTSup 158. Sheffield: Sheffield Academic.

———. 1995. 'Poetic Structure in Leviticus'. In David P. Wright, David N. Freedman and Avi Hurvitz (eds.), *Pomegranates and Golden Bells: Studies in Biblical, Jewish, and Near Eastern Ritual, Law and Literature in Honor of Jacob Milgrom*. Winona Lake: Eisenbrauns, 239–56.

———. 1999. *Leviticus as Literature*. Oxford: Oxford University Press.

Dozeman, Thomas B. 2009. *Commentary on Exodus*. ECC. Grand Rapids: Eerdmans.

Dreher, Rod. 2020. *Live Not by Lies: A Manual for Christian Dissidents*. New York: Sentinel.

Duke, Rodney K. 1990. *The Persuasive Appeal of the Chronicler: A Rhetorical Analysis*. JSOTSup 88. Sheffield: Almond Press.

Dunn, James D. G. 1990. 'The Incident at Antioch (Gal 2.11–18).' In *Jesus,*

Paul and the Law: Studies in Mark and Galatians. London: SPCK, 129–82.

Eberhart, Christian A. 2011. *The Sacrifice of Jesus: Understanding Atonement Biblically*. Eugene: Wipf & Stock.

Edwards, James R. 2019. *Between the Swastika and the Sickle: The Life, Disappearance, and Execution of Ernst Lohmeyer*. Grand Rapids: Eerdmans.

Eidevall, Göran. 2012. *Sacrifical Rhetoric in the Prophetic Literature in the Hebrew Bible*. Lewiston: Mellen.

———. 2017. 'Prophetic Cult-Criticism in Support of Sacrifical Worship? The Case of Jeremiah'. In Henrietta L. Wiley and Christian A. Eberhart (eds.), *Sacrifice, Cult, and Atonement in Early Judaism and Christianity: Constituents and Critique*. RBS 85. Atlanta: SBL, 151–67.

Eilberg-Schwartz, Howard. 1990. *The Savage in Judaism: An Anthropology of Israelite Religion and Ancient Judaism*. Bloomington: Indiana University Press.

Ellingworth, Paul. 1993. *The Epistle to the Hebrews: A Commentary on the Greek Text*. NIGTC. Grand Rapids: Eerdmans.

Erbele-Küster, Dorothea. 2017. '"She Shall Remain in (Accordance to) Her Blood-of-Purification": Ritual Dynamics of Defilement and Purification in Leviticus 12'. In Henrietta L. Wiley and Christian Eberhart (eds.), *Sacrifice, Cult, and Atonement in Early Judaism and Christianity: Constituents and Critique*. RBS 85. Atlanta: SBL, 59–70.

———. 2021. 'The Ritual Texts of Leviticus and the Creation of Ritualized Bodies'. In Christophe Nihan and Julia Rhyder (eds.), *Text and Ritual in the Pentateuch: A Systematic and Comparative Approach*. University Park: Eisenbrauns, 240–54.

Erickson, Millard J. 1998. *Christian Theology*. 2nd edn. Grand Rapids: Baker.

Escott, Timothy R. 2019. 'Faithfulness and Restoration: Towards Reading Ezra-Nehemiah as Christian Scripture'. PhD diss., Durham University.

Eskenazi, Tamara C. 1988. *In an Age of Prose: A Literary Approach to Ezra-Nehemiah*. SBLMS. Atlanta: Scholars Press.

Estelle, Bryan D. 2018. *Echoes of Exodus: Tracing a Biblical Motif*. Downers Grove: IVP.

Evans, Craig A. 2001. *Mark 8.27–16.20*. WBC 34B. Nashville: Nelson.

———. 2005. 'Inaugurating the Kingdom of God and Defeating the Kingdom of Satan'. *BBR* 15: 49–75.

Feder, Yitzhaq. 2015. 'Behind the Scenes of a Priestly Polemic: Leviticus 14 and its Extra-Biblical Parallels'. *JHS* 15: 1–26.

Fee, Gordon D. 1987. *The First Epistle to the Corinthians*. NICNT. Grand Rapids: Eerdmans.

Ferch, John G. 2013. 'The Story of Torah: The Role of Narrative in Leviticus's Legal Discourse'. *JESOT* 2: 41–60.

Firmage, Edwin B. 1990. 'The Biblical Dietary Laws and the Concept of Holiness'. In J. A. Emerton (ed.), *Studies in the Pentateuch*. VTSup 41. Leiden: Brill, 177–208.

Firth, David G. 2009. *1 & 2 Samuel*. AOTC 8. Nottingham: Apollos.

Fishbane, Michael. 1988. *Biblical Interpretation in Ancient Israel*. Oxford: Clarendon.

Fitzmyer, Joseph A. 1981. *The Gospel According to Luke (I–IX)*. AB 28. New York: Doubleday.

Fletcher-Louis, Crispin H. T. 2007. 'Jesus as the High Priestly Messiah: Part 2'. *JSHJ* 5: 57–79.

France, R. T. 2002. *The Gospel of Mark: A Commentary on the Greek Text*. NIGTC. Grand Rapids: Eerdmans.

———. 2007. *The Gospel of Matthew*. NICNT. Grand Rapids: Eerdmans.

Frankel, David. 2011. *The Land of Canaan and the Destiny of Israel: Theologies of Territory in the Hebrew Bible*. Siph. 4. Winona Lake: Eisenbrauns.

Fredriksen, Paula. 1999. *Jesus of Nazareth, King of the Jews: A Jewish Life and the Emergence of Christianity*. New York: Knopf.

———. 2021. 'Review of Matthew Thiessen, *Jesus and the Forces of Death*'. *RBL* 1–4.

Frei, Hans W. 1974. *The Eclipse of Biblical Narrative: A Study in Eighteenth and Nineteenth Century Hermeneutics*. New Haven: Yale University Press.

Frymer-Kensky, Tikva. 1983. 'Pollution, Purification, and Purgation in Biblical Israel'. In Carol L. Meyers and M. O'Connor (eds.), *The Word of the Lord Shall Go Forth: Essays in Honor of David Noel Freedman in Celebration of His Sixtieth Birthday*. Winona Lake: Eisenbrauns, 399–414.

Fuhr, Richard Alan, and Gary E. Yates. 2016. *The Message of the Twelve: Hearing the Voice of the Minor Prophets*. Nashville: B&H.

Furstenberg, Yair. 2008. 'Defilement Penetrating the Body: A New Understanding of Contamination in Mark 7.15'. *NTS* 54: 176–200.

———. 2023. *Purity and Identity in Ancient Judaism: From the Temple to the Mishnah*. Bloomington. Indiana University Press.

Gagnon, Robert A. J. 2001. *The Bible and Homosexual Practice: Texts and Hermeneutics*. Nashville: Abingdon.

García Martínez, Florentino. 1996. *The Dead Sea Scrolls Translated: The Qumran Texts in English*. Leiden: Brill.

Gärtner, Bertil. 1965. *The Temple and the Community in Qumran and the New Testament: A Comparative Study in the Temple Symbolism of the Qumran Texts and the New Testament*. SNTSMS 1. Cambridge: Cambridge University Press.

Garvey, Jon. 2019. *God's Good Earth: The Case for an Unfallen Creation*. Eugene: Cascade.

Gerstenberger, Erhard S. 1996. *Leviticus*. Louisville: Westminster John Knox.

Gilchrest, Eric. 2013. 'For the Wages of Sin is … Banishment: An Unexplored Substitutionary Motif in Leviticus 16 and the Ritual of the Scapegoat'. *EQ* 85: 36–51.

Girard, René. 2005. *Violence and the Sacred*. London: Continuum.

Glaim, Aaron. 2017. '"I Will Not Accept Them": Sacrifice and Reciprocity in the Prophetic Literature'. In Henrietta L. Wiley and Christian A. Eberhart (eds.), *Sacrifice, Cult, and Atonement in Early Judaism and Christianity: Constituents and Critique*. RBS 85. Atlanta: SBL, 125–49.

Goldingay, John E. 1989. *Daniel*. WBC 30. Dallas: Word.

———. 2006. *Psalms: Volume 1: Psalms 1–41*. BCOTWP. Grand Rapids: Baker.

———. 2015. *Do We Need the New Testament? Letting the Old Testament Speak for Itself*. Downers Grove: IVP.

Goppelt, Leonhard. 1993. *A Commentary on 1 Peter*. Translated by John E. Alsup. Grand Rapids. Eerdmans.

Greenberg, James A. 2019. *A New Look at Atonement in Leviticus: The Meaning and Purpose of Kipper Revisited*. BBRSup 23. University Park: Eisenbrauns.

Grindheim, Sigurd. 2020. 'Jesus and the Food Laws Revisited'. *JSHJ* 18: 61–76.

Grudem, Wayne. 1994. *Systematic Theology: An Introduction to Biblical Doctrine*. Leicester: IVP.

Gunton, Colin E. 1989. *The Actuality of Atonement: A Study of Metaphor, Rationality and the Christian Tradition*. Grand Rapids: Eerdmans.

Guthrie, George H. 2015. *2 Corinthians*. BECNT. Grand Rapids: Baker.

Habel, Norman C. 1995. *The Land is Mine: Six Biblical Land Ideologies*. OBT. Minneapolis: Fortress.

Haber, Susan. 2008. *'They Shall Purify Themselves': Essays on Purity in Early Judaism*. Atlanta: SBL.

Harper, G. Geoffrey. 2013. 'Time for a New Diet? Allusions to Genesis 1–3 as Rhetorical Device in Leviticus 11'. *STR* 4: 179–95.

———. 2015. 'The Theological and Exegetical Significance of Leviticus as Intertext in Daniel 9'. *JESOT* 4: 39–61.

———. 2018. *'I Will Walk Among You': The Rhetorical Function of Allusion to Genesis 1–3 in the Book of Leviticus*. BBRSup 21. University Park: Eisenbrauns.

———. 2020. '"Do Not Eat the Owl": Hearing Leviticus 11 as Christian Scripture'. *HipNov* 6: 20–32.

———. 2022a. 'Endangered or Dangerous? YHWH's Presence and Impurity in Levitical Perspective'. *JSOT* 46: 480–94.

———. 2022b. *Teaching Leviticus: From Text to Message*. Fearn: Christian Focus.

———. 2024. 'What's Impurity Got to Do with It? Leviticus, Gentiles, and the Council of Jerusalem'. A paper presented to the Kirby Laing Centre/IBR Scripture and Hermeneutics Seminar (26 June).

———. 2025. 'What Hope for the Land? Geospatial Defilement and Cleansing in the Hebrew Bible'. In David G. Firth, Jamie A. Grant and Alison Lo (eds.), *Hope for the World from the Old Testament: Studies in Honour of J. Gordon McConville on His 70th Birthday*. GFS 4. Wilmore: GlossaHouse, 227–39.

———. forthcoming-a. 'Joseph and His Brothers: Genesis 44–45'. In Kit Barker and G. Geoffrey Harper (eds.), *Gospel Shaped Forgiveness: Forgiving One Another as God Has Forgiven Us*. Eugene: Wipf & Stock.

———. forthcoming-b. *Leviticus*. Eugene: Cascade.

———. forthcoming-c. 'Possibilities and Impossibilities in Hebrews 10:4'.

Harrington, Hannah K. 1993. *The Impurity Systems of Qumran and the Rabbis: Biblical Foundations*. SBLDS 143. Atlanta: Scholars Press.

———. 2000. 'The Halakah and Religion of Qumran'. In John J. Collins and Robert A. Kugler (eds.), *Religion in the Dead Sea Scrolls*. Grand Rapids: Eerdmans, 74–89.

———. 2011. 'Purification in the Fourth Gospel in Light of Qumran'. In Mary L. Coloe and Tom Thatcher (eds.), *John, Qumran, and the Dead*

Sea Scrolls: Sixty Years of Discovery and Debate. EJL 32. Atlanta: SBL, 117–38.

Harrison, Roland K. 1980. *Leviticus: An Introduction and Commentary*. TOTC. Leicester: IVP.

Hartley, John E. 1992. *Leviticus*. WBC 4. Dallas: Word.

Hayes, Christine E. 2002. *Gentile Impurities and Jewish Identities: Intermarriage and Conversion from the Bible to the Talmud*. Oxford: Oxford University Press.

Hays, J. Daniel. 2016. *The Temple and the Tabernacle: A Study of God's Dwelling Places from Genesis to Revelation*. Grand Rapids: Baker.

Hays, Richard B. 1993. *Echoes of Scripture in the Letters of Paul*. New Haven: Yale University Press.

———. 2015. *Reading Backwards: Figural Christology and the Fourfold Gospel Witness*. London: SPCK.

Heiser, Michael S. 2015. *The Unseen Realm: Recovering the Supernatural Worldview of the Bible*. Bellingham: Lexham.

Hendel, Ronald S. 2012. 'Away from Ritual: The Prophetic Critique'. In Saul M. Olyan (ed.), *Social Theory and the Study of Israelite Religion: Essays in Retrospect and Prospect*. RBS 71. Atlanta: SBL, 59–80.

Henze, Matthias, and David Lincicum (eds.). 2023. *Israel's Scriptures in Early Christian Writings: The Use of the Old Testament in the New*. Chicago: Eerdmans.

Heschel, Susannah. 2008. *The Aryan Jesus: Christian Theologians and the Bible in Nazi Germany*. Princeton: Princeton University Press.

Hess, Richard S. 2005. *Song of Songs*. BCOTWP. Grand Rapids: Baker.

Hibbert, Richard. 2008. 'Defilement and Cleansing: A Possible Approach to Christian Encounter with Muslims'. *Missiology* 36: 343–55.

Hidiroglou, Patricia. 2000. 'L'eau et les bains à Qoumrân'. *REJ* 159: 19–47.

Hieke, Thomas. 2014. *Levitikus 1–15*. HTKAT. Freiburg: Herder.

Hill, Andrew E. 2003. *1 & 2 Chronicles*. NIVAC. Grand Rapids: Zondervan.

Hillers, Delbert R. 1992. *Lamentations: A New Translation with Introduction and Commentary*. AB 7A. 2nd edn. New York: Doubleday.

Hoffmann, David. 1905–1906. *Das Buch Leviticus I–II*. Berlin: Poppelauer.

Holladay, William L. 1986. *Jeremiah 1: A Commentary on the Book of the Prophet Jeremiah 1–25*. Hermenia. Philadelphia: Fortress.

Hollier, Joel. 2019. *A Place at His Table: A Biblical Exploration of Faith, Sexuality, and the Kingdom of God*. Eugene: Cascade.

Holmén, Tom. 2001. 'The Jewishness of Jesus in the "Third Quest"'. In

Michael Labahn and Andreas Schmidt (eds.), *Jesus, Mark, and Q: The Teaching of Jesus and Its Earliest Records*. JSNTSup 42. Sheffield: Sheffield University Press, 143–62.

Houston, Walter J. 1993. *Purity and Monotheism: Clean and Unclean Animals in Biblical Law*. JSOTSup 140. Sheffield: JSOT Press.

Howell, David B. 1990. *Matthew's Inclusive Story: A Study in the Narrative Rhetoric of the First Gospel*. JSNTSup 42. Sheffield: JSOT Press.

Hubert, Henri, and Marcel Mauss. 1964. *Sacrifice: Its Nature and Functions*. Chicago: University of Chicago Press.

Hulse, Erroll V. 1975. 'The Nature of Biblical "Leprosy" and the Use of Alternative Medical Terms in Modern Translations of the Bible'. *PEQ* 107: 87–105.

Hultgren, Stephen. 2007. *From the Damascus Covenant to the Covenant of the Community: Literary, Historical, and Theological Studies in the Dead Sea Scrolls*. STDJ. Leiden: Brill.

Hundley, Michael B. 2011. *Keeping Heaven on Earth: Safeguarding the Divine Presence in the Priestly Tabernacle*. FAT 2/50. Tübingen: Mohr Siebeck.

Jenson, Philip P. 1992. *Graded Holiness: A Key to the Priestly Conception of the World*. JSOTSup 106. Sheffield: Sheffield Academic.

Jobes, Karen H. 2005. *1 Peter*. BECNT. Grand Rapids: Baker.

———. 2021. *John through Old Testament Eyes: A Background and Application Commentary*. Grand Rapids: Kregel.

Joosten, Jan. 1996. *People and Land in the Holiness Code: An Exegetical Study of the Ideational Framework of the Law in Leviticus 17–26*. VTSup 67. Leiden: Brill.

Josephus. 1987. *The Works of Josephus: Complete and Unabridged*. Peabody: Hendrickson.

Kaplan, Abby. 2022. *Misreading Ritual: Sacrifice and Purity for the Modern-Day Gentile*. Eugene: Resource.

Käsemann, Ernst. 1964. *Essays on New Testament Themes*. Translated by W. J. Montague. London: SCM.

Kateregga, Badru D., and David W. Shenk. 1997. *A Muslim and a Christian in Dialogue*. Scottdale: Herald.

Kazen, Thomas. 2002. *Jesus and Purity Halakhah: Was Jesus Indifferent to Impurity?* ConBNT 38. Stockholm: Almqvist & Wiksell.

———. 2010. *Issues of Impurity in Early Judaism*. ConBNT 45. Winona Lake: Eisenbrauns.

———. 2013a. 'Jesus and the Zavah: Implications for Interpreting Mark'. In Carl S. Ehrlich, Anders Runesson and Eileen Schuller (eds.), *Purity, Holiness, and Identity in Ancient Judaism and Early Christianity: Essays in Memory of Susan Haber*. WUNT 305. Tübingen: Mohr Siebeck, 112–43.

———. 2013b. *Scripture, Interpretation, or Authority? Motives and Arguments in Jesus' Halakic Conflicts*. WUNT 320. Tübingen: Mohr Siebeck.

———. 2014. 'The Role of Disgust in Priestly Purity Law: Insights from Conceptual Metaphor and Blending Theories'. *JLRS* 3: 62–92.

———. 2015a. 'Concern, Custom, and Common Sense: Discharge, Handwashing, and Graded Purification'. *JSHJ* 13: 150–87.

———. 2015b. 'Purity and Persia'. In Roy E. Gane and Ada Taggar-Cohen (eds.), *Current Issues in Priestly and Related Literature: The Legacy of Jacob Milgrom and Beyond*. RBS 82. Atlanta: SBL, 435–62.

———. 2015c. 'Purity/Impurity'. In Robert Segal and Kocku von Stuckrad (eds.), *Vocabulary for the Study of Religion*. Vol. 3. Leiden: Brill, 166–70.

———. 2016. 'A Perhaps Less Halakic Jesus and Purity: On Prophetic Criticism, Halakic Innovation, and Rabbinic Anachronism'. *JSHJ* 14: 120–36.

———. 2018a. 'Levels of Explanation for Ideas of Impurity: Why Structuralist and Symbolic Models Often Fail While Evolutionary and Cognitive Models Succeed'. *JAJ* 9: 75–100.

———. 2018b. 'Purification'. In Risto Uro, Juliette J. Day, Rikard Roitto and Richard E. DeMaris (eds.), *The Oxford Handbook of Early Christian Rituals*. Oxford: Oxford University Press, 220–44.

———. 2021. *Impurity and Purification in Early Judaism and the Jesus Tradition*. RBS 98. Atlanta: SBL.

Keener, Craig S. 2003. *The Gospel of John: A Commentary*. Peabody: Hendrickson.

Kelle, Brad E. 2005. *Hosea 2: Metaphor and Rhetoric in Historical Perspective*. AcBib 20. Atlanta: SBL.

Kellogg, Samuel H. 1891. *The Book of Leviticus*. New York: Armstrong and Son.

Kilchör, Benjamin. 2015. *Mosetora und Jahwetora: Das Verhältnis von Deuteronomium 12–26 zu Exodus, Levitikus, und Numeri*. BZABR 21. Wiesbaden: Harrassowitz.

———. 2020a. 'The Reception of the Priestly Laws in Deuteronomy and Deuteronomy's Target Audience'. In Leslie S. Baker, Jr., Kenneth Bergland, Felipe A. Masotti and A. Rahel Wells (eds.), *Exploring the Composition of the Pentateuch*. University Park: Eisenbrauns, 213–25.

———. 2020b. *Wiederhergestellter Gottesdienst: Eine Deutung der zweiten Tempelvision Ezechiels (Ez 40–48) am Beispiel der Aufgaben der Priester und Leviten*. HBS 95. Freiburg: Herder.

Kistemaker, Simon J. 1984. *Exposition of the Epistle to the Hebrews*. NTC. Grand Rapids: Baker.

Kiuchi, Nobuyoshi. 1987. *The Purification Offering in the Priestly Literature: Its Meaning and Function*. JSOTSup 56. Sheffield: JSOT Press.

Klawans, Jonathan. 1995. 'Notions of Gentile Impurity in Ancient Judaism'. *AJSR* 20: 285–312.

———. 2000. *Impurity and Sin in Ancient Judaism*. Oxford: Oxford University Press.

———. 2006. *Purity, Sacrifice, and the Temple: Symbolism and Supersessionism in the Study of Ancient Judaism*. Oxford: Oxford University Press.

———. 2010. 'Purity in the Dead Sea Scrolls'. In Timothy H. Lim and John J. Collins (eds.), *The Oxford Handbook of the Dead Sea Scrolls*. Oxford: Oxford University Press, 377–402.

Klink III, Edward W., and Darian R. Lockett. 2012. *Understanding Biblical Theology: A Comparison of Theory and Practice*. Grand Rapids: Zondervan.

Knoppers, Gary N. 1995. 'Images of David in Early Judaism: David as Repentant Sinner in Chronicles'. *Biblica* 76: 449–70.

Kohn, Risa Levitt. 2002. *A New Heart and a New Soul: Ezekiel, the Exile and the Torah*. JSOTSup 358. London: Sheffield Academic.

Köstenberger, Andreas J. 2007. 'John'. In G. K. Beale and D. A. Carson (eds.), *Commentary on the New Testament Use of the Old Testament*. Grand Rapids: Baker, 415–512.

Kraemer, Ross S. 1992. *Her Share of the Blessings: Women's Religions among Pagans, Jews, and Christians in the Greco-Roman World*. New York: Oxford University Press.

Kruger, Michael J. 2012. *Canon Revisited: Establishing the Origins and Authority of the New Testament Books*. Wheaton: Crossway.

Kugel, James L. 1996. 'The Holiness of Israel and the Land in Second Temple Times'. In Michael V. Fox, Victor A. Hurowitz, Avi Hurvitz, Michael L. Klein, Baruch J. Schwartz and Nili Shupak (eds.), *Texts,*

Temples, and Traditions: A Tribute to Menahem Haran. Winona Lake: Eisenbrauns, 21–32.

Lakoff, George, and Mark Johnson. 1980. *Metaphors We Live By*. Chicago: University of Chicago Press.

Lam, Joseph. 2016. *Patterns of Sin in the Hebrew Bible: Metaphor, Culture, and the Making of a Religious Concept*. New York: Oxford University Press.

Lane, William L. 1974. *The Gospel of Mark*. NICNT. Grand Rapids: Eerdmans.

Lapsley, Jacqueline E. 2005. *Whispering the Word: Hearing Women's Stories in the Old Testament*. Louisville: Westminster John Knox.

Latz, Andrew B., and Arseny Ermakov (eds.). 2014. *Purity: Essays in Bible and Theology*. Eugene: Pickwick.

Lau, Peter H. W. 2009. 'Gentile Incorporation in Ezra-Nehemiah'. *Biblica* 90: 356–73.

Lau, Te-Li. 2020. *Defending Shame: Its Formative Power in Paul's Letters*. Grand Rapids: Baker.

Leaney, A. R. C. 1958. *A Commentary on the Gospel according to St Luke*. London: Black.

LeFebvre, Michael. 2020. 'The Liturgical Function of Dates in the Pentateuch'. In Leslie S. Baker, Jr., Kenneth Bergland, Felipe A. Masotti and A. Rahel Wells (eds.), *Exploring the Composition of the Pentateuch*. BBRSup 27. University Park: Eisenbrauns, 113–30.

Levenson, Jon D. 1985. *Sinai and Zion: An Entry into the Jewish Bible*. San Francisco: HarperSanFrancisco.

Levine, Amy-Jill. 2006. *Misunderstood Jew: The Church and the Scandal of the Jewish Jesus*. New York: HarperOne.

Levine, Baruch A. 1989. *Leviticus: The Traditional Hebrew Text with the New JPS Translation*. JPSTC. Philadelphia: Jewish Publication Society.

Lightfoot, J. B. 2015. *The Gospel of St. John: A Newly Discovered Commentary*. Downers Grove: IVP.

Loader, William R. G. 2002. *Jesus' Attitude towards the Law: A Study of the Gospels*. Grand Rapids: Eerdmans.

Longman III, Tremper. 2008. *Jeremiah, Lamentations*. NIBC. Peabody: Hendrickson.

Lovell, Nathan. 2021. *The Book of Kings and Exilic Identity: 1 and 2 Kings as a Work of Political Historiography*. LHBOTS 708. London: T&T Clark.

Lucas, Ernest C. 2002. *Daniel*. AOTC 20. Downers Grove: IVP.

Luciani, Didier. 2005. *Sainteté et Pardon: Volume I. Structure Littéraire du Lévitique*. BETL 185A. Leuven: Leuven University Press.

Lundquist, John M. 1984. 'The Common Temple Ideology of the Ancient Near East'. In Truman G. Madsen (ed.), *The Temple in Antiquity: Ancient Records and Modern Perspectives*. Provo: Brigham Young University, 53–76.

———. 1994. 'What Is a Temple? A Preliminary Typology'. In Donald W. Parry (ed.), *Temples of the Ancient World: Ritual and Symbolism*. Salt Lake City: Deseret, 83–117.

Lunn, Nicholas P. 2015. 'Allusions to the Levitical Leprosy Laws in the Jericho Narratives (Joshua 2 and 6)'. *JESOT* 4: 131–44.

Lyons, Michael A. 2009. *From Law to Prophecy: Ezekiel's Use of the Holiness Code*. LHBOTS 507. New York: T&T Clark.

McCarter, P. Kyle. 1973. 'The River Ordeal in Israelite Literature'. *HTR* 66: 403–12.

Maccoby, Hyam. 1999. *Ritual and Morality: The Ritual Purity System and Its Place in Judaism*. Cambridge: University Press Cambridge.

McConville, J. Gordon. 2002. *Deuteronomy*. AOTC 5. Leicester: Apollos.

———. 2016. *Being Human in God's World: An Old Testament Theology of Humanity*. Grand Rapids: Baker.

McDonald Jr., Kelly. 2013. *Clean and Unclean: A Guide to Living the Holy Life*. Maitland: Xulon.

McKnight, Scot. 2007. *A Community Called Atonement*. Nashville: Abingdon.

Magness, Jodi. 2011. *Stone and Dung, Oil and Spit: Jewish Daily Life in the Time of Jesus*. Grand Rapids: Eerdmans.

Malone, Andrew S. 2017. *God's Mediators: A Biblical Theology of Priesthood*. NSBT 43. Downers Grove: IVP.

Marshall, I. Howard. 1978a. *The Epistles of John*. NICNT. Grand Rapids. Eerdmans.

———. 1978b. *The Gospel of Luke: A Commentary on the Greek Text*. NIGTC. Exeter: Paternoster.

Martin, Ralph P. 1988. *James*. WBC 48. Waco: Word.

Meier, John P. 1991. *A Marginal Jew: Rethinking the Historical Jesus*. ABRL. New York: Doubleday.

Michaels, J. Ramsey. 2010. *The Gospel of John*. NICNT. Grand Rapids: Eerdmans.

Milgrom, Jacob. 1990. *Numbers: The Traditional Hebrew Text with the New JPS Translation*. JPSTC. Philadelphia: Jewish Publication Society.

———. 1991. *Leviticus 1–16: A New Translation with Introduction and Commentary*. AB 3. New York: Doubleday.

———. 1993. 'The Concept of Impurity in Jubilees and the Temple Scroll'. *RQ* 16: 277–84.

———. 2000a. 'Impurity is Miasma: A Response to Hyam Maccoby'. *JBL* 119: 729–33.

———. 2000b. *Leviticus 17–22: A New Translation with Introduction and Commentary.* AB 3A. New York: Doubleday.

Miller II, Robert D. 2018. *The Dragon, the Mountain, and the Nations: An Old Testament Myth, Its Origins, and Its Afterlives*. University Park: Eisenbrauns.

Miller, Stuart S. 2015. *At the Intersection of Texts and Material Finds: Stepped Pools, Stone Vessels, and Ritual Impurity among the Jews of Roman Galilee*. Göttingen: Vandenhoeck & Ruprecht.

Miner, Earl. 1994. 'Allusion'. In T. V. F. Brogan (ed.), *The New Princeton Handbook of Poetic Terms*. Princeton: Princeton University Press, 13–15.

Moffitt, David M. 2011. *Atonement and the Logic of Resurrection in the Epistle to the Hebrews*. NovTSup 141. Leiden: Brill.

———. 2022. *Rethinking the Atonement: New Perspectives on Jesus's Death, Resurrection, and Ascension*. Grand Rapids. Baker.

Moo, Douglas J. 1996. *The Epistle to the Romans*. NICNT. Eerdmans: Grand Rapids.

———. 2000. *The Letter of James*. PNTC. Grand Rapids: Eerdmans.

Morales, L. Michael. 2012. *The Tabernacle Pre-Figured: Cosmic Mountain Ideology in Genesis and Exodus*. BTS 15. Leuven: Peeters.

——— (ed.). 2014. *Cult and Cosmos: Tilting toward a Temple-Centred Theology*. BTS 18. Leuven: Peeters.

———. 2015. *Who Shall Ascend the Mountain of the Lord? A Biblical Theology of the Book of Leviticus*. NSBT 37. Nottingham: Apollos.

———. 2019. 'Atonement in Ancient Israel: The Whole Burnt Offering as Central to Israel's Cult'. In Jon C. Laansma, George H. Guthrie and Cynthia L. Westfall (eds.), *So Great a Salvation: A Dialogue on the Atonement in Hebrews*. LNTS 516. London: T&T Clark, 27–39.

———. 2020. *Exodus Old and New: A Biblical Theology of Redemption*. Downers Grove IVP.

———. 2024. *Numbers 1–19*. AOTC 4a. London: Apollos.

Morales, Nelson R. 2018. *Poor and Rich in James: A Relevance Theory Approach to James's Use of the Old Testament*. BBRSup 20. University Park: Eisenbrauns.

Morgan, Christopher W. 2010. *A Theology of James: Wisdom for God's People*. EBT. Phillipsburg: P&R.

Morris, Leon. 1995. *The Gospel According to John*. NICNT. Grand Rapids: Eerdmans.

Moskala, Jiří. 2000. *The Laws of Clean and Unclean Animals in Leviticus 11: Their Nature, Theology, and Rationale: An Intertextual Study*. ATSDS. Berrien Springs: Adventist Theological Society.

———. 2001. 'Categorization and Evaluation of Different Kinds of Interpretation of the Laws of Clean and Unclean Animals in Leviticus 11'. *BR* 46: 5–41.

Mounce, William D. 2000. *Pastoral Epistles*. WBC 46. Nashville: Thomas Nelson.

Nanos, Mark D., and Magnus Zetterholm. 2015. *Paul within Judaism: Restoring the First-Century Context to the Apostle*. Minneapolis: Fortress.

Neusner, Jacob. 1973. *The Idea of Purity in Ancient Judaism: The Haskell Lectures, 1972–1973*. Leiden: Brill.

———. 1994. *Purity in Rabinnic Judaism: A Systematic Account*. SFSHJ 95. Atlanta: Scholars Press.

Newton, Michael. 1985. *The Concept of Purity at Qumran and in the Letters of Paul*. SNTSMS 53. Cambridge: Cambridge University Press.

Neyrey, Jerome H. 1986. 'The Idea of Purity in Mark's Gospel.' *Semeia* 35: 91–128.

Ng, Wai-Yee. 2001. *Water Symbolism in John: An Eschatological Interpretation*. StBibLit 5. New York: Lang.

Nihan, Christophe. 2007. *From Priestly Torah to Pentateuch: A Study in the Composition of the Book of Leviticus*. FAT 2/25. Tübingen: Mohr Siebeck.

Nihan, Christophe, and Julia Rhyder (eds.). 2021. *Text and Ritual in the Pentateuch: A Systematic and Comparative Approach*. University Park: Eisenbrauns.

Nolland, John. 2005. *The Gospel of Matthew: A Commentary on the Greek Text*. NIGTC. Grand Rapids: Eerdmans.

Olyan, Saul M. 2000. *Rites and Rank: Hierarchy in Biblical Representations of Cult*. Princeton: Princeton University Press.

Osborne, Grant R. 2002. *Revelation*. BECNT. Grand Rapids: Baker.

Oswalt, John N. 2003. *Isaiah*. NIVAC. Grand Rapids: Zondervan.

Pagola, José A. 2009. *Jesus: An Historical Approximation*. Translated by Margaret Wilde. Miami: Convivium.

Paschen, Wilfried. 1970. *Rein und Unrein: Untersuchung zur biblischen Wortgeschichte*. SANT 24. München: Kösel-Verlag.

Paschke, Boris. 2018. 'The Land in the New Testament'. In Hendrik J. Koorevaar and Mart-Jan Paul (eds.), *The Earth and the Land: Studies about the Value of the Land of Israel in the Old Testament and Afterwards*. EDIS 11. Berlin: Lang, 277–304.

Peres, Caio. 2021. 'Bloodless "Atonement": An Exegetical, Ritual, and Theological Analysis of Leviticus 5:11-13'. *JHS* 20: 1–36.

Péter-Contesse, René. 1993. *Lévitique 1–16*. CAT3A. Geneva: Labor et Fides.

Peterson, David. 2009. *The Acts of the Apostles*. PNTC. Grand Rapids: Eerdmans.

Petterson, Anthony R. 2010. 'The Shape of the Davidic Hope across the Book of the Twelve'. *JSOT* 35: 225–46.

———. 2021. 'Exile and Re-exile in the Book of the Twelve'. In George Athas, Beth M. Stovell, Daniel C. Timmer and Colin M. Toffelmire (eds.), *Theodicy and Hope in the Book of the Twelve*. LHBOTS 705. London: T&T Clark, 40–65.

Philip, Tarja S. 2006. *Menstruation and Childbirth in the Bible: Fertility and Impurity*. StBibLit 88. New York: Lang.

Philo. 1993. *The Works of Philo: Complete and Unabridged*. Peabody: Hendrickson.

Pierce, Madison N. 2020. *Divine Discourse in the Epistle to the Hebrews*. SNTSMS 178. Cambridge: Cambridge University Press.

Poirier, John C. 2003. 'Purity beyond the Temple in the Second Temple Era'. *JBL* 247–65.

Porter, Stanley E. 1993. 'Holiness, Sanctification'. In Gerald F. Hawthorne, Ralph P. Martin and Daniel G. Reid (eds.), *Dictionary of Paul and His Letters*. Downers Grove: IVP, 397–402.

Postell, Seth D. 2011. *Adam as Israel: Genesis 1–3 as the Introduction to the Torah and Tanakh*. Eugene: Pickwick.

Provan, Iain. 2001. *Ecclesiastes/Song of Songs*. NIVAC. Grand Rapids: Zondervan.

Pugh, Ben. 2014. *Atonement Theories: A Way through the Maze*. Eugene: Cascade.

Radner, Ephraim. 2016. *Time and the Word: Figural Reading of the Christian Scriptures*. Grand Rapids: Eerdmans.

Reasoner, Mark. 1999. *The Strong and the Weak: Romans 14:1-15:13 in Context*. SNTSMS 103. Cambridge: Cambridge University Press.

Redditt, Paul L. 2001. 'Recent Research on the Book of the Twelve as One Book'. *CR:BS* 9: 47–80.

Reeve, Joshua D. 2018. 'Blemished Bodies in Sacred Space: Disability in Leviticus 21:16–24'. PhD diss., Sydney Missionary and Bible College.

Regev, Eyal. 2016. 'Washing, Repentance, and Atonement in Early Christian Baptism and Qumranic Purification Liturgies'. *JJMJS* 3: 33–60.

Reid, Andrew. 2011. 'Evangelical Hermeneutics and Old Testament Preaching: A Critical Analysis of Graeme Goldsworthy's Theory and Practice'. ThD diss., Ridley.

Relph, Edward. 1976. *Place and Placedness*. London: Pion.

Rendtorff, Rolf. 2003a. 'Leviticus 16 als Mitte der Tora'. *BI* 11: 252–58.

———. 2003b. 'Nadab and Abihu'. In J. Cheryl Exum and H. G. M. Williamson (eds.), *Reading from Right to Left: Essays on the Hebrew Bible in Honour of David J. A. Clines*. JSOTSup 373. London: Sheffield Academic, 359–63.

Renz, Thomas. 2002. *The Rhetorical Function of the Book of Ezekiel*. Boston: Brill.

Riley, Jason A. 2014. 'Does YHWH Get His Hands Dirty? Reading Isaiah 63:1–6 in Light of Depictions of Divine Post-Battle Purification'. In Brad E. Kelle, Frank Ritchel Ames and Jacob L. Wright (eds.), *Warfare, Ritual, and Symbol in Biblical and Modern Contexts*. AIL 18. Atlanta: SBL, 243–267.

Rimmon-Kenan, Shlomith. 2002. *Narrative Fiction: Contemporary Poetics*. London: Routledge.

Robinson, Armin L. (ed.). 1944. *The Ten Commandments: Ten Short Novels of Hitler's War against the Moral Code*. London: Cassell.

Rodriguez, Angel Manuel. 1979. *Substitution in the Hebrew Cultus*. Berrin Springs: Andrews University Press.

Rogan, Wil. 2023. *Purity in the Gospel of John: Early Jewish Tradition, Christology, and Ethics*. LNTS 679. London: T&T Clark.

Romney Wegner, Judith. 2003. '"Coming before the LORD": The Exclusion of Women from the Public Domain of the Israelite Priestly Cult'. In Rolf Rendtorff, Robert A. Kugler and Sarah Smith Bartel (eds.), *The Book of Leviticus: Composition and Reception*. VTSup 93. Leiden: Brill, 451–65.

Rooke, Deborah W. 2015. 'The Blasphemer (Leviticus 24): Gender, Identity and Boundary Construction'. In Francis Landy, Leigh M. Trevaskis and Bryan D. Bibb (eds.), *Text, Time, and Temple: Literary, Historical and Ritual Studies in Leviticus*. HBM 64. Sheffield: Sheffield Phoenix, 153–69.

Sanders, E. P. 1990. *Jewish Law from Jesus to the Mishnah: Five Studies*. London: SCM.

———. 1992. *Judaism: Practice and Belief 63 BCE–66 CE*. London: SCM.

Sanders, James A. 1976. 'Adaptable for Life'. In Frank M. Cross (ed.), *Magnalia Dei*. Garden City: Doubleday, 531–60.

Scarlata, Mark W. 2021. *A Journey through the World of Leviticus: Holiness, Sacrifice, and the Rock Badger*. Eugene: Cascade.

Schellenberg, Annette. 2014. 'More Than Spirit: On the Physical Dimension in the Priestly Understanding of Holiness'. *ZAW* 126: 163–79.

Schenck, Kenneth L. 2007. *Cosmology and Eschatology in Hebrews: The Settings of the Sacrifice*. SNTSMS 143. Cambridge: Cambridge University Press.

Schnittjer, Gary E. 2021. *Old Testament Use of Old Testament: A Book-by-Book Guide*. Grand Rapids: Zondervan.

Schürer, Emil. 1891. *A History of the Jewish People in the Times of Jesus Christ*. New York: Scribner.

Selvidge, Marla. 1990. *Woman, Cult, and Miracle Recital: A Redaction Critical Investigation on Mark 5:24–34*. Lewisburg: Bucknell University Press.

Shea, William H. 1986. 'Literary Form and Theological Function in Leviticus'. In F. Holbrook (ed.), *The Seventy Weeks, Leviticus, and the Nature of Prophecy*. DRCS 3. Washington DC: Biblical Research Institute, 131–68.

Shead, Andrew G. 2012. *A Mouth Full of Fire: The Word of God in the Words of Jeremiah*. NSBT 29. Nottingham: Apollos.

Shepherd, David J. 2023. *King David, Innocent Blood, and Bloodguilt*. Oxford University Press: Oxford.

Shepherd, Jerry E. 2021. *Leviticus*. SGBC. Grand Rapids: Zondervan.

Shinall, Myrick C., Jr. 2018. 'The Social Condition of Lepers in the Gospels'. *JBL* 137: 915–34.

Sklar, Jay. 2005. *Sin, Impurity, Sacrifice, Atonement: The Priestly Conceptions*. HBM 2. Sheffield: Sheffield Phoenix.

———. 2013. *Leviticus*. TOTC. Nottingham: IVP.

Sloane, Andrew. 2008. 'Aberrant Textuality? The Case of Ezekiel the (Porno) Prophet'. *TynBul* 59: 53–76.

Smith, Christopher R. 1996. 'The Literary Structure of Leviticus'. *JSOT* 70: 17–32.

Smith, Katherine M. 2017. 'The Persuasive Intent of the Book of Leviticus'. PhD diss., University of Bristol and Trinity College.

———. 2018. 'Biblical Purity and Worldview: Understanding and Living Our Story'. *WWS* 2: 80–107.

Smoak, Jeremy D. 2015. *The Priestly Blessing in Inscription and Scripture: The Early History of Numbers 6:24–26*. Oxford: Oxford University Press.

Sommer, Benjamin D. 2001. 'Conflicting Constructions of Divine Presence in the Priestly Tabernacle'. *BI* 9: 41–63.

———. 2011. 'Dating Pentateuchal Texts and the Perils of Pseudo-Historicism'. In Thomas B. Dozeman, Konrad Schmid and Baruch J. Schwartz (eds.), *The Pentateuch: International Perspectives on Current Research*. FAT 78. Tübingen: Mohr Siebeck, 85–108.

Sonia, Kerry M. 2020. *Caring for the Dead in Ancient Israel*. ABS 27. Atlanta: SBL.

Soskice, Janet M. 1985. *Metaphor and Religious Language*. Oxford: Clarendon.

Starling, David I. 2016. *Hermeneutics as Apprenticeship: How the Bible Shapes Our Interpretive Habits and Practices*. Grand Rapids: Baker.

Stephens, Mark B. 2011. *Annihilation or Renewal?: The Meaning and Function of New Creation in the Book of Revelation*. WUNT 2/307. Tübingen: Mohr Siebeck.

Stevenson, Kalinda R. 1996. *The Vision of Transformation: The Territorial Rhetoric of Ezekiel 40–48*. Atlanta: Scholars Press.

Stökl Ben Ezra, Daniel. 2003. *The Impact of Yom Kippur on Early Christainity: The Day of Atonement from the Second Temple to the Fifth Century*. WUNT 163. Tübingen: Mohr Siebeck.

Strahan, Joshua. 2024. 'Did Jesus Nullify the Torah and Declare Nonkosher Foods Clean? Toward a Better Reading of Mark 7:19b'. *BBR* 33: 259–80.

Strawn, Brent A. 2017. *The Old Testament Is Dying: A Diagnosis and Recommended Treatment*. Grand Rapids: Baker.

Talbert, Charles H. 1992. *Reading John: A Literary and Theological Commentary on the Fourth Gospel and the Johannine Epistles*. New York: Crossroad.

Taylor, Joan E. 1997. *The Immerser: John the Baptist within Second Temple Judaism*. SHJ. Grand Rapids: Eerdmans.

Thiessen, Matthew. 2018. 'The Legislation of Leviticus 12 in Light of Ancient Embryology'. *VT* 68: 297–319.

———. 2020. *Jesus and the Forces of Death: The Gospels' Portrayal of Ritual Impurity within First-Century Judaism*. Grand Rapids: Baker.

———. 2023. *A Jewish Paul: The Messiah's Herald to the Gentiles*. Grand Rapids: Baker.

Thomas, Bruce. 1994. 'The Gospel for Shame Cultures'. *EMQ* 30: 284–89.

Thompson, Alan J. 2011. *The Acts of the Risen Lord Jesus: Luke's Account of God's Unfolding Plan*. NSBT 27. Nottingham: Apollos.

Thompson, John A. 1980. *The Book of Jeremiah*. NICOT. Grand Rapids: Eerdmans.

Thompson, Marianne M. 2001. *The God of the Gospel of John*. Grand Rapids: Eerdmans.

———. 2017. 'Baptism with Water and the Holy Spirit: Purification in the Gospel of John'. In R. Alan Culpepper and Jörg Frey (eds.), *The Opening of John's Narrative (John 1:19–2:22): Historical, Literary, and Theological Readings from the Colloquium Ioanneum 2015 in Ephesus*. WUNT 385. Tübingen: Mohr Siebeck, 59–78.

Tiemeyer, Lena-Sofia. 2006. *Priestly Rites and Prophetic Rage: Post-Exilic Prophetic Critique of the Priesthood*. FAT 2/19. Tübingen: Mohr Siebeck.

———. 2009. 'The Priests and the Temple Cult in the Book of Jeremiah'. In Hans M. Barstad and Reinhard G. Kratz (eds.), *Prophecy in the Book of Jeremiah*. BZAW 388. Berlin: de Gruyter, 233–64.

Tomson, Peter J. 2001. *'If This Be from Heaven...': Jesus and the New Testament Authors in Their Relationship to Judaism*. BibSem. Sheffield: Sheffield Academic.

Towner, W. Sibley. 1984. *Daniel*. Atlanta: John Knox.

Trevaskis, Leigh M. 2011. *Holiness, Ethics and Ritual in Leviticus*. HBM 29. Sheffield: Sheffield Phoenix.

Trummer, Peter. 1991. *Die blutende Frau: Wunderheilung im neuen Testament*. Freiburg: Herder.

Ulrich, Eugene, John W. Wright, Robert P. Carroll and Philip R. Davies (eds.). 1992. *Priests, Prophets and Scribes: Essays on the Formation and Heritage of Second Temple Judaism in Honour of Joseph Blenkinsopp*. JSOTSup 149. Sheffield: Sheffield Academic.

Vaughn, Brad. 2022. *The Cross in Context: Reconsidering Biblical Metaphors for Atonement*. Downers Grove: IVP.

Walton, John H., and D. Brent Sandy. 2013. *The Lost World of Scripture: Ancient Literary Culture and Biblical Authority*. Downers Grove: IVP.

Walton, John H., and J. Harvey Walton. 2017. *The Lost World of the Israelite Conquest: Covenant, Retribution, and the Fate of the Canaanites*. Downers Grove: IVP.

———. 2019. *Demons and Spirits in Biblical Theology: Reading the Biblical Text in Its Cultural and Literary Context*. Eugene: Wipf & Stock.

Warning, Wilfried. 1999. *Literary Artistry in Leviticus*. BIS 35. Leiden: Brill.

Wassén, Cecilia. 2013. 'Do You Have to Be Pure in a Metaphorical Temple? Sanctuary Metaphors and Construction of Sacred Space in the Dead Sea Scrolls and Paul's Letters'. In Carl S. Ehrlich, Anders Runesson and Eileen Schuller (eds.), *Purity, Holiness, and Identity in Judaism and Christianity: Essays in Memory of Susan Haber*. Wunt 305. Tübingen: Mohr Siebeck, 55–86.

———. 2016a. 'The (Im)purity Levels of Communal Meals within the Qumran Movement'. *JAJ* 7: 102–22.

———. 2016b. 'The Jewishness of Jesus and Ritual Purity'. *SIDA* 27: 11–36.

Watkin, Christopher. 2017. *Thinking Through Creation: Genesis 1 and 2 as Tools of Cultural Critique*. Phillipsburg: P&R.

Watts, James W. (ed.). 2001. *Persia and Torah: The Theory of Imperial Authorization of the Pentateuch*. SBLSS 17. Atlanta: SBL.

———. 2007. *Ritual and Rhetoric in Leviticus: From Sacrifice to Scripture*. Cambridge: Cambridge University Press.

———. 2013. *Leviticus 1–10*. HCOT. Leuven: Peeters.

———. 2017. *Understanding the Pentateuch as a Scripture*. Hoboken: Wiley Blackwell.

———. 2023. 'Pollution in the Bible and in Cognitive Science: A Review of Recent Works by Thomas Kazen and Yitzhaq Feder'. *VT* 73: 793–98.

Watts, John D. W. 1985. *Isaiah 1–33*. WBC 24. Waco: Word Books.

———. 1987. *Isaiah 34–66*. WBC 25. Waco: Word Books.

Webb, Barry G. 2000. *Five Festal Garments: Christian Reflections on the Song of Songs, Ruth, Lamentations, Ecclesiastes and Esther* NSBT 10. Leicester: Apollos.

Webb, Robert L. 1991. *John the Baptizer and Prophet: A Socio-Historical Study*. JSNTSup 62. Sheffield: JSOT.

Weiss, K. 1954. 'Priester der christlichen Kultgemeinde'. *TLZ* 79: 355–64.

Welch, Edward T. 2012. *Shame Interrupted: How God Lifts the Pain of Worthlessness and Rejection*. Greensboro: New Growth.

Wellhausen, Julius. 1885. *Prolegomena to the History of Israel*. Edinburgh: Adam & Charles Black.

———. 1958. *Israelitische und jüdische Geschichte*. Berlin: de Gruyter.

Wenham, Gordon J. 1979. *The Book of Leviticus*. NICOT. Grand Rapids: Eerdmans.

Werman, Cana. 1997. 'Jubilees 30: Building a Paradigm for the Ban on Intermarriage'. *HTR* 90: 1–22.

Werrett, Ian C. 2007. *Ritual Purity and the Dead Sea Scrolls*. STDJ 72. Leiden: Brill.

Williams, James G. 1991. *The Bible, Violence, and the Sacred: Liberation from the Myth of Sanctioned Violence*. San Francisco: HarperSanFrancisco.

Williams, Jarvis J. 2017. 'Cultic Action and Cultic Function in Second Temple Jewish Martyrologies: The Jewish Martyrs as Israel's Yom Kippur'. In Henrietta L. Wiley and Christian A. Eberhart (eds.), *Sacrifice, Cult, and Atonement in Early Judaism and Christianity: Constituents and Critique*. RBS 85. Atlanta: SBL, 233–63.

Williams, Logan. 2024. 'The Stomach Purifies All Foods: Jesus' Anatomical Argument in Mark 7.18–19'. *NTS* 70: 371–91.

Williamson, H. G. M. 1985. *Ezra, Nehemiah*. WBC 16. Waco: Word Books.

———. 1997. 'Chronicles 1, 2: Theology of'. *NIDOTTE* 4:466–74.

Winkle, Ross E. 2017. '"You Are What You Wear": The Dress and Identity of Jesus as High Priest in John's Apocalypse'. In Henrietta L. Wiley and Christian A. Eberhart (eds.), *Sacrifice, Cult, and Atonement in Early Judaism and Christianity: Constituents and Critique*. RBS 85. Atlanta: SBL, 327–46.

Witherington, Ben. 1998. *The Acts of the Apostles: A Socio-Rhetorical Commentary*. Grand Rapids: Eerdmans.

Witt, William G., and Joel Scandrett. 2022. *Mapping Atonement: The Doctrine of Reconciliation in Christian History and Theology*. Grand Rapids: Baker.

Wolterstorff, Nicholas. 1995. *Divine Discourse: Philosophical Reflections on the Claim That God Speaks*. Cambridge: Cambridge University Press.

Wood, Bryant. 1984. 'To Dip or Sprinkle? The Qumran Cisterns in Perspective'. *BASOR* 256: 45–60.

Wray Beal, Lissa M. 2014. *1 & 2 Kings*. AOTC 9. Nottingham: Apollos.

———. 2019. *Joshua*. SGBC. Grand Rapids: Zondervan.

Wright, David P. 1987a. 'Deuteronomy 21:1–9 as a Rite of Elimination'. *CBQ* 49: 387–403.

———. 1987b. *The Disposal of Impurity: Elimination Rites in the Bible and in Hittite and Mesopotamian Literature*. SBLDS 101. Atlanta: Scholars Press.

———. 1991. 'The Spectrum of Priestly Impurity'. In Gary A. Anderson and Saul M. Olyan (eds.), *Priesthood and Cult in Ancient Israel*. JSOTSup 125. Sheffield: Sheffield Academic, 150–81.

———. 1992. 'Unclean and Clean'. In David Noel Freedman (ed.), *Anchor Bible Dictionary*. New York: Doubleday, 6:729–41.

Wright, N. T. 2003. *The Resurrection of the Son of God*. London: SPCK.

Wyatt, Nicolas. 2014. *The Mythic Mind: Essays on Cosmology and Religion in Ugaritic and Old Testament Literature*. London: Routledge.

Zangenberg, Jürgen K. 2013. 'Pure Stone: Archaeological Evidence for Jewish Purity Practices in Late Second Temple Judaism (Miqwa'ot and Stone Vessels)'. In Christian Frevel and Christophe Nihan (eds.), *Purity and the Forming of Religious Traditions in the Ancient Mediterranean World and Ancient Judaism*. DHR 3. Leiden: Brill, 537–72.

Zenger, Erich (ed.). 2008. *Einleitung in das Alte Testament*. 7th edn. Stuttgart: Kohlhammer.

Zenger, Erich, and Christian Frevel. 2008. 'Die Bücher Levitikus und Numeri als Teile der Pentateuchkomposition'. In Thomas Römer (ed.), *The Books of Leviticus and Numbers*. BETL 215. Leuven: Peeters, 35–74.

Zissu, Boaz, and David Amit. 2008. 'Common Judaism, Common Purity, and the Second Temple Period Judean *Miqwa'ot* (Ritual Immersion Baths)'. In Wayne O. McCready and Adele Reinhartz (eds.), *Common Judaism: Explorations in Second-Temple Judaism*. Minneapolis: Fortress, 47–62.

Scripture acknowledgments

Scripture acknowledgments

Index of authors

Index of Scripture references

Note: Primary discussions of a passage are often indicated in **bold**.

Daniel

Hosea

Mark

Luke

Titles in this series:

1 *Possessed by God*, David Peterson
2 *God's Unfaithful Wife*, Raymond C. Ortlund Jr
3 *Jesus and the Logic of History*, Paul W. Barnett
4 *Hear, My Son*, Daniel J. Estes
5 *Original Sin*, Henri Blocher
6 *Now Choose Life*, J. Gary Millar
7 *Neither Poverty Nor Riches*, Craig L. Blomberg
8 *Slave of Christ*, Murray J. Harris
9 *Christ, Our Righteousness*, Mark A. Seifrid
10 *Five Festal Garments*, Barry G. Webb
12 *Now My Eyes Have Seen You*, Robert S. Fyall
13 *Thanksgiving*, David W. Pao
14 *From Every People and Nation*, J. Daniel Hays
15 *Dominion and Dynasty*, Stephen G. Dempster
16 *Hearing God's Words*, Peter Adam
17 *The Temple and the Church's Mission*, G. K. Beale
18 *The Cross from a Distance*, Peter G. Bolt
19 *Contagious Holiness*, Craig L. Blomberg
20 *Shepherds After My Own Heart*, Timothy S. Laniak
21 *A Clear and Present Word*, Mark D. Thompson
22 *Adopted into God's Family*, Trevor J. Burke
23 *Sealed with an Oath*, Paul R. Williamson
24 *Father, Son and Spirit*, Andreas J. Köstenberger and Scott R. Swain
25 *God the Peacemaker*, Graham A. Cole
26 *A Gracious and Compassionate God*, Daniel C. Timmer
27 *The Acts of the Risen Lord Jesus*, Alan J. Thompson
28 *The God Who Makes Himself Known*, W. Ross Blackburn
29 *A Mouth Full of Fire*, Andrew G. Shead
30 *The God Who Became Human*, Graham A. Cole
31 *Paul and the Law*, Brian S. Rosner
32 *With the Clouds of Heaven*, James M. Hamilton Jr
33 *Covenant and Commandment*, Bradley G. Green
34 *Bound for the Promised Land*, Oren R. Martin
35 *'Return to Me'*, Mark J. Boda
36 *Identity and Idolatry*, Richard Lints
37 *Who Shall Ascend the Mountain of the Lord?*, L. Michael Morales

38 *Calling on the Name of the Lord*, J. Gary Millar
40 *The Book of Isaiah and God's Kingdom*, Andrew T. Abernethy
41 *Unceasing Kindness*, Peter H. W. Lau and Gregory Goswell
42 *Preaching in the New Testament*, Jonathan I. Griffiths
43 *God's Mediators*, Andrew S. Malone
44 *Death and the Afterlife*, Paul R. Williamson
45 *Righteous by Promise*, Karl Deenick
46 *Finding Favour in the Sight of God*, Richard P. Belcher Jr
47 *Exalted Above the Heavens*, Peter C. Orr
48 *All Things New*, Brian J. Tabb
49 *The Feasts of Repentance*, Michael J. Ovey
50 *Including the Stranger*, David G. Firth
51 *Canon, Covenant and Christology*, Matthew Barrett
52 *Biblical Theology According to the Apostles*, Chris Bruno, Jared Compton and Kevin McFadden
53 *Salvation to the Ends of the Earth (2nd edn)*, Andreas J. Köstenberger with T. Desmond Alexander
54 *The Servant of the Lord and His Servant People*, Matthew S. Harmon
55 *Changed into His Likeness*, J. Gary Millar
56 *Piercing Leviathan*, Eric Ortlund
57 *Now and Not Yet*, Dean R. Ulrich
58 *The Glory of God and Paul*, Christopher W. Morgan and Robert A. Peterson
59 *From Prisoner to Prince*, Samuel Emadi
60 *The Royal Priest*, Matthew Emadi
61 *Life in the Son*, Clive Bowsher
62 *Answering the Psalmist's Perplexity*, James Hely Hutchinson
63 *'Egypt My People . . . and Israel My Inheritance'*, Daniel C. Timmer
64 *Impossible to Be Restored?*, Marcus A. Mininger
65 *'You Shall Be Clean'*, G. Geoffrey Harper

An index of Scripture references for all the volumes may be found at http://www.thegospelcoalition.org/resources/nsbt.